SANCTIONING APARTHEID

Edited by Robert E. Edgar

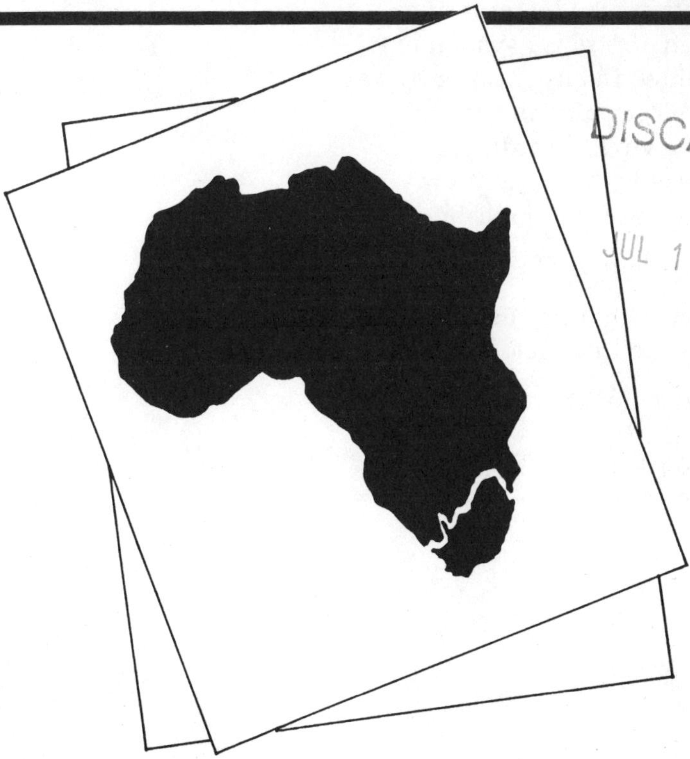

Africa World Press, Inc.
P.O. Box 1892
Trenton, New Jersey 08607

Africa World Press, Inc.
P.O. Box 1892
Trenton, N.J. 08607

First Printing 1990

Cover Design by Ife Nii Owoo

Type formatted from editor's disk by Malcolm Litchfield

Library of Congress Catalog Card Number: 90-80151
ISBN: 0-86543-162-0 Cloth
0-85543-163-9 Paper

CONTENTS

ACKNOWLEDGEMENTS

In September 1986, the U.S. Congress adopted the Anti-Apartheid Act over President Reagan's veto. A year later, a two-day international conference featuring eleven panels and some forty presentations was held at Howard University to evaluate the impact of the Act and to assess whether sanctions generally were having their intended impact on South Africa. This volume has emerged from the deliberations at that conference. A number of the chapters presented in this volume were delivered at the conference in abbreviated form. We had invited participants to submit briefing papers which could be digested easily at the conference and then distributed to Congressional offices. As this volume took shape, we then invited contributors to write up lengthier essays. Then, as other sanctions-related research came to our attention, we invited researchers to include their essays in this collection. These include the chapters by Benjamin Beit-Hallahmi, Douglas Anglin, David Hirschmann, Richard Knight, James Cobbe, Jack Parson, and Alan Booth. The latter three were presented at a panel at the African Studies Association in 1987.

The conference could not have taken place without the generous support and backing of a number of individuals and groups. Financial support was provided by the African Studies and Research Program, the Department of International Affairs, the Graduate School of Arts and Sciences, and the Moorland-Spingarn Research Center at Howard University; the International Center for Development Policy; Lutheran World Ministries; Maryknoll Fathers; the National Council of Churches of Christ (Africa Office); the Presbyterian Church (U.S.A.) Division of International Mission; the Carnegie Corporation; and the United Nations Centre Against Apartheid.

Numerous individuals helped plan and facilitate the conference. I would especially like to acknowledge the contributions of Nzongola-Ntalaja, who was a convenor of the conference, Sulayman Nyang, Director of the African Studies and Research Program, Adwoa Dunn, Barbara Harmel, Ann Brown, Anita Baker, Mellenia Jones, who showed remarkable patience in dealing with the financial maze that we encountered, and Joanne Jackson, who humored me by typing up the manuscript for this volume.

SANCTIONING APARTHEID

In September, 1986, the US Congress passed the Comprehensive Anti-Apartheid Act over the veto of President Reagan. The law was a major victory for American anti-apartheid groups, which had labored for many years to pass tough sanctions legislation against South Africa. But it was also a testament to a resurgence of resistance inside South Africa to the apartheid regime, since it was the resistance—and the government repression of it—that caught the attention of the American public and brought the issue before Congress. Despite a broad consensus that some action had to be taken to express a popular sentiment against the apartheid system, there was still considerable disagreement within Congress about the kinds of messages it wanted to send. The Anti-Apartheid Act won passage because it was worded in such a way as to appeal to the widest number of legislators, especially moderate Republicans, who had to be convinced that it was important enough to override an anticipated Reagan veto. In its final form, the Act's provisions expressed a number of (and sometimes conflicting) sentiments about the apartheid system and how to confront it. Key components of the law included:

1. Providing financial assistance through scholarships for "victims of apartheid," grants for community organizations in "disadvantaged communities," and assistance for political detainees and their families.

2. Directing the Export-Import Bank to assist black businesses and making sure that American businesses strictly adhered to the Code of Conduct (formerly known as the Sullivan Principles) on fair employment practices for black employees.
3. Prohibiting the following: the importation of Krugerrands; the importing of South African-made weapons or military vehicles or any product made by a South African parastatal; loans to the government of South Africa; air links between the United States and South Africa; the sale of computers to various arms of the South African government (military, police, prison system); the sale of nuclear material or technology; importing of uranium, coal, iron, and steel; no new investments in South Africa; and the export of crude oil and petroleum.

During the first year of the law's operation, Congress refrained from introducing any additional sanctions measures. A critical juncture came a year after the law's passage, when the Reagan administration was mandated to submit a report assessing whether the South African government had taken any positive steps to dismantle apartheid and, if not, to make recommendations for additional measures that should be implemented. The President's report of 6 October 1987 concluded that "significant progress has not been made toward ending the system of apartheid," but it went on to reiterate the administration's belief that sanctions were not an effective tool in moving the South African regime away from apartheid and that the Anti-Apartheid Act had actually worsened, not improved the situation.[1]

As several contributions to this volume make clear, this line of argument is hard to follow because the Reagan administration has severely hampered the Act's effectiveness by not fully implementing it. For instance, Gay McDougall demonstrates that the Reagan administration took the Act's loosely worded amendments and interpreted them in a manner that undermined their intent. She identifies specific areas where this has happened: the prohibition of new investment by American businesses in South Africa; the ban on imports produced by South

African parastatals and on South African uranium oxide; and the prohibition of certain exports such as computers, oil, arms, and nuclear material from the US. She concludes that because the executive and legislative branches were split over the law, "selective sanctions invite(d) misinterpretation and evasions" by the executive branch. In other words, half-measures halfheartedly imposed cannot be expected to have much of an impact.

Adding weight to McDougall's concerns is a 1989 General Accounting Office (GAO) report that found that while the State Department had given the US Customs Service the names of 106 South African government agencies and parastatals, it had failed to provide a list of the products produced by these institutions. The GAO's conclusion was that "Customs does not know which South African products could have come from parastatals . . . and so cannot devote special enforcement attention to them."[2]

Several chapters in this collection examine in more detail the questions McDougall raises about computers and strategic minerals. For instance, Thomas Conrad's examination of American computer sales to South Africa is a case in point of how ambiguously worded restrictions have little practical effect. In 1978, the US government toughened the arms embargo by placing restrictions on which agencies in the South African government certain high tech items like computers could be sold to. Despite these regulations, US computers make their way to the South African military and police, who use computers for control of South Africa's black community. McDougall shares Conrad's concern about controlling computer sales. She argues that because the Anti-Apartheid Act prohibits U.S. computers to "apartheid enforcing agencies" does not mean that the computers will not eventually make their way to precisely the branches of the government that should be off limits.

The Reagan administration had designated ten minerals imported from South Africa as exempt from the provisions of the Anti-Apartheid Act. Sanford Wright considers three of the metals—chromium, vanadium, and the platinum group metals—and concludes that while Western countries rely heavily on some of South Africa's strategic minerals, there are domestic and international alternative sources of supply. Moreover, the US has sufficient stockpiles of these minerals to meet demand until new sources are identified or tapped. A study by Paul Jourdan of Zimbabwe's Institute of Mining Research provides added support to Wright's argument, as he has determined that Zimbabwe alone can provide most of Western countries' chromium and platinum needs and that southern African states can provide many of the other strategic minerals.[3]

Another provision of the legislation which has not been aggressively monitored is Section 508, which called for identifying violators of the international arms embargo against South Africa and for terminating US military assistance to countries that transgress. The provision had the most impact on Israel, which has had an extensive military and trade relationship with South Africa. In response to the US government's finding that Israel (and several other countries) were not observing the arms embargo, the Israeli government moved to stave off problems with US military assistance by announcing in March 1987 several measures curtailing the South African connection, but, as Benjamin Beit-Hallahmi shows, the new prohibitions on buying Krugerrands, on government loans, and on the sale of oil to South Africa are really a sleight-of-hand trick, since the measures have little consequence and do not alter an ongoing military relationship highlighted by an October 1989 NBC News report that Israel had supplied technology from its Jericho-2B intermediate-range missile to South Africa. But Israel's pronouncement has been successful in heading off any punitive measures from a US Congress reluctant to disrupt the special relationship with Israel.

The Anti-Apartheid Act also advised the US government to confer with other "industrialized democracies" about finding cooperative areas where sanctions could be imposed against South Africa. Given the Reagan administration's opposition to sanctions, it was probably anticipated that it would not carry out this objective. Yet, for American sanctions at any level to have an impact, it is important for sanctions to be implemented in a coordinated manner with other nations, especially those nations—Japan, France, West Germany, Great Britain, Taiwan, and Switzerland—which have the most extensive economic ties with South Africa. In addition to providing a comprehensive analysis of the impact of varying degrees of sanctions on the South

African economy, Roger Riddell makes a series of specific recommendations. Among them are: tightening restrictions on bank loans to South Africa and making it difficult for South Africa to roll over its current debts; preventing new foreign investment and reinvestment of profits; closing off avenues for South African sanctions busting and diversions of trade to countries not participating in sanctions; cutting off South African exports of iron and steel, coal, textiles, agricultural products, and uranium; shutting down loopholes in the oil embargo; and keeping the price of gold from rising. The key to his recommendations is that major industrialized countries will have to coordinate their actions on sanctions measures before they can exert the most effective pressures on the South African government.

Several essays in this volume probe some of the specific sanctions that the international community can impose. One critical area, for instance, is the debt owed by the South African government, parastatals, and private sector to foreign banks. This debt expanded rapidly in the late 1970s and early 1980s to $24 billion. It reached a critical point in mid-1985 when foreign banks refused to roll over their short-term loans and froze new credits for South Africa. The South African government responded in September 1985 by declaring a moratorium on repaying the short-term debt of $14 billion that it owed. An agreement reached between banks and South Africa allowed for 5% of the principal to be repaid by June 1987, an additional 13% by June 1990, and the rescheduling of the remaining debt in June 1990. Although anti-apartheid groups had called on European and American creditor banks to exact concessions from the South African government as a price for rescheduling debt, South African Reserve Bank governor Chris Stals announced in October 1989 that South Africa had succeeded in negotiating a new debt package, which called for 20.5% of the $8 billion due in June 1990 to be paid in eight installments over a 3 1/2 year period.The banks can also turn the rest of the short-term debt into long-term loans, but these loans could not be rolled over again.

South Africa has apparently escaped one debt-related bind, but there are other facets of the debt problem that can be utilized as pressure points. For instance, the debt problem has lowered

South Africa's credit rating and it has had to turn to trade credits as a key source for financing its international trade and for importing capital goods. Six countries—Great Britain, the United States, West Germany, Switzerland, France, and Japan—supply most of these credits. John Lind and David Koistinen show that trade credits have given South Africa breathing space and that if they were all cut off at once, South Africa would be put in a major predicament as it would have to raise $4 billion to $7 billion in foreign exchange to finance trade, an almost impossible task.

Another area in which South Africa is vulnerable is oil importation, where, despite South African efforts to achieve self-sufficiency through its coal-to-oil conversion plants, it still depends on imports for about two-thirds of its liquid fuel needs. Moreover, liquid fuels are funnelled to a few critical areas: the transport sector and the police and military. Jaap Woldendorp details the extensive programs and laws South Africa has initiated to meet its oil needs. The United Nations has adopted an oil embargo, but it has not been effectively carried out, largely because of the opposition of the United States and the United Kingdom in the U.N. Security Council, and because there are oil-producing countries, oil traders, and shipping companies that are willing to supply South Africa's needs at a premium price. An August 1989 report prepared for the Commonwealth Committee of Foreign Ministers on Southern Africa concluded that if the loopholes in oil exportation to South Africa were tightened, it would add another $2 a barrel to the price South Africa pays for oil.[5]

A third pressure point is gold. South Africa provides over a third of world gold production and gold yields about 35% to 40% of all of South Africa's foreign exchange earnings. Moreover, an elevated gold price on world markets allows South Africa to cushion the shock of sanctions. It has long been argued, however, that the implementation of sanctions against South African gold would be a complex challenge because of the difficulty of tracing the origin of gold and because it would disrupt the world gold market. But Ian Lepper and Peter Robbins present an imaginative plan for a ban on South African gold that can be implemented through the cooperation of nations and by carefully monitoring bullion refiners and "middlemen" who might try to sell the gold, and compensating for the loss of the 600 tons of gold that South Africa annually produces by drawing on the large reserves of gold which most nations keep.

The question is often raised as to how black people in South Africa perceive the sanctions issue. A number of polls have been taken which have raised even more controversy since in a number of cases the questions asked in the polls have been framed in such a way as to elicit a certain answer. The most recent survey was done by the South African Chamber of Mines and not surprisingly it found that 80% of black South Africans were opposed to disinvestment and sanctions (and the results were fortuitously released as a delegation of South African clergymen was meeting with President Bush).[6] David Hirschmann takes a different tack. His chapter is based not on a poll, but on intensive interviews with a focus group: 93 second- and third-level urban African leaders representing a wide range of organizations and viewpoints. The strength of Hirschmann's research is not that he reduces the views of the people he interviewed to some easily quantifiable result, but that he provides their testimony on a series of issues. He does identify some trends in thinking which are worth noting: that this group of black South Africans was generally suspicious of US policy despite the passage of the Anti-Apartheid Act, that they were aware of the sophistry of American corporations in divesting from South Africa, that hostility towards American policy in South Africa had not abated, and that more and more blacks were identifying apartheid with capitalism.

Opponents of sanctions argue that, because the Anti-Apartheid Act has been ineffective, sanctions are an ineffective and inappropriate tactic to combat apartheid. But contributions to this volume provide ample testimony that the Act has not been as effective as it might have been because of how it has been interpreted and implemented, compared to its original intent. Despite all the reservations that have been raised about the Act, a case can be made that it played a very positive role in forcing the Reagan administration to reexamine its decided tilt in favor of the South African regime. The Act reflected a genuine outpouring of American public sentiment against the apartheid system and Congressional dissatisfaction with the manner in which the executive branch was dealing with the South African government's twin policies of internal repression and regional destabilization. As a result of this, the Bush administration has moved to heal the serious breach that had developed between Congress and the Executive branch over South Africa by acknowledging that the Act has sent a strong message to South African government officials. Herman Cohen, the new Assistant Secretary of State for African Affairs, has stated: "Sanctions have had a very major impact, I believe, on the development of new thinking in South Africa."[7] The tone of his statement is a significant departure from those of the Reagan administration, but it should not be interpreted as an enthusiastic embrace of sanctions, but as a tactic to derail the drive in Congress for additional sanctions.

The primary intent of the Anti-Apartheid Act was to express American outrage over the apartheid system and not to put undue economic pressure on South Africa. But the Act has worked to restrict the importation of certain trade products such as coal, iron and steel, uranium, textiles, and agricultural products. A General Accounting Office report concluded that South African exports to the United States had declined $417 million between the first three quarters of 1986 and the same period in 1987. And South Africa did not recover these losses through expanding trade elsewhere. One should not exaggerate the economic impact of the Act, but when combined with other external economic pressures on a stagnating South African economy, it has taken its toll, as reflected in statements by South African government officials that political reform may have to be a precondition for restoring the country's economic linkages to the international community.

The Act also put a measure of pressure on American corporations by prohibiting new investment, but a little noticed amendment to the Budget Reconciliation Act in 1987 sponsored by Charles Rangel (D-NY) has had more important consequences. The Rangel amendment withdrew tax credits for taxes paid by American corporations to the South African government. This effectively raised the rate of taxation from 58% to 72%. Several American corporations—Mobil Oil, Hewlett-Packard, NCR, St. Paul

Companies, and Goodyear Tire and Rubber—have pulled out of South Africa in 1989 because the higher taxes spelled lower profits, and there is the likely prospect that other American corporations will follow suit.

Discussion of the Rangel amendment highlights the fact that some 200 American (and over 60 British) firms have already pulled out of South Africa since 1984. But a "pullout" does not necessarily mean a complete severing of ties with South Africa, as revealed in Richard Knight's and Ann Seidman's chapters. Licensing, franchising, and distribution agreements between American and South African firms allow the former continued access to South African markets. Moreover, 200 American companies remain in South Africa and have an important role in such vital industries as oil, computers, automobiles, and electronics.

Congress and Sanctions in 1988

As I have noted, the Anti-Apartheid Act mandated that the Reagan administration submit a report a year later to Congress detailing whether the South African government had made any progress in ending apartheid and calling on him to recommend new sanctions if it had not. The report confirmed that no progress had been made, but it sidestepped the question of new sanctions. That set the stage for a host of new sanctions bills to be introduced in Congress in early 1988, but, over time, efforts concentrated on passing H.R. 1580 (the Anti-Apartheid Act Amendments of 1988), popularly known as the Dellums bill after its sponsor, Ron Dellums, a black Democratic congressman and a long-time champion of anti-apartheid causes. Despite the fact that the State of Emergency in South Africa had dampened overt resistance there and that South African restriction on news reporting had taken South Africa off the front pages of American newspapers and off the evening TV news, a concern over South Africa still existed in Congress, even though as the bill moved through committees in the House of Representative, it passed, largely with Democratic support. Eventually eight committees—Foreign Affairs, Armed Services, Banking, Intelligence, Public

Works, Ways and Means, Interior, and Energy—all reviewed the bill and added amendments. In its final form, H.R. 1580 significantly tightened the language of the 1986 Act and added tougher provisions, including: that no American can hold or acquire any investment, including loans, in South Africa 180 days after the law is passed and that American businesses with over 24 employees have 90 days to terminate their business; that no article from South Africa can be imported into the U.S. (exempted are strategic metals); that no U.S. goods can be exported to South Africa (exempted are humanitarian and charitable materials); and that no American can assist in the transporting of crude oil or petroleum to South Africa.

When the bill came to a floor vote in the House on 11 August 1988, it passed 244 to 132 and was sent to the Senate where an identical bill, S. 2756, was introduced by Sen. Alan Cranston (D-CA) in the Senate Foreign Relations Committee. A provision to prohibit any oil company selling oil to South Africa from acquiring new federal oil leases was deleted, but the bill did make it out of committee—by a slim 10-to-9 margin on strictly party lines. But when it came before the full Senate, it succumbed to a variety of problems. First, the Senate Majority Leader, Robert Byrd (D-WVa), who had the power to decide which bills would come up for a floor vote, did not support the bill, and second, the bill did not have the support of moderate Republicans, who had been willing to go along with limited sanctions in 1986. It is doubtful whether they would have gone along with tougher sanctions in any event, but coming as it did in the midst of the 1988 Presidential campaign, no Senate Republican was willing to put President Reagan in a bind again or undercut the campaign of George Bush. The campaign also had an impact on Democrats. The Democratic candidate, Michael Dukakis, strongly supported tougher sanctions, and he would have been embarrassed by Democrats who voted against the bill if it had come to a vote. Finally, the bill got caught up in international controversies. Several newspapers editorialized that passage of the bill would have alienated South Africa at a time when delicate negotiations over Namibia were in progress (ignoring the fact that sanctions and the threat of tougher sanctions had played a constructive role in bringing South Africa to the negotiating table in the first place). And countries like Britain vociferously opposed provisions like the one that "banned the issuing of new oil, coal, and gas leases to US subsidiaries with investment in South Africa or which export oil to South Africa." That provision would have had an adverse effect on the American business of British Petroleum and Shell, two British oil firms with considerable commitments in South Africa.[8]

The sanctions legislation that died in the Senate in 1988 was reintroduced in 1989. The expectation was that the House would back the measure again and that the Senate would be the key battleground for passage of any legislation, so the legislation was first introduced in the Senate Foreign Relations Committee. The measure did not emerge from the committee during the 1989 congressional session. Although the sanctions debate will be renewed in the 1990 session, it remains to be seen whether any sanctions legislation will emerge intact or with modification.

Sanctions and Southern Africa

With sanctions becoming a real possibility by the mid-1980s, southern African states had to confront the hard choices of how they stood on the issue. Douglas Anglin demonstrates how the sanctions issue became interlinked with SADCC, Commonwealth, and international relations and how southern African states, individually and collectively, have weighed the implications for sanctions for their national and regional economies. Despite the desire of leaders like Robert Mugabe of Zimbabwe and Kenneth Kaunda of Zambia to push for sanctions, they have had to deal with the reality that those regional states which implement sanctions will have to pay a high price in the form of South African reprisals and destabilization. Nevertheless, Anglin believes that there are several modest ways in which southern African states can support the sanctions effort: through aggressively monitoring South African sanctions busting at a national level, by joining in a modified air ban on South African air links with the rest of the world, and by restricting financial transfers to residents of South Africa.

The difficulty of southern African states participating wholeheartedly in sanctions is exemplified by Roger Riddell's case study of Zimbabwe, SADCC's strongest national economy. Its government has been a leader in calls for sanctions and, unlike most other southern African states, it could implement measures to counteract South African pressure:

> For instance it could halt the outflow of South African profits, interests and dividends (valued at over $20m a year), freeze the interest and principal repayment of the $120m loan owed to South Africa, interrupt the over $35m worth of annual pension and annuity remittances of former residents now living in South Africa, confiscate the remaining financial assets of the 60,000 people who have emigrated to South Africa since Independence in 1980 or even more dramatically, nationalise the over $850m worth of South African capital assets in the country, confiscate the South African locomotives and rolling stock on Zimbabwe's rail system and take action against the upwards of 4,000 people in Zimbabwe who have South African citizenship of the right to South African passports.[9]

The Zimbabwe government is also committed to de-linking its economic ties with South Africa. Some progress has been achieved towards that end, most notably in the areas of tourism, investment, transport routes, and trade. Despite the fact that Zimbabwe has improved its bargaining position vis a vis South Africa, it still retains substantial ties to South Africa and remains vulnerable to South African destabilization. If a showdown occurred between Zimbabwe and South Africa, the latter would have the upper hand.

The remarkable thing about southern African states is that, despite South African destabilization, most of them have consistently called upon the international community to implement sanctions. Even Lesotho, which James Cobbe shows, is expected to carry out a pragmatic relationship with South Africa because of its vulnerable position, supports sanctions which take into account the need to compensate southern African states for their losses. As King Moshoeshoe II has argued:

> The international community should continue to press for change in South Africa's racial policies, deploying sanctions or other peaceful measures. But its members must not fail to build into such actions consideration for the special needs of South Africa's neighbors, willing as we are to sacrifice, but not to die as nations, in order to help bring an end to apartheid.[10]

However many areas of leverage South Africa has on its neighbors, sanctions are still a double-edged sword. On the one hand, South Africa can punish states that support sanctions; on the other hand, South Africa needs regional trade even more to offset losses elsewhere, and its ability to soften the impact of sanctions is directly related to its ability to evade them through neighboring countries. In other words, as Jack Parsons puts it, the "management of the sanctions environment" is a necessity for the South African government, and he shows how complex this is in the case of Botswana. The Botswana government has had a very consistent policy on supporting international sanctions, but, at the same time, Botswana has a petty bourgeoisie with extensive ties to South African capital, which may, wittingly or unwittingly, aid South African sanctions-busting efforts. At the same time, Botswana has benefitted in some ways from sanctions through added international flights between Botswana and Europe, the relocation of multinationals from South Africa, and the development of local industries such as the soda ash deposits at Sua Pan. The latter presents a dilemma to the Botswana government because the soda ash deposits are being exploited due to South African fears that the US will cut off soda ash deposits to South Africa at some point. In this case, Botswana has acquired one more card for bargaining with South Africa, while South Africa is better able to escape the sting of sanctions.

Of all southern African states, Swaziland has been the most receptive to working with South African companies to circumvent sanctions. Alan Booth shows that Swazi businesses countered an economic downturn in Swaziland by courting transnational corporations such as Coca Cola, which have relocated their plants from South Africa to Swaziland, but still tap the South African market and by attracting South African investors, who, in turn, have been able to send their goods through Swaziland and take advantage of a provision of the Anti-Apartheid Act that exempts goods produced in South Africa's neighbors and exported through South Africa from any restrictions. As Booth explains, "the exemption encompassed such products of Swaziland as were 'transported, graded, packaged, repackaged, marked, containerized, or otherwise serviced' in South Africa; and it included goods produced in Swaziland by private South African capital." Since Swaziland does not enforce local content regulations, it is also possible for South African firms to ship their goods to warehouses in Swaziland, place a "Made in Swaziland" stamp on them, and export them to unsuspecting countries.

Southern African states are an obvious starting point for sanctions-busting efforts, but, as John Daniels has argued elsewhere, there are many other outlets—Israel, Taiwan, the Comores Islands—that South Africa uses. He also pinpoints Anglo American's subsidiary, MINORCO, the key arm for Anglo's investments in Western Europe and North America, which allows Anglo to "sanitize its investment" and "operate from a secure base."[11] An indicator of the importance that South Africa places on evading sanctions is that 5,700 of 8,000 registered South African exporters were established in the last two years.[12]

Cultural Boycott

The campaign for imposing economic sanctions on South Africa has attracted the most discussion in recent years, but it should not detract from an equally vital debate over the cultural boycott with South Africa. Over the years, the cultural boycott—of sportspersons, musicians, academics, playwrights, and writers performing or having their works performed in South Africa—has been highly successful. But, as Larry Shore and Mbulelo Mzamane argue, as cultural resistance inside South Africa has escalated in recent years and has proved to be a major challenge to the apartheid regime, it has become necessary for representatives of the mass democratic movement inside and outside South Africa to modify the boycott and come up with a viable alternative that promotes and does not stifle cultural activities. The new policy that has evolved declares that the isolation of apartheid institutions will continue, while direct contacts and exchanges between anti-apartheid groups inside and outside the country can be broadened so that the "culture of liberation" can flourish. The National Executive of the African National Congress has endorsed this policy and organizations associated with the mass democratic movement have created a cultural desk with elected representatives from cultural organizations which will make policy and make decisions on specific boycott issues. This does not necessarily mean that there will always be clarity on which events, groups or individuals will be given a blessing, but an important shift has taken place.[13]

Although the focus of this collection is on the external pressures that can be brought to bear on the South African regime, the contributors understand full well that, in the final analysis, the challenges mounted by opposition movements within South Africa will be more decisive in determining the manner in which the apartheid system is ended. Sanctions are not a secret weapon that can magically topple the apartheid regime on their own. They contribute more when they operate in tandem with the efforts of the South African Mass Democratic Movement to force the South African regime to recognize the necessity of totally dismantling and not merely reforming the edges of the apartheid edifice. F. W. de Klerk's reformist moves have not been inconsequential, but he remains a dogged defender of group rights—which is a cornerstone of apartheid—and he has not addressed the necessity for fundamental political and socioeconomic change. A recent report prepared for the Commonwealth nations puts the argument for sanctions this way:

> Sanctions are a diplomatic tool. They are a spur to the negotiating process, not an alternative to it. . . . The ultimate goal of sanctions is political—to promote negotiations. The intermediate goal is to create a growing group of people who will press for genuine talks, and thus help to build a lobby for negotiations. . . . We see the role of sanctions as making it increasingly difficult to maintain even a "reformed" apartheid, thus forcing white South Africans to realize that fundamental change must take place.[14]

Despite the mounting evidence that sanctions, if properly applied, can be a constructive force for change in South Africa, many governments remain ambivalent about imposing strong sanctions against South Africa. The argument is not understanding the nature of the apartheid system, since all governments make ritualistic condemnations of it; it is, rather, about what steps to take to bring an end to it. The situation reminds me of the joke in Woody Allen's film, *Annie Hall*, about the fellow who goes to consult a psychiatrist, complaining about his brother who thinks he is a chicken. The psychiatrist says the solution is simple: commit the brother to a mental hospital. And the patient responds, "That's fine, but I need the eggs." Everyone agrees that the apartheid is an insane system, but there are too many interests which still want South Africa's eggs, especially the golden ones. Until governments are willing to take the necessary steps to challenge the apartheid regime, they will go on "sanctioning" apartheid instead of imposing the sanctions necessary to help bring about its demise.

Notes

1. For instance, some critics of the Anti-Apartheid Act have identified it as a key reason why the white electorate lurched to the right in the 1987 South African election. But sanctions are conveniently ignored when it comes to analyzing the drift to the center of the white electorate in the 1989 election.

2. *Washington Post*, 20 August 1989.

3. *Africa News*, 19 September 1988.

4. Congressman Walter Fauntroy (D-Washington, D.C.) has introduced the South Africa Financial Sanctions Act of 1989 (H.R. 3458) in the House of Representatives. The Act would prohibit US banks from rescheduling debt and the conversion of short-term into long-term loans; require South Africa to pay 20% of the principal of

outstanding debt annually; and set limits on trade finance and correspondent banking services.

5. *Africa News,* August 1989.

6. *Weekly Mail,* 26 May-1 June 1989.

7. *Newsweek,* 25 September 1989; *Washington Post,* 4 October 1989.

8. For more detailed analyses of the congressional battle over sanctions in 1988, see Steven McDonald, "Washington Pauses to Reassess the South African Sanctions Issue," *CSIS Africa Notes,* Number 94 (20 January 1989) and Imani Countess, "Sanctions Supporters Face Uphill Battle in 1989," *Africa Information Network Washington Report* (December 1988-January 1989), 1-3, 6-7.

9. "Sanctions and South Africa's Neighbours," Overseas Development Institute (London), *Briefing Paper,* May 1987, 6.

10. *New York Times,* 5 July 1988.

11. John Daniel, "Sneaking Around Sanctions," *Southern Africa Report,* IV, 5 (1989), 22-23.

12. *Washington Post,* 20 August 1989.

13. See articles on the cultural boycott in the *Weekly Mail,* 7 July-13 July 1989, 14 July-20 July 1989, and 21 July-27 July 1989.

14. *Africa News,* August 1989.

IMPLEMENTATION OF THE ANTI-APARTHEID ACT OF 1986*

Gay McDougall

Introduction

Background

On October 2, 1986, the Comprehensive Anti-Apartheid Act of 1986 ("the Act"), 22 U.S.C. §§ 5001-5116 (Supp. IV 1986), became law.[1]

The purpose of the Act, as set forth in the statute, is:

> [T]o set forth a comprehensive and complete framework to guide the efforts of the United States in helping to bring an end to apartheid in South Africa and lead to the establishment of a nonracial, democratic form of government.

22 U.S.C. § 5002 (Supp. IV 1986).

---

*This chapter was excerpted from a longer report issued by the Southern Africa Project of the Lawyers' Committee for Civil Rights Under Law in June 1988, to which a number of people contributed.

In summary, the Act bans imports into the United States of textiles, agricultural products, iron and steel, coal, and uranium from South Africa, as well as any article that is grown, produced, manufactured, marketed or otherwise exported by a parastatal organization of South Africa and Namibia.[2] In addition, the Act prohibits new investment in South Africa, bans new loans to the Government of South Africa or to organizations controlled by the Government of South Africa and revokes U.S. landing rights for South African-owned aircraft, as well as the rights of U.S. owned aircraft to provide service between the United States and South Africa.

The Act also codifies, and in some cases extends, the sanctions contained in President Reagan's Executive Orders Nos. 12,532[3] and 12,535, of September 9, and October 1, 1985, that ban the importation of Krugerrands; the importation of arms, ammunition or military vehicles made in South Africa; the export of computer software and related items to South Africa for use by Government agencies; the making or approval of loans by U.S. banks to the Government of South Africa; and the export to South Africa of nuclear power equipment and supplies.[4] Executive Order No. 12,532 also requires the implementation of fair labor practices by U.S. nationals employing more than 25 individuals in South Africa.[5]

Under the Act, sanctions are not to be lifted until South Africa meets a number of specified conditions related to achieving a negotiated political settlement with representatives of the black majority and the dismantling of the apartheid system. If within one year the South African Government has not made substantial progress in ending apartheid, the Act provides that the President shall recommend which of the additional sanctions listed in the Act should be imposed.[6]

On October 27, 1986, President Reagan issued Executive Order No. 12,571 to implement the Act (hereinafter the "Implementing Order"). It delegates to respective Executive Branch agencies responsibility for implementing each section of the Act. The Office of Foreign Assets Control ("OFAC") of the Department of the Treasury, which customarily implements restrictions on import and financial transactions with other countries, was charged with implementing the import and financial transactions prohibitions contained in the Act.[7]

The Limited Nature and Impact of the Sanctions

U.S. sanctions against South Africa differ radically from U.S. sanctions against other countries. Although there is some variation among their provisions, U.S. sanctions that have been imposed against North Korea, Cambodia, Vietnam,[8] Cuba,[9] Iran,[10] Nicaragua,[11] and Libya[12] are uniformly comprehensive; they are intended to prohibit virtually all trade and financial transactions with the designated countries as a means of expressing U.S. disapproval with and desire to effect change in the political and economic systems of such countries.[13]

Although the sanctions imposed in the Comprehensive Anti-Apartheid Act seek goals similar to U.S. sanctions against other countries, they are significantly more limited in their scope and application. They do not impose a comprehensive trade embargo, nor do they mandate U.S. corporate withdrawal from South Africa or the cessation of all financial transactions between the U.S. and South Africa. Rather, the import restrictions skirt significant pressure points in the South African economy. While the Act prohibits gold coin imports, for example, it does not prohibit the import of gold in other forms—South Africa's major export commodity.[14] Even the ban on gold coin imports was not significant, since Krugerrand sales in the United States had been dropping steadily prior to the imposition of the ban since their peak in 1984.[15]

The Act's ban on investment also has had limited immediate effect. Foreign investment in South Africa was already in a significant decline by the time the Act was implemented, as were American exports to South Africa.[16] For example, the U.S. share of the computer market in South Africa has been dropping substantially since 1980.[17] Further, the potential impact of U.S. sanctions against South Africa has been circumscribed generally by the lack of effective multilateral coordination on sanctions.[18]

The experience, however, with regard to sanctions against Rhodesia confirms that even when sanctions are comprehensive and multilateral, they are a medium- to long-range strategy. Sanctions are not expected to have a sudden dramatic impact.

Indeed, they may have limited, even inverse impact in the early stages. Over the long term, however, they have a corrosive effect on the economy and become a significant additive to other international and internal pressures on a Government.[19]

To some extent, the political realities that weighed on Congress when it voted for less than comprehensive sanctions against South Africa can be understood and the limited nature of the resulting sanctions accepted. In some respects, their limited nature represents an attempt by Congress to direct their impact on the South African Government, as opposed to the South African people. The South African sanctions also represent the first time in recent history that Congress, not the President, has imposed substantial sanctions on another country. Other U.S. sanctions have been imposed by Executive Order. The experience under the Act teaches that when there is a fundamental divergence of views between the President and Congress with respect to the necessity or nature of sanctions, the statutory provisions must be drafted with precision to guarantee that Congressional intent is fulfilled.

Less understandable or acceptable, however, are the other processes that have eroded the effectiveness of the sanctions that Congress did impose. After passage of the Act, its implementation was entrusted to an Administration which publicly and vehemently opposed sanctions against South Africa. This generated understandable concern among members of Congress and Americans supporting sanctions against South Africa that Congressional intent with respect to the sanctions would receive less than full and faithful implementation.

An in-depth assessment of Executive agency action reveals that, in part, this concern has been realized. With regard to some of the sanctions, little or no issue can be taken with the Executive Branch implementation of the statutory language and Congressional intent. With respect to other provisions, however, significant problems have arisen that call into question the Administration's faithful adherence to the letter and the spirit of the Act and reveal differences that are hard to reconcile between the manner in which certain sanctions against South Africa are interpreted and the manner in which similar sanctions against other countries have been interpreted.

In short, the current sanctions are indeed inadequate for two reasons. First, the sanctions are too limited in their scope and application to be effectively implemented. Second, the Reagan Administration has created glaring loopholes through regulations promulgated to implement the law by Executive branch agencies. An examination of implementation of several provisions of the Act will support these conclusions.

Prohibition on New Investments by U.S. Entities in South Africa

Potentially the most far-reaching of the provisions of the Act is Section 310 which states:

> [n]o national of the United States may, directly, or through another person, make any new investment in South Africa.[20]

"New investment" is defined as:

> (i) a commitment, or contribution of funds or other assets, and a loan or other extension of credit.[21]

"New investment" does not include:

> (i) the reinvestment of profits generated by a controlled South African entity[22] into that same controlled South African entity or the investment of such profit in a South African entity;[23] (ii) contributions of money or other assets where such contributions are necessary to enable a controlled South African entity to operate in an economically sound manner without expanding its operations; or (iii) the ownership or control of a share or interest in a South African entity or a controlled South African entity or a debt or equity security issued by the Government of South Africa or a South African entity before October 2, 1986, or the transfer or acquisition of such a share, interest or equity security if any such transfer or acquisition does not result in a payment, contribution of funds or assets, or credit to a

> South African entity, a controlled South African entity, or the Government of South Africa.[24]

In effect, U.S. companies are permitted to reinvest their profits earned in South Africa and are allowed to make certain new investments necessary to maintain their operations. This implies that U.S. companies are not required to divest their South African business interests. Americans are also permitted to hold debt or equity securities issued by a South African entity as long as such securities were issued before October 2, 1986. However, trading in South African securities issued on or after October 2, 1986 is prohibited, whether by direct purchase, purchase of American Depository Receipts evidencing such securities, mutual fund investment or reinvestment, or otherwise.[25]

Some of the most difficult regulatory and enforcement questions regarding the Act arise in the context of the prohibition of "new investments," specifically, what is the scope to be given to the exceptions to the ban on new investments.

Seller-Financed Withdrawals of Corporations From South Africa

One problem of interpretation of Section 310 relates to its application to what had become a standard practice for U.S. companies withdrawing from South Africa. The problems faced by such U.S. parents include the following:

> —A company, having been involved in manufacturing, rather than a trade or service industry, has substantial assets in South Africa for which it wants to be compensated and for which it, at least, wants to minimize its losses.
>
> —There is no South African purchaser with sufficient capital.
>
> —Even if a purchaser with sufficient capital is found, the value of the transaction for the U.S. parent is diminished substantially by the fact that proceeds from the sale of assets must be exchanged at the financial exchange rate, the lower of the two-tier foreign exchange rate introduced by South Africa in 1985.

The solution adopted by several corporations which withdrew from South Africa prior to the effective date of the Act was seller-financing. In essence, the seller (the U.S. parent company) extended a loan or credit for the purchase price of its South African assets to the South African buyer. To circumvent the lower rand exchange rate, repayment was sometimes disguised as part of fees for licensing agreements, giving the South African purchaser access to the U.S. parent's manufacturing processes, technology, equipment, spare parts, managerial services, or in some instances, its trademark.[26] Payments on such licensing arrangements, as well as for trade, were exchanged at the higher commercial exchange rate.

An example of such a transaction occurred in October 1986, when General Motors Corp. and IBM Corp. announced plans to withdraw from South Africa. Both transactions involved loans to the South African buyers to finance their purchases. Repayment of principal and interest was to be made over a period of years out of working capital and profits. In the case of IBM, the loan will be paid over a five year period. The new company holds the IBM exclusive franchise in South Africa, and a contract for importing and selling IBM products and services. The deal also guarantees the new company access to future IBM technology.

General Motors sold its subsidiary to a group headed by local management. The U.S. parent reportedly paid approximately $45 million to cover its subsidiary's debts and agreed to a delay of as much as 18 months for the payment of the purchase price out of anticipated profits. In exchange for the investment, the parent company receives GM license fees for the use of its trademarks and continued income from the sale of automobile kits and components and its exclusive franchise arrangement with the new South African company.[27]

When the Act went into effect, OFAC had to determine whether arrangements such as these violated Section 310's ban on new investments. While there was no evidence that Congress specifically considered the question, it was thought that Congress would be inclined to grant an exemption for such transactions, since to do otherwise would appear to contradict the spirit of disinvestment. The Treasury Department regulations issued to implement Section 310 were, however, silent as to whether seller-financed withdrawals would be interpreted as violations of the Act.

According to OFAC officials, "new investment" by a U.S. national for the purpose of withdrawal shall be reviewed on a case-by-case basis, although new investment will not be permitted in a South African entity even for the purpose of disinvestment. The proposed withdrawal transaction is to be presented to OFAC. If the plan is approved, OFAC will issue a "letter of comfort."

Investments To Continue Operations In a Sound Economic Manner

The statute also fails to state what is meant by the exemption from the prohibition on "new investment" for contributions of money or other assets "necessary to enable a controlled South African entity to operate in an economically sound manner without expanding its operations."[28] That exemption and the question of the Act's application to seller-financed withdrawals were central issues in the debate that took place in December 1987 regarding the Ford Motor Company's[29] plan to withdraw from South Africa.

In 1985, Ford merged its South Africa operations with a branch of the Anglo American Corporation to form the South African Motor Corporation, "Samcor." Ford took a 42% ownership in Samcor. Both Anglo American and Ford South Africa had been experiencing losses generated by the declining South African economy and automobile market. Samcor experienced substantial losses in 1985 and 1986 and, as a consequence, incurred heavy debt. To cut its losses and in response to the demands of the anti-apartheid movement, Ford was ready to fully withdraw from South Africa.

Ford's withdrawal transaction had several elements. Twenty-four percent of Ford's equity interest in Samcor was to be placed in a trust for Samcor's employees.[30] The remaining 18% was to be transferred to the Anglo American Corporation for $1.00. Ford products would continue to be sold in South Africa through a network of 146 dealers. Ford would supply Samcor with necessary components, licensed use of the Ford trademark, plus management and technical assistance.

The controversial aspect of the plan involved a cash "contribution" by Ford to Samcor of R203.3 million or roughly $61 million. The "contribution" was considered a "fundamental precondition" to implementation of the withdrawal plan and was "conditional upon U.S. Treasury acquiescence."[31] Briefing materials distributed by Ford made five arguments in favor of the cash contribution.[32] Anglo American stated its intention to close Samcor if the contribution was not made.

In asserting the legality of its withdrawal plan under the Act, Ford sought refuge under the exception to the "no new investment rule" allowing contributions to a "controlled South African entity" to enable it to continue its operations in "an economically sound manner".[33] The application of that exception to the no-new-investment rule has always been unclear.

In general, the exceptions to the new investment ban appear to support the view that, while Congress wanted to restrict the growth of U.S. investment in South Africa, it did not intend the Act to mandate corporate withdrawal. Congress was willing to make certain concessions, therefore, to permit U.S. corporate subsidiaries in South Africa to continue their operations. While the Act does not define what operating in "an economically sound manner" may be, the Senate Report on S.2701, the Senate Bill which was eventually enacted as law, says simply that this "allows an extension of funds or assets in the event of a flood, fire or other occurrence which would force the operation to shut down or operate at [an] uneconomical level."[34] It goes on to say that "[u]nder no circumstances, however, does this exception permit investment designed to expand existing operations or increase profitability." On the floor of the House on September 12, 1986, Congressman Roth described this provision as permitting "investment necessary to maintain continuing operations" and that it was meant to allow U.S. companies to "continue to conduct their businesses in South Africa at the current level of operations."[35]

This legislative history suggests at least four prerequisites to the application of this exception: 1) the recipient must be a South African subsidiary controlled by a U.S. corporation; 2) the U.S.

corporation must be continuing its operations in South Africa; 3) there must be an event which necessitates an emergency replacement of capital; and 4) the contribution from the U.S. parent corporation must be solely to return the subsidiary to its operating level prior to the event.

The Ford transaction did not appear to meet any of these prerequisites. First, Ford held only a 42% equity interest in Samcor, and it is not clear that Ford "controlled" Samcor.[36] For example, the State Department concluded that Ford did not "control" Samcor for the purpose of compliance with the Code of Conduct set out in the Act with respect to employment practices.[37]

The second prerequisite for an exception to the ban on new investment is that the U.S. parent must be continuing its operations in South Africa. Even Ford's legal counsel conceded: "Congress intended that new investment be limited to contributions essential for the continuation of existing U.S. owned business; a condition precedent to the contribution."[38] There can be no doubt that the Ford Motor Company was withdrawing from South Africa. To obfuscate its failure to meet this fundamental requirement, Ford engaged in a fictitious analysis: instead of viewing its disinvestment scheme as one transaction, it was viewed as two separate and distinct actions. In the first, Ford, *which is continuing its operations in South Africa,* made a permissible new investment that met the statutory requirements. In the second, which took place immediately after the first transaction, Ford withdrew.

The meaning of the third prerequisite, the occurrence of an event which necessitates an emergency replacement of capital, is ambiguous. The Senate Report refers to natural disasters, acts of God: "in the event of flood, fire or other occurrences which would force the operation to shut down or operate at an uneconomical level."[39] Ford's senior attorney argued that in the absence of statutory language creating limits, it would be an unwarranted artificial construction of the Senate Report to confine the course to natural disasters. Ford's counsel reasoned: "It would be illogical to assume that natural disasters were carved out as taking precedence over economic disasters. The standard should be and is one of effect on the South African entity. The Act and regulations give that standard as 'necessary . . . to operate in an economically sound manner.' The Senate Report amplifies, but not necessarily clarifies, that standard to one which 'would force the operation to shut down or operate at an uneconomical level'."[40] Ford argued, then, that the inability of a heavily leveraged, perennially unprofitable company to finance a competitively necessary product action should be considered a causative factor under the Act equal to a natural disaster.

Ford did not dispute the fourth prerequisite, that is that the contribution from the U.S. parent must be solely to return the subsidiary to its operating level prior to the event. When the event is determined to be long-term unprofitability, however, the requirement appears to be inapposite.

The Treasury Department acquiesced to the Ford withdrawal plan and it was implemented in full. The Department declined to make a public record of its decision.

The Ford deal sets a dangerous precedent. It appears that the Treasury Department has interpreted the exemption to permit new investments in companies in South Africa to cure the effects of long-term unprofitability. The ramifications of such an expansive interpretation of the exception to the prohibition on new investments could be enormous. With respect to the Ford transaction, the result has been that an otherwise impermissible infusion of $61 million was made into the South African economy. This violates the letter and the spirit of the Act.

In light of the Ford ruling, this potentially crippling loophole should be closed. The Act should be amended to eliminate the exception to the ban on new investments for replacement capital to allow a company to "continue to operate in an economically sound manner." At a minimum, specific language should be added that clearly limits its application to situations where the local business has been damaged by natural forces. Complete elimination of the exception would not derogate from what appears to be Congress' understandable intention to assure investors who invested in South Africa prior to the enactment of the statute that they would not be unduly penalized if their investments were wiped out by causes over which they had no control. Insurance exists precisely for such purposes. Congress could authorize U.S. Government insurance bodies such as the

Overseas Private Investment Corp. to issue policies covering such catastrophic conditions. If such insurance is unavailable, then the statute and the implementing regulations should specifically categorize those situations where, and the circumstances under which, the exception would be available to U.S. investors.

Import Restrictions

The Act includes several prohibitions on imports into the United States of goods produced in South Africa. Section 303(a) of the Act prohibits the import into the United States of any "article which is grown, produced, manufactured by, marketed, or otherwise exported by a parastatal organization of South Africa," with the exception of "those strategic minerals for which the President has certified to the Congress that the quantities essential for the economy or defense of the United States are unavailable from reliable and secure suppliers."[41] Section 303(b) defines a "parastatal organization" as "a corporation or partnership owned or controlled or subsidized by the Government of South Africa," but not one "which previously received start-up assistance from the South African Industrial Development Corporation but which is now privately owned."

The State Department, charged by the President with responsibility for determining what South African organizations are parastatal,[42] has published definitions of the operative terms and a list of organizations it has identified as parastatal.[43]

The State Department has defined an entity "owned" by the South African Government as one in which "the South African Government holds more than 50% of the outstanding voting securities of the corporation, partnership, or entity concerned."[44] State Department regulations define a corporation, partnership or entity as "controlled" by the South African Government if the South African Government controls in fact the corporation, partnership or entity concerned.[45] This would include situations where the South African Government has the authority to manage, direct or administer the affairs of a corporation, partnership or entity.[46]

The State Department determined that a corporation, partnership or entity "subsidized" by the South African Government is one "at the present time receiving any financial assistance on preferential terms from the South African Government, other than that generally available to the public. A corporation, partnership, or entity that is receiving a *de minimis* amount of assistance from the South African Government is presumed not to be 'subsidized' by the South African Government for purposes of the Act."[47]

The parastatal/non-parastatal distinction in Section 303 was intended by its Congressional sponsors as a type of targeting "to pressure the South African Government" specifically, rather than "those who bear no responsibility for and have no influence with that Government."[48] The distinction made by Congress is based on the assumption that a clear division can be made between public and private enterprises in South Africa. Congress assumed that South African Government enterprises could be affected while holding the private sector immune. That basic assumption, however, is inconsistent with the realities of the South African economy.

The South African economy is one in which private industry has been pervasively aided by the Government. It is not realistic to attempt to distinguish corporations or other entities entangled with the Government in an economy where Government assistance is common and its forms widely varied. The goal of not trading with South African Government enterprises, consequently, requires a much broader approach than that taken in the statutory or regulatory definition of parastatal.

The South African Government is involved in industry in crucial ways excluded by the State Department's definition of "subsidized." To encourage industries to locate in areas near the "homelands," for example, the Government has provided financial assistance such as tax concessions, loans, reduced railway rates and exemptions from wage regulations.[49] Government assistance of this nature, however, is apparently not covered by the State Department's definition of "subsidized": assistance "on preferential terms" and not "generally available to the public."[50] Similarly, the Act expressly excludes as a determinant of parastatal status the start-up assistance that is frequently provided by South Africa's Industrial Development Corporation.[51]

Furthermore, even trading with a company not receiving direct South African Government assistance inures to the Government's direct benefit. For example, in the 1984-85 fiscal year, income taxes and lease payments by the privately owned gold mines alone accounted for 8.3% of Government revenues, while income taxes from all other companies totaled only 16.9% of revenues.[52] Thus, although these privately owned companies are not parastatals, *per se*, they give direct economic support to the Government and, consequently, to the maintenance of its policies of apartheid.

Finally, two points must be noted about the effect of the parastatal/non-parastatal distinction. While clearly Congressional intent with respect to Section 303 was to penalize the South African Government rather than to establish as broad a trade embargo as possible, it should not escape attention that banning trade with narrowly defined parastatals results in a minimal trade embargo.

Data is not available on the percentage of South Africa's exports to the U.S. prior to the Act that were from parastatals. However, few of the major segments of South African industry that are owned directly by the Government, and thus covered by the existing parastatal provision, produce goods that are exported to the U.S. For example, 40% of South Africa's fuel requirements are produced by the three oil-from-coal plants built by the South African Coal, Oil and Gas Corporation ("SASOL"),[53] and 93% of the country's electricity is supplied by the state-controlled Electricity Supply Commission ("ESCOM").[54] South Africa, however, exports neither oil nor electricity to the United States. Additionally, South African State President P. W. Botha has recently announced a goal of privatizing the South African government-owned corporations.[55] The effect would be to nullify Section 303.

Because of the extent of the interrelationships between Government and private enterprise in South Africa, the goal of pressuring the South African Government is not accomplished by limiting the import ban to products of organizations "owned, controlled or subsidized" by the Government. The only realistic way to affect the Government, taking into consideration its relationship to private industry, is to ban all imports from South Africa.

In addition, the parastatal/non-parastatal distinction as to imports is administratively unworkable. First, it has proved impossible to gather significant data necessary to determine which entities meet the statutory and regulatory definition.

Statistics on ownership of South African corporations are published and readily available. Staff at the United States Embassy in South Africa has found it virtually impossible, however, to obtain information about Government control or subsidization of these corporations.[56] There is no independent source of such data, and the companies at issue are—not surprisingly—unwilling to supply it. There is thus no way to ensure that the State Department's list of parastatal organizations is complete or accurate. No revisions to the Act or the regulations could cure the problem of access to the necessary data.

Additional problems arise at the port of entry to the United States. Neither the U.S. importer of a particular product, nor the Customs official responsible for determining the product's status, can make an independent determination regarding the producer of every South African commodity imported into the United States. Both must rely on the exporter's characterization of the product's source.[57]

Such problems in administration and enforcement have a significant impact on the integrity of the prohibition. Clearly, a comprehensive ban on the import of goods from South Africa, or an embargo that makes distinctions on an item by item basis rather than a focus on the identity of the producer, would greatly facilitate administration and enforcement.

Ban on Uranium Imports

In the years prior to the Act, South Africa earned substantial amounts of U.S. dollars from uranium exports to this country. Section 309(a) of the Act, however, prohibits the importation of "uranium ore [and] uranium oxide . . . produced or manufactured in South Africa."[58] Section 309 was intended to terminate all uranium trade with South Africa. As Senator Edward M. Kennedy (D-Mass.), a chief sponsor of the legislation, stated on the floor of the Senate on October 18, 1986, the purpose of the Act was "to cut off all imports of the items specified, no 'and, ifs or buts' and no loopholes either."[59] Following the Act's passage, the Treasury Department was assigned Executive Branch responsibility for implementing the provisions of Section 309.[60]

The use of the term "uranium oxide" by Congress must be read to prohibit all processed forms of uranium and not to create a technical distinction between a specific uranium oxide compound and other related compounds which result from intermediate and necessary steps in the enrichment process. Similarly, "uranium ore" as used in Section 309 of the Act refers to all unprocessed forms of uranium. This clear Congressional intent, however, has been subverted by the implementing regulations promulgated by the Department of the Treasury.

The Treasury Department issued a "Final Rule" interpreting Section 309, which concluded that by using the terms uranium "ore" and "oxide" in the Act, Congress did not intend to establish a comprehensive ban on the importation of all forms of uranium from South Africa. Rather, the Treasury Department narrowly construed the statute to distinguish between uranium ore and oxide-related compounds, such as uranium hexafluoride, which are essentially interchangeable and which serve no commercial purpose other than as fuel for nuclear reactors.[61]

In promulgating the Final Rule, Treasury sought to distinguish between these various chemical compounds of uranium on the theory that Congress intended to ban some but not all of them. Treasury's Final Rule stated that "[a]rticles such as uranium hexafluoride, which are produced from uranium ore or uranium oxide and which the U.S. Customs Service determines to have been substantially transformed outside the United States, are not subject to the import prohibition."[62]

The issue of whether uranium hexafluoride is encompassed within the definition of uranium ore or oxide is of great significance, as any construction of Section 309 which would limit its effect to those forms of uranium found only at the beginning and end of the enrichment process, while leaving intermediate forms of uranium free to enter the United States, would effectively nullify the Congressional prohibition on the import of uranium. The Treasury Department's interpretation permits easy circumvention of the sanction. The conversion of uranium yellowcake into uranium hexafluoride involves an expenditure of less than 4% of the total cost it takes to produce nuclear fuel. Therefore, the ore can be readily and easily transformed into uranium hexafluoride in Europe or Canada and then transported into the United States for further processing.

The legal rationale employed by the Department of the Treasury—the doctrine of "substantial transformation"—does not support the Final Rule. This doctrine was developed in the context of customs law to determine the country of origin of an import for duty purposes and has previously been used solely to categorize various commodities in order to assess tariffs and trade quotas. Substantial transformation has never been involved in the context of an absolute prohibition on imports of a particular product from a particular country.

Even if reference to the doctrine of substantial transformation were appropriate in this case, Treasury's decision to apply the doctrine to uranium oxide and hexafluoride runs counter to well-settled principles of customs law. The courts and the U.S. Customs Service have most commonly examined a number of factors to determine if substantial transformation has occurred: whether a new commodity has been created with a distinct character, independent use or value, and a new name.[63] While different nomenclature distinguishes hexafluoride from oxide, the change undergone in processing from a concentrate to hexafluoride does not affect its basic character as uranium. Processing adds no foreign element. Nor does it significantly alter its utility. Hexafluoride has no independent use or value outside of the nuclear fuel enrichment cycle. It is its character as uranium which makes the ultimate product, fuel rods, valuable—not its chemical form as hexafluoride or oxide.

The effect of the rule permitting the importation of South African uranium hexafluoride was a sudden increase in requests for authorization to import that form of uranium. Shortly after the Act went into force, applications for eight licenses to import South African uranium hexafluoride were filed with the Nuclear Regulatory Commission (NRC), an independent Government agency that controls the uranium trade in the United States.[64] The applicants sought licenses to import a total of 3,708 metric tons of uranium, 2,708 tons or 73% of which was to be in the form of hexafluoride. By contrast, prior to the Act, in 1985 and 1986, hexafluoride comprised only about 10% and 9%, respectively, of the overall uranium imports from South Africa.[65] Despite legal challenges by the Lawyers' Committee for Civil Rights Under Law and others[66] to the new license applications and to existing licenses, the Nuclear Regulatory Commission granted three of the pending license applications to import South African uranium hexafluoride on September 21, 1987.[67] The Commission concluded that:

> . . . [S]ection 309(a) of the Anti-Apartheid Act, 22 U.S.C. 5059(a), bars the import of uranium ore and uranium oxide, regardless of its intended end use. Importation of other forms of uranium is not barred by section 309(a). South African-origin uranium oxide which is transformed into uranium hexafluoride or other substantially transformed uranium compounds before it is imported into the United States is also not barred.[68]

The grant of those licenses by the NRC created the potential that twice as much South African uranium may be imported into the United States now than was actually imported in the year prior to sanctions. The three licenses will permit a total of 1,167.732 metric tons of South African-origin uranium hexafluoride to be imported over a three-year period. At the same time, the NRC had under consideration a petition to revoke 11 pre-existing licenses to the extent that they authorized the importation of South African-origin uranium. The NRC declined to limit those existing licenses with respect to South African-origin hexafluoride.[69]

The NRC's grant of these licenses is currently under review by the United States Court of Appeals for the District of Columbia Circuit. Regardless of the court's ultimate ruling on the issue of the abuse of the "substantial transformation" doctrine, however, Congress should act to prevent future abuses in interpretation by amending the language to explicitly ban the importation of all South African uranium, regardless of its form, processing or end-user.

Import Restrictions on Other Products

The Act prohibits the importation of certain other products such as coal, textiles, agricultural products, iron, steel, and sugar. Unfortunately, both the regulations implementing these import prohibitions and the "country-of-origin" rules used by the Customs Service undercut the effectiveness of the sanctions.

Section 320 of the Act prohibits the importation into the United States of "iron or steel extracted in South Africa."[70] On November 19, 1986, the Treasury Department issued guidelines for the U.S. Customs Service to determine which products are subject to the import bans imposed by the Act.[71]

The regulations do not include ferroalloys, such as ferrochromium and ferromanganese.[72] By excluding ferroalloys from the list of banned products, the regulations diminish the effectiveness of the sanctions. In 1986, ferroalloys were South Africa's sixth leading export, exceeding its iron ore exports.[73] In addition, South Africa is the world's dominant supplier of ferrochromium, with an export value of approximately R500 million a year.[74] In 1985, South Africa produced 852 metric tons of ferrochromium and 331 metric tons of ferromanganese.[75] Thus, in a manner probably not anticipated by Congress, the regulations fail to restrict the importation into the United States of a substantial percentage of iron products from South Africa.[76]

Export Restrictions

The Act's approach to the use of exports as an economic weapon against apartheid is highly selective. The export of only four classes of goods are embargoed: (1) computers, computer software, or goods or technology to manufacture computers, if the computer product is intended for use by agencies of the South African Government engaged in the enforcement of the apartheid policies of that Government;[77] (2) nuclear materials and nuclear technology;[78] (3) items on the U.S. Munitions List that are not exported for commercial purposes;[79] and (4) crude oil and refined petroleum products.[80] Many of these prohibitions, moreover, merely codify prohibitions already in place prior to the passage of the Act.

With regard to administrative enforcement, the administering agencies—primarily the Department of Commerce and the State Department—simply made minor modifications to existing regulations.[81] On the whole, it is not clear that the Act has dramatically closed prior loopholes, nor that the Act has resulted in the taking of steps by the administrative bodies charged with its enforcement that they would not, otherwise, have undertaken.[82]

The only new export restriction is imposed in Section 321, which bans the export of "crude oil or refined petroleum products which is subject to the jurisdiction of the United States, or which is exported by a person subject to the jurisdiction of the United States."[83]

The statutory ban on the export of crude oil and refined petroleum products appears to be, on its face, complete. It covers products within the jurisdiction of the United States, and those under the control of persons subject to U.S. jurisdiction. However, Commerce Department regulations require that, in order for the sanction to come into effect, the product must be subject to the jurisdiction of the United States, *and* the decision maker must also be subject to the jurisdiction of the United States. These regulations exempt re-export from third countries as long as such re-export is not undertaken by a U.S. incorporated entity, or a U.S. national (including a U.S. permanent resident) acting on his own behalf, or export to the third country was undertaken with the intent to circumvent the prohibition.[84] Further, the Commerce Department has defined the export restriction narrowly, to exclude from the export ban petrochemicals.[85] This is clearly not consistent with Congressional intent.

These export restrictions are very limited and hardly merit the descriptions "punitive" or "comprehensive." Even within their narrow scope, however, there are substantial loopholes.[86]

The shortcoming of an overly restrictive approach to the use of export sanctions is illustrated by the ban on computer products and related technology. Despite the overriding importance of computer technology to the maintenance of the apartheid system and the South African economy, and the ease with which access to computers can be manipulated, the Act simply bans exports to "apartheid enforcing agencies." The remainder of the South African Government is at liberty to obtain U.S. computers and computer technology as long as the Government (which has openly expressed the view that it is entitled to take any steps whatever to evade foreign sanctions) gives an end-user certification that it would not transfer the computer and related products to its apartheid enforcing agencies. Moreover, the South African private sector retains unlimited access to U.S. computer technology.[87]

A complete prohibition on the export of U.S. computers and computer technology to South Africa—South African Government and private entities alike—is imperative. In the absence of that there should be, at a minimum, a complete ban on exports to the South African Government. At the same time, the end-user certification requirement, and particularly its enforcement—through both pre-and post-shipment inspections—should be strengthened to ensure that private recipients do not divert computers to the South African Government.[88]

With regard to the ban on the export of crude oil and petroleum products, there should be a clear prohibition on the export or re-export of crude oil from the U.S., and of any product produced from crude oil that originated in the U.S., regardless of the nationality of the individual or entity with control over that product. Further, the statute should be amended to expressly require the Commerce Department to include petrochemicals in the definition of "refined petroleum products."

Additionally, while Congressional unwillingness to burden U.S. exporters with the imposition of restrictions on their exports to South Africa is, perhaps, understandable in this age of substantial trade deficits,[89] yet the limitation on U.S. export bans to the four discrete and well-tested areas of computers, arms, nuclear material, and petroleum products is too narrow. Specifically, Congress should at the least include a ban on shipment of capital goods to South Africa.[90] In 1986, machinery and transport equipment represented 27.2% of all South African and Namibian imports.[91] The United States is the fourth largest supplier of machinery to South Africa.[92] As a South African businessman has pointed out, restrictions on South Africa's access to capital goods would significantly affect its economy;[93] and this could be done at relatively small cost to the U.S.

economy. Moreover, as has been the case in other areas, the U.S. lead is likely to put pressure on other industrialized countries to adopt comparable restrictions on the export of machinery.[94]

Multilateral Measures

When Congress passed the Act, it recognized that multilateral cooperation was necessary for effective sanctions. Therefore, Section 401 of the Act states "[i]t is the policy of the United States to seek international cooperative agreements with the other industrialized democracies to bring about the complete dismantling of apartheid." It also called on the President or the Secretary of State to convene an international conference with other industrialized democracies to develop a coordinated strategy no later than 180 days after the Act went into force. It stated further that it was the sense of Congress that the United States Ambassador to the United Nations sponsor a Security Council resolution that would mandate that all nations impose sanctions similar to our own.

The language of this Section of the Act was interpreted by the State Department as not legally binding on the President's authority to conduct foreign affairs. Attempts by Congress particularly to mandate Presidential actions with respect to bilateral or multilateral negotiations may raise complex issues.[95] There are several precedents, however. They include, for example, a provision in the Bretton Woods Agreement Act, by which Congress mandates the President to instruct the Executive Director to the International Monetary Fund to oppose the extension of credit to South Africa, unless certifications are made to Congress relating to the effects of apartheid on labor, capital mobility, balance of payments, and related standards.[96]

The "Gonzalez Amendment" to the International Development Association Act is another example. It requires the President to instruct the U.S. Executive Directors of the International Bank for Reconstruction and Development and the International Development Association to vote against loans to any country which has nationalized property owned by or which has repudiated contracts with a U.S. national.[97]

In this case, the Reagan Administration disregarded the Congressional wishes to negotiate multilateral cooperation on sanctions against South Africa. Not only has the Administration failed to comply with the spirit of the law, it has actively worked to subvert and undermine the efforts of other nations to achieve precisely the kind of multilateral cooperation contemplated by the statute. Since the Act came into force, the State Department has made no effort to convene an international conference or to coordinate anti-apartheid policies among the industrialized nations of the world. Instead, and totally inconsistent with the intent of the Congress, on February 20, 1987 and again on April 9, 1987, the Administration vetoed resolutions in the United Nations Security Council that would have made the same sanctions that exist in U.S. law mandatory for other countries.[98] The U.S. is one of six industrialized countries that account for 84% of South Africa's trade.[99] If a coordinated strategy had been achieved among those nations, the impact on the South African economy would have been staggering.

Conclusion

Based on the above analysis, action is warranted on three levels: the Executive Branch agencies must improve implementation of the sanctions through tighter regulations; Congress must take legislative initiatives to close those loopholes that were unintentional and Congress must also grapple with the reality that selective sanctions invite misinterpretations and evasions. Effective implementation is most easily achieved with comprehensive multilateral sanctions.

Notes

1. The history of the Act is as follows: On June 18, 1986, the House passed a bill (H.R. 4868) that would have required the U.S. to

impose a comprehensive trade embargo of South Africa and forced all U.S. companies to leave South Africa within 180 days of enactment. On August 15, 1986, the Senate passed S.2701, which sought to impose more limited sanctions than the House bill. The House adopted this version without changes, thereby eliminating the need for a House-Senate conference. The President vetoed the bill on September 26, 1986, and, in turn, was overridden by the House on September 29, 1986 and the Senate on October 2, 1986. Comprehensive Anti-Apartheid Act of 1986, Pub. L. No. 99-440, 100 Stat. 1086 (1986).

2. Section 3(6) of the Act defines South Africa as including "any territory under the administration, legal or illegal, of South Africa . . . ." Namibia is an international territory under the *de jure* authority of the United Nations but the illegal occupation of South Africa. For all purposes, therefore, the sanctions imposed by the Act apply to Namibia. The "bantustans" or "homelands," to which South African blacks are assigned on the basis of ethnic origin are also deemed to be part of South Africa for purposes of the Act. The so-called "independent" homelands include Transkei, Bophuthatswana, Ciskei and Venda.

3. Executive Order No. 12,532 cites as its statutory authority, *inter alia*, the International Emergency Economic Powers Act, 50 U.S.C. {{ 1701-1706, and the National Emergencies Act, 50 U.S.C. {{ 1601-1651.

4. Some of the sanctions contained in the 1985 Executive Order merely reaffirmed sanctions already in place by existing legislation. For example, since 1982, the U.S. has prohibited the export of computers to the South African military, police and apartheid-enforcing entities (the "Berman Amendment" to the Export Administration Act.). Since 1964, the United States has restricted military exports to the Republic of South Africa and to Namibia. The restrictions on conventional military hardware are administered and monitored by the Office of Munitions Control ("OMC") of the Department of State. The Arms Export Control Act, 22 U.S.C. § 2778 (1982), is the statutory authority for export controls on military items. Controlled items constitute the United States Munitions List, 22 C.F.R. § 121.1 (1987), which is regulated by the Office of Munitions Control. *Id.* §§ 120.1, 120.4. In addition, export controls existed on a category of non-military goods, technology, and dual-use items, *i.e.*, items which have both civilian and military

uses, when the end-user is the South African military, police or paramilitary. These controls are administered by the Commerce Department under the authority of the Export Administration Act. The Export Administration Amendments Act of 1979, 50 U.S.C. app. § 2405(a) (1982). *See* 15 C.F.R. §§ 371.2, 373.1 (1988).

5. These fair labor practices are based on a code of conduct for U.S. companies in South Africa commonly referred to as the "Sullivan Principles." Introduced in 1977 by Rev. Leon Sullivan, they seek voluntary commitments from U.S. companies to desegregate their facilities, pay equal wages to blacks, improve training and advancement and the quality of their workers' lives.

6. On October 2, 1987, pursuant to Section 501 of the Act, President Reagan transmitted to Congress a report on the extent to which significant progress has been made by South Africa toward ending the system of apartheid and the impact that U.S. sanctions have made. He concluded that no such progress had been made. Rather than recommending additional sanctions as required by the Act, however, he stated that "the imposition of additional economic sanctions at this time would not be helpful . . . ." He recommended instead a return to constructive engagement, a "period of active and creative diplomacy . . . ." *Report To Congress Pursuant to Section 501 of the Comprehensive Anti-Apartheid Act of 1986*, at 7, 8.

7. Since the early 1960s, the Treasury, through OFAC, has been responsible for the implementation and enforcement of several prohibitions on financial transactions with foreign states ordered by the Executive Branch: *e.g.*, the Foreign Assets Control Regulations restricting financial transactions with certain countries governed by Communist Party dominated governments such as North Korea, Vietnam, and Cambodia 31 C.F.R. pt. 500 (1987); the Cuban Assets Control Regulations blocking access to and dealings in financial and other assets of Cuban nationals maintained in the U.S. or held by U.S. nationals, *id*. pt. 515; the Iranian Assets Control Regulations which froze Iranian assets held by U.S. regulated institutions, *id*. pt. 535; and the Libyan Sanctions Regulations restricting transactions—financial and otherwise—with Libya, *id*. pt. 550.

8. *See* Proclamation 2914, 3 C.F.R. 99 (cum. supp. 1949-1953); 50 U.S.C. app. at 171 (1982) (Proclaiming the Existence of a National Emergency); 31 C.F.R. pt. 500 (1987) (containing the Foreign Assets

Control Regulations); 15 C.F.R. § 385.1 (1987) (implementing the Department of Commerce restrictions on exports involving North Korea, Vietnam, Cambodia and Cuba).

9. *See* Proclamation 3447, 27 Fed. Reg. 1085 (1962) (imposing embargo on all trade with Cuba); 31 C.F.R. pt. 515 (1987) (containing the Cuban Assets Control Regulations); 15 C.F.R. § 385.1 (1987) (implementing the Department of Commerce restrictions on exports involving North Korea, Vietnam, Cambodia and Cuba).

10. *See* Proclamation 4702, 44 Fed. Reg. 65,581 (1979) (on imports of petroleum and petroleum products); Exec. Order No. 12,170, 44 Fed. Reg. 65,729 (1979) (blocking Iranian Government property); Exec. Order No. 12,205, 45 Fed. Reg. 24099 (1980) (prohibiting certain transactions with Iran); Exec. Order No. 12,221, 45 Fed. Reg. 26,685 (1980) (further prohibiting transactions with Iran); Exec. Order No. 12,276, 46 Fed. Reg. 7913 (1981) (termination of the sanctions); Exec. Order No. 12,294, 46 Fed. Reg. 14,111 (1981) (suspension of litigation against Iran); and Exec. Order No. 12,613, 52 Fed. Reg. 41,940 (1987) (prohibiting imports from Iran); 31 C.F.R. pt. 535 (1986) (containing the Iranian Assets Control Regulations); 15 C.F.R. § 390.6 (1988) (preventing the use of special licensing procedures for aircraft controlled by Iran).

11. *See* Exec. Order No. 12,513, 50 Fed. Reg. 18,629 (1985) (prohibiting trade and certain other transactions involving Nicaragua); 31 C.F.R. pt. 540 (1987) (containing Nicaraguan Trade Control Regulations).

12. *See* Exec. Order No. 12,543, 51 Fed. Reg. 1354 (1986) (prohibiting trade and certain transactions involving Libya); 31 C.F.R. pt. 550 (1987) (containing the Libyan Sanctions Regulations); 15 C.F.R. §§ 385.7, 390.7 (1988) (implementing the Department of Commerce restrictions on exports involving Libya).

13. The recently imposed sanctions against Panama are not comprehensive, however. *See* Exec. Order No. 12,635, 53 Fed. Reg. 12,134 (1988).

14. In 1986, 40% (R16,719 million) of all South African exports were gold. For a discussion of the difficulties connected with an embargo on gold. *See* Lipton, *Sanctions and South Africa: The Dynamics of Economic Isolation*, 47 (The Economist Intelligence Unit, Special Report No. 1119, 1988).

15. Goshko, "Presidential Action Restricts Bank Loans, Technology Exports," *Washington Post*, Sept. 10, 1985, at A1, col. 4, A10, col. 1. In 1984, Krugerrand sales to the United States peaked at $484 million. In the first six months of 1985, only $87.8 million worth of Krugerrands were sold in the United States; Krugerrand sales have been prohibited since October 1985.

16. *Id.* While United States exports to South Africa for the first six months of 1984 were worth $1.28 billion, the exports for the same period in 1985 amounted to only $675 million.

17. *Id.* The U.S. share of the computer market in South Africa dropped from 70% in 1980 to 48% in 1984.

18. To date, the United States has the strongest sanctions of South Africa's four largest trading partners, i.e., West Germany, United Kingdom and Japan. In 1986, Denmark was the first Western country to impose a total ban on trade with South Africa. Norway and Sweden adopted comprehensive trade and investment embargoes (with some exceptions) in 1987. Outside of Western Europe, India has had a complete ban on trade with South Africa since 1946. Cyprus, Singapore, Malaysia and Jamaica (and others) also have a total boycott. *See* Lipton, *supra* note 14, at 19; J. Hanlon & R. Omond, *The Sanctions Handbook* 51, 199 (1987).

19. Hanlon & Omond, *supra*, at 204-211; Lipton, *supra*, note 14, at 75-78.

20. 22 U.S.C. § 5060 (Supp. IV 1986).

21. *Id.* § 5001(4)(A).

22. A "controlled South African entity" is defined as "a corporation, partnership, or other business association or entity organized in South Africa and owned or controlled, directly or indirectly, by a national of the United States," or "a branch, office, agency, or sole proprietorship in South Africa of a national of the United States." *See id.* § 5001(2).

23. Defined as "a corporation, partnership, or other business association or entity organized in South Africa," or "a branch, office, agency, or sole proprietorship in South Africa of a person that resides or is organized outside South Africa." *Id.* § 5001(7).

24. *Id.* § 5001(4)(B).

25. *Id.* § 5060; 31 C.F.R. § 545.415(a) (1987).

26. Of the 158 U.S. companies that have withdrawn from South Africa since January 1, 1984, 72 have maintained ties with their former subsidiaries through licensing and distribution agreements. J. Kibbet & D. Hauck, *Divestment Non-Equity Ties: The Changing Pattern of U.S. Corporate Involvement in South Africa* (Investor Responsibility Research Council, June, 1988). Arm's length purchases and sales of goods, services and technology on normal commercial terms do not contravene the prohibition on new investments. 31 C.F.R. § 545.418 (1987). Such sales between a withdrawing parent and a remaining subsidiary, however, could hardly meet the "arms length" test.

27. Claiborne, "IBM, GM Map Restructuring in S. Africa," *The Washington Post*, Oct. 23, 1986, at A1, col. 6, A26, col. 1; Leas, "I.B.M. Still Bolsters Apartheid," *N.Y. Times*, Apr. 4, 1988, at A21.

28. 22 U.S.C. § 5001(4) (Supp. IV 1986).

29. Ford Motor Company of Canada Limited was the parent entity. Ford Motor Company Briefing on South Africa Disinvestment, Letter from Donald Peterson to investors (Nov. 25, 1987).

30. The plan also included a $10 million contribution by Ford to a number of programs aimed at improving educational and housing opportunities and free legal assistance to black South Africans.

31. *See* letter agreement signed by Leslie Boyd, Executive Director of the Anglo American Corporation of South Africa Limited and W.D. Broderick for Ford Motor Company (Nov. 24, 1987).

32. (i) The equity contribution was to be employed to retire Samcor debt of an equal amount prior to disinvestment by Ford; (ii) the contribution amount was established through analysis of Samcor's financing requirements to operate in an economically sound manner, and would not enable Samcor to expand its business; (iii) the R203.3 million was Ford's proportionate share of Samcor's financing requirement, but it preceded Anglo's contribution because the Ford contribution had to be made before disinvestment, while the Anglo contributions were to be made as required

by Samcor; (iv) the contribution was necessary because Samcor, with its heavy debt burden, could not sustain additional debt necessary to finance a replacement vehicle for the Escort-size car that accounted for 61% of its volume, and that vehicle needed to be replaced because the primary supplier, Mazda, was discontinuing component production; and (v) Anglo was to assume full financial responsibility for Samcor after the Ford disinvestment would not allow Samcor to commit to tooling and development contracts unless Samcor's viability had been restored through the Ford equity contribution.

Ford Motor Company Briefing on South Africa Disinvestment (Dec. 7, 1987).

33. 22 U.S.C. § 5001(4)(B)(ii) (Supp. IV 1986).

34. S. Rep. No. 370, 99th Cong., 2d Sess. 9 (1986).

35. 132 Cong. Rec. H6765 (daily ed. Sept. 12, 1986) (statement of Rep. Roth).

36. The term "controlled South African entity" is defined under Section 3(2) of the Act to mean:

    A) a corporation, partnership, or other business association or entity organized in South Africa and owned or controlled, directly or indirectly, by a national of the United States; or

    B) a branch, office, agency, or sole proprietorship in South Africa of a national of the United States.

37. 22 U.S.C. §§ 5034, 5035 (Supp. IV 1986). In determining "control", the State Department regulations require that a company:

    (a) Employ at least 25 individuals in South Africa and Namibia;

    (b) Own or control more than 50% of the outstanding voting securities of a foreign subsidiary or other entity that employs at least 25 individuals in South Africa and Namibia; or

    (c) Control in fact any other foreign entity that employs at least 25 individuals in South Africa and Namibia. Such control consists of the authority or ability of the domestic concern to establish or direct the general policies or day-to-day operations of a foreign subsidiary or entity in South Africa and Namibia. Such authority or ability will be presumed under the circumstances described below, subject to rebuttal by competent evidence provided to the Department of State at the time of registration:

(1) The domestic concern beneficially owns or controls (whether directly or indirectly) 25% or more of the voting securities of the foreign subsidiary or entity, if no other person owns or controls (whether directly or indirectly) an equal or larger percentage;

(2) The foreign subsidiary or entity is operated by the domestic concern pursuant to the provisions of an exclusive management contract;

(3) A majority of the members of the board of directors of the foreign subsidiary or entity are also members of the comparable governing body of the domestic concern;

(4) The domestic concern has the authority to appoint the majority of the members of the board of directors of the foreign subsidiary or entity; or

(5) The domestic concern has the authority to appoint the chief operating officer of the foreign subsidiary or entity.

See 22 C.F.R. § 60.2 (1987).

38. Letter from Judith H. Scott, Senior Attorney, Ford Motor Company to W.D. Broderick (Aug. 18, 1987).

39. S. Rep. No. 370, 99th Cong., 2d Sess. 9 (1986). *See* M.A. Fishburne, South African Sanctions: What Are the Loopholes and Which Non-Governmental Organizations Are Policing the Implementation of the 1986 Anti-Apartheid Act? 2 (paper prepared for the Procedural Aspects of International Law Institute) [hereinafter "International Law Institute Paper"].

The problem remains that the provision is still ambiguous. A liberal construction of the phrase "or other occurrence", as used in the Senate Report, would result in the creation of several exceptions to the prohibition. It is instructive to note that a South African periodical has interpreted the phrase to mean that if a "U.S.-owned plant is destroyed by accident or sabotage, the parent will only be permitted to restore it to its original, often outdated, condition if using outside funds". *Id.*

40. Letter from Judith H. Scott, Senior Attorney, Ford Motor Company, to W.D. Broderick (Aug. 18, 1987).

41. 22 U.S.C. § 5053(a) (Supp. IV 1986). The paragraph includes two other exceptions as well. First, agricultural products are stated to be exempt from the import ban for twelve months from the date of enactment. *Id.* { 5053(a)(1). This provision was effectively nullified by Section 319, which prohibited importation of agricultural products effective upon the date of enactment. According to OFAC Regulations, a more restrictive import prohibition supersedes a less restrictive provision. 31 C.F.R. § 545.413 (1987).

    Second, imports pursuant to a contract entered into before August 15, 1986 were exempt from the import ban until April 1, 1987. 22 U.S.C. { 5053(a)(2) (Supp. IV 1986).

42. Exec. Order No. 12,571, 51 Fed. Reg. 39,505 (1986).

43. South African Parastatal Organizations, 51 Fed. Reg. 41,912 (1986); 52 Fed. Reg. 9982 (1987).

44. South African Parastatal Organizations, 51 Fed. Reg. 41,912, (1986).

45. 51 Fed. Reg. 41,912 (1986).

46. *Id.*

47. 51 Fed. Reg. 41,912 (1986).

48. 132 Cong. Rec. S11,622 (daily ed. Aug. 14, 1986) (statement of Sen. Lugar). *See also id.* at S11,650 (statement of Sen. Dodd); *id.* at S11,677 (statement of Sen. Lugar).

49. Katzen, *infra* note 53, at 908.

50. South African Parastatal Organizations, 51 Fed. Reg. 41,912 (1986).

51. 22 U.S.C. § 5053(b) (Supp. IV 1986).

52. Katzen, *infra* note 53, at 918.

53. Katzen, "Economy," in *Africa South of the Sahara 1987*, at 906, 909 (16th ed. 1986). SASOL, established as a state-owned entity, became

a publicly held corporation in 1979. *Id.* Nevertheless, "Sasol Three (Pty) Ltd." remains on the State Department's parastatal list, although "Sasol Ltd.," which appeared on State's first list, was removed when the list was revised. "South African Parastatal Organizations," 52 Fed. Reg. 9982, 9984 (1987).

54. Katzen, *supra,* at 910. ESCOM is a parastatal organization on State's list. 52 Fed. Reg. 9982, 9983 (1987).

55. South African State President P.W. Botha announced in a statement at the opening of Parliament on February 5, 1988 a package of economic reforms. Among them were plans to privatize large government-owned corporations. Joffe, "Understanding Bothanomics," *The Weekly Mail,* Feb. 12, 1988, at 14, col. 1.

56. Telephone conversation with former State Department staffer (Feb. 15, 1988).

57. Telephone conversation with officer in Custom's Fraud Investigation Division (Apr. 29, 1988); telephone conversation with former State Department staffer (Feb. 15, 1988).

58. 22 U.S.C. { 5059(a) (Supp. IV 1986).

59. 132 Cong. Rec. S17,319 (daily ed. Oct. 18, 1986) (statement of Sen. Kennedy).

60. Exec. Order No. 12,591, 51 Fed. Reg. 39,505 (1986).

61. After mining, uranium ore is milled into a concentrate, known as "yellowcake," which is an oxide form of uranium. The concentrate is then converted into a gaseous form of uranium—uranium hexafluoride—to render it usable in the enrichment process. After enrichment, the uranium hexafluoride is reconverted into an oxide form of uranium in order to be fabricated into fuel rods. *See generally* Energy Information Administration, *The Uranium Industry Annual 1986,* DOE/EIA-0478 (1986).

62. 31 C.F.R. { 545.425 (1987).

63. *See e.g., C.S.D. 86-28,* 20 Cust. B. & Dec. 656, 658 (1986); *C.S.D. 84-112,* 18 Cust. B. & Dec. 1106, 1108 (1984).

64. On December 29, 1986, four applications were filed by Braunkohle Transport USA (License Application numbers IU-87001, IU-87002, ISNM-87003, ISNM-87004). On January 9, Advanced Nuclear Fuels Corporation submitted an application (License Application number ISNM-87005). Edlow International Company filed applications for three licenses on January 14, 1987 (License Application numbers ISNM-87008, IU-87007, IU-87006).

65. *See* M. Levy, *Issue Brief: Update on U.S.—South African Uranium Trade* 2-3, 9 (Nuclear Control Institute, Feb. 1987); *NRC Releases Figures on 1985-86 Imports of South African Uranium*, Nuclear Fuel, May 4, 1987, at 11.

66. Those joining in the challenge include Congressmen Ronald V. Dellums, Mervyn M. Dymally, William H. Gray, III, Edward J. Markey, Charles B. Rangel, Bill Richardson and Howard Wolpe; the Nuclear Control Institute; the American Committee on Africa; TransAfrica, Inc.; the Washington Office on Africa; Robert L. Chavez, an unemployed uranium miner; Carlos P. Cisneros, a state senator from New Mexico; and Henry Eric Isaacs, a South African exile.

67. Of the eight applications filed with the NRC in December 1986 and January 1987 (*see supra* note 64), Braunkohle Transport USA withdrew on July 29, 1987 three of its License Application numbers IU-87001, IU-87002 and ISNM-87003. Previously, on March 13, 1987, it had withdrawn License Application number ISNM-87004. On September 17, 1987, Edlow International Company withdrew its License Application number IU-87006.

68. *Advanced Nuclear Fuels Corp.*, Docket No. CLI-87-9, at 5 (N.R.C. Sept. 21, 1987).

69. *Edlow Int'l Co.*, Docket No. CLI-87-10 (N.R.C. Sept. 21, 1987).

70. 22 U.S.C. § 5070 (Supp. IV 1986). The effective date of this section was October 2, 1986. The regulations specify that any iron or steel imported pursuant to a contract entered into before August 15, 1986 is exempted provided that the shipment is made before December 31, 1986. 31 C.F.R. § 545.206 (1987).

71. The regulations specify that the following fifteen categories of products are included within the ban on iron and steel:

    1. Iron ore—TSUS 601.24.
    2. Iron or steel waste and scrap—TSUS 606.08-606.11.
    3. Pig iron, cast iron and spiegeleisen—TSUS 606.13-606.19.
    4. Sponge iron, iron and steel powders, grit and shot—TSUS 606.55-606.64.
    5. Ingots, blooms, billets, stabs and sheet bars—TSUS 606.67-606.69.
    6. Iron or steel forgings—TSUS 606.71-606.73.
    7. Bars of iron and steel—TSUS 606.75-606.99.
    8. Hollow drill steel—TSUS 607.05-607.09.
    9. Wire Rods—TSUS 607.14-607.59.
    10. Plates, sheets and strip—TSUS 607.62-609.17.
    11. Wire—TSUS 609.20-609.76.
    12. Angles, shapes, sections, and sheet piling—TSUS 609.80-609.98.
    13. Rails, joint bars and tie plates—TSUS 610.20-610.26.
    14. Pipes and tubes, including blanks and fittings—TSUS 610.30-610.92.
    15. Wire products—TSUS 642.02, 642.08, 642.11-642.16, 642.20.

    South African Transactions Regulations—Product Guidelines, 51 Fed. Reg. 41,911 (1986).

72. The term "ferroalloy" is defined as "any of various alloys of iron used in the manufacture of steel: named from the added metal, as ferrochromium, ferromanganese, etc." *Webster's New World Dictionary*, 516 (2d ed. 1986).

73. International Law Institute Paper, *supra* note 39, at 6.

74. *Id.*

75. U.S. Dep't of the Interior, *The Mineral Industry of the Republic of South Africa* 3 (1985), *preprinted from Bureau of Mines Mineral Yearbook* (1985).

76. In *Springfield Industries Corp. v. United States*, 633 F. Supp. 128 (Ct. Int'l Trade 1987), the Court of International Trade held that prestressed concrete strand ("PC strand") was not "steel" within the meaning of Section 320 of the Act and that the Department of Treasury's inclusion of PC strand in the regulations exceeded the

scope of its authority in promulgating the regulations. *Id.* at 138. However, this decision was reversed by the U.S. Court of Appeals for the Federal Circuit. *Springfield Ind. Corp. v. United States,* 842 F.2d 1284 (Fed. Cir. 1988). The Federal Circuit stated that "as long as the Executive interpretation of the statute is not manifestly contrary to the terms of the statute," that interpretation must be given deference, especially in the situation where the interpretation is made by the agency charged with administration of the statute and when the agency action is in the foreign affairs arena. *Id.* at 1285-86. Accordingly, the court held that the government's ban on imports of PC strand from South Africa was not arbitrary or capricious. *Id.* at 1286.

77. 22 U.S.C. § 5054(a) (Supp. IV 1986).

78. *Id.* § 5057.

79. *Id.* § 5067.

80. *Id.* § 5071.

81. *See, e.g.,* 52 Fed. Reg. 2105 (1987), Department of Commerce, International Trade Administration-Export Administration, amending 15 C.F.R. pts. 371-373, 377, 379, 385-387, 389, 399; 51 Fed. Reg. 47,013 (1986), Department of State, International Traffic in Arms Regulations, amending 22 C.F.R. pts. 121, 123-128.

82. *See generally,* General Accounting Office, "South Africa: Status Report on Implementation of the Comprehensive Anti-Apartheid Act of 1986" (Oct. 21, 1987) [hereinafter "GAO Report"].

83. The performance of contracts entered into prior to October 2, 1986, is, however, exempted from the prohibition.

84. *See* 52 Fed. Reg. 2105, amending 15 C.F.R. { 385.4(a)-(13). The regulatory definition of covered persons expressly excludes U.S. citizens and permanent residents acting on behalf of non-U.S. entities, and also excludes, by implication, non-U.S. affiliates—subsidiaries and branches—of U.S. corporations; Conversations with Commerce Department General Counsel's Office, May 11 and May 12, 1988.

85. *See* 15 C.F.R. pt. 399.1, Supp. 1, Group 7, pt. 377 Supp. 2 (1988).

86. Interestingly, the Departments of Justice and Commerce found during the first year of the Act that of fourteen investigations for its violation, thirteen could have been investigated (and if necessary, prosecuted) under existing export laws; the remaining investigation related to the ban on export of crude oil and refined petroleum products. 1987 GAO Report at 20-21.

87. International Business Machines, Inc., despite its purported withdrawal from South Africa, continues to sell and service virtually all of its products in South Africa through a trust arrangement. *See, e.g.*, Leas, "I.B.M. Still Bolsters Apartheid," *N. Y. Times*, Apr. 4, 1988, at A21.

88. The weakness of the current pre- and post-shipment inspection performance is illustrated by the GAO findings reported in its October, 1987 report to the Congress. The GAO found that only three percent of all world-wide pre-shipment inspections conducted in the U.S. in 1986, and four percent in 1987, involved exports to South Africa. Moreover, while 21 percent of the world-wide post-shipment investigations were carried out in South Africa in 1986, and 27 percent in 1987, there was virtually no investigation in third countries directed at ferreting out illegal diversions through re-exports from those third countries. Even in South Africa, such post-shipment inspections tended to focus on assuring that the physical product was on the premises or in the hands of the person to whom it was licensed; not whether it was being used in the manner and for the purpose for which it had been licensed. Much of the short fall in the effective enforcement of these provisions of the Act was directly attributable to lack of resources, compared to the resources being spent on investigation of the flow of other controlled substances such as narcotics, illegal high-tech exports to Eastern Europe and other controlled destinations, pornography, and financial irregularities in customs declarations. 1987 GAO Report, App. III.

89. *See, e.g.*, "South Africa: Whatever Happened to Sanctions?," *The Economist*, Aug. 22-28, 1987, at 38.

90. Capital goods may be defined as machinery and equipment used in the production of other goods.

91. In 1986, the Rand amount of imports of machinery and transport equipment by South Africa (including Namibia) was R7,318

million, or 27.2% of all South African imports. In value this was the most important of all items imported by South Africa. Lipton, *supra* note 14, at 32 (numbers based on data from Comm'r for Customs & Excise; South African Reserve Bank; Minerals Bureau).

92. In 1985, the total of South African imports of machinery and transport equipment from OECD countries was $3,894 million. Imports from the U.S. totalled $573 million, representing 14.7% of total South African imports of machinery from the OECD. This makes the U.S. the fourth largest supplier of machinery to South Africa. West Germany comes first with 29%, Japan second with 17.8%, and U.K. third with 15.9% *Id.* at 34-35. (numbers based on OECD data).

93. Interview with Anthony H. Blum, "Managing Against Apartheid," *Harvard Business Review*, Nov.-Dec., 1987, at 49. In 1985, U.S. exports of machinery to South Africa (a significant component of any capital goods trade) amounted to about half a billion dollars with another three-quarters of a billion dollars consisting primarily of manufactured articles and chemicals. United States exports made up approximately 10 percent of South African imports for that year. *See* John E. Lind, "Trade Credits Economic Pressure Points on South Africa" (Paper presented at the South Africa and Sanctions Conference, Howard University, Oct. 30-31, 1987).

94. Seventy percent of all South African imports come from OECD countries, primarily Japan, Germany, Italy, the United Kingdom and France. Lind, *supra*.

95. *See generally* Henkin, "Foreign Affairs and the Constitution," *Foreign Affairs*, Winter 1987/88, at 284.

96. 22 U.S.C. 286aa (Supp. I 1983). *See also* Export-Import Bank Act Amendments of 1986, 12 U.S.C. § 635(b)(2) (Supp. IV 1986).

97. 22 U.S.C. § 284j (1982). *See also,* the "Hickenlooper Amendment" of the Foreign Assistance Act, 22 U.S.C. § 2371 (1982).

98. From February 17-20, the United Nations Security Council met on the topic of the internal situation in South Africa. A resolution that would have imposed on South Africa as mandatory the same sanctions imposed by the Act was vetoed by the United States and Britain. U.N. Doc. S/18705 (1987). On April 9, 1987, the United

States and Britain vetoed a second Security Council Resolution that would have imposed mandatory sanctions. U.N. Doc. S/18785 (1987).

99. *U.S. Sanctions Against South Africa: Hearings Before the Committee on Foreign Relations of the United States Senate* 3 (June 24, 1988) (Statement of Allan I. Mendelowitz, Senior Associate Director, National Security and International Affairs Division of the United States General Accounting Office).

THE SOUTH AFRICA-ISRAEL ALLIANCE, 1986-1988: PUBLIC RELATIONS AND REALITY

Benjamin Beit-Hallahmi

Over the past two years, something has changed in the South Africa-Israel alliance in terms of public relations and propaganda, but nothing has changed in terms of the substance. We will review here some recent developments in order to illustrate the gap between propaganda and reality.

Recent events in South Africa have made it clear that the apartheid regime is in trouble and its end is in sight. For Israel, such a prospect is truly frightening. The fall of apartheid will be for Israel not only a psychological blow, but also a strategic setback of incalculable consequences.

In an article entitled, "Why South Africa?" A. Schweitzer expressed the views of the "liberal" Israeli elite regarding the apartheid crisis and Israel's alliance with the apartheid regime. His prognosis for the future of apartheid is positive, and presumably comes from government evaluations: "It seems that Israel's government, which continues its contacts with South Africa does have a good idea of the outcome of a race between white existence in South Africa and the doom predicted by its domestic critics." And he gives another reason why Israel should support apartheid in its hour of crisis: "The Third World, with Soviet guidance and Arab financing, has been carrying on for years an offensive against two states tied to the West: Israel and South Africa . . . . It should be clear that the fall of one of the two will lead to storming the other one. We will not do ourselves a favor if we hasten to eulogize South Africa, or accelerate its decline through our deeds, diplomatic or other. On the contrary, we have to hope that it will overcome the current crisis."[1]

In line with this thinking, a new domino theory is making the rounds in Israel. It states quite bluntly that the fall of the Portuguese colonies led to the fall of Rhodesia, the fall of Rhodesia is leading to the fall of South Africa, and the fall of South Africa will lead to the greatest crisis Israel has ever faced. The essential correctness of this domino theory cannot be denied. Given that, Israel's reaction to the apartheid crisis is comprised of an offensive on two fronts. On the public one, Israel will try to put more distance between itself and South Africa. On the secret front, Israel will mount a campaign to help the survival of apartheid by all means. This involves helping South Africa with 'public relations' and substantive help in military and counterinsurgency measures.

The recent public relations campaign started in response to the worldwide campaign against apartheid and the imposition of economic sanctions on the part of many countries. The anti-apartheid struggle in the United States was a most important stimulus, as the Israel-South African alliance was drawing more attention. The pro-Israel lobby in Washington recognized that a problem existed, especially following the Congressional adoption of the Comprehensive Anti-Apartheid Act on 2 October 1986. Section 508 of the Act required that a report be submitted to Congress on 1 April 1987, dealing with the extent to which the international embargo on the sale and export of arms and military technology to South Africa was being violated. While the Act was being debated by Congress, this section was the subject of aggressive lobbying by Israel's friends, but, due to time, pressure, and oversight, it became a part of the final Act. In early 1987, the prospect of a report to Congress, which would necessarily name Israel as the number one violator of the international arms embargo, created a mini-panic in the Israeli lobby.

On 18 March 1987, the "inner cabinet" of the Israeli government released a statement, reporting a decision to "refrain from new undertakings, between Israel and South Africa, "in the realm of defense." When Foreign Minister Shimon Peres, a former Defense Minister whose visits to South Africa number many scores, presented the March declaration to the Knesset, he emphasized Israeli relations with the United States as the main reason for issuing it. Mr. Peres lied to the Knesset on that occasion when he denied any Israeli nuclear collaboration with the apartheid regimes, and when he stated that South African jets did not come from Israel.[2]

Typical of reactions inside Israel to the announcement of 18 March is the cartoon reproduced here, published in Israel's most popular daily two days after the announcement. In it we can see Prime Minister Yitzak Shamir leaning on a stack of papers, representing the existing military cooperation contracts with South Africa, and making it clear that this cooperation would continue.

Tom Dine and Bob Asher, the leaders of American-Israel Political Action Committee, the Israeli lobby group in Washington, met with Prime Minister Shamir in July 1987 to press upon him the urgency of making further public relations moves to ward off any possible pressures in Congress. In response, on 16 September 1987, the Israeli government announced several measures, later described as "sanctions" or "restrictions" covering relations with South Africa. These measures were described when they were first made public as "symbolic" and "meaningless."[3] To see how "symbolic" and "meaningless" these measures were, let us examine the major ones in detail. The first two articles of the official cabinet decision follow:

1. No new investments in South Africa will be approved. Proposed exceptions will be brought to a committee consisting of the Ministry of Finance, the Bank of Israel, and the Ministry of Foreign Affairs.

2. The Government will:

A. Prohibit the granting of government loans;

B. Prohibit the sale and transfer of oil and all its products;

C. Prohibit the import of krugerrands (*sic*).

All of the above measures are similar to the decisions of the Common Market in these matters.

To appreciate the senselessness of article 1, one should recall that all foreign investments by Israeli individuals or corporations are severely controlled and restricted. The volume of Israeli investments in South Africa in the past has been insignificant, and South Africa in 1987 did not look like a good place to invest in any case.

Concerning article 2, one must remember that the Israeli government has never given any loans to anybody in South Africa and, with a foreign debt of over $25 billion, is in no position to do that. To appreciate the true meaning of article 2B, one should recall that Israel has never sold any oil to South Africa, for the unfortunate reason that Israel has no oil to sell to anyone. The only oil product that Israel could conceivably sell would be olive oil.

Article 2C, which received the most attention in the media, is similarly ridiculous. By Israeli law, the importation and sale of any gold coins are strictly forbidden, so no Krugerrands have ever been sold in Israel. The true significance of these prohibitions has been noted in the Israeli press, but has not been probed by the media in the United States.

It is important to realize that the various declarations about "bans," "restrictions," or "sanctions" on trade with South Africa are not backed by any legal machinery, unlike the measures adopted by the American Congress or by European governments. The September declaration was discussed by Knesset member, Uzi Landau, as follows:

> I can see the logic . . . the measures are more declarative than substantive . . . I can see the logic in passing decisions calculated to ward off external criticism, but such decisions should not entail anything more than the barest minimum of substance. It is in Israel's interest to preserve ties with South Africa in military and commercial fields alike.[4]

Even the two "meaningless" declarations issued during 1987 drew public criticism from Israelis who found them superfluous and objectionable. Some critics regarded these moves as a shameful surrender to the United States. An editor of the *Jerusalem Post*, Israel's English language daily, wrote:

> America has cut off links and Israel is expected to follow suit. Is that not asking too much, and do we have to obey our mentor submissively? . . . we have not been supplying arms to America's enemies. The springboks are in the Western camp . . . . America decided, for reasons of its own, to blackball South Africa. Our offense is that we did not automatically comply. . . . Obligations are one thing, servility another; and a critical red line separates the two.[5]

However, the recent public relations campaign has brought about some successes, notably in the US Congress and at the

United Nations. In the world body, a resolution dealing with the alliance, adopted in 1987, was milder in tone than one adopted a year earlier.[6] Significantly, the text of the resolution included reference to Israeli "restrictions" and takes them at face value.

The report issued by the US Department of State on 2 April 1987 (there was also a secret report) noted that Israel was indeed actively engaged in supporting the military efforts of the apartheid regime. It mentioned that private companies in other countries were also maintaining military ties with South Africa, but it made it clear that, in the case of Israel, ignoring the embargo was a matter of government policy. But the report also noted the decision of 18 March which thus proved its propaganda value and served its intended purpose.[7]

Describing Israel's leaders in January 1987, an Israeli journalist said: "They have not learned anything from Irangate—that you don't play games with the Congress."[8] What Israeli leaders have actually learned is that where the Israel-South Africa alliance is concerned, you can play games and thumb your nose at Congress. The 18 March declaration, viewed in Israel as a joke, was welcomed and praised by Congressman Mickey Leland, the chairman of the Congressional Black Caucus. The September declaration, with the phony restrictions on trade and contacts, was just as well received. The lesson to be drawn from this affair is that Israel can get away with what it has been doing because Congress will not dare touch it.

And what of the continuing reality of the Israel-South Africa alliance? What of the substance? Even now, thousands of Israelis are working to insure the continuing survival of apartheid. They work as military advisors and instructors, as technicians and engineers, as production workers, and as diplomatic advisors. An article by an Israeli columnist dealing with the Israel-South Africa alliance is appropriately titled "Shall Old Acquaintance Be Forgot?"[9] And indeed the alliance is an old one and not a recent development.

The alliance between Israel and South Africa is unique because no other nation except Israel has ever had such intimate relations with the apartheid regime and such a comprehensive commitment to its survival. The most significant aspects of the alliance are in the fields of military, nuclear, and intelligence collaboration. The total Israeli commitment to supporting the apartheid regime has not changed, and is not likely to change. The specific forms of aid are determined by the specific needs of South Africa. Following a long tradition, Israel hastens to fill any new need and any new deficiency. The Israeli military advisors are still there, and will be there as long as the regime survives. The South African Defense Forces enjoy every Israeli achievement in military technology, and much of the light and heavy ammunition used to defend apartheid comes from Israel.

As we observe the South African Defense Forces in the townships, in Namibia, or on their parade grounds, we are likely to see Israeli weapons, Israeli tactics, and Israeli strategies.[10] The South African infantry carries the Israeli Galil rifle, the South African navy uses Israeli missile boats, and the South African Air Force flies the Israeli Kfir jet, known in South Africa as the Cheetah (Kfir in Hebrew for "young lion," which shows that the South Africans were not terribly original even in their zoological choice). The nuclear collaboration program, which has been in force for more than a generation, continues to move forward towards fourth- and fifth-generation nuclear weaponry. Only recently, Israeli officers have been seen on Marion Island in the southern Indian Ocean, where South Africa and Israel are building a nuclear test site.[11]

In civilian matters, the Israeli presence is less substantial, but no less friendly. When the United Nations published a blacklist of artists who have performed in South Africa despite the international boycott, 26 nations were included. Of these, Great Britain was first, the United States second, and Israel third. Visits by Israeli artists and athletes to South Africa have been continuing at the same pace. Israeli tourism to South Africa, which is one way in which Israelis gain a direct experience of apartheid, has been growing. It increased by 18% during the first half of 1987, and was expected to rise by 20% for the whole year.[12] South Africa remains a favorite destination for Israelis who want to go on a foreign vacation, those who want to work in a foreign country temporarily, and those who are looking for a new homeland. Even today, when South Africa does not look like an attractive new home for immigrants, and when native

South Africans are leaving, Israelis in search of a promising future continue to settle in the land of apartheid.

Israel's support for grand apartheid has been expressed in the form of continuing contacts with the Bantustan leadership. Despite the fact that Israel does not accord them diplomatic recognition, the leaders of the TVBC states (Transkei, Venda, Bophuthatswana, and Ciskei) have remained welcome visitors to Israel. Only a few Americans have heard of such entities as KwaNdebele or Lebowa, but quite a few Israelis find these obscure names meaningful, as government officials and academics continue their contacts in South Africa and Bantustan leaders go on enjoying Israeli hospitality.

The Inkatha movement, led by Chief Gatsha Buthelezi, has enjoyed Israeli support for years. Buthelezi, the Reagan administration's model of a "moderate" black leader in South Africa, visited Israel in 1985 in what was really the beginning of a joint propaganda campaign designed to benefit the Chief, the Israeli government, and the apartheid regime. Members of Inkatha enjoy the hospitality reserved for other Bantustan leaders.

Several government-to-government economic agreements were renewed in 1986. They covered such areas of mutual interest as fishing rights, export credits, and capital investments. These biannual agreements were renewed in the summer of 1988.

Israel has not played a major role in South Africa's attempts to bypass economic sanctions, but it was not because of any lack of readiness to do so. As early as February 1978, before any significant economic sanctions were being contemplated, the Israeli Finance Minister, Simha Ehrlich, announced during an official visit to South Africa that Israel would be happy to serve as a conduit for South African goods destined for the European Common Market and the United States, thus avoiding both import duties and political sanctions.[13] This generous offer has been renewed many times, usually in private. An Israeli economic delegation, headed by the Director-General of the Finance Ministry, Emmanuel Sharon, went to South Africa in August 1986 and again made this offer, but was turned down. The reason South Africa does not need Israel's good services now is that other convenient conduits much closer to home are available.

Israel's direct and open support for the apartheid regime in its hour of need is especially appreciated by those U.S. leaders whose own support cannot be equally direct. In this case, Israel is playing the role of the most valuable surrogate the U.S. may have. As in other cases, Israel can provide vital services with reliability and dedication. Those—and they are numerous—within the US executive branch who are concerned about the survival of South Africa as a valuable ally are heartened by what they know of Israel's activities. But many pro-apartheid Americans do not even know half of what Israel is really doing.

Israel has become part of the history of South Africa, an active partner in the war over the future of apartheid. A black South African said to an Israeli journalist, "Tell your generals in the Israeli army that they are in a losing war."[14] But the end of that war will have momentous implications for Israel, together with the rest of the world. It is important to realize how deeply concerned Israel's leaders are about the survival of apartheid. Theirs is not the concern of foreign corporations worried about their investments. It is a true commitment to something which is vital to the survival of their own country. This is much more than most foreigners feel about apartheid. We can expect this commitment to continue in various forms, most of which will be unpublicized. Israel will also continue to play the role of the middleman between South Africa and the United States.

Notes

1. A. Schweitzer, "Shall Old Acquaintance Be Forgot?" *Haaretz* (Hebrew), 4 October 1987.

2. A. Ben-Vered, "Peres: Israel Must Consider U.S. Attitudes Towards South Africa," *Haaretz*, 20 March 1987.

3. A. Eldar, "The Cabinet Will Discuss Today Symbolic Measures Against South Africa," *Haaretz*, 8 July 1987.

4. B. Morris, "Cabinet Plans Pretoria Sanctions," *The Jerusalem Post*, 17 September 1987.

5. D. Krivine, "The Pollard Affair South African parallel," *The Jerusalem Post*, 2 April 1987.

6. P. Lewis, "U.N. Toning Down an Anti-Israeli Resolution," *New York Times*, 19 November 1987.

7. US Department of State. *Report to Congress pursuant to Section 508 of the Comprehensive Anti-Apartheid Act of 1986: Compliance with the U.S. Arms Embargo*, 1 April 1987.

8. T. L. Friedman, "Israelis Reassess Supplying Arms to South Africa," *New York Times*, 29 January 1987.

9. Schweitzer, "Shall Old Acquaintance."

10. Benjamin Beit-Hallahmi, *The Israeli Connection* (New York: Pantheon, 1987).

11. Y. Tzur, "Military Officials at RSA 'Nuclear Test Site'," *Al Hamishar* (Hebrew), 8 November 1987.

12. A. George, "Israeli Group 'Laundering Steel Imports From South Africa'," *The Guardian*, 25 August 1987.

13. C. Murphy, "Israeli's Visit Bolsters Ties With South Africa," *Washington Post*, 8 February 1978; see also Beit-Hallahmi, *The Israeli Connection*.

14. Y. Litani, "Black Fear Enters a White Heart," *Hadashot* (Hebrew), 13 November 1987.

SANCTIONS, DISINVESTMENT, AND US CORPORATIONS IN SOUTH AFRICA

Richard Knight

Future historians may date mid-1984 as a turning point in the history of South Africa. Massive protests inside South Africa combined with escalating pressure internationally to force substantial capital flight and perhaps the greatest challenge to the continuation of white minority rule in recent history. In the five years since then, some 200 US and more than 60 British companies have withdrawn from South Africa, international lenders have cut off Pretoria's access to foreign capital, and the value of the rand, South Africa's currency, has dropped dramatically. South Africa's economic relations with the international community have been significantly altered.

This chapter will attempt to discuss the effects of sanctions and disinvestment over the last five years and highlight some of the continuing U.S. financial links to South Africa. Finally, I will attempt to draw some conclusions as to the effectiveness of international attempts to pressure the white minority government through sanctions and disinvestment.[1]

The Political Context

Undoubtedly the greatest challenge to white minority rule came from the explosion of political resistance which followed Pretoria's introduction of a new constitution in 1983 with a complex set of segregated parliaments. In a total rejection of apartheid, black South Africans mobilized to make the townships ungovernable, black local officials resigned in droves, and the government declared a State of Emergency in 1985 and used thousands of troops to quell the "unrest." Television audiences throughout the world were to watch almost nightly reports of massive resistance to apartheid, the growth of a democratic movement, and the savage police and military response. This escalation of popular resistance sparked a dramatic expansion of international actions to isolate apartheid, actions that combined with the internal situation to force dramatic changes in South Africa's international economic relations. US corporate executives, who hoped that if they just held on for a few years apartheid would slowly disappear, were forced to face the reality of a long drawn out confrontation. The writing on the wall spelled trouble ahead in South Africa and at home. As a result, the agenda of South Africa's new State President, F. W. de Klerk, is dominated by efforts to counter the democratic movement and international pressures.

The US Anti-Apartheid Movement

In the US, the long established movement to impose economic isolation on South Africa gathered dramatic momentum in this period. Activists seeking to stop corporate collaboration with apartheid found the way blocked in Washington and had developed other strategies for exerting pressure on the corporations. One major focus of this effort was the divestment campaign, aimed at moving individuals and institutions to sell their holdings in companies doing business in South Africa. Already strong on the campuses across the US, new student protest surged after 1984 and the number of colleges and universities at least partially divesting jumped from 53 prior to April 1985 to 128 by February 1987 to 155 by August 1988.

The divestment movement was not limited to the campuses. Concerned legislators and anti-apartheid activists built strong networks in cities and states and by the end of 1989 25 states, 19 counties, and 83 cities had taken some form of binding economic action against companies doing business in South Africa. These activities include divestment by public pension funds of stocks of companies that do business in South Africa and pressure exerted via selective purchase policies, whereby cities give preference in bidding on contracts for goods and services to those companies who do not do business in South Africa.

All this local activity helped generate the thrust for a victory in 1986 when passage of the Comprehensive Anti-Apartheid Act was won over the veto of President Reagan. What made the Congressional override more surprising is that it happened while the Republican Party controlled the Senate. The Act banned new US investment in South Africa, sales to the police and military, and new bank loans, except those for the purpose of trade. Specific measures against trade include the prohibition of the import of agricultural goods, textiles, shellfish, steel, iron, uranium and the products of state-owned corporations. The Act has had some effect in cutting US imports from South Africa, which declined by 35% between 1985 and 1987. However, in 1988, US imports from South Africa increased by 14% to $1.5 billion. US exports to South Africa increased by 40% between 1985 and 1988. Some of the increase in US imports may be due to lax enforcement of the 1986 Act. A 1989 study by the General Accounting Office concluded that the US government had failed to enforce the Act adequately. A major weakness of the Act is that it does little to prohibit exports to South Africa, even in such areas as computers and other capital goods.

In 1987, the Budget Reconciliation Act included an amendment by Rep. Charles Rangel ending the ability of US firms to claim tax credits in the US for taxes paid in South Africa. This effectively imposed double taxation on US corporate operations in South Africa. The sums of money involved are large. According to the Internal Revenue Service, taxes involved in 1982 were $211,593,000 on taxable income of $440,780,000. The US Chamber of Commerce in South Africa has estimated that the measure increases the tax bill for US companies from 57.5% to 72% of profits in South Africa. Mobil Corporation cited the Rangel Amendment as a major factor in its decision to withdraw from South Africa.

Table 1
Trade With South Africa, 1985-1988 ($ million)

	US Exports	*US Imports*
1985	1,205.0	2,070.8
1986	1,158.3	2,364.5
1987	1,281.2	1,345.5
1988	1,690.3	1,529.6

In August 1988 the House of Representatives passed a new sanctions bill mandating the withdrawal of all US companies from South Africa, the sale by US residents of all investments in South African companies and the end of most trade, except for the import of certain strategic minerals. The bill did not reach the Senate floor but the fact that such a sweeping bill got as far as it did alerted both the South African government and US business that significant further sanctions were likely to be forthcoming.

The impact of the anti-apartheid movement has clearly been felt by US companies. It has significantly raised the cost of doing business in South Africa, adversely affecting corporate image, threatening the ability to raise capital and maintain domestic markets. Gone are the days when, as in 1980, David Packard of Hewlett Packard stated, "I'd rather lose business in Nebraska than with South Africa."

US Investment

Some 200 US companies have disinvested from South Africa in the last five years and US direct investment has declined from $2.3 billion at the end of 1982 to $1.3 billion at the end of 1988. However, many of those companies which have disinvested continue to do business through licensing, franchising, and distribution agreements.

Table 2
US direct investment in South Africa by type of industry
($million)

End Year	*All Industries*	*Petroleum*	*Manufacturing*	*Wholesale Trade*	*Banking*	*Finance and Insurance*	*Services*	*Other*
1982	2,281	S	998	295	S	46	18	S
1983	1,987	S	963	210	S	56	20	158
1984	1,440	S	777	79	S	53	21	162
1985	1,394	S	568	227	S	48	12	162
1986	1,567	S	633	291	S	61	26	139
1987	1,590	S	707	186	0	74	32	S
1988	1,270	S	508	80	0	69	S	S

Legend

S = suppressed. Direct investment is a measure of the value of the foreign subsidiaries or associates of US companies. Department of Commerce figures include only those companies whose ownership goes directly from the US to South Africa. Not included would be a company which has a subsidiary in a third country, which in turn has a South African subsidiary.

Source: US Department of Commerce

Despite the large number of corporate withdrawals and the prohibition of new US investment, which came in effect in the fourth quarter of 1986, the value of US direct investment in South Africa actually increased between 1985 and 1987. However, the basic trend is down. A number of major disinvestments took place in 1989, very likely bringing direct investment below $1 billion.[2]

A Vulnerable Economy

Not only are US corporations disinvesting, but, as the accompanying table shows, those of many other countries as well. Since mid-1984, South Africa has suffered considerable capital flight, as a result of corporate disinvestment and because of the repayment of foreign loans. Net capital movement out of South Africa was R9.2 billion in 1985, R6.1 billion in 1986, R3.1 billion in 1987, and R5.5 billion in 1988. This trend is continuing, with R1.7 billion in capital outflow in the first two quarters of 1989. One effect of this capital outflow has been a dramatic decline in the international exchange rate of the rand. This means that imports are increasingly expensive. It has also helped fuel South Africa's inflation rate, which at 12-15% per year, is much higher than its major trading partners.

The South African government has attempted to limit the amount of capital outflow. In September 1985 it imposed a system of exchange control and a debt repayments standstill. Under exchange control, South African residents are generally prohibited from removing capital from the country and foreign investors can only remove investments via the financial rand, which is traded at a 20% to 40% discount compared to the commercial rand. This means that companies that disinvest get significantly fewer dollars for the capital that they withdraw.[3]

Few argue against the thesis that the South African economy was developed with foreign capital. This was especially true of the gold mining industry, which is central to the apartheid economy. Most South African economists agree that without foreign capital, South Africa will not be able to fund the necessary imports for economic growth at more than a marginal rate. This is because in order for the economy to grow, South Africa must import capital goods and other inputs for production. Currently it has difficulty in paying for everything it wants to do. The modest economic expansion in the South African economy in the first half of 1988 put such a strain on the current (trade) account, that in August 1988, Pretoria slapped a hefty surcharge on capital goods imports. At the same time, the government increased fuel prices by 15%, despite the fact that the world price for petroleum had been dropping. If South Africa had a net inflow on the capital account (especially loans and investment), it would be able to fund the necessary imports for economic growth.

Table 3
Cumulative disinvestment from South Africa and/or Namibia, with number of corporations at end of 1987

	Disinvestment	*Divesting*	*Remaining Number*
Australia	17	—	32
Canada	21	3	12
France	6	1	15
West Germany	10	—	128
Netherlands, Norway Sweden, Denmark	12	3	27
Switzerland	2	—	32
UK	92	7	266
US	250	21	178
Total	410	35	66

Source: *Business International,* based on UN Economic and Social Council E/1988/23, 8 February 1988. The figures in this table do not match those cited in the text for several reason, including that of the time period covered.

South Africa needs not only foreign capital but also foreign technology. South Africa imports 95% of all computer equipment, and could not build a car, truck, or other sophisticated item without imported technology and components. While some South Africans have talked about a "siege economy," in reality

South Africa is heavily dependent on foreign input. The South African Board of Trade and Industry notes that although import replacement has long been government policy, merchandise imports as a percentage of gross domestic product has only declined from 20% to 19% between 1960 and 1986. South Africa's economy is simply not large enough to develop high-tech products. Even the mining industry depends on capital goods imported from the U.S. and other countries. Henri de Villers, chairman of the Standard Bank Investment Corp, put it succinctly "In this day and age there is no such thing as economic self-sufficiency and we delude ourselves if we think different . . . South Africa needs the world. It needs markets, it needs skills, it needs technology and above all it needs capital."

A Way to Go

US investment in South Africa is clearly not at an end. More than 130 US companies still have subsidiaries in South Africa. And products of US companies are available via licensing, franchising, and distribution agreements. As a result, US companies and their products are found across the spectrum in South Africa. Supermarkets in South Africa often look like supermarkets in the US with Kellog's cereals, Colgate toothpaste, and Coca-Cola. South African miners use continuous miners, drill bits and other equipment from such companies as Joy Technologies, Baker Hughes, and Dresser Industries. The chemical products might well come from American Cyanamid Co. or E. I. Du Pont de Nemours and Co. Computers come from IBM and Hewlett-Packard. A person reading a magazine will see advertisements designed by J. Walter Thompson.

Petroleum Industry

Nowhere is the strategic nature of US investment in South Africa more clearly shown than in the oil industry. This remains the case today, although several US companies, including Mobil, have disinvested. For many years the largest US investors in South Africa were Mobil and Caltex (a joint venture of Chevron and Texaco). In 1985, US petroleum companies (primarily Mobil and Caltex) had a net income after taxes of $75 million, approximately one-half of all US non-bank affiliates in South Africa.

Caltex Petroleum Corp., the US parent of the Caltex group of companies, is 50% owned by Chevron Corp. and 50% owned by Texaco Inc. Up-to-date information on Caltex is difficult to come by as the company is extremely secretive about its operations in South Africa. Caltex is estimated to have $350 million in assets in South Africa, and is reported to service 1,185 filling stations, of which some 393 are company owned. These filling stations give Caltex a 20% share of the South African market. In 1980 Caltex Oil (SA) (Pty.) Ltd. had 2,257 employees or 17% of Caltex's employees world-wide. Caltex operates a 100,000 barrel per day refinery, which represented about 6.3% of the company's world-wide capacity in 1980. Caltex also owns 34% of South African Oil Refinery (Pty.) Ltd., a 3,000 barrels per day lube oil refinery.

The US presence in the South African oil industry would be much larger if it were not for the efforts of the anti-apartheid movement. Ashland Oil sold all its South African operations in mid-1986. For a short time, Ashland had maintained licensing and distribution agreements, including the sale of $300,000 a year in Valvoline products. However, when faced with the possible loss of a $12 million contract with the City of Los Angeles, Ashland quickly terminated its ties to South Africa. "Our relationship with Los Angeles was clearly more important than our small and somewhat limited relationship in South Africa," said Ashland corporate attorney John Biehl.

In 1989, Mobil Oil, which had over $400 million in assets in South Africa, disinvested. Because of its strategic involvement, Mobil had been one of the foremost targets of the anti-apartheid movement. Mobil had also headed corporate efforts to oppose sanctions and disinvestment. Mobil's disinvestment is a major victory for US anti-apartheid activists.

US oil companies have claimed in the past that they were not responsible for the actual importation of the oil into South Africa, which is done by the government, but they did refine and market petroleum. The US companies, combined with the UK company British Petroleum and the UK/Netherlands company

Royal Dutch/Shell, refined the vast majority of petroleum consumed in South Africa.

US oil companies have never denied that they sell to the South African police and military. They get around the US government restrictions prohibiting sales to the police and military because the oil they sell in South Africa has not been exported or reexported from the US. Justifying selling oil to the police and military has not been a problem for US oil companies. As recently as 1981, Mobil told its shareholders: "Total denial of supplies to the police and military forces of a host country is hardly consistent with an image of responsible citizenship in that country. The great bulk of the work of both police and military forces in every country, including South Africa, is for the benefit of all its inhabitants."

The oil companies have been out in front as companies attempting to present an image of opposition to apartheid. Shell takes out advertisements in the *Weekly Mail*, an "alternative" newspaper in South Africa, saying it is for a free press. Mobil had been one of the leading companies behind the Sullivan principles, and, after the abandonment of the principles by the Rev. Sullivan, the principles' rebirth as the "Statement of Principles."

Motor Industry

South Africa's reliance on foreign technology is clearly demonstrated in the motor industry. There is no such thing as a "South African" car. Despite years of a "local content" program, 40% to 50% of the value of input into cars produced in South Africa is imported. Two of the largest US investors, Ford and General Motors, have withdrawn from South Africa but their products continue to be made in South Africa under license. Ford vehicles have long been sold to the police and military. In 1986, in its last proxy statement before ending ownership in South Africa, Ford stated that if it ceased sales to the police and military in South Africa, it would lose all government sales and no longer be economically viable. Ford has made it clear that although it no longer has any ownership, it is going to continue to provide not only the design, but the management and retooling assistance, without which, Ford maintains, the South African operations would likely not be able to continue.

General Motors (GM) had made a loss in South Africa for several years prior to its withdrawal. Now GM cars are made under license by its former subsidiary, renamed Delta Motor Corp., which now also assembles Isuzu trucks.

Early in 1988, as international pressure on companies doing business in South Africa continued to grow, the Japanese company Toyota announced that it will limit the number of cars made in South Africa. South African motor companies, recognizing their own vulnerability and the danger of increasing pressure on their suppliers, recently agreed to suppress sales data, the publication of which, they said, was aiding advocates of sanctions. "With sales rising, SA companies don't want to put more pressure on their Japanese principles. Delta SA, for instance, represents Isuzu's second biggest market outside Japan," observes the *Financial Mail*.

Computers

All US computer companies have ended their direct investment in South Africa, but almost all have continued licensing and distribution agreements. US mainframe computers represent almost 50% of the market. South Africa is totally dependent on imported computers and South African businessmen display increasing concern about the possibility of computer sanctions. "Mainframe computers are one of the items most vulnerable to sanctions and this cannot be replaced by a locally manufactured product," noted one South African business executive recently. "This year we are able to import computers but who knows what the situation will be next year." Despite the US ban on the sales of computers to the police and military, sales are not prohibited to any of the 1,000 private sector companies which handled up to 60% of military production in South Africa.

Companies that no longer have ownership in South Africa, but continue to do business through distribution agreements include Amdahl Corp. (divested in 1987), Control Data Corp. (1988), Honeywell Inc. (1986), International Business Machines (1986), and Unisys (1988).

International Business Machines (IBM) sold its South African subsidiary in October 1986. The South African company was renamed Information Services Management (ISM) with ownership vested in an employee trust named ISM Trustees. By October 1987 ISM had formed a joint venture with a large South African conglomerate, Barlow Rand, a company with close ties to the South African military. This new company is called Technology Systems International (TSI). ISM Trustees and Barlow Rand each own 28%, the remainder is publicly owned. TSI has two subsidiaries, ISM and Reunert Computers, which had previously been a subsidiary of Barlow Rand. The one, Reunert Computers, sells Japanese-made Hitachi IBM plug-compatible mainframe computers in apparent competition with IBM computers sold by ISM. This ISM-Barlow Rand marriage appears to have been designed to circumvent sanctions. Brian Mehl, the managing director of ISM, commented, "What we've done with Technology Systems International is create the best of all worlds for our customers in that we've immediately created an alternative source—we've got IBM and we've got the leading IBM-compatible supplier."

IBM products continue to play an important role in the South African computer market. An estimated 40% of South Africa's installed mainframe computer base is of IBM origin, and the company had a 1985 market share of 20%.

The terms of the Unisys disinvestment demonstrate the concern South African companies have about being cut off from their source of supply. In August 1988 Unisys sold its South African subsidiary to a local company, Mercedes Datakor, for R132 million. Mercedes Datakor, which will continue as the Unisys distributor, insisted on some protection for itself from a possible future cutoff of Unisys products. Unisys received only R82 million in cash immediately, the balance to be placed in trust in Europe and paid to Unisys in quarterly installments over four years, provided Unisys continues to supply the South African company. In addition, Mercedes Datakor demanded a ten year distributing agreement, where the normal Unisys agreement needs to be renewed annually. Such a long-term agreement makes it more difficult for Unisys to unilaterally stop supplying its products to the South African company.

The disinvestment of Control Data Corp. in November 1988 was very similar to that of Unisys. Control Data sold to a South African company. Only 60% of the purchase price was paid immediately, the rest to be paid over five years, provided Control

Data continues to supply its former subsidiary. Control Data cited US law prohibiting the financing of any expansion of its South African operations as the reason for its disinvestment. Control Data retains the right to re-enter South Africa if conditions warrant.

South Africa is dependent on the US for computer software as well as hardware. Most Japanese mainframe computers sold in South Africa are IBM-compatible and run IBM or other US software. Software from most major producers is distributed in South Africa. The software they produce is central to the running of a modern economy. In March 1987, ISM became the sole South African distributor for Hogan Systems, a US company that specializes in software for banks. Since Hogan runs on IBM mainframe computers, the use of Hogan by these banks helps hardware sales. For example, Volkskas, which uses Hogan, recently purchased R60 million worth of hardware from ISM.

This continued availability of software raises some interesting questions about the implementation of corporate decisions to distance themselves from apartheid. Microsoft, the maker of the computer operating systems MS-DOS and OS/2, announced in April 1986 that it had ended "direct shipment of its software to the Republic of South Africa and terminated its relationship with its local distributor." Yet clearly Microsoft products are available in South Africa, as without them no IBM or IBM compatible personal computers could operate. Lotus Development Corp. has taken a stronger position and considers the use and sale of its software products in South Africa a violation of copyright.[4]

Electronics

Westinghouse Electric Corp. closed its South African office in 1987 but still has contracts with ESCOM for the Koeberg nuclear power plant. In addition, Westinghouse has several distributors and licensees in South Africa, primarily for electrical equipment.

The Motorola case is another victory for the antiapartheid movement. Motorola sold its South African operations to Allied Technologies (Altech), a South African electronics company. Motorola products are now made under license in South Africa, including its highly regarded two way radios. However, as a result of pressure from municipal governments in the US, Motorola has announced that it would not renew its licensing agreements with Altech when they expire in 1990.

Sounding a Confused Retreat

It is impossible in this chapter to look at each of the corporate withdrawals. In general, where a manufacturing corporation with plant in place withdraws, the company sells its South African subsidiary either to local management or to a South African company. In these cases actual disinvestment does take place and capital leaves South Africa, but in most cases the product remains through licensing and distribution agreements. In some cases no actual disinvestment has taken place. A number of companies have simply sold all or part of their South African operations to European or other US companies, frequently as part of a corporate restructuring.

It seems that the basic trend of US companies disinvesting from South Africa will continue. And as the number of companies declines, it will be increasingly difficult for those who remain to justify their continued presence in South Africa. Some companies will sever all ties. However, it is also true that many of those who do withdraw from South Africa will continue to do business through non-equity ties. This continued collaboration with the apartheid economy will be a focus of the US anti-apartheid movement.

Bank Loans

South Africa's foreign debt increased significantly in rand terms between 1983 and 1985, although the increase in dollar terms was less dramatic. By the end of 1984 US bank loans had reached $4.7 billion, about 20% of South Africa's foreign debt.

But as anti-apartheid pressure in the U.S. grew, an increasing number of US banks modified their lending policies, some prohibiting loans to the South African government, others stopping all loans to South Africa. By the end of 1985, fourteen

Table 4
Foreign debt of South Africa

End Year	*Rand (million)*	*Dollar (million)*
1982	24,289	22,609
1983	29,116	23,945
1984	48,230	24,294
1985	60,142	23,473
1986	49,513	22,593
1987	43,593	22,618
1988	50,380	21,185

Source: South African Reserve Bank

states, nine counties, and 58 cities had adopted policies either withdrawing funds or limiting other business with banks making loans to South Africa. The pressure to deny future loans to South Africa was not taken seriously at that time by the South African government, but it made a major impact on the thinking of US banks. Banks were also concerned about the South African economy and by the rapid rise in South Africa's debt. Real gross domestic fixed investment had been declining since 1982. The structure of the South African debt was particularly disturbing. Debt with a maturity of less than one year jumped from 56% in 1982 to 68% in 1985 to 82% in 1986. South African banks were borrowing money internationally with short-term maturity and loaning it out as long-term loans in South Africa, on the assumption that the loans would automatically be rolled over as they matured.

In December 1984, Seafirst adopted a policy of no new loans to South Africa, followed by the Bank of Boston in March 1985 and First Bank System, also in 1985. Even more significantly, in July 1985, North Carolina National Bank Corp., the regional bank with the largest lending to South Africa and the only regional bank to have an office in South Africa, ended all new loans. It appears that many other banks, while not acting publicly, limited their loans in this period.

The rapid rise in US bank loans to South Africa came to an abrupt halt in mid-1985. Between March and September 1985, US bank loans to South Africa declined by $757 million. In August 1985, Chase Manhattan quietly told its customers in South Africa it would not roll over loans. Most US banks which had not already ended new loans to South Africa quickly followed Chases' action.

Table 5
US bank loans to South Africa

End Year	*$millions*	*Percent of South Africa's Total Debt*
1982	3,676	16.3
1983	4,637	19.4
1984	4,704	19.4
1985	3,240	13.8
1986	2,957	13.1
1987	2,888	12.8
1988	2,510	11.8

Source: Federal Financial Institutions Examination Council

The US banks' actions caused a panic in South Africa. At the time, US banks had outstanding loans of $3.5 billion, of which $2.8 billion had a maturity of one year or less. Faced by the prospect of massive capital flight, the South African government stepped in, and in September 1985, it imposed a debt standstill and reimposed exchange controls.

Two "Interim Arrangements"—the second one expires in June 1990—were negotiated between the South African government and a "Technical Committee" of fifteen international banks, representing some 300 banks. The US representatives on the Technical Committee were Citicorp, Manufacturers Hanover, and J. P. Morgan.

The exact terms of the two interim arrangements are not known. According to press reports, the Second Arrangement lasted for about three years, during which only 13 percent of capital was repaid. Citicorp told the Africa Fund in early 1989 that it had received only about 5% of its principal back.[5]

Despite the fact that anti-apartheid activists put pressure on banks to use the debt arrangements to put pressure on the South African government to push ahead with reforms, a Third Interim Arrangement was announced in October 1989 that effectively reschedules $8 million of South Africa's foreign debt inside the standstill. The new arrangement runs from 1 July 1990 to 1 January 1993. During that period, South Africa will have to pay foreign banks approximately 20%—or $1.5 billion—of the debt inside the standstill. By 1994, a fourth agreement will have to be reached for the repayment of the remaining $6.5 billion.

South Africa's problem is that it owes about $12 billion outside the standstill, some $2 billion of which is due in 1990. The debt repayment schedule under the Third Interim Arrangement is aimed at limiting the amount of debt inside the standstill that needs to be paid during this key period. Chris Stals, chairman of the South African Reserve Bank, commented: "I am relieved we no longer face a crisis in June 1990, but this does not mean there is less pressure on the balance of payments. We will meet our new commitments as we did the previous ones—with difficulty. Economic policy will have to remain restrictive, especially considering the large payments of debt outside the net falling due next year."

In order to get this agreement, South Africa had to work hard. F. W. de Klerk released eight long-term political prisoners, including Walter Sisulu, in October 1989. The US government advocated "giving F. W. a chance" and a grace period of at least six months. But the Mass Democratic Movement in South Africa issued a strong call for financial sanctions and for no debt rescheduling and Walter Sisulu condemned the new agreement.

It should be noted, however, that South Africa did not get everything its way. Despite the fact that the dollar figure of money covered by the standstill has dropped from $12 billion to $8 billion, it will be paying back slightly more than during the last agreement. In fact, 20% of outstanding capital will be paid back during the coming 3 1/2 year period compared to 13% during the last three year period. Combined with payment of debt outside the standstill, South Africa will be faced with considerable capital outflow. Minister of Finance Barend du Plessis admitted, "All South Africans must realize that the country faces tough times in the next four years in which we have to pay back $8 billion in foreign debt." He also said that South Africa would have to adopt strict internal policies to limit the growth of the economy.

No information has been provided on the interest rate to be paid. One British banker told the *New York Times* that "the rates are relatively high .... They are penalty rates of interest." The same banker noted that when banks renegotiate terms of loans to Latin American countries, they often reduce the rate paid.

Exit Loans

The new agreement also has a provision whereby banks can remove their debt from the standstill by converting their debt to long term loans. Under this provision, banks will get no principal payments for 7 1/2 years and then will be paid back in equal six month payments over the following 2 1/2 years. A similar clause existing in the Second Interim Arrangement was exercised by Citicorp. South Africa is encouraging banks to take this option as it eases the immediate payment problems. Chris Stals remarked: "We already faced substantial liabilities up to 1997 and it was prudent to avoid more pressure during this period. The repayment of these loans will be bunched in three years beginning in 1998."

It is difficult to determine how many banks have exercised the exit clause, but US bank loans with a maturity of over five years have increased from $37 million in March 1987 to $747 million in June 1989. This implies that at least $710 million has been converted under the Second Interim Arrangement to long-term loans.

Citicorp and Manufacturers Hanover are two prominent banks which have converted some of their outstanding loans. In February 1989, Citicorp exercised one of the exit clauses by converting $660 million in short-term loans covered by the Second Interim Arrangement into a ten year loan. Citicorp will receive no repayment of principal until 1992, with full payment by 1997. Citicorp was criticized for this action because it removed the immediate pressure on South Africa at a time when it was facing serious capital outflows. To protest Citicorp's action, Westchester County, New York withdrew $40 million from Citicorp.

Maintaining pressure on banks that continue to collaborate with South Africa is also the objective of a bill which Congressman Walter Fauntroy (D-Washington, D.C.) introduced in the House of Representatives shortly before the announcement of the Third Interim Arrangement. If enacted, the bill would impose a series of financial sanctions against South Africa. It would require US banks to insist that "not less than 20 percent of the principal" on loans be paid back each year; prohibit converting loans to long-term loans under the exit clauses and holding exit loans after 31 December 1992; and ban trade financing.

It is clearly very important for South Africa to keep its connections to the major banks of all its trade partners. South Africa continues to be able to get trade credits and to have other links with international banks. South Africa has been able to raise some $600 million in loans backed by gold reserves held by the South African Reserve Bank. In early October 1988 then State President P. W. Botha used the opportunity presented by the funeral of West German leader Franz Josef Strauss to visit Europe and meet with Swiss bankers and businessmen. In late October the Johannesburg city council announced that it expected to secure a $19 million loan. Anti-apartheid activists are keenly aware that foreign banks will make loans to South Africa if they seem profitable and if they do not face anti-apartheid pressure.

Portfolio Investment

US investment in South African companies listed on the South African stock exchange is over $4 billion. W. I. Car, the London stockbroker, estimates that about 25% of South African gold mining shares, worth about $2.5 billion, are owned by US citizens. Davis Borkkum Hare, a Johannesburg stockbroker, estimates US ownership in all South African mining shares (not just gold mining) at 14%, worth R14.3 billion ($4.1).

This stock is owned in a number of different ways. A number of gold and other mutual funds own stock in South African gold mines. In this case, investors buy shares in the US mutual fund, that then invests in South African gold shares. Two such mutual funds are International Investors and the Franklin Gold Fund with some $300 million and $69 million respectively, invested in South African gold shares. One company, ASA Ltd., owned some $998 million in South African stock, primarily in gold mines, in August 1987. Unlike a mutual fund, US investors buy ASA stock on the US stock market. Stock in many South African companies is also available through American Depository Receipts (ADRs). ADRs are receipts issued by a US depository bank to promote trading in a foreign security. The bank holds the foreign securities and the ADRs are issued against them. Dealers in ADRs of South African companies include Citicorp, Chemical Bank, Irving Trust, Morgan Guaranty Trust and the Bank of New York.

The Anti-Apartheid Act's prohibition on new investment in South Africa has been interpreted to mean that American residents cannot purchase South African stock issued after the effective date of the Act. Stock issued prior to that date can be bought and sold. The August 1988 bill passed by the US House of Representatives would mandate the sale of all this stock. The possibility of such sanctions has had a depressing effect on South African gold share. Notes W. I. Car, "the threat of further U.S. disinvestment has made South African gold shares unacceptable to the international investor." If Americans were forced to sell this stock, if would have a significant downward pressure on South African gold stocks, and limit the ability of the gold mines to raise much needed new capital.

Conclusion

South Africa has a continuing need for foreign capital. Without new foreign capital, in terms of loans and investment, South Africa's economy cannot grow at a more than marginal rate. A few examples are worth citing.

The gold mining industry has historically been developed with foreign capital. With gold providing 40% of South African exports, it is vital to the economy. Yet South Africa's gold production declined 40% between 1970 and 1987. To even maintain current production levels, South African mining companies will have to invest large sums of money in exploration and new mines. When South African companies need to raise money to finance new mines, they usually issue stock, much of which is purchased overseas. Already US citizens are prohibited from buying new stock and if such sanctions are extended, it would be difficult to see how South Africa could afford to undertake the necessary expenditure to develop new mines.

Prior to the imposition of the debt standstill, South African state corporations, such as ARMSCOR (armaments), ESKOM (electricity), SASOL (oil), and ISCOR (steel) all borrowed extensively overseas. Many South African companies also borrowed on the international market. All have had to drastically revamp their capital expansion programs as a result of being cut off from the foreign capital markets. They now have to depend on the domestic capital market.

Foreign technology is as important to South Africa as foreign capital. The anti-apartheid movement has been less successful in blocking technology than it has been in forcing companies to withdraw. But South African businessmen are increasingly concerned that they will be cut off from needed foreign technology.

The development of the Mossel Bay gas field demonstrates the link between foreign capital and technology. At least 20% of Mossel Bay will be foreign sourced, without which the development could not be undertaken. Without the necessary trade finance, this key foreign input cannot be purchased.

Unless South Africa abandons apartheid, the logic of the situation is that there will be more sanctions in the future, not less. Although the Bush administration opposes additional sanctions, this does not mean that it will be in a position to stop such legislation. While welcoming the fact that the Republican Party maintained control of the White House, South African Foreign Minister Pik Botha cautioned, "A Bush victory does not mean that South Africa has escaped sanctions."

South Africa's new President, F. W. de Klerk, faces a series of contradictions in his effort to modernize apartheid. If he eases up and allows more political activity, the world will once again see massive demonstrations against so-called change which does not lead to a unitary democratic state. But if it does not ease up, no changes made will have the slightest credibility either at home or abroad.

A combination of growing resistance and capital flight has severely challenged the long term survival of the apartheid system. The withdrawal of numerous US and UK companies is a significant victory for the anti-apartheid movement. Yet many companies continue to operate in South Africa, either through direct investment or through licensing, franchising, and distribution agreements. Recent event have demonstrated how vulnerable the South African government is to international pressure. Now is the time to increase that pressure until the end of apartheid and the installation of a unitary democratic state.

Notes

1. Disinvestment is defined as the selling of equity ownership in South Africa. A company disinvests if it sells its ownership in a South African subsidiary (50% or more owned) or affiliate (less than 50% owned). An individual or company (such as a mutual fund) may also own shares in a South African company, the selling of which is also considered disinvestment. Divestment is the process where an individual or an institution sells its securities (stocks or bonds) in a company that does business in South Africa. Non-Equity ties are licensing, distribution or management agreements between US companies and South African companies. A distribution agreement can be indirect, such as a case where a US company gives a European company world rights outside the US.

2. The primary reason for the increase between 1985 and 1987 was the reinvestment of profits by those companies which had not disinvested was greater than the capital outflow from South Africa as a result of disinvestment. Another factor is the change in the

rand/dollar exchange rate, which also changes the dollar value of US investment. The General Accounting Office (GAO) has computed the value of US direct investment in South Africa, adjusted for exchange rate fluctuations, as having increased from $2.04 billion in 1984 to $2.23 billion in 1986 before declining to $2.12 in 1987.

3. Because the financial rand rate fluctuates considerably at a discount of between 20% to 40% of the commercial rand rate, this also makes it difficult to convert the rand to dollars for companies disinvesting. Moreover, the author does not know the date the money is actually removed from South Africa.

4. Lotus products, especially Lotus 123, are widely available. It would be interesting for Lotus to try to sue users of its products in South Africa for violation of copyright.

5. Following the debt standstill, Citicorp had ended new cross border loans to South Africa and, in mid-1987, sold its South African subsidiary to First National Bank of South Africa. First National, the largest bank in South Africa, is the former subsidiary of Barclays Bank. Citicorp was the only US bank to have an actual subsidiary in South Africa, although several others did have offices.

THE IMPACT OF SANCTIONS AND DISINVESTMENT ON BLACK SOUTH AFRICAN ATTITUDES TOWARD THE UNITED STATES

David Hirschmann

"The more things change the more they stay the same."

ALPHONSE KARR*

Introduction

In clarifying the specific purposes of this chapter, it is necessary to make reference to and distinguish it from two surveys of black South African opinion on disinvestment. Based on a survey of black production workers carried out in 1984, Lawrence Schlemmer concluded that roughly 75% were opposed

---

*Karr, as quoted by the First National Bank of South Africa in a brochure explaining to its clients the significance of the change from Barclays, which had withdrawn from South Africa, to First National, which had taken over Barclays' interests.

to disinvestment and roughly 25% were in favor.[1] In a 1985 study, Mark Orkin found that 24% supported disinvestment, 26% opposed it, and 48% favored conditional disinvestment. (When asked if they would still support disinvestment if there were serious job losses for blacks 26% said yes, 26% said yes only if there were a few jobs lost, and 48% said they were opposed if there were any loss of jobs.[2]) There have been criticisms of Schlemmer's methodology and questioning of Orkin's interpretation that his results demonstrated a majority commitment to disinvestment. It is possible to argue that the results are not as contradictory as they might appear and that their meaning is as follows: About 25% support disinvestment unconditionally, about 25% oppose it, and about 50% both support it if it will help end apartheid and oppose it if it will cause serious economic disadvantage to black South Africans. This apparent contradiction might be difficult for policy makers to deal with, but it may well approximate the reality.[3]

The study on which this chapter is based had a broader purpose, namely, to assess black South African attitudes toward the US, the extent to which they may have been changing, the reasons for these changes, and to relate the changes to increased radicalization. In-depth interviews were conducted with 93 urban black South Africans comprising a reasonably representative cross-section of ideological tendencies, political affiliations, professions, and age categories. With the exception of five or six people who may be regarded as national leaders, the groups were made up mainly of second- and third-level regional and local leaders and organizers.[4]

The results of the first round of interviews—with 45 people during the period June through August 1986—revealed a very widespread and dramatically increased hostility toward the US on the part of those interviewed. This was as true for younger as for older people and for both more and less radical members of the group. In simple terms the US—and most pointedly the Reagan administration—was seen as a serious hindrance rather than a source of support for black liberation. There was considerable anger and disappointment contained in these responses. The only exceptions were supporters of Chief

Buthelezi's Inkatha movement, who were consistent in their support for the US and its policies toward South Africa.

In the months of June through August 1987 a second round of interviews were conducted with 65 people, 17 of whom were also interviewed in 1986. Between the two rounds of interviews four noteworthy events occurred which related to US-South African relations. These were the Anti-Apartheid Act passed by Congress, the acceleration in the pace of American companies disinvesting, the meeting between the US Secretary of State, George Shultz, and the President of the ANC, Oliver Tambo, and the appointment for the first time of a black American Ambassador to Pretoria.

Because of the legislative restrictions included in the state of emergency regulations, it was decided in 1986 not to ask direct questions about sanctions and disinvestment. It was nevertheless abundantly clear from the responses that most of those interviewed were in favor of both. President Reagan's opposition to these steps was without doubt a major cause of their feeling of hostility toward him and his administration. So too was the US failure to have any high level official contact with the ANC. The possibility of the appointment of a black ambassador was discussed with only a few people; they were all opposed to the idea.

On the surface, at least, the US appeared in the interim to have complied to some extent with these demands. In the course of the second round of interviews questions were therefore asked about each of these steps, and their overall impact on attitudes to the US. In simple terms, did they cause people to change their minds? This chapter is based on the 65 interviews carried out in the second round. The first and main part—specifically on responses to the sanctions legislation and disinvestment—is not intended to be of statistical value. As explained, because of legislative restrictions, interviewees were not asked directly to express approval or disapproval of these acts. Rather they were asked to give their opinions on certain questions relating to these issues. The purpose therefore is to convey something of the content and tone of the debate about sanctions and disinvestment that has been taking place among black South Africans. The second, concluding section is intended to have some statistical relevance: people were asked directly whether these new policies and actions amounted to a meaningful change in policy and whether this had influenced their attitudes toward the US.

The Sanctions Act of October 1986

In October 1986, overriding the veto of the President, the US Congress passed the Comprehensive Anti-Apartheid Act of 1986. Interviewees were asked whether they thought sanctions had any impact, material, psychological or otherwise, and whether they thought black South Africans had been pleased by the passing of the Act.

A large proportion of the group were clearly not familiar with the contents of the Act. Most of those who were specifically asked about this admitted that they did not know much detail about the Act, and they did not think that most others did. A university research associate said: "People are pleased with anything anti-South African. If it puts South Africa on trial, good. But people are not familiar with the details. Even I am not familiar with the details and I am a researcher."

The explanations given for this apparent lack of attention to an Act which, the previous year, had been seen as so important were varied. One interpretation (mentioned by a few people) related to the coinciding of the passing of the Act with a moment of great pressure on black South Africans. Also, because of the state of emergency, black organizations were not allowed to call meetings to inform their followers of the contents of the legislation. People had come to rely on their organizations for the dissemination of this kind of information. Sanctions came at a time of severe official restriction on black political communication; there was little opportunity to explain or to hold open discussion. A few people commented that their lack of knowledge resulted from their having been in prison at the time of enactment and for a further eight or nine months thereafter. Yet others argued that they themselves, as well as people they knew, did not take the contents seriously because of a deeply felt mistrust of and cynicism about American actions in South Africa.

This last point was confirmed by the fact that one of the most common responses (mentioned 34 times) expressed some form of suspicion about the motives behind the Act. Other comments varied from charges that the sanctions were too weak and implementation was ineffective, to arguments that any gains had already been eroded by intensified pressure and that sanctions were more an "American football" than a method of liberation, and to the acknowledgement that there may have been exaggerated expectations of what sanctions could achieve.

Suspicion of American motives was expressed by a number of people. A middle-aged woman from the eastern Cape maintained that "even a vote of Congress we can't believe. We want to discover what the trick is." A young university lecturer said:

> Anti-Americanism is so deeply felt. America would not do anything that is not in America's interest. Also this was an election year in America and this decision was part of that process.

An official of a trade union affiliated with COSATU remarked:

> The Black worker is very suspicious of the sincerity of American policy. What is passed in America and what is implemented are very different things. We also know that sanctions are very difficult to police firmly . . . . The West has a tendency to go public in terms of propaganda on these decisions . . . still it was welcomed by the working class . . . only afterwards they learnt it was meaningless.

An almost equal number of comments (32) indicated a positive response to the passing of the Act. Some of these respondents went on to say that they later became disillusioned because of the apparent lack of impact or of implementation. A journalist observed:

> People are rejoicing to see tensions build up between Pretoria and Washington. People rejoice when they see the South African Government lose friends. America, being one of the biggest allies of South Africa,

> one has watched the fiery exchange and hostile attitudes developing from Pretoria and Washington.

He went on to explain that for a variety of reasons—mainly that sanctions were not producing results—local issues had become more pressing and relevant. An Azapo official said that it had been a step in the right direction, but that lack of coordination with Western governments would render it ineffective. A professional man in Durban, while acknowledging that no material impact was discernible, nevertheless felt that it was seen as a "positive signal" to progressives in South Africa. It had also introduced South Africans to the complexities of American politics, to the differences between the Reagan administration, the Congress, and the people. He saw it as a victory for the Anti-Apartheid Movement in the teeth of opposition from the President. Two others who were positive about the passing of the Act based their satisfaction on the defeat of Reagan, rather than on the significance for South Africa.

Assessments of the impact on South Africa of the sanctions may be divided into four main types: no impact; a negative impact on blacks; a negative impact on whites; and an inability to assess. The most common response (mentioned 34 times) was that it had no or very little impact. (Ten said no effect; four, very little impact; four, no effect on the South African government; eight, no economic effect; four, very little economic effect; three, it would not bring the government down; and three, the government had prepared in advance and therefore it could have no impact.) A professional level manager said that South Africa had stockpiled strategic supplies in advance, and observed further that the South African economy had long been structured in response to political and ideological demands rather than to market forces, and therefore it would be able to adapt to the new pressures. A researcher said that South Africa had done its "homework" and was ready; and a community organizer commented:

> The South African Government is very strong. Unemployment was very high anyway. It has made very little difference to our suffering. It affected the Government on a very low scale. People were pleased

> because they thought the Government was not as strong as it is. We have learnt quickly.

As regards impact on the black population, a senior level manager stated:

> Black people accept it. The Black man is hungry whether he is working or not working. When he gets sacked we are sorry, but his brothers and sisters will help. Nobody is going to die. We will help.

Twenty of the responses included comments to the effect that black people had suffered as a consequence of sanctions (13 said that it had caused unemployment; five, that it had worsened working conditions; and two, that black people were not pleased by its effects). The interviewees that were most convinced of its having a deleterious effect on blacks were primarily people who were opposed to it in the first place. In the words of an Inkatha organizer:

> It is having effects. But the effects it is having are not the ones intended. It has hurt Blacks more than Whites. Next door is the manpower building dealing with unemployment. People in large numbers are lining up outside. Sanctions helped Whites to rally round the Government—they felt threatened and became more conservative. This was reflected in the election. The Progressive Federal Party was washed away and the Conservative Party became the official opposition. The National Party won an outstanding majority. And South African troops are hitting neighboring countries. Black people are still detained in large numbers. People in the forefront [of Black politics] are thinking twice about this. People are not pleased. And the social programs of these companies are ended or reduced.

Fifteen comments referred to some negative effects on whites or/and the government (six said that it had threatened the government in some way; five, that it had affected the economy negatively; three, that whites had suffered; and one that whites had suffered psychologically). "The Government did panic," said one middle aged woman. A graduate student agreed:

> Government felt threatened. It knows the consequences of sanctions, and the power of sanctions in arousing militancy and revolutionary instincts on the part of the exploited and unemployed, and that it breeds anger.

A university researcher:

> It has had an effect on the economy. It has actually stalled quite a few things. There is a lot of uncertainty about the continuation of American companies and on projected investment.

A community activist in Cape Town:

> I am very happy the bill passed. It has had effects. Thousands of people have lost jobs, not only Blacks, but also Whites, and certain White firms have gone bankrupt.

A worker supervisor in a private organization:

> I have to mix sanctions and disinvestment. People are pleased with both. In the short term it will harm Blacks but in the long term it will bring liberation. White people will also suffer because firms will close down. If I lose my job I will be pleased because the White man will also be in trouble; because I will become a criminal and deal with the White man directly. Whenever he is at work he will have to employ a guard at home and so will have to pay for it. He will realize that he is forced to do all this because of Government policy.

By contrast, four people made the point that the major impact of sanctions on whites was to mobilize and unify them. "It mobilized [them] in order to overcome it. It sent Whites back into the laager and caused more hatred."

It was clear from most of the comments that concrete and conclusive evidence on the effects of sanctions was in short supply. Ten answers specifically included this point: it was "too soon" or "too early" to be able to assess the effects; "no data were available"; "there was an economic recession unrelated to sanctions"; "open debate on this is restricted"; and "the Government and the White media control the facts." Certainly at the time the interviews were undertaken, analyzing short- and long-term impacts and distinguishing between different causes or specific consequences remained very problematic.

Disinvestment by US Firms

In 1984 seven US companies pulled out of South Africa, in 1985 this rose to 40, in 1986 to 50, and in the first half of 1987 (at which stage the second round of research was undertaken) 33 more companies left. This brought the total number of companies which had disinvested to 130, and indicated an accelerating trend.[5] Interviewees were requested to structure their answers around the questions of whether they considered the disinvestments to be having any impact of any kind and whether they felt black people were pleased by the departure of the companies. Answers, quite appropriately, were multifaceted and therefore difficult to classify and quantify.

By far the most common response (mentioned 35 times) was that the processes involved did not amount to disinvestment. Eighteen comments, many made in conjunction with the first point, claimed that disinvestment had had no effect, political or economic. Twenty responses, by contrast, stated that blacks had suffered as a consequence. Included in the answers were ten comments asserting that black people were pleased; and ten disagreed. Ten argued either for more careful targeting of sectors, or for a different form of disinvestment more advantageous to workers, and six people said that COSATU and other leaders were rethinking the whole issue.

The dominant point made was that the companies that had announced they were withdrawing were not in reality disinvesting. What would have satisfied the definition of real disinvestment was not made clear. Based on my understanding of discussions in 1986, it was generally anticipated that disinvestment would amount to a closing down of facilities and a complete withdrawal of the companies, together with their products, their technology, and their expertise. Unavoidably, this would cause hardship for black people who would be unemployed, but whites would also suffer, and it was necessary to put pressure on the South African economy and on the government. With the exception of Kodak (which many people confirmed had withdrawn in a real sense), most companies had not done this, leading to considerable cynicism and doubt about the intentions and sincerity of these companies. What then was actually happening, and how did the interviewees interpret the process? First, a senior manager (strongly pro-private enterprise) with a firm in the eastern Cape:

> It amounts to a management buy-out. General Motors becomes Delta Motors, and the current White managers are put in a position where they can purchase the company outright. Young people, Afrikaners, could not have bought the companies in their individual capacity. The South African Government has become involved in assisting them. Volkskas Bank has risen to prominence as a merchant bank—from being a small savings bank for the Afrikaans community. So the Government, through Volkskas helped these people to buy these companies. Immediately the new owners could make bold statements that they would renew contracts with the South African Government and Defence Force—US companies could not do that—and they were not bothered with the response of Black trade unions to that. In addition those corporations that left did so for economic reasons, not political ones. They were not profitable any more, partly because wages are not as low as they used to be.

He proceeded to give the example of Ford, which, he said, had built a recreation center for black workers "to gain Brownie points under the Sullivan Code." When the company left, it reneged on its commitment to its black workers by allowing these facilities to pass into white hands. An Azapo supporter explained:

> When we investigate these actions we see a perpetuation of control by one superior race over another. It is just a change of masters .... They are indigenizing oppression. Now Afrikaners will be more cruel because they are not responsible to international public opinion. Azapo is for total disinvestment. People should pack up and leave the country because we are in a campaign to isolate South Africa. We are not interested in selective or conditional disinvestment.

A businessman who had gone to considerable length to find ways for black businessmen to take over some of these companies' interests agreed despite a very different approach to the topic:

> We are seeing management buy-outs, which have not included Blacks. Top White guys in management have become instant millionaires, and Blacks remain sloggers as before. It is racism. The White people who take over are not putting their own money into it. We tried to take over Coca Cola. Financial institutions, banks, here and in the US refused us. They opened their checkbooks and signed for Whites, but not for Blacks. So far there is no unemployment because it is all a trick. Kodak is the only exception.

In agreeing with the above comments a man who worked for the UDF added that the forces calling for disinvestment now found that they had lost control of the process, and had become alarmed at the way in which it was being handled.

> Our view is that the transfer of ownership is not ending American involvement in South Africa. There is a minimum degree of upset for the ruling class, but it still has access to the products and the technology. Disinvestment has been worked out with the local ruling class and we have lost control. Now they are opening up share markets to Blacks. One company is placing shares in trust so that employees can buy up the shares over time. This is positive in the sense of creating involvement of the indigenous middle class,

> but at the same time it is undermining and dividing some of the forces of the opposition. They have opposed the State's attempts to create and coopt a Black middle class; so now disinvesting companies are trying to do the same thing. So the trade unions want consultation on this before companies leave. We don't know what the new parameters are going to be.

The notion that this selling to white management amounted to a public relations trick—"They are not withdrawing. They are not disappearing. Their products go on being made."—was widely accepted. Further there was a feeling that to the extent that they acted at all these corporations were responding to economic realities at home or/and in South Africa, rather than in support of black liberation.

The next most frequently mentioned comment was that black people had suffered as a result of the disinvestments. A senior executive with a private foundation explained:

> There has not been much effect on the economy. At the same time as the companies are being taken over by South African private enterprise, Black workers are not enjoying the same privileges as before. Workers are also unhappy about not being informed in good time of the withdrawal. Now there is a cry: Why do you leave us? People are scared of losing the privileges they had under the Sullivan Code.

An Inkatha official also saw the results as negative. He gave as an example his own brother, a father of many children, who had lost a job. "This is why people are becoming hoboes." The only person who attempted to present some kind of statistical evidence on this topic was a trade unionist who supported disinvestment. He felt that the results had not been significant. "Possibly 3000 workers have lost jobs as a result compared to 3 million unemployed in total."

Ten comments claimed that black South Africans were pleased by announcements of disinvestment. A woman student in Cape Town, while acknowledging that there did not seem to be much change, said that blacks were very pleased to see anything that helped end apartheid. A legal adviser explained her sense of satisfaction in this way.

> Suffering has not increased because of disinvestment. The companies which are leaving are the same ones which did not pay a living wage and exploited Black workers. If they had paid a living wage we would welcome them to stay. Blacks were not better off when they were here. We are very happy when they go. People are pleased because they see the pressure building up.

Interviewees who argued that blacks were positive also asserted that disinvestments were having an impact on whites. A trade union organizer said that it had made a psychological impact on the government, which had led to strong anti-American feeling in Pretoria. A graduate student argued that when Barclays Bank announced that it was disinvesting, many Afrikaners woke up to the fact that in the 1980s things had changed.

A unionist affiliated to COSATU felt that it had created uncertainty among whites and that this could be seen in the number of whites, particularly professionals, taking the "chicken run," that is, emigrating. About ten comments supported the opposing view, namely that blacks were not pleased by the disinvestment. There were also a number of people who admitted to mixed feelings about the experience so far. For example, a lawyer employed by a legal advice bureau said:

> Obviously some people have lost jobs. It must affect them because there are no other jobs. My concern is that they are taking away our workers' efforts in the form of profits. We fear that capital created by workers is leaving the country.

And a priest in the eastern Cape:

> It raises lots or problems. Workers have fears, but they also see that the Government fears disinvestment more than they do. Others feel a better option would have been to strengthen the military wing of the ANC. Most people in the democratic movement feel that the

> military option cannot be openly encouraged and therefore we are restricted to encouraging disinvestment . . . but we have been discouraged by these companies simply being bought out.

There was also a group of people who were of the opinion that COSATU in particular, but also other leaders, were rethinking their strategy on disinvestment. A researcher in Durban explained the significance of this: "It all depends on COSATU. People don't so much have their own opinions as they depend on significant actors, and they follow suit—Tutu, Mandela, COSATU can say anything—and it is taken as correct." A manager argued that leaders who had earlier called for sanctions would not now openly admit their error because they would lose face. "I suspect though that there is less enthusiasm for it." An official of a union affiliated to COSATU suggested:

> People are re-thinking and coming with ideas of how the campaign should be handled. We don't want money to go out of the country, or that we should lose jobs. This won't remove the Government, and putting people out of work is not going to solve the problem . . . . What people would like to see happening, if possible, is to have companies pull out so as to leave a direct impact on the South African Government rather than affecting the employees only and immediately. For example, if access to technology could be limited it could cause problems for their projects, and the Government would be forced to do something. We are not looking for something dramatic like thousands losing jobs per day and then wait and see if the Government will take notice. There is rethinking about this in COSATU: they want a more concrete approach than just a generalized support for anything that puts pressure.

These opinions came both from people who supported and people who did not support COSATU and disinvestment. It is however important to emphasize that COSATU has since stressed on a number of occasions that its policy remains unchanged.

The large majority of the group interviewed would have been in favor of disinvestment and sanctions the previous year.

This was a key reason for the hostility felt towards the US then, particularly the Reagan administration. Clearly, a good number of them still did believe in this strategy. For these people, the ineffectiveness of sanctions resulted from their very partial and insincere implementation. For them, then, strengthened and more comprehensive sanctions and complete disinvestment were required to have an impact on the South African government. Another group would acknowledge the lack of effectiveness and seriousness of purpose of those withdrawing, and in consequence would be looking for more carefully targeted, and maybe selective actions: actions that operate more directly against white interests and the government and less immediately against black people. Others again have become cynical that capital will ever respond substantively and positively to their struggle, and feel that other strategies need to be stressed. Yet others fear that eventually capital might effectively withdraw, and their reading of even the minimal effects experienced so far frightens them into believing that growing numbers of black workers will be unemployed and will in fact suffer seriously. The minority, primarily Inkatha members and some management personnel, opposed these measures from the start, and believe their arguments have proved to be well-founded. They claim that blacks are already suffering from these actions and will continue to do so as long as they are being implemented. Facts are in very short supply—and, where and when available, are and will be difficult to analyze. So at this stage perceptions are all important. It is very early to make assessments, and extremely problematic given the pressures brought to bear on black leadership over the previous 15 months or so.

1986/87: A Meaningful Change in US Policy?

Question: If you take account of the following actions of the US during the past year—the sanctions law, the rapidly increased pace of disinvestment, the meeting between Shultz and Tambo, and the appointment of a Black Ambassador—do you see all of this as amounting to a change in American policy toward South Africa? And if so, how meaningful is that change?

Asked: 64; No change at all: 35 (56%); A very minor change: 11 (18%); A small change: 11 (18%); A substantial change: 5 (8%); Uncertain/conditional: 2.

Question: Have these actions caused you to change your assessment of the US? In other words, have you become less critical or more critical or has your attitude remained unchanged?

Asked: 63; Attitude remained unchanged: 52 (84%); More critical: 3 (5%); Less critical: 3 (5%); Wait and see: 1 (2%); Uncertain/conditional: 4 (7%).

Since there was so overwhelming a negative response to the appointment of a black ambassador, and this seemed of less importance than the other actions taken, it seemed wise (after a few responses to the first question indicated that this was likely to detract from the point of the question) to refrain from including this in the list of US actions taken. Given the hostility expressed during the 1986 interviews, the most significant issue of concern to the second of these questions was whether there may have been any reduction in the degree of criticism.

In brief, these results mean that three-quarters of the group saw no or precious little change in US policy; and about 90% had not reduced the level of hostility felt towards the US as a consequence of the actions referred to. Very clearly these four steps had made almost no impact on black attitudes towards America. The concluding section of the chapter will attempt to suggest explanations for the lack of impact and the continuing hostility.

President Reagan's opposition to the Anti-Apartheid Act and to disinvestment detracted from its impact on black South Africans. The fact that Congress took the—at that stage—unusual step of overriding the President's veto was not seen as a victory. Possibly, for the interviewees the fact that the most important leader in the US, both substantively and symbolically, is opposed to these actions may mean that they therefore carry less weight. Black South Africans were obviously suspicious of the sincerity with which the law would be implemented under these circumstances. It would seem that in this regard they had good reasons for doubt, since many of the provisions have not been put into practice, or have been interpreted in such a way as to limit their impact.

The fact that corporations have disinvested under pressure both political and economic, rather than doing so in order to strengthen the cause of liberation, has reduced their meaning for black South Africans. There is a widely held view that companies are leaving because profits are down, or because they are under threat of losing business abroad. The manner in which disinvestment has been taking place has strengthened these doubts. Management sellouts to local white managers, or to local or foreign companies, at discounted prices and with all production systems and licensing arrangements continuing, have meant that disinvestment has turned out to be a very different process from that anticipated. Corporations are not leaving; no crisis is resulting; pressure on the government is not that significant; some white businessmen are in fact benefitting; and some black workers, probably not many in number yet, are suffering. Blacks called for a particular type of action against apartheid. They feel they have been tricked.

The Reagan administration's continuing call on the ANC to renounce violence continues to cause hostility. It was widely seen in the following terms: as selective, since the US itself uses violence when it deems this necessary and supports violence when it thinks it is advantageous to its interests (the US should by now be aware that black South Africans have a very long history of peaceful resistance which made no headway); as unrealistic, given the government's handling of black opposition; and, ultimately, as serving as an excuse for refusing to support the movement. The overt support given to UNITA also continues to cause a great deal of anger among black South Africans. This is seen as putting the US firmly into a military alliance with the South African government. For some it therefore becomes difficult to see how the US can ever sincerely oppose the government when it has chosen to fight on the same side.

Capitalism, with which America is so closely identified, is under increasing suspicion in South Africa. As this study has demonstrated elsewhere, blacks are coming to identify capitalism with apartheid. In tandem these systems have exploited them for a long time. There are those who make the point that true private enterprise does not operate in the country. Nevertheless most people interviewed do appear to identify the system as such and to feel that it has brought very few benefits to black South Africans. Those among the interviewees who identify America as imperialist therefore go on to make the case that America will not willingly undermine a capitalist system from which it is profiting.

Anger toward the US has been growing for some time now, possibly for a decade, and more particularly since the Reagan administration has been in office. The reasons for this change in attitude emerge from the interviews. Suspicion is therefore high. Ulterior motives for any apparently positive move are therefore always sought. (It remains to be seen whether the Bush administration's actions will change these attitudes.)

Finally, the history of events over the last two years inside South Africa will have affected the response. The South African government has effectively and cruelly delayed the progress of the black struggle. There has been a great deal of suffering. This may be only a temporary setback. But in the meantime blacks look around and see increased oppression and a deteriorating political situation, and they must come to the conclusion that, whatever foreign powers are doing, it is having no positive impact.

Notes

1. Lawrence Schlemmer, *Black Worker Attitudes. Political Options, Capitalism, & Investment in South Africa* (Durban, Center for Applied Social Sciences, University of Natal, 1984), 33-41.

2. Mark Orkin, *Disinvestment, the Struggle and the Future. What Black South Africans Really Think* (Johannesburg, Ravan Press, 1986), 12-13.

3. See Merle Lipton, *Sanctions and South Africa. The Dynamics of Isolation* (London, The Economic Intelligence Unit, Special Report No. 1119, 1988), 119.

4. The full study provisionally entitled *Changing Attitudes of Black South Africans toward the United States of America,* will be published in the near future.

5. *Weekly Mail* (Johannesburg), 24 July 1987, 17.

THE IMPACT OF NEW SANCTIONS AGAINST SOUTH AFRICA*

Roger C. Riddell

The debate about imposing or extending the range of economic sanctions on South Africa[1] needs to be placed first in the context of the likelihood of achieving the objectives desired and, second, in relation to other, alternative methods of achieving those objectives. In the case of externally imposed sanctions against South Africa, the ultimate objective is to move the country forward to the establishment of a free democratic society.

In relation to the means chosen, the first question to raise is whether and to what extent South Africa is vulnerable to sanctions taken by other countries which will, either directly or indirectly, affect the country's economic performance. Briefly, the answers are that South Africa is extremely vulnerable to a range of sanctions which, as a whole, have already had a major impact on the prospects for economic growth through adversely

---

*An earlier version of this article was presented as testimony at hearings before the African Sub-Committee of the US House of Representatives, March 1988.

affecting business confidence in that country. As the President of the South African Foundation stated at the end of 1987:

> . . . there is no doubt that the (sanctions) package has had an adverse effect on domestic confidence. This lack of confidence is again and again emerging as the most important single factor inhibiting growth in this country.[2]

Additionally, specific sanctions have had a more direct impact on different sub-sectors of the economy even if their precise outcome is difficult to determine because of the complexity of factors. Continuing sanctions and extending their range is likely to deepen these effects. In general, the more measures taken by increasing numbers of South Africa's economic partners, the greater is likely to be the effect and the less likely that either evasive action or counter-measures or other adverse trends will over-ride the effect of sanctions.

Assessing and determining the precise impact of different measures is complicated by a range of factors. Five of these in particular need to be highlighted. First, at present and in the foreseeable future not all countries are likely to impose comprehensive sanctions against South Africa; hence, the immediate effects of sanctions imposed by one country will be counterbalanced (to a greater or lesser degree) by other measures taken by third countries wishing to gain from the initial economic intervention. Second, South Africa's economy is affected externally by a host of factors other than the sanctions currently imposed or likely to be imposed, such as the price of gold, the value of the American dollar, and the prospects for world trade; in some cases these can reinforce the effects of sanctions, in others they can reduce the effects. Third, the impact of sanctions can be affected by the extent to which countervailing action is taken by the South African authorities and business community. Fourth, the impact of sanctions will be affected by the time period in which the sanctions are imposed. And in this regard, experience from other countries suggests that where sanctions are not comprehensively imposed by all economic partners or where there is not one dominant economic partner, it will require some considerable time—a number of years—before the adverse effects of the sanctions begin to bite. Fifth, and finally, experience also shows that it is frequently not necessary for sanctions to have the widespread economic impact intended for the political outcome to be achieved: if the sanctioned country is convinced that the threat of imposing sanctions is genuine, and if the country is vulnerable economically to such action, this is often sufficient for progress towards the desired political action to be set in motion.[3] It is within this context of some uncertainty over specific results of sanctions that the discussion about their effectiveness and of possible new measures must be conducted.

The South African Economy

In common with most modern developing economies, South Africa has an economic structure vulnerable to external influence and conditions. Its growth and development have been and continue to be determined to a large extent by its external economic, financial, transport, and technological relationships. High and sustainable levels of growth and development can only be achieved in the context of continuing these international relationships; without them, low levels of growth and development will ensue, which will be unsustainable because of their fueling the already serious levels of political unrest and repression. With radical changes to South Africa's internal structures, dependence upon these external relationships could, in theory, be reduced, and some people in South Africa at least have placed this issue on the agenda for discussion. It needs to be stressed, however, both that there is no evidence that the necessary radical steps to effect substantial structural change are being taken and that even if they were taken it would be five years or more before their impact would be felt.

The best way to appreciate the external vulnerability of the South African economy is to look at its growth and development in historical context. For much of the 1960s, the South African economy achieved growth rates of 6% or more each year; in the 1970s (and in common with many other similarly-structured economies and for similar reasons) average growth rates fell to 3% a year. In the period 1980 to 1987, however, annual growth rates have dropped to just over 1.2% a year. In 1987, the South African economy grew by an estimated 2.5%; for 1988, year projections and estimates vary from 2.5% to an (optimistically) high rate of 4%.

The high growth rates of the early period were made possible by the following factors: a rapid expansion in external trade; large inflows of foreign capital, skills, and technology; and the development of external transport routes. While South Africa was adversely affected by the oil price rises and high levels of inflation of the 1970s, positive growth rates were sustained not only by the maintenance of its external trade, technology, and skills-absorption policies but, additionally, by substantial foreign borrowing.

Looking ahead, for a number of years there has been a consensus that in order to absorb all its work-seekers/school-leavers, the South African economy will have to grow by between 5% to 6% a year. To the extent that this fails to occur, overall unemployment will increase.

With levels of low economic growth recently achieved, the expansion in black employment has been minimal: there has been no net increase in black employment since 1977 and only in the gold mining industry have net additions (some 30,000 in the 1980s) taken place. Between 1982 and 1986, only some 22,000 new jobs were created each year whereas over 300,000 were needed to absorb all the job-seekers. Recent estimates are that black unemployment in 1987 totalled at least two million, over 25% of the total black workforce. But in the urban areas, where recent levels of violence have been most pronounced, both aggregate and especially youth unemployment rates among blacks are even higher—in Pietermaritzburg 30% and 85%, respectively, in mid-1986.[4]

The Overall Implications of Sanctions for the Economy

The dilemma South Africa faces is this: high levels of economic growth are required to absorb increasing numbers of job seekers, but this requires further external economic and financial contacts, especially with the industrialized and more advanced industrializing nations of the world. Lower levels of external contact will lead to lower levels of domestic economic growth, raising unemployment levels and fueling domestic unrest. It is here that the "sanctions element" comes into the economic equation. Impeding or restricting South Africa's exports, cutting off or reducing its crucial imports, restricting, reducing, and halting loan finance, including trade credit, impeding the transfer of technology, disrupting transport and communications links—all these have the effect of lowering growth rates for the economy.

At present, given the past accumulation of commercial foreign debt, South Africa requires expanding levels of exports to run a quite substantial current account surplus on its balance of payments to honor its debt repayments while at the same time importing the oil, machinery, and equipment it needs for high levels of sustained growth. Recent figures and those projected for 1988 indicate that South Africa has been quite successful in achieving a current account surplus.

Table 1

Year	*Current Account Surplus*	
	Rand (Billion)	*US$ (Billion)*
1985	5.7	2.6
1986	7	3.1
1987	6	3.0 (estimate)
1988	3-4.6	1.5—3.5 (forecast)

Initially it would appear that success in managing the current account has occurred because of a rapid rise in exports. Indeed the value of South Africa's total exports has risen from R20 billion in 1980 to R25 billion in 1985 and to R42 billion in 1986. However, measured in SDRs, South African exports fell by 25% from SDR 21 billion in 1980 to SDR 15.7 billion in 1986 (a large part of the sustaining of exports being due to the predominant place and world price of gold, gold accounting for some

35% of total export earnings). Nonetheless South Africa managed to record a healthy merchandise trade surplus, which in large part sustained its overall current account surplus, because of very substantial cuts in imports. In US$ terms, total imports fell by over 33% at current prices, from $16.7 billion in 1980 to $11.1 billion in 1986.

The falling level of imports was a cause of the low levels of aggregate growth achieved in the South African economy in the 1980s. They were themselves due in no small measure to the dramatic fall in aggregate investment levels of the economy: as a ratio to GDP, gross fixed investment fell from 28% in 1980/81 to 22% in 1985/86, a fall of 17% in real terms with a 50% fall in the manufacturing sector. There is no doubt, however, that the low and falling levels of real investment in the South African economy have been due in large measure to the actual and anticipated action of the international community against South Africa, which has seriously and adversely affected the business climate and level of confidence among investors and potential investors.

Three factors stand out in this regard: first, the decision of foreign banks not to roll over South Africa's foreign debt in 1985; second, the decision of many (largely US firms) to disinvest from South Africa; and, third, the action—taken by a number of countries, most notably the United States and some European Economic Community (EEC) and Scandinavian countries—to impose various trade sanctions against South Africa.

So concerned have the South African authorities been about both low levels of aggregate growth and investment that they have followed twin policies of cheap money and increased state spending to attempt to stimulate growth: interest rates were lowered from 21.75% in May 1985 to 9.5% at the end of 1987 while government spending has annually increased by over 15% in recent years and inflation rates have only fallen from over 20% in the mid-1980s to an anticipated 14% in 1988. In 1987, however, although these policies led to a rise in consumer spending, they also led to an increase in imports required to sustain the higher growth level achieved. Concerned about this rise in the imports, in February 1988 the authorities announced lower targets for money supply growth followed in early March with a reversal of their four year policy of "easy" money by raising interest rates to 10.5%. While the effect of such policies will be to reduce the pressure on imports, it will also dampen down aggregate growth in the economy. Economists from the Anglo-American Corporation judge that for South Africa to grow at the required 5% a year some 10% of all investment will have to come from abroad, amounting at 1985 prices to about R3 billion a year to the end of the decade.

As highlighted in the February 1988 edition of the Standard Bank's *Economic Review* of South Africa, the seriousness of the balance of payments constraint necessitates controlling the rate of economic expansion. However, it continues, "unless conditions change significantly in South Africa's favor, the surplus on the current account of the balance of payments will probably be sufficient to support a satisfactory rate of domestic growth only for this year." It is within this context that consideration needs to be given to particular sanctions.

The Vulnerability of South Africa to Particular Sanctions

I shall look briefly in turn at three areas of sanctions—general finance, private investment, and external trade—concentrating in more detail on external trade sanctions.

General Financial Sanctions

There is no doubt that the decision of major international banks in July 1985 to call in short term loans and freeze new lending to South Africa not only had a major impact on worsening the already adverse business climate within South Africa but sent shock waves through the authorities because it raised the possibility of South Africa being isolated from access to foreign finance. More concretely, it led the authorities to declare a moratorium on debt repayment and to freeze repayments on $14 billion (58%) of its total outstanding debt of $24 billion. Nonetheless efforts to stem the outflow of capital have been far from successful; thus it is estimated that South Africa has sustained a net loss of capital of some R15.5 million (US$7 million) in 1985 and 1986 (equivalent to some 6% of gross domestic product) due to dividend outflow, a net outflow of capital and those debt repayments which have been permitted.

By early 1988, and following agreement with the banks in March 1986 and February 1987, total outstanding debt still stood at some $22 billion (despite repayment in excess of $5 billion since 1985, largely because of changes in the rate of the Rand against the US dollar). Under the latest agreement—repaying interest on the frozen debt and interest and principal on the outstanding debt—South Africa will have to pay out some $1.2 billion a year to 1990 in debt repayments. On current trends this would give a debt service ratio of around 10% a year. However, since January 1988, additional provisions have been announced by the South African authorities which would allow foreign creditors either to use repayment of principal caught in the frozen debt net to buy local property or equity or else to repatriate money through the medium of the financial Rand. On the basis of current exchange rates, taking up the latter option would reduce repayments in US dollars terms by one-third.

Besides the agreement by the banks to conform to substantial freezing of debt repayments, there is evidence to suggest that external financial restrictions have eased. For instance, South African public corporations managed to raise R695 million ($343 million) in new foreign loans in the first half of 1987, $441 million of short term frozen debt was converted into long term debt between July and September 1987 under the provisions of the 1987 debt rescheduling arrangements and a part of the $3.3 billion (largely, one suspects, export credits) have also been rolled over.

Clearly the most effective means of maximizing the impact of financial measures against South Africa would be a combination of the following: raising the outflow of capital through disinvestment, halting all new loans (including trade credits) to South Africa, banks refusing to eliminate or downgrade their credit position either by taking up the recent offer to liquidate or reduce their credits, and, finally, to raise again the issue of the timetable for repayments by demanding earlier repayment of all due amounts.

Specific actions that could be recommended would include the following:

1. Extending the restrictions currently in force for US banks to embrace trade credits and to tighten the current leeway allowed on rescheduling presently owed debt;
2. Putting pressure on EEC countries, at minimum to extend restrictions on long term lending to South Africa to include short term lending as well;
3. Putting pressure on Japan to strengthen its voluntary ban on bank loans to South Africa and within this area to restrict both long term and short term lending including trade credits of both Japanese banks and trading houses.
4. Putting pressure on Switzerland to advise its banks to adopt restrictive legislation (at present there are no restrictions on Swiss banks).

Private Foreign Investment

There is no doubt that disinvestment by Western (and largely U.S.) companies has added significantly to the undermining of confidence in the South African economy. Clearly, too, the ban (by the U.S. and other countries) on new private investment into South Africa has not only adversely affected confidence but has made and will continue to make a contribution to the shortage of foreign exchange and investment capital in the country. In addition, it has helped to halt the flow of new investment where there is still no domestic legislation to prevent such action.

There are, however, a number of areas causing concern to those wishing to see a more substantial impact of disinvestment on the South African economy. First, the impact of disinvestment on the balance of payments has not been as great as many had expected, partly because the selling of assets has frequently been well below "market" prices but also because of restrictions on the outflow of funds. (These are only permitted through the financial Rand so they usually need to be matched by equivalent inflows from new investment or non-resident transfers.)

The second issue relates to the high proportion of companies which have maintained non-equity and technological ties and agreements with the new companies that have been formed. While these arrangements have certainly put some pressure on the balance of payments, because of far higher royalty payments being paid to the parent companies, it has also meant that the crucial technological, servicing, and market links have not been severed. In addition, the trade legislation does not appear to prevent parent companies with subsidiaries located in countries which do not have an export ban to South Africa from using those subsidiaries to supply former South African subsidiaries. Finally, reports suggests that whereas US legislation prevents US computer and related companies from supplying equipment to institutions of the South African state, where disinvestment has occurred the new companies are now bidding for government contracts. To the extent that equipment and parts originating from the parent company are still supplied to South Africa, the potential for a substantial expansion in trade to assist the efficient operation of the apartheid state is enhanced.

Specific actions to address these and other anomalies would include the following:

1. Extending current US legislation to include a ban on the reinvestment of profits of US companies within South Africa and a ban on subsidiaries in third countries from supplying restricted company products to South Africa;
2. Putting pressure on other countries to tighten their investment bans. In this regard special attention should be given to the case of Taiwan, as some 120 Taiwanese factories have been set up in South Africa's homelands in recent years with total investment of $100 million. Additionally a number of EEC countries, which have only a voluntary ban on new investments into South Africa, should be persuaded to adopt U.S. agreed norms.

Trade Sanctions—South African Exports

Over the last four years South Africa's exports have averaged some 27% of gross domestic product. Recent trends in total exports, in Rand and U.S. dollars, are shown below. They reveal a rising trend in exports after 1985 and the significant fall in South African exports to the United States in 1987 following the passing of the Comprehensive Anti-Apartheid Act of 1986.

Table 2

Year	*Total Exports (billion)*		*Total Exports to US*	
	Rand	*US$*	*US$ (billion)*	*% of SA Exports*
1984	25.3	16.9	2.6	15.4
1985	36.7	16.2	2.1	13.0
1986	42.1	18.3	2.5	13.7
1987	42.7	21.6	1.4	6.5

The most important South African export products banned under current US legislation are: agricultural products, uranium (with dispute concerning uranium hexafluoride), coal, iron and steel products, and textiles. The total export value of all these products from South Africa amounted to $4.3 million in 1985 (26% of total export earnings), but the value of these exported to the United States only amounted to $741 million, 17% of the total export of these products and 4.5% of total South African exports. As can be seen from the table above, the fall in South African exports to the United States in 1987 of $1.1 billion coincided with an overall expansion in the US dollar value of worldwide South African exports of $3.3 billion.

Short of an effective worldwide ban on the importation of all South African produce, three major issues need to be addressed by the United States in the worldwide attempt to restrict the export of South African products: increasing the numbers of countries imposing a ban on products already subject to US legislative restrictions, extending the product range of South African exports subject to legislative restriction, and consideration of action to be taken against third countries through which South Africa channels its restricted exports onto the world market.

I shall look first at the products currently banned by the US legislation. It is clear from a discussion of each of these products that a major requirement is to put pressure on other leading importers of these products (in most cases EEC countries and Japan) to impose measures similar to those currently imposed by the United States. Without such action the impact of the United States' ban will remain weak.

Food and Agricultural Products. These exports account for 6% of total export earnings from South Africa and hence are an important area for restricting the country's foreign exchange earnings. Before the 1986 US trade sanctions were imposed, the United States imported only 13% of South Africa's total exports of food and agricultural products; over 65% went to EEC countries (53%) and Japan (13%). However, with few minor exceptions (Ireland, Denmark), there are no legislative restrictions on imports of these products from South Africa to either the EEC as a whole or to Japan.

Uranium. If all uranium imports from South Africa to the United States were to be banned, this would (on 1985 trade data) account for 46% of all South African uranium exports. However, in total, uranium exports only account for less than 2% of total South African foreign exchange earnings. The current ambiguity concerning US imports and the fact that Britain and France in particular have no legislative ban on either South Africa or Namibian uranium exports point to the need both to remove the ambiguities in regard to the US legislation and to put pressure on the EEC (and Japan) to impose sanctions on the import of this range of products.

Coal. US coal imports from South Africa constituted only 2% of total South African coal exports in 1985. Together Japan and the EEC imported 87% of South African coal exports in 1985. What is more, valued at some $1.3 billion in 1985 and constituting a far more homogeneous product than the wide array of different food and agricultural exports, expanding restrictions on coal exports especially to Britain, Japan, South Korea, Italy, France (where a partial ban does exist), and West Germany will have a major impact on South Africa's export earnings.

Iron and Steel. Prior to the 1986 legislation, the United States imported a significant 31% of all South Africa's iron and steel exports, themselves valued at $1.2 billion and amounting to over 6% of total export earnings from South Africa. While Japan and the EEC have also passed legislation imposing a ban on South African iron and steel products, an important exception relates to ferroalloys. To increase the worldwide impact of restructions on iron and steel products, the ferroalloy exception would need to be removed while, in addition, specific action will need to be taken to persuade Taiwan, which has substantially increased its imports of South African products, to take action to restrict and/or eliminate its imports of these products.

Textiles. Textile exports from South Africa amounted to less than 3% of its total export earnings in 1985, of which less than 20% went to the United States. The bulk of these exports go to the EEC, which imposes no restrictions on such imports, although Denmark, in conjunction with other Nordic countries, forbids such imports as part of its universal ban on South African imports.

Trade Sanctions—South African Imports

Recent trends in South African imports and the U.S. contribution are shown in the table. As with total South African exports, the US contribution is small and has been declining. However, as the previous discussion has highlighted, the potential demand for both total and US imports is higher than the actual figures indicate.

Table 3

Year	*Total South African Imports*		*Of which, US Exports*	
	Rand (billion)	*US$ (billion)*	*US$ (billion)*	*%*
1984	21.7	14.8	2.3	15.5
1985	23.0	10.4	1.2	11.5
1986	27.0	11.2	1.2	10.7
1987	28.7	14.5	1.3	9.0

The exclusion of oil and armament imports for many years in South Africa's detailed import figures, leading to 31% of total imports under the category of "unspecified," means that more detailed analysis of the composition and origin of imports cannot be undertaken. Nonetheless it is apparent that the single most important imported item is oil and that the most important general category of imports is machinery, the latter accounting for nearly 30% of all imports and valued at $3.2 million.

To impose an effective ban on machinery and on technology services in general undoubtedly requires not only a harmonization of action by the United States, the EEC, and Japan, but also and in particular the cooperation of Taiwan, South Korea, and Latin American countries such as Chile, all countries which South Africa has been courting especially since the mid-1980s. In this regard, the partial ban on the export of computer equipment to South Africa by leading producer nations needs to be extended while the United States needs to consider ways of restricting its companies from exporting these goods to South Africa via subsidiaries in third countries.

Oil. About 65% of South Africa's oil requirements are obtained from abroad: oil meets some 20% to 25% of the economy's primary energy needs and accounts for 80% of the energy consumption of the transport sector. It is thus apparent that effective oil sanctions could cause a crippling blow to the South African economy. Until recently, however, international attention on extending oil sanctions and mounting an effective oil blockade of South Africa have been fairly muted. A major reason for this is not because over fifteen years of limited oil sanctions have failed to have an impact on the South African economy—between 1974 and 1984, South Africa had to pay an extra Rand 22 billion (US$10.7 billion) over and above market prices to obtain its oil requirements, a price equivalent to 10% of its export earnings. Rather, the reason has been that conventional wisdom has indicated that the South Africans have between five and seven years' domestic supply of oil from a combination of covert storage and the expansion of the SASOL oil from coal plants.

Recent work, however, by Dr. Conlon of New York,[5] suggests that South Africa has no more than six to seven months' supply of oil. It currently has to import some 14 million tons of crude oil a year. The absence of legal provisions to enforce the oil embargo in some countries, weaknesses of enforcement practices, and the fact that South Africa is able to purchase oil "on the high seas" are three areas that need addressing. Japan and Hong Kong have no ban on the export of crude oil to South Africa, while West Germany operates only a voluntary ban. And of the Arab oil producers, reports indicate that Iran has been supplying South Africa with a proportion of its import requirements.

Further Trade Issues: Combating Sanctions Evasion and Widening the Net

There is no doubt that South Africa is concerned about the impact of trade restrictions, as can be seen from the institutional decisions it has taken recently to respond to the widening of such sanctions. Not only has it attempted to stimulate trade with third countries, most notably those in Asia, but it has established special departments for "unconventional" trade in different ministries with the purpose of assisting in the evasion of sanctions. In addition it has extended even further the list of products which are not individually recorded in its official trade statistics; since September 1987, detailed trade statistics covering over 50% of its external trade are no longer published.

A number of more important features need to be highlighted. First, major successes have been achieved in diverting exports particularly to Taiwan and South Korea, neither of whom publishes detailed trade statistics by country of origin. Total South African-Taiwan trade has risen from $135 million in 1985 to $546 million in 1986 and to $911 million in 1987, accounting in 1987 for 2.6% of total South African trade. Announcements made by Taiwanese officials suggest that plans are in train to expand total trade threefold to reach $3 billion by 1990.[6] Metals, steel, minerals and food and agricultural products top Taiwan's imports. There is thus little doubt that Taiwan, and foreign investors located there, are benefiting indirectly from the US-South African trade ban. It is clear, too, that Israel, at least in the past, has been a major channel of trade for products banned by other countries, such as armaments and steel products. However, it does appear that pressure already applied by the United States has led to an apparent scaling down of these contacts.

In this regard, there is clearly scope for the United States to put pressure on those of its close allies who have traded covertly with South Africa—Israel, Taiwan, and South Korea—at minimum, to publish their detailed trade statistics. More substantially, the possibility of removing bilateral trade preferences (where these exist) should be placed on the agenda for discussion if it can be shown that these these and other countries have benefitted as a result of US-South African sanctions. It should also be possible for the United States to hold discussion with the IMF (of which South Africa is a member) with a view to putting pressure on South Africa to address the issue of the concealment of international trade movements or to restrict regular borrowing.

Mention has been made already of the extent that South Africa trades with Japan. 1987 trade data show that Japan has now become South Africa's largest single trading partner, with total trade valued at $4.27 billion in 1987, 62% higher than total US trade. In Yen terms, Japan's exports to South Africa rose 18% in 1987, although imports from South Africa rose only 1%. Although in Yen terms total South African-Japanese trade has fallen by 24% from 1984 to 1987, it is equally clear that, to extend the effectiveness of trade sanctions against South Africa, Japan will have to play a leading part.

Another issue concerns the disguising of the origin of South African trade. US trade statistics for 1987 reveal, for instance, that US imports from South Africa's neighbor, Swaziland, rose by 116% from US$11 million in 1986 to $24 million in 1987, while Botswana's exports rose by 173% over this period.[7] The senior commercial official of the Swaziland government is on record as complaining of South Africa selling goods under the Swaziland label.

The final question concerning sanctions on South Africa's exports relates to a possible extension of the range of products which could effectively be included in an import ban by South Africa's trading partners, short of a mandatory comprehensive ban. While the more general issues, already discussed, of the significance of the product to South Africa, the likelihood of major trading partners imposing sanctions and the ability to disguise the product's origin would apply to any set of commodities, mention needs to be made in particular of gold.

Gold not only accounts on its own for about 33% of South Africa's total export earnings, but the taxation of the gold companies provides a major source of revenue to the South African government. The importance of gold to the wider issue of trade sanctions becomes clear when it is realized that for every $10 per ounce rise in the gold price, South Africa earns an extra $200 million; in other words, a rise in the gold price from $444 to $480 would in effect cancel out the total effect of the import ban imposed by the United States in 1986.

Without discussing in detail the mechanics and possibilities of imposing gold sanctions against South Africa, a number of points can be highlighted. Although South Africa has conventionally had a reputation for being a low-cost gold producer, this is changing. In 1987, the average cost of producing gold was R29,500 per kilogram and the average price received by the mines was between R29,000 and R30,000. Mining costs, which have risen by over 15% a year since the early 1980s, increased by 18.7% in 1987. To break even in 1988, the mines will require a price of about R34,000 a kilogram. If the rand/$ exchange rate remains at 47 cents (South African), then a gold price of $512 an ounce will be needed for the average mine to remain in profit.[8] The gold price was about $450 an ounce in mid-March 1988. If it does not move up significantly, either the mines will be set to lose money in 1988 or else the government will have to engineer a substantial fall in the value of the Rand (to about 40 cents), which will itself raise the price of imports.

Significantly, too, South Africa's role as a gold mining producer has been eroded in recent years. In 1984, South African gold production was 683 tons, accounting for 59% of total production and 47% of total world supplies of gold (the difference accounted for by Eastern bloc and central bank gold sales). In 1987, South African production dropped to 605 tons, 45% of total world production and only 36% of total supplies. As for 1988, Shearson Lehman Brothers judge that South African production will drop to 585 tons, only 46% of total production. Clearly, for South African gold production to rise again, as the government would like, it is necessary first for the price to rise significantly so that the mining companies can cover their current production costs and for world demand to outstrip supply. However, over the last four years the world supply of gold has exceeded demand by increasing amounts: by 204 tons in 1984, rising to 436 tons in 1987, the latter figure amounting to 32% of total world production.[9]

The implication of this discussion would appear to be that contrary to the view put forward by some commentators that the impact of non-gold trade sanctions will be ineffectual overall, unless simultaneously the gold price were brought down, it may be sufficient merely to attempt to prevent the gold price from rising.

The Impact of Comprehensive Western Sanctions on Black Employment

There are in South Africa no comprehensive data on current employment levels broken down by racial sub-group and the estimates that have been made of employment and unemployment rates both differ markedly from each other and are subject to frequent revision. It should thus be apparent that any attempt to predict with accuracy precise levels of employment and unemployment resulting from the imposition of sanctions and separating these out from other effects on the economy are going to be crude in the extreme. (1985 estimates judge that of 6.4 million people in formal employment, 63% were black; yet although amounting to some 75% of the population, blacks account for only 28% of disposable income, rising to 41% with the inclusion of the Asian and Coloured communities.)

Nonetheless some broad generalizations can be made. As comprehensive sanctions will have a major impact on reducing levels of aggregate growth, they will have an adverse effect on employment: in the absence of government policy to compensate, unemployment levels will increase. As some 63% of all formal sector employees are black and as the dependency ratio for black workers is higher than that for white workers, more black employees and potential employees will be affected by sanctions than their white compatriots. Additionally, as almost all unskilled workers are black and as many of the leading exporting industries involve labor-intensive operations, it would appear that black workers are both absolutely and proportionately more vulnerable to many trade sanctions than white workers.

A number of organizations have analyzed the anticipated loss of black employment resulting from sanctions. For instance, the Federated Chamber of Industries (FCI) has projected forward the growth and employment effects of the imposition of comprehensive sanctions (80% of non-gold and strategic metal trade) over a two-year and a five-year period. The results of the analysis of the FCI indicate that over a two-year period aggregate growth will fall by some 10% and employment will fall by 312,000; over a five year period, aggregate growth will have fallen by nearly 30% and employment losses would total 1.13 million. Of this employment loss, 80% is estimated to occur in secondary industry, services, and commerce, 16% in agriculture, and only 4% from within the mining industry.[10]

One problem with these estimates is that lack of information at the industry level and lack of presentation of detailed assumptions precludes the possibility of checking the projections.[11] Another problem with the projections is that no assumption has (apparently) been made in relation to alternative employment opportunities or to possible government action to stimulate non-trade related employment. A third concern relates to the accuracy of the data on which the projections are based. For instance, since the projections were made, government estimates have revised upwards employment in the manufacturing sector from 1.33 million to 1.5 million. The effect of incorporating these new (and more accurate?) figures into the FCI model would be to alter their numbers by as much as 13%.[12]

But perhaps the most important problem with debating potential job losses in the South African economy as a result of sanctions is that such exercises fail to place the issue of employment and unemployment within its broader context. Without substantial sanctions there are today well over two million unemployed blacks in South Africa and *without* sanctions the economy has failed to absorb between 150,000 and 200,000 new entrants to the labor force each year since the Soweto uprising of 1976. At least 16%—and maybe as high a figure as 30%—of the black workforce is currently unemployed. It was revealed in the official proceedings of the South African parliament in 1984 that the number of people living below the poverty line in South Africa rose from 4.1 million in 1960 to 8.9 million in 1980, accounting in 1980 for some 30% of the total population. In other words, the worst case scenario outlined by the FCI would make little significant difference to what has already been happening in recent years.

It is within this context that one needs to place the evidence of a high proportion of black respondents to opinion surveys and of, for instance, the unanimous declaration of the second annual congress of the Confederation of South African Trade Unions (COSATU) held July 1987, which support the international campaign of sanctions.

To illustrate these sorts of problems, a few brief comments on employment and the coal industry can be made. The coal industry employs about 110,000 people, and about 25% of total coal production was exported in the mid-1980s. The anti-sanctions lobby has made much of the large job losses which it is claimed would result in the industry as a result of coal sanctions. However, some pertinent facts need to be highlighted. First, output levels of coal production doubled to 172 million tons in the past 10 years without any increase in employment. Second, the export losses incurred in 1987 as a result of sanctions were in large measure compensated by higher domestic sales. Indeed, compared with the claim by the South African Chamber of Mines that 30,000 jobs would be lost in the industry as a result of sanctions, the effects so far have been negligible. For instance, the bulletin of the South African Coal Industry, *SA Coal Insight*, stated in its first edition (February 1988) that only 2,708 workers had lost their jobs due to "sanctions compounded by weak markets."

South African Sanctions and the Front Line States[13]

In discussing the sanctions issue in relation to the Front Line States (FLS), three interrelated elements need to be addressed: the effects on these countries of continuing decline of the South

African economy; the vulnerability of the FLS to retaliatory actions which South Africa might take as a result of increased international sanctions; and, finally, the costs to the FLS of the attempts to maintain the apartheid system within South Africa. I will discuss each of them briefly.

There is no doubt that South Africa dominates the regional economy of southern Africa; it generates $3 in wealth for every $1 created by all the nine member countries of the Southern African Development Co-ordination Conference (SADCC) on a quarter of the land area and with one third of the population. Thirty percent of all SADCC imports come from South Africa and it is the destination of 7% of the region's exports. Additionally, about 70% of the extra-regional trade of the land-locked countries of the region passes through South Africa, while South Africa provides employment for probably about 1.5 million foreign nationals from the region. Within the overall grouping, some countries are more dependent upon and interlinked with South Africa than others. Lesotho, Swaziland, and Botswana, joined to South Africa by a common Customs Union, are particularly vulnerable to influences within the South African economy—over 80% of their imports come from South Africa, over 80% of their trade passes through South Africa, and, in the cases of Swaziland and Lesotho, over 40% of their exports are purchased by South Africa.

The simple—but misleading—conclusion to draw from this level of dependence is that sanctions should not be imposed on South Africa, as the SADCC countries will be seriously and adversely affected by such action. If this were the complete picture, it would stand at odds with the most complete joint statement of the grouping in 1986 on the sanctions issue, namely that even though individual SADCC countries may not be in a position to implement their own sanctions, their vulnerability should not be used as an excuse by others for not imposing sanctions.

Besides the political and moral wish of the leaders and people of the SADCC nations to see a quick end to the apartheid system, there are economic and strategic reasons for such a seemingly perverse stance.

South Africa is currently imposing major and significant costs on the economies of the region through its regional policy of destabilization. The dependence of the neighboring states on South Africa's transport network has been intensified by direct and indirect South African action especially over the last eight or nine years, resulting in higher freight and insurance costs and, through the loss of foreign exchange, reduced intra-SADCC trade. Additionally, war damage inflicted on economic and civilian targets by illegal South African incursions deep inside the independent states has reduced production levels and diverted scarce resources to defense, repair, and rehabilitation. As a result, almost one in ten of the populations of these countries have become either refugees or displaced persons over the past eight years.

While it is not easy to accurately assess the economic costs of direct and indirect South African action against its economic neighbors, SADCC data put the cost at $10 billion from 1980 to 1984 and perhaps an additional $9 billion in 1985 and 1986. This is equivalent to about 10% of the combined GDP of the SADCC states. It has in no manner been compensated by foreign assistance. Total foreign aid to the SADCC states in the seven years from 1980 to 1986 amounted to only 80% of the costs of South African destabilization policies.

The SADCC states favor international sanctions because they believe that increased international pressure provides the best hope of bringing apartheid and its regional costs to a rapid end, bringing SADCC's most cost-effective transport and trade routes into operation again, and making possible higher levels of economic growth. It is their assessment that the potential costs of further sanctions against South Africa must be weighed against the extremely high cost of South African destabilization and declining or falling rates of economic growth.

A further factor in the regional equation which merits closer examination is the claim that an escalation of international sanctions will be even more damaging because it will lead to further deliberate action by South Africa, resulting in even greater economic damage. An initial response to such a claim is, of course, to acknowledge not only that this is possible but also that this type of action has already occurred in a systematic way with even the low level of sanctions in the pre-1985 era. The Mozambique population and economy, for example, have simply been laid waste by the combined action of South Africa and the Mozambique Resistance Movement (Renamo). As Chester Crocker explained to Congress in June 1987, South African support for Renamo is the main reason for the spread of banditry and rebellion in that country.

There are, however, reasons why South Africa would not wish to impose—or be seen to impose—widespread additional economic hardship on its neighbors. One factor is that to do so would be likely to encourage the international community in its resolve to damage the apartheid economy. Perhaps a more substantial reason is that South Africa obtains considerable economic benefits from its regional economic relations and these will become relatively more significant to it as restrictions are placed on its non-southern African international trade. For instance, in the mid-1980s, South Africa had a net trade surplus with its SADCC neighbors of about $1.3 billion, roughly equivalent to the total value of 1987 US imports from South Africa. The $1.3 billion constituted over 40% of South Africa's current account surplus in 1987 and exceeds the amount it has committed to set aside for foreign debt repayments to 1990. In short, South Africa has an important long-term interest in not retaliating within the region against sanctions imposed internationally even if short-term military objectives conflict with these objectives.

The preceding discussion provides the context for discussing the steps that might be taken to assist the Front Line States in their striving for peace and prosperity in the region.

There are three areas of action for which the FLS seek the assistance of the international community. These are: the rapid ending of the apartheid system, help in resisting the covert and overt action of Pretoria, and help in assisting in the process of disengagement of the FLS' economies from South Africa required for their sustained economic growth. What is more, to be effective, policies in these three areas need to be coordinated by means of a consistent strategy on the southern African region agreed by, at minimum, the leading Western industrial countries. Specifically this means first, a co-ordinated policy on sanctions against South Africa, second, substantially increased and harmonized official aid programs aimed both at emergency needs and at economic rehabilitation stimulating economic growth and assisted thirdly, by technical assistance, technology transfer, investment, and enhanced trade.

At present, however, the policies of the West are far from harmonized, and in certain respects they are mutually contradictory. Some countries have imposed sanctions against South Africa whereas, in the case of others, South Africa has been able to expand trade to lessen the impact of effective sanctions. Some governments fund development projects which they know risk being destroyed by insurgents out of South Africa or supplied by South Africa. Yet little is done concretely to persuade South Africa to pull back from its escalation of the regional conflict.

From Economic Sanctions to Political Change

That further economic sanctions would have a considerable and adverse impact upon the South African economy is now widely accepted both inside and outside government circles. For instance, as the Minister of Finance observed in his 1988 budget speech, the economy is one "hamstrung by sanctions."[14] It is necessary, however, to ask whether current and extended sanctions will assist in the process of achieving a free democratic society in that country. Some tentative points can be made.

Whatever success sanctions have in moving South Africa further on the path to democracy, the effect of sanctions is likely to be only marginal. While external pressures can help, few if any people believe that their effects will be a major factor in the internal political dynamics that must necessarily remain the crucial element in the process. But will sanctions have a positive (albeit) limited effect in achieving the political objectives sought, or will they, as the critics argue, have a perverse and opposite effect of frustrating even further the achievement of those objectives?

There are a number of factors, some positive and some negative, which support the case for increased sanctions from the viewpoint of the political objectives desired. In the first place, there has been no conclusive evidence during the 1980s that the alternative strategy of constructive engagement or dialogue with Pretoria has led to change in the intended direction. Indeed there is evidence to suggest quite the opposite. For instance, as President Reagan observed in his Fall 1987 statement to Congress, "I regret I am unable to report significant progress leading to the end of apartheid and the establishment of a non-racial democracy in South Africa."[15]

More recently, after two by-elections held in February 1988, the Foreign Minister, Pik Botha, outlined a new tough policy of disregarding criticism from other countries.[16] The effect of this policy was confirmed in mid-March 1988, when former President Botha chose to articulate his intention to ignore considerable pressure from President Reagan, Prime Minister Thatcher, Chancellor Kohl, and the Secretary-General of the United Nations to intervene on behalf of the Sharpeville Six. (It was the actions of the Supreme Court which led to the stay of execution even though under the South African constitution the State President has the power of clemency in such cases.) A week later, former President Botha used his powers to intervene to prevent the trial of six soldiers charged with murder in Namibia.[17]

Not only has it become more evident in the period from 1986 that the South African government has become increasingly unwilling to be influenced by the world's leaders, but events within South Africa suggest that it is likely to be only through punitive action rather than persuasion that the government will move further on the road to creating a democratic free society. A number of factors illustrate this.

In the first place, there has been the increased stifling of black opposition within South Africa. Not only is the state of emergency becoming a permanent feature of South African life, but the action taken in February 1988 to eliminate in effect the power of the seventeen leading, still-functioning democratic and trade union organizations together with the new powers to close down opposition journals and newspapers has dealt a mortal blow to what were already scarcely functioning processes of domestic democratic opposition.

In addition, the government's proposals in relation to furthering the democratic process have been more cosmetic than substantive and have been spurned even by the traditionally cooperative black movements. For instance, the government's proposals of September 1987 to set up a thirty-member national council to advise the President on the constitutional future of South Africa—hailed as "one of the most fundamental reform steps since 1910"—failed to draw support even from either Chief Buthelezi or organizations like the Soweto Civic Association. According to the proposals, no one who has served a prison sentence of a year or more would, in any case, be eligible for election to the proposed council.

Significantly, too, the South African government has made it clear that it is not its intention to oversee voluntarily the ending of the fundamental structures of the apartheid system. As the Report of the Eminent Persons of the Commonwealth observed:

> . . . while the government claims to be ready to negotiate, it is in truth not yet prepared to negotiate fundamental change, nor to countenance the creation of genuine democratic structures, nor to face the prospect of the end of white domination and white power in the foreseeable future. Its programme of reform does not end apartheid but seeks to give it a less inhuman face. Its quest is power-sharing without surrendering overall white control.[18]

Subsequent events confirm that this analysis, as reiterated in the President's report to Congress, is still substantially correct. For instance, in 1987 the South African President's Council advised against dismantling the Group Areas Act—the legislation which determines residential rights on the basis of race. In December 1987, the decision was made to put yet another 500,000 black South Africans under the homeland system. The swing to the right both in the 1987 general election and in two subsequent by-elections confirms that the far right has gained in significance and influence over the past year; indeed the effects of this influence have been spelled out in the restrictions on rights and freedom of association referred to above. As was reported in a restricted report of the South African Catholic Bishops' conference:

> The incomprehensible attitude of the State President at the recent conference with certain of our bishops seems to supply final proof positive that the State President is totally closed to any overtures of reason or moral persuasion.

It appears that the only way that the South African government can be persuaded to give up its racist policies is when it is convinced that such policies can no longer secure the interests of white South Africa. As sanctions raise the cost to South Africa of operating its apartheid system and adversely affect the wellbeing of those who benefit, they have a chance of moving the South African authorities in the direction of change towards the establishment of democracy in that sad country.

Notes

1. Since October 1986, United States' sanctions against South Africa were contained in *Comprehensive Anti-Apartheid Act of 1986*, Public Law 99-440-Oct.2, 1986. The Hearings to which this testimony was addressed took place in the context of a series of bills before the House of Representatives to extend the range of sanctions against South Africa. These were: "To amend the Comprehensive Anti-Apartheid Act of 1986 to prohibit the importation of South African diamonds into the United States", HR 1051 (Mr. Dymally), February 9 1987; "To prohibit investments in, and certain other activities with respect to, south Africa. and for other purposes", HR 1580 (Mr. Dellums), March 12, 1987; "To prohibit United States Intelligence and military cooperation with South Africa", HR 2443, 18 May, 1987 (Mr. Gray); "To require divestiture from the oil industry in South Africa unless certain conditions are met, And other purposes", HR 3317, (Mr. Wise), 21 September 1987; "To prohibit investment in United States capital markets by certain South Africa mining interests", HR 3328,(Mr. Leland), 22 September 1987.

2. *Financial Times* (London), 11 November 1987.

3. For a recent comprehensive assessment of economic sanctions in a number of countries over the past thirty years, see Gary Hufbauer and Jeffrey Schott, *Economic Sanctions Reconsidered. History and Current Policy* (Washington, D.C.: Institute for International Economics, 1987).

4. C. Meth, "Sanctions and Unemployment," Department of Economics, University of Ntal, Durban (mimeo), 1987.

5. See the *Newsletter on the Oil Embargo Against South Africa*, No. 10, January 1988. See also Jaap Woldendorp's chapter in the present volume.

6. *Financial Mail*, 26 February 1988.

7. *African Economic Digest*, 22 November 1988.

8. *Financial Mail*, 12 February 1988.

9. Data from "Gold Metals and Mining," supplement to *Euromoney*, February 1988.

10. An illustration of the degree of judgement used even in assessing the impact of past and present sanctions is that for the period 1985 to 1986, the reputable London-based Economist Intelligence Unit judged that trade levels were 9% lower than what they would otherwise have been, whereas South African business sources put the figure at 3%.

11. See J. P. Hayes, *Economic Effects of Sanctions on Southern Africa* (Brookfield, Vt.: Gover, 1987) and Merle Lipton, *Sanctions and Southern Africa; the Dynamics of Economic Isolation* (London: Economist Intelligence Unit, 1988).

12. C. Meth, "Sanctions and Unemployment."

13. The issues discussed here are analyzed more fully in *Sanctions and South Africa's Neighbours* (Overseas Development Institute Briefing Paper, December 1987).

14. *Financial Times*, 17 March 1988.

15. *Progress Towards Ending the System of Apartheid, Communication From the President of the United States Transmitting the First Annual Report on the Extent to Which Significant Progress Has Been Made Toward Ending Apartheid in South Africa, Pursuant to 22 U.S.C. 509 (b).* 100th Congress, 1st Session, House Document 100-109, 6 October 1987 (Washington, D.C.: Government Printing Office, 1987).

16. *Financial Times,* 5 March 1988.

17. Under the South African constitution, whatever the courts may decide, the State President is at liberty "to pardon or reprieve offenders, either unconditionally or subject to such conditions as he may deem fit, and to remit any fines, penalties or forfeitures." (Constitution Act 1983, Section 6 (3) (d).) Action on behalf of the soldiers was carried out under the Defense Act which exempts members of the security forces from criminal or civilian prosecution if they "acted in good faith in combatting terrorism in an operational area." (*New York Times,* 24 March 1988).

18. *Mission to South Africa. The Findings of the Commonwealth Eminent Persons Group on Southern Africa* (London: Penguin Books, 1986), 122-23.

TRANSNATIONAL MANUFACTURING-FINANCE LINKS

Ann Seidman

In the postwar era, especially after the Sharpeville massacre in 1960, transnational corporations, backed by bank finance, invested heavily in South African manufacturing industries. They played a major role in transforming South Africa into an industrialized subcenter, strengthening the minority regime's capacity not only to repress the black majority at home but to dominate the entire region.[1] The contradictory consequences rendered South Africa's economy both more capable of manufacturing many of its own modern-sector requirements and more externally dependent and vulnerable to international pressures.

Examination of these contradictory tendencies may contribute to insights needed to design more effective sanctions which the US could impose either unilaterally or in cooperation with the other developed countries, especially the EEC and Japan.

President Reagan's assertion that the 1986 Congressional sanctions did not work reflects his own administration's refusal to implement them and utilization of every possible loophole to reduce their effectiveness.[2] Nevertheless, the addition of particular features could enhance their effectiveness. Furthermore, as Randall Robinson emphasized, if—instead of joining Britain to veto UN Security Council sanctions—the administration pursued Congress' recommendation that it take the initiative in introducing and enforcing international measures, sanctions would have a far greater impact.[3]

This chapter focuses primarily on the potential use of sanctions to end the role of US transnational manufacturing corporations, backed by US banking capital, in building up South Africa's minority-controlled military-industrial complex. It adopts Richard Moorsom's criteria for judging sanctions' potential effect:

> The timescale for sanctions to be effective depends crucially on the level of internal resistance: they would be one pressure of many bearing on the apartheid regime. They could exert considerable pressure. Furthermore, the dislocation would be cumulative .... The specific effects are not predictable, but almost any measures would have a morale-boosting effect on those struggling for justice and democracy, since even a minor sanction can cause a sudden loss of business confidence and the economic equivalent of panic .... At a minimum, serious sanctions could force South Africa into major and costly adjustments to a siege economy, and in the longer run grind it down. When added to the internal confrontation that appears unavoidable in view of the rejection by the South African government of paths towards peaceful change sanctions could be decisive.[4]

Adopting this view, this chapter examines: the way transnational corporate manufacturing investment fostered the transfer of high technology into South African industrial growth, heightening minority control while aggravating black unemployment; the implications for the potential effectiveness of sanctions on the intensification of South Africa's industrial dependence on foreign technology, capital, and markets; South Africa's possibilities of utilizing transnational corporate and banking links for sanctions busting; and the benefits for US workers of sanctions that effectively block off US transnational firms and financial institutions' contributions to industrialization under apartheid.

Manufacturing Growth and the Dichotomization of South Africa's Economy

Fueled by transnational corporate capital and technology, the rapid growth of South Africa's manufacturing sector in the 1960s and 1970s accelerated the dichotomization of South Africa's political economy along race and class lines. On the one hand, it accelerated the concentration and centralization of capital in the hands of fewer firms, dominated by locally based mining finance houses, particularly the Anglo American Group.[5] On the other hand, it contributed to the further unemployment and marginalization of the black labor force that intensified pressures for liberation. By the late 1970s, direct transnational corporate investment had multiplied to almost 40 percent of all manufacturing investment. US oil majors helped the state expand South Africa's oil refining capacity to the largest on the continent. Although their initial capital inflow spurred the post-Sharpeville boom, however, their South African business never constituted much more than one percent of their worldwide sales.[6] Furthermore, increasingly, instead of bringing in new capital, the transnationals reinvested a share of their locally generated profits and local capital.

More important than the new capital they invested, the transnationals transferred to South Africa increasingly sophisticated, capital-intensive technologies. As Table 1 shows, they sold most of their $7 billion worth of South African output inside South Africa. A large part of these sales constituted advanced technologies that augmented the productivity of the minority-controlled modern sector without necessitating the upgrading of black skills.

The US oil majors made about a third of US South African affiliates' total sales, helping South Africa evade the international oil boycott by refining and selling imported crude oil.[7] Other manufacturing affiliates made two fifths of the sales, half of them selling chemicals, machinery, and transport equipment. Despite

Table 1
Sales of US affiliates[a] operating in South Africa, by sector, 1984 (in millions of dollars and as percent of total U.S. Sales in South Africa)

Affiliates in:	*Sales ($ million)*	*% of Sales*
All industries	7,407	100.0
Within Southern Africa	6,825	92.1
Petroleum	2,524	35.1
All manufacturing	3,068	41.4
Food and kindred products	641	8.6
Chemicals and allied products	475	6.4
Primary and fabricated metals	200	2.7
Machinery except electrical	333	4.5
Electrical and electronic equipment	98	1.3
Transportation equipment	847	11.4
Other	475	6.4
Wholesale trade	1,576	21.3
Finance[b]	50	0.6
Services	114	1.5
Other industries	75	1.0

Notes
a. Includes only majority-owned affiliates of non-bank United States parent companies: i.e., it would not include firms, like Chrysler, which retained a minority share in its affiliate when it sold it to the Anglo American Group's Sigma.
b. Excludes banking, but includes insurance and real estate.
Source: U.S. Department of Commerce, *United States Direct Foreign Investments Abroad—Operations of U.S. Parent Companies and Their Foreign Affiliates,* Preliminary 1984 estimates (Washington, D.C.: U.S. Department of Commerce, 1985).

the growth of their investments in manufacturing, however, the importance of US affiliates' wholesale trade suggests their sales of imported machinery and equipment continued to be important to South Africa.

Those who object that sanctions might hurt blacks never point out that, on balance, US manufacturing investment served to reduce black employment. At the peak of their South African investment, US firms directly employed less than two percent of South Africa's black labor force. At the same time, their import and manufacture of high tech machinery and equipment enabled relatively scarce skilled white personnel to manage the expanding modern sector and the growing military machine while maintaining and heightening controls over an increasingly restive black labor force.[8] To put it bluntly, their advanced technical inputs served directly to help build up the integrated military-industrial complex that perpetuated minority rule.

The rapid spread of computers throughout South Africa—giving it one of the highest, if not the highest, per (white) capita use in the world—represents only one aspect of the accelerated introduction of advanced technologies supplied by US transnational corporations. The modernization of the domestic transport industry facilitated the shipment of goods to and from ports and cities throughout the nation and the region, as well as the movement of troops and police throughout the townships and to the borders. The increased use of electronic devices facilitated automation of manufacturing, mining and even agricultural operations, augmenting productivity while reducing the number of blacks employed per unit of output. The chemicals industry not only produced synthetics that replaced locally grown, more labor-consuming cultivation of fibers, but helped South Africa acquire the potential for manufacturing napalm and other chemical weapons.

By the 1980s, the South African regime's deliberate policy of encouraging investment to "reduce dependence" on black labor, coupled with the impact of the international crisis, had generated growing numbers of black unemployed. Official statistics do not adequately record black unemployment. They particularly ignore the special plight of black women, forced to supplement their families income by leaving home to take wage employment for whites. Unofficial data suggest that by the mid-1980s as many as 30 to 40 percent of the black labor force had access to neither paid jobs nor land.[9] Forced removals and unemployment pushed about 12 to 14 million blacks—about half of the black population—into a struggle for bare survival in the bantustans. For blacks, the spread of mechanization and automation throughout the economy, spurred by US transnational corporate injections of capital and technology, spelled fewer job opportunities and growing hunger.

Increased External Dependence

The post-Sharpeville growth of South Africa's manufacturing industry strengthened minority control of the economy, but in three respects rendered the economy, if anything, more externally dependent and hence more subject to the impact of sanctions. The new factories required imported inputs which the local economy could not produce; the foreign exchange to finance them; and expanding external markets in which to sell their output.

First, as the large share of US business in wholesale trade (see Table 1) suggests, South Africa remained particularly dependent on transnationals for sophisticated electronics equipment and parts, transportation machinery, and chemical inputs. Its domestic industries achieved neither the economies of scale required to render a basic chemicals industry viable, nor the technological sophistication to design and manufacture advanced electronics and transportation equipment and machinery. As Table 2 shows, in the 1980s, South Africa imported large amounts of these from the US. In exchange, the US bought crude materials, including uranium, coal, steel products, and "miscellaneous" manufactures.

Furthermore, South Africa's manufacturing industry, and particularly the transport sector, required oil. The US transnational, Fluor, engineered South Africa's giant oil-from-coal project, SASOL. The South African *Financial Times* reports SASOL "was financed with state money and, though privatization took place some years ago, the company is effectively controlled by government through the state's residual 30 percent equity stake." Yet, under the 1986 sanctions act, the US State Department removed SASOL from the list of South African parastatals barred from US trade.[10] SASOL, however, produces only part of South Africa's oil needs. For the rest, South Africa has to rely on expensive backdoor deals to import all the oil refined in its transnational corporate and parastatal-owned refineries. As Table 1 shows, US oil majors conduct a major share of US business in South Africa, refining and selling oil imported from sources outside the US in violation of international boycotts.

If more effective sanctions measures ended South African import of more sophisticated equipment, chemicals and oil, they would impact important sectors of the minority-run modern economy. At the same time, since the majority of the black population neither buys the output nor works in the more sophisticated industries, most would remain relatively unaffected. In fact, the former Rhodesian (now Zimbabwe) experience suggests sanctions might benefit blacks by forcing white-owned mines, farms and manufacturing industries to rely more heavily on more labor-intensive, locally-devised technologies.[11]

Moreover, South Africa's manufacturing sector required external markets to sustain its profitability. In the 1970s and early 1980s, as long as the market absorbed the manufacturing industries' growing output, transnational manufacturing firms reaped profit rates two to three times those in their home countries.[12]

But apartheid imposed sharp limits on the domestic South African market. The black majority, unemployed or earning wages below the poverty line, could afford to buy only a fraction of the manufacturing sector's growing output. The main civilian component, the high-income minority of five million whites, remained less than half the size of the population of New York City. Although the military budget multiplied six times in the 1960s, and six times again to exceed $3 billion by 1983,[13] it provided too narrow a market for South Africa's burgeoning industry. In the 1980s government borrowing, devaluation of the rand, and rising import prices stimulated inflation, further reducing the domestic market.

The neighboring countries, especially Botswana, Lesotho, Swaziland, and Namibia within the South African Customs Union, however, remained captive markets. Table 3 shows that

Table 2
Major United States Exports To and Imports From South Africa, 1983-85 (in millions of dollars and as percent of total)

	1983		1984		1985	
	$	%	$	%	$	%
US Exports to South Africa						
Chemicals	262	12.3	259	11.4	192	15.9
Manufacturers, including electrical	177	8.3	173	7.6	93	7.7
Machinery, transport equipment	1,106	51.9	972	42.9	573	47.5
(Aircraft, etc.)	(245)	(11.5)	(73)	(3.2)	(59)	(4.9)
(Data proc., etc.)	(122)	(5.7)	(124)	(5.4)	(80)	(6.6)
Misc. mfrs.	187	8.8	193	8.5	121	10.0
Sub-total	1,732	81.3	1,597	70.4	979	81.1
All exports to SA	2,129	100.0	2,265	100.0	1,205	100.0
US imports from South Africa						
Crude materials	164	7.8	184	7.1	190	8.7
Mineral fuels, etc.	51	2.3	48	1.8	76	3.4
(Coal, peat moss)	(30)	(1.4)	(24)	(0.9)	(43)	(1.7)
Chemicals, etc.	223	10.6	189	7.3	193	(8.9)
(Uranium, etc.)	(198)	(9.4)	(146)	(5.7)	(140)	(6.4)
Manufactured goods by chief material	1,044	49.7	1,429	55.4	1,324	60.8
(Iron, steel mfrs.)	(253)	(12.1)	(321)	(12.4)	(287)	(13.1)
(Aluminum and alloys)	(15)	(0.7)	(34)	(1.3)	(22)	(1.0)

(Nickel and alloys)	(21)	(1.0)	(19)	(0.7)	(14)	(0.6)
Misc. mfrs.	462	22.0	516	20.0	159	7.2
Sub-total	1,944	92.4	2,366	91.8	1,942	89.1
All imports from SA	2,098	100.0	2,577	100.0	2,179	100.0

Source: United States Department of Commerce, *U.S. Foreign Trade Highlights*, 1985 (U.S. Department of Commerce, 1986)

Table 3
Botswana, Lesotho, and Swaziland as markets for South African goods, 1982 (in millions of dollars and as a percent of their exports and imports)

	Imports from South Africa		Exports to South Africa		Deficit in trade with South Africa	
	$	%	$	%	$	%
Botswana	595	84	56	17	539	76
Lesotho	435	97	21	47	388	86
Swaziland	481	83	126	37	355	61

Source: Calculated from Joseph Hanlon, *Apartheid's Second Front: South Africa's War Against Its Neighbors* (Middlesex: Penguin Books, 1986), using 1982 UK-US exchange rate.

Botswana, Lesotho, and Swaziland all depended on South Africa for over 80 percent of their imports, while their exports to South Africa remained far less.

Malawi, Zimbabwe, and Zambia, the latter pressured by the International Monetary Fund (IMF),[14] provided additional outlets for surplus South African goods. Nevertheless, the majority of their impoverished populations only buy a limited share of South Africa's manufactured products. Their narrow high income groups buy some sophisticated consumer items. The mines (often partly government owned, but managed by transnational corporate partners) and commercial farms (still predominantly white-owned) buy machinery, equipment, chemical inputs, and refined oil products.

Table 4 indicates that in the 1980s, the independent African countries outside the South African Customs Union bought a little over five percent of South Africa's exports. Economic difficulties, as well as their governments' efforts to reduce their dependence on South Africa, cut their imports from South Africa to a 1984 low of $616 million worth of goods. By 1986, however, as South Africa's surrogates, UNITA in Angola and MNR in Mozambique, targetted alternative transport networks, they increased the dollar value of their imports from South Africa.[15] Furthermore, they purchased far more than they sold to South Africa, building up a chronic deficit. Even when they reduced their purchases, South Africa reduced its imports from them, so substantial deficits remained.

Even when added together with the imports of Botswana, Lesotho and Swaziland, the independent African countries purchased little more than 10 percent of South Africa's exports. However, they bought a much higher proportion—probably 45 percent—of its manufactured exports, making a major contribution to the viability of South Africa's manufacturing sector.[16] In addition, the hard currency payments they make to cover their chronic balance of trade and payments deficits with South Africa contribute foreign exchange that helps South Africa purchase the capital goods and equipment its manufacturing industry requires to remain operational.

Table 4
South African trade with Africa, 1980-1986 (in millions of dollars and as percent of South African trade)*

	1980		*1982*		*1984*		*1986*	
	$	*%*	*$*	*%*	*$*	*%*	*$*	*%*
Exports	1,412	5.4	834	4.7	616	3.5	808	4.0
Imports	371	2.0	305	1.8	284	1.8	243	2.1
Africa's deficit	1,041	3.4	529	2.9	332	1.7	565	1.9

Note
*Excludes South African trade with Botswana, Lesotho, Swaziland, and Namibia, all within the South African Customs Union and hence much more heavily reliant on imports from South Africa; (b) the independent African countries as a whole buy far more (mostly manufactured goods) from South Africa than they sell to it (mostly crude materials).
Source: International Monetary Fund, *Direction of Trade Statistics Yearbook, 1987* (Washington, DC: IMF, 1987).

The dependence of South Africa's manufacturing industry on the neighboring states underscores the importance of two types of complementary measures required to make sanctions against South Africa effective. First, the independent landlocked southern African states need assistance to develop alternative routes to the sea to import manufactures they now buy from South Africa (as well as export their own crude materials). In particular, the US Congress should prohibit all forms of direct and indirect support for the South African puppet force, UNITA, which has set as a primary target the Benguela railway.[17] Likewise, Congress must reject proposals to aid the MNR which, like UNITA, deliberately disrupts road and rail transport to Mozambique's ports.

Second, Congress and the anti-apartheid movement should exert pressure on the US government, international agencies,[18] and US transnationals to assist the independent countries to build up their own industries and facilitate their efforts to buy the manufactured imports they require from sources other than South Africa. US government measures should include not only reaching double taxation agreements with South Africa's neighbors, but also opening up consular offices to assist US exporters and investors to find viable opportunities within the national and regional plans of the SADCC member states,[19] and providing export credit through the US Export-Import Bank to finance the sale of appropriate US equipment and machinery to facilitate implementation of those plans.[20]

Third, in the late 1970s and in the 1980s, South Africa became increasingly dependent on foreign loans to finance its continued import of essential capital goods, including electronics, transport equipment, and chemical materials, as well as its oil and military imports—the last two categories rendered more expensive by UN sanctions. Eurocurrency consortia, frequently organized by the US-based Citicorp, the world's largest bank, provided loans to South African government agencies and parastatals as well as the private and banking sectors.

As their most important function, these loans financed the continued imports on which South Africa's military-industrial growth depended. Since money (including hard currency) is fungible, it mattered less which sector—public or private—received these loans than that they freed foreign exchange which the South African government and its parastatals, as well as private firms, used to buy essential oil and strategic military hardware or the machinery and equipment required to produce it.

The international anti-apartheid movement successfully focused on ending bank loans, first to the South African government, then to the private sector. The 1986 US compromise sanctions have now prohibited both kinds of long term loans. But two important features of the banks' continued role in financing the South African regime remain untouched—trade finance and the rescheduling of outstanding loans.

Chris Stals, South Africa's Minister of Finance, underscored the importance of trade finance when he observed:

> If the world banking community should effectively exclude South Africa from international trade and payments systems, it would be a much more effective

> sanctions measure than the trade sanctions applied by governments. It would put us on a barter system overnight.[21]

An amendment to the 1986 compromise sanctions, introduced by Senator Charles Mathias, permits US banks to continue to provide crucial short-term trade finance to South Africa. Even those US banks that sold their South African assets to South African interests still retain correspondent bank relationships and continue to provide short term loans to finance South Africa's imports and exports. Repeal of the Mathias amendment and extension of sanctions to halt the banks' continued financing of South African imports constitutes a necessary step to help end the inflow of strategic sophisticated technologies.

The second feature of the largest banks' continued financial assistance to South Africa has been to reschedule its large outstanding debt to Western banks, estimated at $13 billion. Bishop Tutu and Reverends Boesak and Naude publicly requested the banks not to reschedule the loans. In response to anti-apartheid pressures, the banks initially made a big play about refusing to roll over South Africa's debt, so South Africa simply stopped payments altogether. And, as the South African Finance Minister noted, a number of small American creditor banks earlier in 1987 formally declared some South African loans to be "non-performing" and moved to "attach" (seize) South African assets. The move could have easily started a world-wide scramble to attach South African assets. But the affair was hushed up by some of the big US banks, which moved quickly to pacify smaller creditors by taking over their South African loans.[22]

Under a shroud of secrecy, the big banks then proceeded to reschedule South Africa's foreign debts twice, once in February, 1986, and again in late March, 1987. The current arrangement, due to expire March 1990, gives South Africa repayment terms that look generous when compared to those imposed on Latin American governments.[23] Over the next three years, South Africa must repay only $1.4 billion of the $13 billion it owes the transnational banks.[24] The US Congress could prohibit further rescheduling and provide for seizure of South African assets in this country if South Africa again refuses to repay.

Sanctions Busting and Transnational Corporate Links

In response to international anti-apartheid pressures, including the 1986 US sanctions, US transnational manufacturing corporations and banks altered the channels through which they transfer and finance the high tech South Africa's minority needs. To close them entirely will require specific measures, some of which may necessitate further research.

By 1987, about 130 US firms had taken steps to reduce their visible presence in South Africa. Most manufacturing firms, however, agreed to continue to supply technological knowhow, inputs, and, in some cases, finance, to South African firms.[25] For example, after IBM and General Motors sold their South African affiliates to local firms they continued to sell their technologies to them. The local firms can sell their output to the South African government and its agencies as well as to private buyers.

Several US companies like Ford sold their South African holdings to the Anglo American Group's Sigma, increasing that group's monopolistic domination in the transport sector of the South African economy. Chrysler had earlier sold a majority of the shares in its South African affiliate to Sigma. Both Chrysler and Ford companies continue to sell their technologies to Sigma, taking advantage of US banks' short-term trade finance in the process.

The transnationals also helped the Anglo American Group to further centralize its control over South African financial institutions.[26] In 1987, the British Bank, Barclays, which together with Standard owned about two thirds of South Africa's banking assets, sold its South African business in its entirety to the Anglo American Group.[27] Citicorp, which had links with Anglo through MINORCO (see below), followed suit. The Group united their holdings to create the National Bank of South Africa. This change of legal status gave the Bank more freedom to deal with South African government agencies and parastatals. It did not end either former parent company's continued provision of trade finance to keep essential imports coming into South Africa.

Recognizing that financial institutions play a critical role in South Africa's efforts to evade sanctions, Pretoria selected Desmond Krogh to coordinate its secret measures to circumvent the present round.[28] During UDI, the South African government had seconded Krogh to head the Rhodesian (now Zimbabwe's) Reserve Bank, a key institution for directing scarce foreign exchange to finance circuitous trade routes; he held that post for almost two years after Zimbabwe attained independence. His appointment suggests that South Africa intends to draw on his extensive experience of assisting Rhodesia to evade UN sanctions by strengthening its direct control over banks and other financial institutions.

The potential implications of the transfer of US manufacturing and financial assets to the Anglo American Group requires special emphasis. Anti-apartheid activists have pointed out that transnational manufacturing firms, like the big tobacco transnational, Rothmans, may use their overseas affiliates, including those in the United States, to market South African products abroad in violation of sanctions.[29] The Anglo American Group, however, has far more extensive links overseas, including those in the United States than any other South African-based transnational. In the 1970s it turned over many of its US holdings to MINORCO.[30] Through MINORCO, the Anglo Group cemented ties with Citicorp, whose former head, Walter Wriston, sat on MINORCO's board. It also acquired shares in Wall Street's biggest investment house, Phibro Salomon.

In addition to its links with the highest financial circles in the United States, the Anglo American Group has a history of cementing political ties with leading US government officials. Its longstanding connections with the Englehard Company for many years provided it with contacts in Democratic administrations.[31] The Anglo Group owns a controlling share in the US Newmont Mining Company[32] which provides it with another channel to the White House. Newmont shares ownership with the Bechtel Corporation in Peabody, the largest US coal mining firm. Before joining President Reagan's Cabinet, both former Secretary of Defense Casper Weinberger and Secretary of State George Shultz worked for Bechtel.

Scraps of evidence suggest that in the past, Caribbean ties in relatively unsupervised Caribbean off-shore bases have aided South Africa to evade the international community's efforts to impose sanctions. For example, violating the UN embargo on military exports to South Africa, the US Space Research Company illegally shipped US manufactured military weapons through Antigua to South Africa.[33] Both the Netherlands Antilles and Dominica served as transshipment points for tankers to load up with oil to evade international attempts to block oil flows to South Africa.[34] In the face of growing anti-apartheid sentiment directed at transnational banks, MINORCO, Anglo's relatively unsupervised Bermuda offshore finance platform, may provide a convenient location for laundering continued financial transactions. This possibility requires further research.

Meanwhile, however, given the potential use of transnational corporation networks to evade sanctions, the Congress should propose measures to prohibit their direct or indirect participation in continued sales, servicing or financing the transfer of advanced technologies to South Africa. These measures should include prohibitions on any kind of licensing agreement to employ US technologies, as well as the seconding of US personnel or training South African personnel to operate technologies previously sold there.

Since the United States played a leadership role in designing and implementing NATO sanctions devised to thwart the transfer of sophisticated technologies to the Soviet Union and Eastern Europe, its administrative agencies have experience in formulating and implementing these kinds of measures. Given the administration's failure to enforce the 1986 sanctions, however, the Congress must provide a monitoring mechanism to ensure the formulation and implementation of appropriate measures in this case.

Why US Workers Should Support Sanctions on South African Manufacturing

Some British opponents of sanctions argue that sanctions will cost British workers jobs.[35] A case study of the shift of manufacturing jobs from the US southeast to South Africa suggests, in contrast, that—especially within the framework of appropriate industrial and agricultural development strategies—sanctions could contribute to increased employment and incomes in the United States.[36] In economic sectors as widely different as tobacco cultivation, coal mining, strategic minerals, steel, textiles, high tech, and finance, US transnational corporations took advantage of the post-World War II technological revolution to shift manufacturing operations away from low wage areas like the US southeast to still lower wage regions like South Africa. Besides aggravating unemployment in the US southeast, where jobless rates exceed the national average, in a real sense these shifts put the wages and working conditions of that region[37] into competition with those of near-slave labor shaped by apartheid.

To summarize its findings in four relevant areas, the study shows that in the early twentieth century, taking advantage of low wages and cheap iron and coal,[38] the United States Steel Company introduced steel production in Birmingham, Alabama, transforming that city into the "Pittsburgh of the South." After World War II, however, instead of investing to improve productivity in its Birmingham plants, it transferred a share of its profits to four subsidiaries in South Africa, helping to build up that country's steel industry. By the 1980s, as South Africa began to ship steel to US markets,[39] US Steel (just before renaming itself USX) closed down the last of its Birmingham steel works. The multiplier effect raised Birmingham's official unemployment rates a third above the national average.

Secondly, a global shift in the textiles and apparels industry culminated in a 1986 loss of 43 jobs a day in North Carolina, the primary beneficiary of an earlier movement of US firms seeking lower wages inside the country. US transnationals helped move some of these jobs to South Africa in two ways. First, US firms like Celanese established subsidiaries to sell imported synthetic fibers to South African firms for making textiles and apparel. Second, US merchandising firms like Sears Roebuck[40] bypassed US textiles firms to import cheap textiles from South Africa. By 1987, Taiwan textiles companies had established 75 factories in South African bantustans where they paid wages equivalent to $7 a week—only a little more than North Carolina workers earned in an hour. Detective work is needed to determine how much of the textiles sold in the US with a "made in Taiwan" label may actually come from South Africa.

Thirdly, in the 1970s and 1980s, high tech firms and military contractors, attracted by the US southeast's low wages, moved to its urban centers, contributing to a marginalization of the rural, largely black population, and a dichotomization of the regional economy not unlike that in South Africa. In the early '80s, some of the biggest firms, like IBM, ITT, GE, and Burroughs, expanded their assembly and sales of high tech items in South Africa while closing down plants in the US southeast. Some also contracted with smaller southeast firms that kept costs, including wages down. For example, SCI of Huntsville, Alabama, contracting to manufacture IBM personal computers, threatened to move if its employees unionized. When IBM sold its South African assets to a local South African firm, it arranged for the continued local assembly and sale of its products on a contractual basis not unlike that with SCI. This enabled IBM to shift its manufacturing processes—at no risk to its own capital—to whichever region offered the lowest wages.

Affiliates of a number of the US southeast's leading military contractors—including United Technologies, Goodyear Tire and Rubber, General Electric, General Motors' Hughes Aircraft—operated in South Africa. Presumably, they transferred there some of the high tech discoveries made through military-related research paid for by US taxpayers; whether this transferral ended when some (not all) of these firms sold their South African assets remains a pressing question for further research.[41]

Finally, several US transnational financial institutions loaned funds deposited by their US clients to finance the shift of the region's manufacturing capacity to South Africa. Citicorp, the world's biggest bank, led in mobilizing international capital for loans to South Africa after the Soweto uprising. But the leading southeastern regional bank, North Carolina National Bank (NCNB), actually loaned more of a percentage of its assets to South Africa (including the government) than any other US bank. Even after Citicorp sold its South African assets to the Anglo American Group, NCNB retained its South African office in Johannesburg.[42]

NCNB's chairman, Hugh McColl, commented, "I think it's [South Africa's] one of the most wonderful countries in the world . . . ."[43]

From this perspective, US workers stand to benefit from sanctions that hasten the liberation and development of South and southern Africa. On the one hand, they would no longer face the unfair competition fostered by transnational corporate efforts to maximize profits without regard to the welfare of the people on either side of the Atlantic. On the other hand, development and rising incomes of the independent states of Southern Africa, and eventually of a liberated South Africa, itself, will foster far greater mutually beneficial trade.

From a more positive viewpoint, southern Africa, including South Africa, comprises a land area as big as the United States, with a population of over 100 million people. Available data suggests that the US sells about eight times as much goods, per capita, to developed countries as to Africa. Once the South African people win their liberation, they will undoubtedly establish a floor under their wages, ending the unfair competition that acts as a drag on the working and living conditions of US workers. As the peoples of South and southern Africa work together to build a balanced, integrated regional economy, they will provide a growing market, up to eight times as large as at present, for US machinery and equipment. In short, the full liberation and development of South and southern Africa would lay the foundations for increasingly productive employment opportunities and rising living standards on both sides of the Atlantic.

Notes

1. See Ann Seidman and Neva Makgetla, *Outposts of Monopoly Capital: Southern Africa in the Changing Global Economy* (Westport, CT: Lawrence Hill, 1980).

2. *New York Times*, 2 October 1987.

3. "Turn Up Heat on Pretoria," *New York Times*, 5 October 1987.

4. Richard Moorsom, *The Scope for Sanctions—Economic Measures Against South Africa* (London: Catholic Institute for International Relations, 1986), 62.

5. Duncan Innes, *Anglo American and the Rise of Modern South Africa* (New York: Monthly Review Press, 1984) details Anglo American's role in this process.

6. See source of Table 1.

7. While the US Department of Commerce lists these sales under "petroleum," South Africa possesses no oil deposits; almost all these sales relate to oil refined, that is, manufactured in plants built by the oil majors in South Africa.

8. In addition, the taxes US affiliates paid, subsidized by the double taxation agreement between South Africa and the US government, helped to finance increasingly oppressive state structures.

9. *Survey of Race Relations*, 1983 (Johannesburg: South African Institute of Race Relations, 1983), 132ff.

10. *Link*, II, 2.

11. See research on Zimbabwe's industrial structures, Economics Department, University of Zimbabwe, mimeo, 1981-2.

12. US Department of Commerce, Survey of Current Business, August 1982.

13. Solidarity News Service (Botswana), "South Africa—The Militarism of a Society," (SNS Special Paper) March 1984.

14. In the late 1970s, Zambia had reduced its purchases of South African exports, mainly manufactures, to about 10 percent of its imports; but one of the first requirements imposed by the IMF was to reopen the channels to South African goods, which, by the 1980s, once again constituted almost a third of its imports. (Marcia Burdette, "The Political Economy of Zambia," University of Zambia, mimeo, 1982).

15. The data does not reveal how much inflation affected the actual amounts of goods purchased.

16. Moorsom, *The Scope for Sanctions,* 53.

17. The Irangate hearings revealed evidence suggesting that, even prior to the Clark amendment, the U.S. might have illegally channeled aid to UNITA, as well as Nicaragua, via third countries.

18. Like the World Bank and IMF, in which the U.S. because of its financial contribution exercises a major voice.

19. Southern African Development Coordination Conference, an organization of the nine independent Southern African states, with its head office in Botswana, which seeks to foster coordinated development among themselves while reducing dependence on South Africa. For more details, see Ann Seidman, *The Roots of Crisis in Southern Africa,* especially chapters 4, 6, and 7.

20. For an example of the possible kinds of regional industry and changes required for transnationals to contribute to its realization, see Tom Ostergard, *Southern African Regional Integration: the case of the tractor industry.* (M.A. Thesis International Development Program, Clark University, 1987.)

21. *Euromoney,* December 1986, 97.

22. Ibid., 98.

23. This information is based on interviews Patrick Bond of the Johns Hopkins University Coalition for a Free South Africa conducted with South African bank officials (Letter of Patrick Bond to author, 1 October 1987).

24. *Link,* II, 2. South Africa continues to repay the additional $10 billion it owes the IMF and other favored creditors on the original basis.

25. John D. Battersby, "U.S. Goods in South Africa—Little Impact of Divestiture," *New York Times,* 27 July 1987.

26. See Innes, *Anglo American,* for the Group's financial holdings prior to the 1980s.

27. Anglo had previously acquired a growing share of its stock, and for decades had been represented on Barclays' International board of directors.

28. *Business Day* (South Africa), 6 November 1986.

29. *Anti-Apartheid News* (London), May 1987.

30. The Anglo Group initially set up MINORCO using funds obtained by the sale of 51 percent of its shares to the Zambian government, and transferred to it additional funds obtained by various pricing manipulations through affiliates in Zimbabwe and elsewhere. See Innes, *Anglo American* for details.

31. Ann and Neva Seidman, *South Africa and U.S. Multinational Corporations* (Westport, CT: Lawrence Hill, 1977).

32. Newmont has consistently violated UN resolutions by mining copper in Namibia's biggest copper mine, Tsumeb.

33. Tom Berry, Deb Preusch, and Beth Wood, *The Other Side of Paradise: Foreign Control in the Caribbean* (New York: Grove Press, 1984), 28.

34. Ibid., 233.

35. Moorsom argues that, despite the much longer interlinked development of South Africa and England, they grossly overestimated the effects of sanctions on British employment. See Moorsom, *The Scope for Sanctions*, Chapter 8.

36. This section is based on the results of a research project summarized in Ann Seidman, *Militarization and the Changing International Division of Labor: The case of the U.S. Southeast and South Africa* (Trenton, NJ: Africa World Press, forthcoming). It is hoped that research along similar lines, conducted in other regions of the United States, will help to expose the myth that US citizens stand to gain from policies like "Constructive Engagement" and military intervention in support of groups like UNITA in Angola.

37. Although wages there already average roughly a third less than for the US as a whole.

38. It was cheap because of low wages in those then non-unionized industries.

39. In 1984, South Africa ranked seventh among the importers of steel other than semi-finished under the Voluntary Restriction Agreements with the US government; by 1985, it had moved up to sixth place. In addition, in the latter year, South Africa shipped an additional 55,106 short tons of semi-finished steel to the United States. (See *Monthly Reports on the Status of the Steel Industry, Report to the Subcommittee on trade,* Committee on Ways and Means on Investigating No. 332-220 under Section 332 of Tariff Act of 1930—US ITC Public 1852, Tables 8,9 (Washington, DC: US International Trade Commission, 1986).

40. Although not primarily a financial institution, Sears also made credit available to South Africa, becoming that country's twenty-second largest creditor in 1984.

41. John Battersby, "U.S. Goods in South Africa—Little Impact of Divestiture," *New York Times,* 27 August 1987.

42. This information is derived from photographs taken by Patrick Bond in the summer of 1987.

43. *Charlotte Observer,* 10 February 1985.

THE OIL EMBARGO AGAINST SOUTH AFRICA: EFFECTS AND LOOPHOLES

Jaap Woldendorp

> Oil is a key factor in the racist regime's illegal occupation of Namibia, in the acts of aggression against the People's Republic of Angola and other neighbouring states, and in the terror, repression and death meted out against the peoples of Namibia and South Africa.
>
> PRESIDENT SAM NUJOMA AND PRESIDENT O. R. TAMBO*

Without a doubt, oil is South Africa's most vulnerable point of dependence on the international community. Oil is the only strategic raw material not found in exploitable quantities, yet it is vital for the South African economy, its military forces, and police apparatus. South Africa has to import about two thirds of its need for liquid fuel—about 14 million tons of crude oil a

---

*This was a joint appeal by President Sam Nujoma of SWAPO and President O. R. Tambo of ANC to impose and enforce an oil embargo against South Africa, 7 March 1985.

year—from overseas by means of large oil tankers. The remaining third is covered by production from three South Africa Coal, Oil, and Gas Corporation (SASOL) plants converting indigenous coal into liquid fuels. South Africa has spent large sums of money on oil exploration, mainly offshore, without striking sizeable oil finds.

As a result of the enforced reorganization of energy consumption due to the replacement of oil by coal, SASOL products, nuclear energy, and contingency measures, the use of oil has now become concentrated in those areas where it is virtually impossible to substitute liquid fuels. These areas are the transport sector and the military and police forces. Official statistics on oil consumption are not available, but estimates show that the transport sector accounts for the largest proportion of total consumption—about 80 percent. Traffic by road, sea, and air is totally dependent on liquid fuels. Even the railways, despite the extensive coal-based electrification program, have to rely on diesel fuel for 30 percent of their total energy consumption. The other main consumers of liquid fuels—the military and police forces—account for about 10 percent of total consumption.

Oil is a strategic and essential commodity for the survival of the South African government. Without oil, the South African military could not maintain its army, air force, and navy. Without oil, the military and police could not invade and occupy the black townships inside South Africa and maintain the system of apartheid. Without oil, South Africa could not continue its invasions and bombings in Angola, Botswana, Lesotho, Mozambique, Swaziland, Zambia, and Zimbabwe.

A mandatory oil embargo against South Africa, imposed by the United Nations Security Council, has not yet been implemented because of opposition from two permanent members, the United States and the United Kingdom. France, which in the past repeatedly vetoed a mandatory oil embargo, abstained from voting in the Security Council meeting of 8 March 1988. However, there does exist a voluntary international oil embargo supported by an overwhelming majority in the UN General Assembly as was shown on all occasions when the oil embargo was discussed as a separate issue. The resolution of 20 November 1987 on the oil embargo was adopted by 130 to 4 votes, with

12 abstentions. The member states voting against were the United States, the United Kingdom, France, and the Federal Republic of Germany. In addition, the oil embargo is endorsed by all main oil-exporting countries, including member states of the Organization of Petroleum Exporting Countries (OPEC) and the Organization of Arab Petroleum Exporting Countries (OAPEC). An oil embargo has also been included in a package of restrictive measures against South Africa by the European Community and by the Commonwealth.[1]

South Africa's Counterstrategy

The existing voluntary oil embargo has forced the South African government to develop a counterstrategy aimed at reducing its dependence on imported crude oil. The result has been that the government centralized and restructured its oil procurement apparatus and reorganized energy consumption in several economic sectors. Furthermore, the oil embargo has resulted in the emergence of an elaborate system of officially enforced secrecy and legislation, both to protect the identities of the suppliers of embargoed crude oil and to insure the smooth operation of the oil procurement apparatus.

The main impact of the oil embargo, however, has been the financial burden on South Africa's economy. Circumventing the oil embargo has forced South Africa to take costly measures in the field of synthetic fuel production (SASOL), to pay large premiums above the price of imported crude oil to traders and middlemen, and to establish an extensive strategic stockpile of oil.

Oil-From-Coal Production (SASOL)

The construction of three SASOL plants at an estimated cost of $10,000 million has reduced South Africa's crude oil imports by 25 to 30 percent. This partial self-sufficiency, however, tends to decrease in time. This is partly caused by a steady growth in domestic consumption of petrol and diesel and partly by a decline in the production capacity of the SASOL installations due to a drop in their thermal efficiency. As a result, according to

SASOL's chairman, D. P. de Villiers, South Africa's dependency on imported crude oil will steadily grow in the years ahead:

> The fuel consumption of the Republic of South Africa is increasing and the ability of SASOL to bring about production increases in its three existing factories will decrease in time. This makes South Africa more dependent on imported petroleum.[2]

SASOL's exploitation is also highly unprofitable. The price at which SA SASOL produces liquid fuels is estimated at $75 per barrel of oil equivalent. Lastly, a major problem with the SASOL process is that it produces too much petrol and too little diesel, a ratio of 23:1, against a 1:1 ratio from oil refineries. Road transporters and the police and military require diesel, not petrol.

No additional plants using SASOL technology are planned by the South African government or by private companies. South Africa cannot afford to build more capacity in order to achieve even near autarchy in fuel production. To bring about 70 percent self-sufficiency in 1995, it has been estimated that another investment of $16-20,000 million would be required. From 1995 onward, one new plant would have to be constructed every three years to maintain the then existing level of production capacity.

As a strategic response to the oil embargo, new synthetic fuel projects are under consideration by the South African government. All of these are still in the feasibility-study phase, and no definite decisions have yet been made. These projects have in common that, if carried through, they would largely be dependent on foreign technology and capital.

Oil and Gas Exploration

In its search for oil, the South African government, through the state owned company, SOEKOR, has already spent at least R850 million, mainly on offshore exploration. However, sizeable and commercially viable oil deposits have not been found since SOEKOR started its operations at the end of the 1960s. Only a relatively small deposit of gas has been found south of Mossel Bay. According to SOEKOR, the Mossel Bay field has reserves of 1,220 billion standard cubic feet. SOEKOR expects to yield a production of 25,000 barrels a day in 1992 by conversion of gas into liquid fuels. This volume would meet about 5 percent of South Africa's total liquid fuel consumption. Total costs of the Mossel Bay project are estimated to be in excess of R5,500 million.[3]

Strategic Stockpile of Oil

The South African government has also built up an excessive stockpile of oil, which is reported to be about five times the size of a stockpile used in similar industrialized countries. In several facilities spread over the country, oil estimated to cover about fifteen months of crude oil consumption (16 to 17 million tons) is stored. In reality, the stockpile fluctuates under the influence of world market prices of crude oil and of the Rand-Dollar rate.

Facing a sharp fall of the Rand against the US Dollar during 1984 and 1985, the South African government tried to keep the petrol pump price at its 1984 level by heavily drawing on the strategic stockpile. However, this could be merely a temporary measure. In January 1985, the government was forced to raise the petrol price by more than 40 percent, which boosted the domestic rate of inflation (which was already 15 percent) even higher. Compared with 1983, the cost of imported crude oil for South Africa doubled by the end of 1985. The South African government has taken advantage of the drastic fall of world market prices of crude oil in 1986 and replenished its strategic stockpile.[4]

Recent research findings by Paul Conlon, a well-known New York oil consultant, suggest that South Africa's strategic stockpile of oil is in fact considerably smaller than presently presumed. According to him, the total strategic oil storage capacity in South Africa "is under no conditions more than 50-60 million barrels," or between 7 and 8 million tons—equivalent to six or seven months of crude oil imports.[5]

Official Secrecy and Draconian Legislation

Secrecy rules the oil trade with South Africa. On the one hand, the South African government insists on strict secrecy and protects it suppliers, because the country's vulnerability to an oil embargo must not be revealed to the outside world. Therefore, it has passed numerous laws which make it illegal for anyone in South Africa to disclose any information on oil-related matters. People infringing these laws face heavy fines and possible jail terms. On the other hand, the oil companies, oil traders, shipping companies, and other suppliers involved are anxious not to lose their hidden identities because they fear exposure as violators of the oil embargo.

Changing market conditions in the international oil and shipping trades, an oil glut, and the overcapacity of tankers have not altered the rule of secrecy. This was expressed by the South African Minister of Mineral and Energy Affairs, Danie Steyn:

> We are receiving more offers because the oil is running out of the suppliers' ears, and they do not know what to do with it. However, every offer contains the clause: We will give you oil but nobody must know about it.[6]

In South Africa, oil companies are regulated from top to bottom. Longstanding laws direct the manner in which oil companies produce, transport, distribute, and price their products. Regulations govern everything, from the number of service stations a company may open to whether a firm must maintain its own security forces to protect it from possible sabotage. Companies face heavy penalties if they reveal whether the South African government has compelled them to sell their products to controversial buyers such as the police and the army. The government also requires companies to participate in its program to build up a strategic stockpile of oil.

The main laws regulating South Africa's oil procurement apparatus, the strategic stockpile of oil security, secrecy, and its system of financing crude oil purchases are briefly discussed below.

The National Supplies Procurement Act was passed soon after November 1977, when the United Nations declared an arms embargo against South Africa. The government can use regulations of this law to force foreign-owned companies to produce strategic oil products for South Africa. Oil companies are required to set aside a certain portion of their refined oil for government purchase. In compliance with the South African regulations, the oil companies remain silent on the role they play in South Africa. Danie Steyn explained the reason for this:

> We are still in an embargo situation; there is no question about that. No oil company would happily supply to South Africa because they would know that they would be in a lot of trouble in their own country.[7]

The National Key Points Act covers oil companies and allows the government to take over company facilities and place military personnel on the premises during emergencies. The Act empowers the Minister of Defense to declare as a national key point any place or area which is of strategic importance to the functioning of the South African state. Once such a declaration has been made, the owner of a key point is legally obliged to take steps to secure it with measures which must be adequate to satisfy the Minister of Defense.

The Petroleum Products Act of 1977 assures oil suppliers that their business is kept strictly confidential. The act was tightened even further in 1979 and 1985. It carries a penalty of up to seven years imprisonment and/or fines up to R7,000 against anybody "who discloses information relating to the sources, manufacture, transportation, destination, storage, consumption, quantity or stock level of any petroleum product acquired or manufactured for or in South Africa." Explaining to Parliament why new provisions were added in the Petroleum Products Act of 1985, Danie Steyn said that publications in his country could confirm allegations made overseas. He explained that oil traders were sensitive to such a possibility and were concerned that the coupling of their names with South Africa could jeopardize their contacts with other countries.

> They made it very clear that, if we did not put an immediate end to the publication of their name in our newspapers, they would discontinue their oil supply to us.[8]

The State Oil Fund Act of 1977 was special legislation to create a state-controlled structure by which the South African government could evaluate its involvement in the procurement of crude oil, in particular the raising and monitoring of secret funds. The main funds involved are: the State Oil Fund (SOF) (which was transformed into the Central Energy Fund [CEF] in 1985), the Strategic Fuel Fund (SFF), and the Equalisation Fund. The volume of these funds are kept secret, although they are raised by taxpayers' and petrol consumers' money. The funds are financed by various levies on liquid fuel consumption.

The SOF was established to finance the construction of SASOL plants two and three. Because these plants are on stream now, the SOF was changed in 1986 into the CEF, which covers the costs of research and development and construction of all energy projects in South Africa, including all expenses for SOEKOR. CEF subjects the whole structure of crude oil purchases and all connected financial transactions to control by the government, which appoints CEF's board of directors. It is significant that these directors control not only CEF, but also the Equalisation Fund and the SFF.

The SFF was originally created to purchase oil and stockpile it for strategic purposes. Since 1977, however, SFF has become the state's monopoly agency for South Africa's oil purchases from abroad.

The Equalisation Fund was established to compensate the subsidiaries of Western oil companies refining oil in South Africa for their abnormal costs of crude oil purchases from abroad.

The Costs of the Oil Embargo for South Africa, 1979-1987

> Between 1973 and 1984 the Republic of South Africa had to pay R 22 billion more than it would have normally spent. There were times when it was reported to me that we had enough oil for only a week. Just think what we could have done if we had that R 22 billion today . . . what could have been done in other areas? But we had to spend it because we couldn't bring our motor cars and our diesel locomotives to a standstill as our economic life would have collapsed. We paid a price, which we are still suffering from today.[9]

The following table lists the estimated costs the South African government has had to make to import the crude oil the country needs.[10]

Table 1

Year	*Estimated Cost of Crude Oil (in US$ million)*	*Estimated Cost of Embargo (in US$ million)*
1979	3,800	2,360
1980	3,800	2,360
1981	3,000	2,000
1982	3,000	2,000
1983	3,000	2,300
1984	3,000	2,300
1985	3,000	2,300
1986	1,300	2,200
1987	1,730	2,150
Total	25,630	19,970

During the past nine years, South Africa has had to pay at least US $20,000 million extra to circumvent the present voluntary oil embargo. Part of the cost is not included in the above table. Due to the introduction of SASOL products on the South African market, existing refineries owned by Western oil companies are forced to operate below capacity. The oil companies are compensated for this underutilization of their refining capacity by the South African government. Furthermore, the loss of potential export earnings on coal which is now consumed by SASOL (about 35 million tons per year) could be included. Other extra costs are caused by the polluting effects of SASOL's chemical processes on the environment. For example, SASOL consumes 100 million liters of water a day, while the country is short of water resources, particularly during drought periods. Finally, other costs which are not quantified here should be taken into consideration. Among them are the expenses for repairs due to sabotage and the costs of preventive security measures.

Loopholes in the Oil Embargo

All major oil-exporting countries have a policy that their oil should not reach South Africa. There is virtually no more "non-embargoed" crude oil available on the world market. Nevertheless, South Africa still manages to obtain crude oil from the outside world, albeit at considerable cost, through a number of loopholes related to the origin of the crude oil, shipping companies, oil traders, the transfer of technology and capital for oil and gas exploration, and oil majors with South African subsidiaries.

Research by the Shipping Research Bureau indicates that the bulk of the oil shipped to South Africa until January 1985 originated in a very limited number of oil exporting countries, especially in the Persian Gulf area: Saudi Arabia, the United Arab Emirates, Oman, and Iran. The other main source of South Africa's crude oil imports until late 1986, was the Far Eastern Sultanate of Brunei. Obviously, monitoring and enforcing publicly proclaimed embargo policies of the above mentioned countries is urgently needed.

The embargoed crude oil is carried to South Africa in tankers owned by mainly Western shipping companies. Norwegian shipping companies have especially been heavily involved in this secret trade. According to the Shipping Research Bureau's research findings, up to 35 percent of South Africa's need for imported crude oil has been carried on Norwegian owned or managed ships. Shipping companies based in a range of other mainly Western countries, especially Greece, the United Kingdom, the U.S., the Federal Republic of Germany, and Singapore, have also been involved.

Except for Denmark and Norway, no other (shipping) nation has taken any steps to prevent shipping companies under their jurisdiction to sail to South Africa with oil. And even the Norwegian measure leaves a large loophole: it covers only instances where shipowners are aware at the time of concluding a charter party that the final destination of the cargo(es) involved is either South Africa or Namibia.

The crude oil on board the tankers is usually sold to South Africa's SFF by oil traders. Three companies deserve special attention: Transworld Oil, based in the Netherlands and Bermuda and owned by the Dutchman, John Deuss; Marc Rich and Co., A.G., based in Switzerland and owned by Marc Rich; and Marimpex, based in the Federal Republic of Germany and owned by Gert Lutter. During 1979-1983, Transworld Oil delivered at least 25 percent of South Africa's need for imported crude oil. In October 1987, the company issued a statement to the effect that the company had recently stopped delivering crude oil to South Africa. According to the Shipping Research Bureau's research findings for 1981-1985, Marimpex delivered at least about 9 percent of South Africa's needs, and Marc Rich (still personally wanted for tax evasion in the US) at least about 6% since 1979. The Bureau has not been able to identify the owners of the remaining 60% of imported volume.

Despite their prominent involvement in the secret oil trade with South Africa, these companies appear to have no difficulties in trading with those oil-exporting countries whose oil, contrary to their official policies, regularly ends up in South Africa.

In the field of oil exploration, a large number of companies, especially from the United Kingdom and the Federal Republic of Germany, are involved in the transfer of technology to South Africa. At the same time, a small number of British-based subsidiaries of South African companies are participating in North Sea oil production. The huge SASOL plants could not have been built without capital and technology transferred by companies based in the Federal Republic of Germany, France, and Switzerland. None of these countries have taken any steps to prevent companies under their jurisdiction from assisting the South African government with capital and technology in its search for oil.

Lastly, the oil embargo is violated daily by the subsidiaries of five Western oil majors owning refineries in South Africa: Royal Dutch/Shell, British Petroleum, Caltex (Socal and Texaco), and Total Oil.

Tightening the Oil Embargo

It is clear from the examples given above that legislation, monitoring, and enforcement are still urgently needed to close the loopholes in the oil embargo against South Africa. To quote the United Nations Intergovernmental Group to Monitor the Supply and Shipping of Oil and Petroleum Products to South Africa:

> 20. It has been noted that many States have not introduced legislation or comparable measures to enforce the oil embargo. In some cases, even declared policies have not been fully observed.
> 21. Technical measures such as 'end user' certification and other restrictive destination clauses in oil contracts would, if scrupulously implemented, assist in halting the flow of oil and petroleum products to South Africa. However, these clauses are in many cases either not implemented, neglected or subjected to cheating and falsification. Furthermore, legal action against companies and individuals involved in violating the oil embargo is rarely undertaken and penalties are not frequently imposed.[11]

Legislative or comparable measures to tighten the oil embargo are enumerated in great detail in UN General Assembly Resolution 42/43F of 20 November 1987. In paragraph 3, members states are requested:

> (a) To apply strictly the 'end users' clauses and other conditions concerning restriction on destination to ensure compliance with the embargo;
> (b) To compel the companies originally selling or purchasing oil or petroleum products . . . to desist from selling, reselling, or otherwise transferring oil and petroleum products to South Africa and Namibia, whether directly or indirectly;
> (c) To establish strict control over the supply of oil and petroleum products to South Africa and Namibia by intermediaries, oil companies and

traders by placing responsibility for the fulfillment of the contract on the first buyer or seller of oil and petroleum products who would, therefore, be liable for the action of these parties;

(d) To prevent access by South Africa to other sources of energy, including the supply of raw materials, technical know-how, financial assistance and transport.

(e) To prohibit all assistance to apartheid South Africa, including the provision of finance, technology, equipment or personnel for the prospecting, development or production of hydrocarbon resources, the construction or operation of oil-from-coal plants or the development and operation of plants producing fuel substitutes and additives such as ethanol and methanol;

(f) To prevent South African corporations from maintaining or expanding their holdings in oil companies or properties outside South Africa;

(g) To terminate the transport of oil to South Africa by ships flying their flags, or by ships that ultimately are owned, managed or chartered by their nationals or by companies within their jurisdiction.

With respect to monitoring and enforcement of embargo policies, the resolution requests member states:

(h) To develop a system for registration of ships, registered or owned by their nationals, that have unloaded oil in South Africa in contravention of embargoes imposed;

(i) To impose penal action against companies and individuals that have been involved in violating the oil embargo;

(j) To gather, exchange and disseminate information regarding violations of the oil embargo.

Clearly, as long as important Western states such as the US, the United Kingdom, the Federal Republic of Germany, France and Switzerland do not support a mandatory oil embargo against South Africa, loopholes will remain. However, it is equally obvious from the findings of the Intergovernmental Group that if a number of states which do support the oil embargo would see to it that their officially proclaimed embargo policies were strictly adhered to, the present oil embargo could be tightened substantially.

Notes

1. The call for an oil embargo is also widely supported by many international organizations such as the Non-Aligned States, the Organization of African Unity (OAU), the League of Arab States, the World Council of Churches (WCC), the Lutheran World Federation (LWF), the Workers' Group of the International Labour Office (ILO), international trade union bodies like the International Confederation of Free Trade Unions (ICFTU) and the World Federation of Trade Unions (WFTU), the International Transport Workers' Federation (ITF), Western seafarers' and dockers' unions represented by the Maritime Unions Against Apartheid, the Organization of African Trade Union Unity (OATUU), the European Parliament, the Association of Western European Parliamentarians for Actions Against Apartheid (AWEPAA) and the Socialist International (SI).

2. *Financial Mail*, 4 October 1985.

3. See the *Shipping Research Bureau's Newsletter*, Nos. 7 and 8. The Shipping Research Bureau (SRB) was founded in 1980 by two Dutch non-governmental anti-apartheid organizations, the Holland Committee on Southern Africa (HCSA) and the Working Group Kairos (Christians against Apartheid). The SRB conducts research and publishes reports on the ways in which South Africa tries to obtain its crude oil imports to counter the embargo which is imposed by virtually all oil-producing countries. Additional objectives are to do research on legislative and other measures making the oil embargo more effective and to inform governments, intergovernmental and non-governmental organizations about findings in order to strengthen the existing oil embargo. The main

reports published by the SRB contain extensively verified data regarding all identified crude oil deliveries to South Africa which took place within a specific period. The main report, *South Africa's Lifeline, Violations of the Oil Embargo,* was published in September 1986, and covers the period January 1983 to January 1985. A follow up report, covering 1985, 1986 and the first six months of 1987, was published in late 1988. The SRB also releases occasional surveys detailing current developments regarding crude oil supplies to South Africa.

4. *SRB Newsletters* Nos. 5 and 6.

5. *SRB Newsletter* No. 10. For Conlon's findings see his *South Africa's Offshore Oil Exploration* (UN Centre Against Apartheid, Notes and Documents 8/85, October 1985); *South Africa's Attempts to Reduce Dependence on Imported Oil* (UN Centre Against Apartheid, Notes and Documents, 9/85, October 1985); and *The SASOL Liquefication Plants: Economic Implications and Impact on South Africa's Ability to Withstand an Oil Cutoff* (UN Centre Against Apartheid, Notes and Documents, 10/85, October 1985).

6. *House of Assembly Debates* (Hansard South Africa), Col. 2587, 21 March 1985.

7. Ibid., Col. 5855, 20 May 1985.

8. Ibid., Col. 5863, 20 May 1985.

9. President P. W. Botha, quoted in the *Windhoek Advertiser,* 25 April 1986.

10. The table is based on the following assumptions: that between 1979 and 1982, oil imports averaged 15 million tons per year and the average stockpile was 30 million tons (2 years consumption); and that between 1983 and 1987, oil imports averaged 14 million tons per year and the average stockpile was 17 to 18 million tons (15 months consumption). In 1979 and 1980 the average price of a barrel of crude oil was US $35 with South Africa paying an average premium of $6 per barrel. In 1986, the average price per barrel

was $13 with an average premium per barrel of $2. In 1987, the average price per barrel was $17.30 with an average premium of $1.50. (For these calculations, see *Secret Oil Deliveries to South Africa 1981-1982* (Shipping Research Bureau, 1984) and *South Africa's Lifeline Violations of the Oil Embargo 1983-1984* (Shipping Research Bureau, 1986).

HIGH-TECH SANCTIONS: MORE BARK THAN "BYTE?"

Thomas Conrad

Introduction

There are few products that are intrinsically violent or repressive by their nature. Weapons—which are manufactured expressly to kill and cause pain—are an exception. But even things that are not intrinsically repressive can be used to violate human beings if they get into the hands of the wrong people. A clamp used by a plumber to stop a leak in a pipe can also be used by the police as a thumbscrew to extract a confession from a political prisoner. Similarly, computers, which can be used for a variety of helpful applications, can also be used to design weapons, file fingerprints, or store names for segregated voters' roles. In the hands of the practitioners of apartheid, computers are vital to white minority rule in South Africa.

High-Tech Sanctions: A Look At the Record

The high-tech sector is the one area in which the United States has had the longest experience enforcing sanctions against

South Africa. Thus a look at sanctions in this sector may be instructive as we discuss expanding sanctions to other areas. Have controls on high-tech exports to South Africa served to distance the United States from apartheid? Have they prevented American technology from reaching the military or being used to enforce apartheid?

Sanctions in the form of export restrictions against Pretoria were first put in place by the United States in 1963 in response to the United Nations arms embargo. In a corollary to the arms embargo, US controls were expanded to bar certain high-tech exports to military and certain government end-users in 1977. These controls were most recently tightened in 1986 pursuant to the Comprehensive Anti-Apartheid Act. Thus the United States has had ten years of experience enforcing a partial ban on high-tech sales to South Africa, and nearly 25 years of experience enforcing the arms embargo against Pretoria. In evaluating the effectiveness of these sanctions it is important to look not only at the last year, but the last several years.

The record of implementation and enforcement has essentially yielded mixed results. One area of success has been a halt in official US government-to-government arms transfers to South Africa pursuant to the United Nations arms embargo. Most official arms transfers are handled under the Pentagon's Foreign Military Sales program of the Military Assistance Program. These transactions are subject to public scrutiny and there is no indication that there have been any such shipments to Pretoria for several years.

Whatever comfort may be taken in the fact that official government-to-government arms shipments have been stopped is offset by the volume of private high-tech sales to South Africa. This commercial trade in military, dual-use, and other advanced technology overshadows whatever other success the United States may have had in distancing itself from apartheid. Its strategic significance for the survival of the status quo in South Africa cannot be overstated. Because of this trade, Pretoria has continued to enjoy access to a vast array of crucial products including computers, software, laser technology, electronics, instrumentation, and communications equipment, which are exported by American companies under licenses issued by the US government.

The "Wiring" of South Africa: An Overview

Computers have undergirded South Africa's white power structure since they were first introduced to the country in the 1950s. Pretoria was quick to recognize the value of the computer in streamlining government operations and managing its majority population. IBM South Africa received its first order for an "electronic tabulator" in 1952 from the government's Division of Electronics.[1] Since then, IBM and other US and European suppliers have helped "wire" South Africa, putting strategic technology at the disposal of the government and private end-users who have used it to consolidate their power.

Imported computers have played a key role in engineering the very system of racial classification that has made apartheid possible. By 1955, Pretoria had already automated its population register, streamlining the hated passbook system which covered all people designated as Africans. IBM had bid on the passbook system in 1965 but lost to its British competitor, ICL.[2] As a consolation, Pretoria gave IBM the contract for the "Book of Life," an identity system which covered all other groups, including Indians, "Coloureds," "Cape Coloureds," and whites. US suppliers such as Burroughs, NCR, and Control Data outfitted other branches of the South African government with advanced hardware.

US equipment also found its way into the inventory of the security forces. Before US controls were expanded in the late 1970s, IBM sold hardware to the South African Defence Force and installed equipment at the Simonstown Naval installation. Mohawk Data Sciences sold equipment to the South African police for use in a nationwide suspect tracking system.[3]

In the face of the international arms embargo, South Africa's indigenous arms industry has made great strides in the local manufacture and assembly of counter-insurgency arms (many of them modelled on foreign weapons) and other military systems. Imported computers and electronics have been critical to this effort. Through the 1970s and early 1980s, companies such as Mohawk Data Systems, Sperry, and Hewlett-Packard sold equipment directly to ARMSCOR, South Africa's government-owned weapons conglomerate. IBM, Control Data, and Amdahl helped supply Pretoria's largest research agency, the Council for Scientific and Industrial Research.

Although Siemens, ICL, and other European firms also play an important role in South Africa, on balance, non-US companies have been no match for American computer firms. At the end of the 1970s, US companies together essentially controlled South Africa's computer market. By 1980, a local industry survey showed that US companies were selling 75 percent of all the computers in the country and handling 77 percent of all the rentals.[4]

US companies say they have lost some business because of government controls on exports to South Africa, but they have remained a driving force in the market. According to the 1986 *South African Computer Users Handbook*, IBM was still in first place in 1985, followed by ICL, with Burroughs in third place and Sperry in fifth (Burroughs and Sperry have since merged).[5] While their home offices were dealing with strong public anti-apartheid sentiment, US computer vendors in South Africa were doing a brisk business: in 1985, no fewer than six of the top ten computer vendors in South Africa were US-owned.[6]

The Pretoria government is itself one of the biggest consumers of imported computers in South Africa. According to local industry sources, government purchases make up more than 40 percent of all electronics purchases in South Africa (which include computers and other technology).[7] IBM said in 1987 that less than ten percent of its sales were to the government.[8] More than 50 percent of Control Data's sales and approximately 30 percent of Burroughs' sales were to the public sector.[9]

Because the South African government regards computers and electronics as strategic commodities, Pretoria has publicly embraced a "Made in South Africa" campaign, seeking to stimulate the development of a local high-tech industry. Strides have been made in the local production of microchips, and in electro-optics; locally made peripherals have begun to appear on the market. Yet despite official encouragement, the South

African high-tech sector is far from self-sufficient. In fact, the campaign may well have been designed as much to boost public morale at home and project a spunky "go it alone" attitude to overseas suppliers and foreign critics, for South Africa is still overwhelmingly dependent on US and other international suppliers.

When all is said and done, 75 percent of South Africa's high-tech products are still imported—most of them by foreign companies.[10] Disinvestment by US computer companies is not likely to have had a significant effect on the predominance of US computer companies in South Africa. In most cases, although the companies have packed up, their products continue to be available.

The US minicomputer company Wang Laboratories figured out how to "stay in while getting out," pioneering a strategy of "South Africanization" that has been adopted by other US companies facing disinvestment pressure. Nearly ten years ago, Wang announced its "withdrawal" from South Africa, leaving its sales to be managed by a local firm, General Business Systems. Wang has for several years been able to claim that it doesn't have a subsidiary in South Africa, yet sales of Wang hardware have been brisk, increasing as much as 45 percent some years. "Far from hurting us, I feel the withdrawal has probably strengthened us in the South African marketplace," said a representative of Wang's South African distributor.[11] Wang says that it has since ended its relationship with its South African distributor.

The Impact of Export Controls: Dealing with the "Computer Siege"

Not long after the Commerce Department tightened controls on computer sales to South Africa in 1978, a South African business analyst explained why computers are Pretoria's Achilles' Heel: "No other sector of the economy is as utterly dependent as the computer industry is on the multinationals . . . it is a sector through which stranglehold can be applied on the whole economy," warned the specialist in an article entitled, "How to Beat a Computer Siege."[12]

Despite the new US restrictions, the computer siege never fully materialized. How was South Africa able to maintain its access to US technology? Pretoria was evidently able to circumvent Washington's ban on direct sales to the police and security forces by exploiting weaknesses in the US regulations. In addition to Pretoria's own resourcefulness, though, evidence suggests that the US companies themselves may have helped thwart US controls. According to a South African study cited in a cable from the US mission in Pretoria which was released to the American Friends Service Committee under the Freedom of Information Act,

> Multinationals, including U.S. subsidiaries, are determined to undercut any sanctions action and have already made plans to camouflage their operation through subterfuges arranged with affiliates in other countries.[13]

Throughout the past ten years, US vendors have insisted that they have abided by US export regulations. Yet an admission by a local industry leader in 1986 cast serious doubt on these claims. Pointing to the 1978 restrictions on sales to the police and military, she said, "It is interesting to note that despite the 1978 legislation, a substantial amount of U.S. computer equipment is currently installed in South Africa in those very entities which were embargoed."[14]

Are the Current Sanctions Viable?

In assessing the effectiveness of current export controls it is helpful to look at a few case studies—instances in which advanced US technology found its way into the hands of objectionable or repressive end-users in South Africa before the regulations were expanded. How have these transactions occurred? Is it probable, or even possible, that the new regulations implementing the Anti-Apartheid Act of 1986 could prevent them from recurring? The answers to these questions will help determine whether the current sanctions are accomplishing what they are supposed to. This chapter will examine three cases:

Case One: US Technology for "Commercial, Non-Military Use"

In 1980, the *Financial Mail* reported on an advanced new workplace surveillance system that was taking South Africa's mining industry by storm.[15] The innovative new "Labour Information System" is a locally assembled electronic network which automatically reads workers' coded identification cards, and "provides full information on every worker, from his ethnic group to his merit rating, and also keeps tabs on where every worker is at any one time." A microprocessor made by the US manufacturer Ontel functions as the most crucial part of the system—the "electronic brain" which controls the network. The "Labour Information System" has been installed in 25 South African mines.

"A general-purpose computer could have many applications," said a US Ontel representative. "We don't have knowledge of what they use it for," he added. Ontel stopped selling equipment in South Africa after it arranged for a local corporation to manufacture the microprocessor.

This case apparently involved a straightforward commercial transaction in which Ontel simply sold its microprocessor to the makers of the "Labour Information System" and later sold the know-how for the microprocessor itself. Despite the repressive potential of such a system, it seems unlikely that the expanded US export regulations put in place in the wake of the Anti-Apartheid Act would prevent any transaction of this type from recurring because Ontel's partner is apparently a civilian entity. The Commerce Department regulations have little effect on US sales to civilian companies and end-users in South Africa.

Case Two: US Technology for "Non-Military Government Use"

For several years, IBM computers have provided the brains for much of South Africa's transportation system. In 1978, it was reported that the railways had established a new computerized tracking system based on two IBM central processing units that linked up 600 terminals across the country.[16] The network, which also uses Data General and Westinghouse equipment, permits operators to monitor the exact load, location, and destination of any freight in the country. In January 1986, the government announced that it planned to spend at least R13.7 million on IBM hardware and R5 million for IBM software (it was unclear if the new acquisition upgraded the existing rail monitoring system or whether it was for a new application).[17]

In South Africa, government operations that may seem harmless and non-objectionable often are crucial to the smooth functioning of apartheid and the security establishment. South Africa's transportation system is formally under civilian control but it is of enormous strategic significance to crucial industries and the South African military. The railway system has obvious civilian value. But it is also the chief means of moving weapons and military supplies around the country.

The strategic significance of the rail system was especially evident in the case of the military occupation of Namibia. According to a South African military journal, approximately 90 percent of the weapons and military equipment arriving at the Defence Force's huge logistics base in Grootfontein, Namibia, came by rail—80 to 90 freight cars every month.[18] Thus the railway played a vital role in the war system, and because the network was hosted on IBM equipment, IBM was directly implicated.

In addition to sales to national agencies, US vendors have saturated government agencies on the local level with US hardware.[19] Often overlooked, these local white-controlled government bodies are in many ways the "shock troops of apartheid." Their front-line role in implementing the repressive system has largely escaped scrutiny. NCR, in particular, has had great success in penetrating this market. NCR hardware is used for "public administration" in the municipalities of Stellenbosch, Lydenburg, Zeerust, Kokstad, Bloemfontein, Walvis Bay (Namibia), and many others. Burroughs, IBM, and Wang equipment is also installed at local agencies.[20]

It must be assumed that "non-objectionable" government agencies and parastatals front for those state agencies that are clearly off limits for US suppliers. According to one local specialist, "There is a lot of underutilized capacity in government computer installations, and there is no way the U.S. authorities will be able to prevent this capacity from being shared by the defence and police departments."[21]

There are numerous other instances of commercial sales of equipment to government departments, parastatals, and local agencies—entities which, because they are ostensibly non-military, are assumed not to be involved in repressive, militarily significant or other strategic activities. Although some of these types of transactions may receive additional scrutiny because of the Anti-Apartheid Act, these sales have apparently not been stopped. Assurances from South African government agencies can hardly be taken seriously. Yet as long as the vendor receives a pledge from a government agency that it won't divert equipment to other embargoed government users, and as long as the agency agrees to an end-use check, the transaction is likely to be licensed by US officials.

Case Three: US Technology for Non-Governmental (Commercial) Arms-Makers

The 1986 issue of an annual guide to the computer industry in South Africa shows several installations of US hardware at companies involved in local military production.[22] Samples include:

Company	*Area of Expertise*	*US Hardware Installed*
ESD[23]	Specialized Electronics	Digital Equipment; IBM
Trivetts/UEC	Naval Communications	Digital Equipment
Grinel	Counterinsurgency communications gear	Hewlett-Packard
Sandock-Austral	Naval Strike Craft and armored vehicles for police and military use	Burroughs (Unisys)

Fuchs	Components for anti-personnel and other projectiles	Data General; Hewlett-Packard

These are five of approximately 800 local military subcontractors that supply the South African Defence Force and provide goods and services to the government-owned ARMSCOR weapons conglomerate. Access to advanced imported computers is of profound strategic importance to Pretoria in overcoming the arms embargo. Given the size of South Africa's indigenous weapons industry (now the world's tenth-largest) and the relative freedom US vendors have had to do business with it, these installations probably represent the tip of the iceberg. The hardware listed above was installed before the Anti-Apartheid Act went into effect, but even the previous US export controls were supposed to have prohibited sales of equipment that could be used by or for the security forces.

Do Hewlett, Digital Equipment, Unisys, and the other companies listed (or their representatives) continue to provide software, services, and spares for these installations? Are US companies, or go-between firms that represent them, still permitted to sell advanced technology of this kind to civilian arms-makers? Although systematic public monitoring of these transactions is impossible, it seems unlikely that the new regulations will have halted or seriously hampered commercial sales of this type. South African arms companies are undoubtedly prepared to provide any end-use guarantees required to get the hardware they need. Once the companies control the equipment, the United States is powerless to prevent them from using it for military applications.

Conclusion

As has been shown, despite the sanctions that have been put in place over the past several years, Pretoria has managed to maintain access to much of the US technology it needs. While the restrictions imposed pursuant to the Anti-Apartheid Act of 1986 were a step in the right direction, they have not halted the flow of computers, advanced electronics, and other "strategic inputs" to South Africa.

Perhaps one of the greatest weaknesses of US high-tech sanctions to date has been the implicit assumption that Pretoria will quietly abide by them. "Boikot Breken"—sanctions busting—is a national pastime in South Africa. It is fostered by the government and it involves government agencies, local commercial firms, and multinationals. Pretoria knows the stakes are high and has vowed to "fight dirty" to maintain access to foreign technology,[24] a point that was driven home recently when the press reported that an official of a South African civilian firm, Avitech Pty. Ltd., and others, were indicted for having provided 79 loads of military aircraft components to the South African Air Force from 1980 to 1987.[25]

It is axiomatic that once US technology reaches South Africa, it is potentially at the disposal of the South African government, its security forces, and its arms industry. Given Pretoria's willingness to engage in subterfuge, and given the companies' complicity, it must be assumed that virtually any US product destined for any end-user in South Africa can be diverted or used repressively, regardless of what promises have been made, or what post-shipment inquiries take place. Under these conditions, to license high-tech exports to South Africa is to wink at trade in repression. When all is said and done, the one element that would make high-tech sanctions work has been in shortest supply: the political will to make sanctions stick.

Notes

1. *South African Computer Users Handbook,* 1980 (hereafter *CUH*).

2. *Washington Post,* 30 September 1976.

3. Additional details about government and military sales are contained in *Automating Apartheid—U.S. Computer Exports to South Africa and the Arms Embargo* (Philadelphia, NARMIC/American Friends Service Committee, 1982).

4. *Management*, December 1979.

5. *CUH*, 1986.

6. Ibid.

7. *CUH*, Special Section, 1986.

8. Company Report, "International Business Machines Corporation," Investor Responsibility Research Center (IRRC), 1987.

9. Company Reports, "Control Data Corporation" and "Unisys Corporation," IRRC, 1987.

10. Michael Brzoska, "Shades of Grey: 10 Years of South African Arms Procurement in the Shadow of the Mandatory Arms Embargo," paper delivered at the *Institut fur Politische Wissenschaft*, University of Hamburg, no date.

11. *Datamation*, June 1979.

12. *Sunday Times* (*Business Times*), 26 March 1978.

13. Cable to Secretary of State from the U.S. Embassy, Pretoria, 13 October 1978.

14. *Financial Mail* (Supplement), 28 November 1986.

15. *Financial Mail*, 11 July 1980.

16. *Electronics and Instrumentation*, August 1978.

17. Company Report, "International Business Machines Corporation," IRRC, May 1978.

18. *Paratus*, May 1978.

19. These vendors include Sperry, NCR, and Hewlett installations at the South African Reserve Bank; IBM and Control Data installations at the Council for Scientific and Industrial Research; IBM installations at the Department of the Prime Minister and Department of Statistics; and Control Data installations at ESCOM. These examples are cited in *Automating Apartheid.*

20. *CUH,* 1986.

21. *Sunday Times, (Business Times),* 26 March 1978.

22. *CUH,* 1986.

23. An international arms journal notes that ESD has "designed machines that emulate U.S. producers—a move necessitated by the arms embargo applied since 1977." (*International Defense Review,* May 1985).

24. *Johannesburg Star International Airmail Weekly,* 14 May 1980.

25. *New York Times,* 29 October 1987.

GOLD AND INTERNATIONAL SANCTIONS AGAINST SOUTH AFRICA

Ian Lepper and Peter Robbins

Introduction

Gold was first produced in South Africa almost exactly a century ago. Since then the metal has become inseparable from the history, economic structure, and foreign relationships of South Africa and from apartheid itself. It provides about half of South Africa's foreign income and 13% of its Gross Domestic Product (GDP). Of the South African government's tax revenues, 13% comes directly from the gold mines and perhaps another 10% from taxes on associated economic activity such as the mine supply industry and income tax of workers in the gold sector.

The profits of gold mining in South Africa far exceed the cost of miners' wages, an almost unique phenomenon in such a labor intensive industry. However, the interests of the black mineworkers, whose labor provides these riches, are hardly considered by the mining companies. Thirty-five thousand of them have died in mine accidents. In 1986 alone, there were 702 such deaths. Many times this number have been injured and have received little or no compensation. The black mineworkers' wages average one seventh those of the white miners, and the majority are paid far below the poverty line. The gold mining companies, bastions of South African "free market enterprise," have, with government assistance, constructed mechanisms and laws to prevent any competition for labor. Above all, practically every black mineworker and his family must suffer the untold miseries of the migrant labor system.

The reaction to a century of this kind of injustice in the lust for gold and the failure to diversify from a gold-based economy has now made South Africa extremely vulnerable to a gold sanction (see Appendix 1).

South Africa is unquestionably important as a gold producer, providing over a third of world supply. But only 5% of all new gold appearing on the market each year is put to any practical industrial use; further, almost all the gold ever produced in the history of the world (equivalent to 50 years of present output) is available to the market. Gold is so central to the South African economy that it alone can provide sufficient profits for the sustained oppression of the country's black majority. Hence, effective sanctions in this area would have more effect than other measures short of military action. If all gold sales from South Africa ceased tomorrow, it would have no impact on industrial activity in the rest of the world. On the other hand, the South African economy would be catastrophically damaged.

The authors of this chapter are convinced that powerful trade sanctions against South Africa are a necessary part of the struggle to get rid of apartheid with the least possible bloodshed and damage to the industrial infrastructure of that country. It is not, however, the purpose of this chapter to prove that point or even to argue for it.

There is no doubt that an effective gold sanction would be an extremely powerful measure. It is the practical problem of implementing such a sanction, in order to make it effective, that this chapter tries to address. Just ten jumbo jets would be required to export all of South Africa's gold production each year and there is likely to emerge considerable scope for smuggling of that gold on to world markets. Furthermore, the scope of such smuggling would be enhanced as the gold price rose with every new act of trade and other forms of economic sanctions against the apartheid regime. Gold sanctions should be constructed with a view to maximize the negative impacts on the South African economy at the minimum cost to the rest of the world, including other gold producers. In addition, there would be no point in taking any step which would bring into question the role of gold in the world's monetary system; indeed, there is no reason to do so. The aim would not be to depress the international price of gold, but only the price received by South Africa. A key feature of this proposed policy is that it does not fundamentally conflict with the interests of the gold market. The more countries that adopt the policy, the greater will be the incentive for the markets to participate in policing it.

Our strategy is designed to fulfill these objectives. Its effectiveness would be insured as more countries adopted it. However, even if a small number of countries boycotted apartheid gold, it would make a significant impact. In doing so, these countries would demonstrate that action could be taken to reduce the benefits to South Africa of its most valuable export and set an example for ever wider international acceptance. A further positive aspect is that the economies of countries adopting the policy would in no way be damaged.

The key elements of the strategy are as follows:

1. A ban on all imports of newly mined South African gold or gold shipped directly from South Africa, including products containing such gold;
2. The release of gold from national reserves of sanction-taking countries, on a monthly basis, of equivalent quantities that would otherwise be imported from South Africa; and
3. The establishment of a fund to finance a training program for students chosen by the South African liberation movement to learn the advanced skills of mining and marketing gold.

The source of gold is difficult to trace, unlike most metals. Its detailed chemical composition (including trace elements) cannot readily be identified with the country in which it was mined (see Appendix 2). This means that if South Africa chose to smuggle its gold, cast in molds and stamped to look as though it has been produced in Mexico in 1926, it would take a great deal of scientific investigation to prove that it was not. Even the most rigorous scientific tests could not distinguish between newly mined South Africa gold and gold that had been mined in South Africa fifty years ago. Although the South Africans would need the cooperation of some unscrupulous international gold dealers they could smuggle at least some of their gold into the market even if all countries decided to ban its import. There seems, therefore, no point in making a sanctions program totally dependent on preventing all smuggling. Doing so may well prove counterproductive. If a large part, but not all, of South Africa's gold were smuggled, the shortage of gold in the market would drive up the price of the gold that was sold to a high enough level to compensate for the loss of volume.

A realistic strategy must allow for the danger of price increases due to sanctions and for the probability of some of South Africa's gold being smuggled onto the gold market with the assistance of the dealers. The policy must, therefore, insure that the world price is kept steady and that the dealers charge the South Africans an extremely high price for their cooperation. The price obtained by South African exporters will then be reduced rather than enhanced.

In spite of cheap labor, South African gold mines are now less profitable than gold mines in most other parts of the world. This is because of geological factors and difficulties that South African mining companies have in adopting new technology due to the low level of the Rand and other trade and financial sanctions. With a gold price of $US 400 or less, the mines on average are barely profitable. However, at present, the gold mines are a massive contributor to government funds. Even a moderate fall in the income which the mining companies derive from gold sales would present the government with a serious dilemma. It would either have to subsidize the gold industry or allow the value of the Rand to fall to the level which would keep the mines profitable. The first choice would entail the government either losing the necessary funds that it needs for the oppression of the black population or taxing whites (the only real source of income tax revenue) to compensate for this massive loss of income. The second choice would cause a massive rise in the cost of all imports and serious extra inflation. Whatever happens, the economy is severely damaged. So let us look at the strategy in detail.

1. A ban on all imports of newly mined South African gold or gold shipped directly from South Africa, including products containing such gold

This ban should apply nationally. At an international level, this should be supported by a United Nations Security Council resolution for legislative embargoes to be imposed on imports of South African gold and products containing such gold from a certain date. In addition, pressure would be needed to insure the support of certain non-governmental institutions such as bullion refiners. There are only fifty gold refineries in the world whose product is acceptable to international gold dealers, so the South Africans would have to use at least one of these to disguise smuggled metal coming into the market.

There would be no point in disallowing the movement of gold exported from South Africa in previous years, since this would only distort gold prices. There would always be the chance that a certain country may collaborate with the South Africans by buying its new gold and exporting its old gold to sanctions-taking countries. This could not be done indefinitely, however, because of the large quantities needed to be sold each year. It would also become quickly obvious which country was doing this substitution, and steps would need to be taken to ban imports of any gold from that country. It is unlikely, however, that any country would wish to build up massive stocks of unsalable metal.

Even with the ban on newly mined gold, importing countries could expect some to enter their markets in disguised forms; but by making this illegal the onus for compliance can be thrown on to the individual gold importers. Conviction for committing such an offense should result in confiscation of the gold (and a suitable prison term), and the gold should then be sold by the government concerned. Such a policy would have particular repercussions in the world's gold trading centers (see Appendix 2).

The ban would create a secondary market in new South African gold. The price discount between this secondary market and the open market could be substantial, due to widespread implementation of the ban. The South African government and mining companies would have to find "middlemen" prepared to circumvent the ban. Naturally such people would demand a large compensation for taking the risks involved, with the heavy cost falling on the mining companies and the South African government. The South Africans would have the further problem of finding middlemen—who would need to be criminally minded to take on the task—who could be trusted with the $US 8 billion worth of credit needed to shift enough gold to represent present earnings (see Appendix 3).

2. *The release of gold from national reserves of sanctions-taking countries on a monthly basis of equivalent quantities of gold that would otherwise be imported from South Africa*

The cost to South Africa of avoiding sanctions may be compensated for by gold price increases, if measures are not taken to increase gold supplies from other sources to make up for potential reductions in South African sales. This is because the gold market is greatly affected by perceived threats to the supply of gold; this is magnified by the effects of hoarding and dishoarding. The mere threat of trade sanctions at present tends to push up the gold price, on the assumption that supplies must be affected in the long term. Any sanctions on gold must therefore compensate for this by guaranteeing a long term extra supply of gold, to take the wind from the speculators' sails.

Fortunately the huge international stocks of gold, particularly in national and international reserve holdings, facilitate this. Almost all countries of the world have, for historical reasons, kept a large part (currently 40%) of their reserves in the form of gold. They have so much of it in fact (35,000 tons in the West alone at the end of 1985 compared with South African annual production of 600 tons) that if they sold even a small proportion it would drive down the price of the unsold balance.

A measured approach to sanctions should use these reserves to exploit the efficiency of the international gold market, rather than fighting it. Countries banning the import of new South

African gold should commit themselves to compensating for the loss of supply to the gold markets, and to using their reserves to do so as necessary. This would mean that they should cease purchasing gold for reserves and compensate for the loss of South African supply to the market with regular monthly sales from their central bank reserves, to be continued until representative government is established in South Africa. As Appendix 4 shows, many countries could sustain such sales for decades. Those with only small stocks should aim to persuade countries with large stocks to "swap" their sales with gold-rich countries to make up the shortfall, and should concentrate generally on ensuring that major gold-holding organizations and countries play their part.

To support this policy, a gold pool could be created based on gold contributions from central banks, the International Monetary Fund (IMF), and the Bank for International Settlements (BIS). The pool would sell gold on a similar basis whenever the price exceeded, or threatened to exceed, a prescribed maximum. Providing that South African gold exports were being effectively policed, the pool could also be permitted to buy in gold solely to replenish stocks when the price fell markedly below this level. The pool could be administered by the IMF.

The threat of such a sales program being implemented would not only discourage increased hoarding, but would have a devastating effect on perceptions for the future of the South African economy under apartheid.

Combined with the ban on imports, the monthly compensatory sales element of the strategy would have many positive aspects:

1. The gold price would fall only if South Africa was allowed to avoid the sanctions despite widespread implementation. This means that in spite of large potential profit margins in sanctions busting, the market would have an incentive to support the sanctions (see 2 below). Price movements would also make the way in which avoidance was being organized apparent so that targets for international pressure, i.e., smuggling countries, could easily be identified.

2. The gold market could well profit from the uncertainty involved without being threatened by it. As soon as implementation began to spread, it would be easier and more profitable for the market to assist in policing the policy than to continue trying to break it. After all, there are 90,000 tons of gold in the world to deal in, so who needs South Africa's 600 tons a year? The market is already tightly controlled. If South Africa lost the support of the dealers, the business of breaking a gold sanction would be nearly impossible.
3. Countries undertaking this type of sanction would not lose money. Converting part of their gold reserves into a mixed basket of international assets should give them adequate security and the added benefit of interest on those securities and reduce gold holding charges.
4. Countries strongly opposed to apartheid could justifiably concentrate calls for action against those countries with the largest gold stocks, such as the US, EEC, and Japan.
5. This policy would effectively demonstrate that South Africa was vulnerable to gold sanctions, even if undertaken by a minority of nations, without any harmful effects to their own economies. The ban on the import of newly mined gold must extend to products containing such gold. This could, of course, apply to such items as gold scrap and alloys containing gold, but the most obvious items would be jewelry.

The United States has long implemented a very successful import boycott of Cuban nickel. This boycott not only covers pure nickel but extends to all products containing this nickel. Importers are required to supply certification that this is so. Any suspect importers must be prepared to submit to an inspection of the books and works of the plant in which the goods were made. Failure to do so would result in losing the US market for all time. World prices for Cuban nickel are consequently very low and, in spite of that country having the second largest nickel deposits in the world, its nickel producing capacity is largely undeveloped. Similar methods of policing gold products containing South African gold should be adopted.

3. The establishment of a fund to finance a training program for students chosen by the South African liberation movement to learn the skills of mining and marketing gold

As the end of apartheid draws near, gold speculators would be expected to buy gold. This is because of the suspicion that gold supplies would be disrupted by sanctions or by unrest at the mines and the speculators' belief that a black government in power in South Africa could not "run" the mines.

There are strong arguments supporting both these predictions. Nevertheless, given the ANC's Freedom Charter declaration to nationalize the mines, a representative government once in power will need loyal and experienced mining engineers, finance experts, geologists, and marketing experts. It is therefore important that a nucleus of personnel be trained—and seen to be trained—to be ready to advise the new government of the policy options that are available to it and to maintain production. A small number of countries could find the resources necessary to do so. Such a move would help destroy the argument that a new democratic government could not run the mines efficiently, discouraging the market from "talking up" the gold price as the apartheid regime crumbles. It would also help the new government to bring the country back from what will inevitably be a very damaged state. Finally, it will help to ensure that South Africa's other mined products will continue to flow to the West after independence.

Conclusions

Gold's key role in sustaining the South African regime economically has profound consequences politically, socially, and militarily for the country. The longer the revenues keep flowing in, the longer it will be before the South African regime is moved to consider any alternative to its present course aimed at maintaining white supremacy over the black majority.

The financial importance of gold has always made it a difficult target for international sanctions. Today, however, we can start to separate South Africa, the largest gold producer, from a market that is many, many times larger than its annual production. South Africa represents a lower and lower percentage of world production each year, so much so that all the needs of the world's jewelry makers and industrial users can be met from other producing countries. The gold market can survive many years without South Africa. The obverse, however, is certainly not true.

Without the protection of gold, white South Africa would not be able to afford either its repressive apparatus or its high living standards. Without gold, the regime would have to switch from empty rhetoric to a real search for a peaceful transition. As this essay shows, the gold revenues can be reduced and, with the right will, can be practically halted.

Appendix 1

The proposition for a gold sanction has only been seriously aired in the last two years. Until then, very little research had been conducted into the effectiveness of such a measure. Recently, however, there seems to be a growing understanding that, far from being protected by its gold-based economy, South Africa has a golden Achilles heel. Gold lost its convertability with major currencies almost two decades ago and the gold market has become much more like the market for any other commodity. Most of the myth and mystery which protected South Africa's role in the world's monetary system by virtue of its supply of gold has been stripped away. In June 1988, representatives of the African National Congress, South West African People's Organization, the British Anti-Apartheid Movement, and the End Loans to South Africa organization set up a body called the World Gold Commission (WGC). This body has the specific task of denying South Africa income deriving from sales of gold. Since the launch of the WGC, Italian jewelry manufacturers (who alone import one-third of all newly mined South African gold) have pledged themselves to find gold from alternative sources, a spokesman for the Union Bank of Switzerland has stated that his bank is looking for different gold, Senator Edward Kennedy has instigated an official inquiry into the feasibility of a gold sanction, and many national and international anti-apartheid and church bodies have called for a serious consideration of a gold sanction.

Appendix 2

Banning the import of new South African gold into the United Kingdom (UK) could pose some difficulties for the world's gold market if not undertaken correctly. The gold markets are unusual because of the homogeneity of the medium, which is measured the world over in terms of units of weight of pure metal. The market is very liquid, because huge quantities of the metal and finance are available to it. Supply or demand can be increased many times over almost instantaneously, simply by moving stacks of bars or currency around in bank vaults or on paper. They are probably the most efficient and purest major markets of any sort in the world. Throughout the day, a true open market price is set at which a large volume of standard purity gold is traded between many participants. The market is accessible to any participant with the necessary resources and has to operate fairly between investors to maintain its credibility. There are only a small number of approved refiners the world over, and movement and registration of bars is meticulously recorded. There is absolutely no possibility of any gold being traded much less used by a customer of the market without total knowledge of the origins of the individual bar being known. In addition, none of the several gold markets in the world, such as Hong Kong, Tokyo, and New York, can operate without maintaining the same general rules as the others. These are ideal conditions for control during the period when sanctions apply. A single gold market, obliged to impose the ban, would police the ban worldwide, motivated by the threat of legal problems in just one dealing center.

In order to distinguish gold mined in one field from that mined in another, it is possible to use a technique known as isotopic analysis. Most gold is refined to a purity of 99.5%. The other 0.5% of the bar is made up of trace elements. These elements in turn consist of the several isotopes in which many elements naturally occur. A mass spectrometer is able to quickly define the ratios of these isotopes to each other. These ratios are a "fingerprint" of the gold, and gold from no two mining areas are the same. It would be costly and time-consuming to analyze every gold bar that passed through customs, but the system could be used where strong supporting evidence of falsification of origin was suspected.

Appendix 3

South Africa produces over one-third of the world's gold and would therefore have to use many smuggling routes in order to spread the sales over a wide range of markets. It could not, for instance, hope to sell its entire production through, say, Singapore and Hong Kong, which have limited gold reserves and no gold production of their own. Suspicion would immediately fall on any country which suddenly became a major gold exporter.

Entrepreneurs who would be the kind of people prepared to do this smuggling work and who operate this kind of unscrupulous business are not internationally renowned for their probity. As was proved many times during the period of UN sanctions on Rhodesia, many instances of major fraud were committed against the Rhodesian government sanctions-busting organizations, which were hardly able to bring legal proceedings against the perpetrators. Furthermore, the people who presently market South Africa's gold are highly experienced and intelligent: it would be unlikely that crooked amateurs could sell gold at anything close to the market price.

So the cost of smuggling South African gold would not simply be the added transport and financing costs involved in sending the metal on its long and circuitous route to the final buyer. There would also be the probable costs of remelting and casting in different molds, restamping, forging specification documents and certificates of origin, huge commissions paid to middlemen, uninsurable losses due to fraud (because middlemen will certainly be unable to pay for the gold before they themselves have been paid and could then abscond with the money), and losses due to far from perfect marketing ability. Even then, only a tiny fraction of present production could be sold in these circumstances.

It is possible that a large existing gold-dealing country like Switzerland could allow its banks and refineries to circumvent gold sanctions. This would be very unlikely, however. In the first place, it would be quickly recognized from the state of the gold market, published trade figures, and the state of financial affairs in South Africa that apartheid gold was getting out to the market. The chances of keeping the shipments hidden from airline and airport workers, van drivers, bank clerks, etc., would be very slim. Any amateur sleuth could easily find out which country was importing the gold. The operation would be so large that the Swiss government would have to be a party to the program. The South African gold trade is an important but very tiny part of world or even Swiss financial activity. The chances of the Swiss government sacrificing its position in the international gold trade to defend apartheid cannot be high. And, as has been stated earlier, the earnings in the gold market would not be affected by a ban on South African imports.

Appendix 4

As Table 1 shows, eight countries (the United States, West Germany, Switzerland, France, Italy, the Netherlands, Belgium, and Japan) and two international organizations (the IMF and the EMCF) hold 27,400 tons of gold, or 80% of the West's reserves, between them. This is equal to 40 years' production from South African mines. Accordingly there should be two "strings" to the sanction: firstly, a measured disposal of part of the national reserves, and, secondly, pressure on these major hoarders to cease their purchases and join the program. In particular, those nations with very little or no gold to sell could seek "swap" sales by countries with a proportionately large holding. India, for instance, with reserves only sufficient to cover seven years' fabrication if new South African gold is excluded, could use its regional importance to press Japan and Taiwan to adjust its policies.

In the last few years the gold price has been propped up by purchases from just two countries, Japan and Taiwan. Although both these countries are very friendly towards South Africa, the first being South Africa's top trading partner and the second being its top new investor, neither country chose to buy the hundreds of tons of gold they have purchased in the last three years directly from South Africa. The purchases were made in the US in a cynical attempt to make both countries' massive positive balance of payments with the US look smaller. These purchases nevertheless helped to increase the price of gold tremendously for a short period just when South Africa needed a high gold price because of its debt crisis. Both buyers have lost a great deal of money with the recent fall of the gold price.

Table 1
Gold Reserves and Consumption

	Reserves, December 1985			Consumption, 1981-1985		
Country	*Million oz.*	*Value ($ million) at $440/oz.*	*Metric Tons*	*Fabrication (tons)*	*Years' Supply*	*Years SA Supply*
US	262.65	105,060	8,169.3	162.22	50.36	92
IMF[1]	103.40	41,360	3,216.1	xx	xx	xx
Germany	95.18	38,072	2,960.4	58.84	50.31	92
EMCF[2]	85.71	34,284	2,665.9	xx	xx	xx
Switzerland	83.28	33,312	2,590.3	26.54	97.60	179
France	81.85	32,740	2,545.8	12.02	211.80	388
Italy	66.67	26,668	2,073.7	196.0	010.58	19
Netherland	43.94	17,476	1,366.7	4.12	331.72	608
Belgium	34.18	13,672	1,063.1	1.46	728.16	1,334
Japan	24.23	9,692	753.6	102.02	7.39	14
Top 10	881.09	352,436	27,404.9	563.22	48.7	89
Austria	21.14	8,456	657.5	4.481	46.77	269
Portugal	20.23	8,092	629.2	2.402	62.18	480
Canada	20.11	8,044	625.5	45.86	13.64	25
UK	19.03	7,612	591.9	29.52	20.43	37
Spain	14.65	5,860	455.7	12.02	37.91	69
Taiwan	12.70	5,080	395.0	17.98	21.97	40
Venezuela	11.46	4,584	356.4	(2.18)	(163.51)	(300)
India	9.40	3,760	292.4	72.04	4.06	7
Lebanon	9.22	3,688	286.8	1.48	193.77	355
Australia	7.93	3,172	246.7	5.40	45.79	84
BIS[3]	6.69	2,676	208.1	xx	xx	xx
Sweden	6.07	2,428	188.8	1.36	138.32	254
Algeria	5.58	2,232	173.6	2.72	65.98	121
South Africa	4.84	1,936	150.5	82.32	1.83	3
Saudi Arabia	4.60	1,840	143.1	35.72	4.01	7
Argentine	4.37	1,748	135.9	(11.88)	(11.44)	(21)
Greece	4.12	1,648	128.1	8.04	15.94	29
Turkey	3.86	1,544	120.1	13.70	8.76	16
Romania	3.82[a]	1,528[a]	118.8[a]	n/a	n/a	n/a
Libya	3.60	1,440	112.0	1.44	77.76	142
Indonesia	3.10	1,240	96.4	22.60	4.27	8

Brazil	3.10	1,240	96.4	3.92	24.60	45
Uruguay	2.62	1,048	81.5	n/a	n/a	n/a
Kuwait	2.54	1,016	79.0	19.60	4.03	7
Thailand	2.49	996	77.4	5.82	13.31	24
Egypt	2.43	972	75.6	28.30	2.67	5
Mexico	2.36	944	73.4	16.32	4.50	8
Malaysia	2.34	936	72.8	6.62	10.99	20
Hungary	2.33	932	72.5	n/a	n/a	n/a
Peru	1.95	730	60.7	1.14	53.20	97
Finland	1.91	764	59.4	0.78	76.16	140
Pakistan	1.90	760	59.1	10.20	8.75	16
Yugoslavia	1.86	744	57.9	8.50	6.81	12
Colombia	1.84	736	57.2	0.82	69.79	128
Denmark	1.63	652	50.7	0.34	149.11	273
Chile	1.53	612	47.6	(0.40)	(118.97)	(218)
Phillipines	1.48	592	46.0	2.02	22.79	42
Norway	1.18	472	36.7	0.20	183.51	336

Note

a. Figures for Romania are doubtful, although given by IMF.

Sources: (1) International Monetary Fund; (2) European Monetary Cooperation Fund; (3) Bank for International Settlements

SANCTIONS AND FINANCING SOUTH AFRICA'S FOREIGN TRADE

John E. Lind and David J. Koistinen

The financing of the import of capital goods is crucial to the maintenance of the South African economy because South Africa produces for export primary products like gold and coal while importing finished goods and the machinery which it needs to keep its mines and industry running.

In September 1987, the governor of the South African Reserve Bank outlined an optimistic scenario for South African growth which required, among other measures, "an increased use by South African importers and exporters of foreign trade and suppliers' credits. . . ." Since there is general agreement concerning the importance of trade credits, this chapter tries to answer in quantitative terms the question: How great would be the damage to the South African economy if all foreign trade finance were cut off?

First, the total amount of trade finance is estimated from the total trade volume, assuming that no general purpose lending is available. The results vary from $5 billion to $8 billion for 1985 to $7 billion to $11 billion for 1987. These numbers are found to be roughly consonant with the foreign debt figures of South Africa, after the trade finance was extracted from the total South

African foreign debt. This extraction was permitted by the currency distribution of the South African debt since 80% of the South African imports are in currencies other than U.S. dollars. That is, the payment of South African imports is usually in the currency of the exporting country. In contrast, 80% of South African exports are denominated in U.S. dollars, but these exports require only a relatively small outstanding amount of trade finance. This knowledge plus two further assumptions permit a rather far reaching analysis of trade finance. These assumptions are: (1) that South African government guarantees for foreign debt primarily cover the debt of the government and parastatal corporations, and (2) that the guarantees of a foreign country are primarily for debt denominated in the currency of that foreign country.

Finally, after knowing the amount of trade finance needed to finance South Africa's foreign trade, the question is: could South Africa easily cover this amount by its present reserves and other foreign assets? At best, the sum of all these assets would be roughly equal to the lower estimates of the necessary trade finance. Thus if all the major trading partners of South Africa, especially the U.K., U.S., Germany, and Japan, were to cut off trade credits together at one time, South Africa would face a major liquidity crisis comparable to the September 1985 banking crisis, but one much more difficult to circumvent. In 1985 the amount of debt was greater, but within a few days, trade credits were exempt from the moratorium, permitting trade to proceed but at a lower volume. Thus it was the trade credits that ameliorated the 1985 crisis and permitted trade to continue.

Part I. Trade Finance: The Volume Required

What Trade Finance Is and How It Works

Trade credits are used to finance almost all international sales of goods. Bulky goods are shipped over long distances, taking from a week to over a month to arrive in the port of destination. Raw materials and semifinished materials such as steel are further manufactured, and imported finished goods must be distributed. The cost of the goods during the transport must be borne by some one, and the cost of the goods during further processing and/or distribution may also be included in this trade finance.

Finally, when a large installation or plant is being built, long term financing is needed until the plant begins to earn revenue. This may include financing to the supplier of goods since there are large production costs which may not be covered by current revenue. Major capital projects typically require finance extending for 5 to 10 years.

When South Africa had a good credit rating in the first half of the 1980s, trade finance for capital projects could often be raised through general purpose borrowing on the capital markets of London, Frankfurt, and Zurich. That is, bonds were issued and large loans from syndicates were available.

Now capital purchases must be financed by trade credits tied to the specific items being purchased. For example, in 1987, the official German export promotion bank Kreditanstalt fuer Wiederaufbau provided a credit of DM33 million ($18 million) for a telephone system for the South African Post and Telecommunications Administration.[1]

In the discussion below, the rather broad time ranges for the terms of trade finance reflect the variations in trade financing arrangements. Some trade credits only cover the period of transport. Others include financing for manufacturing before shipment and some include finance for manufacturing and/or distribution after shipment. The latter processes may be refinanced locally instead of being part of the trade finance. If the export promotion banks in the OECD countries stop guaranteeing trade credits for exports to South Africa, banks and suppliers will be less willing to give generous terms, and local financing will become essential. The choice of the type of trade finance depends on various factors including differences between domestic and international interest rates.

The length of term of trade credits varies according to the type of merchandise being sold. Standard items are:

A. Consumables, small manufactured items, spare parts, raw materials, farm products: 30 to 180 days
B. Industrial and agricultural equipment, general aviation aircraft: 180 days to five years

C. Industrial plants, commercial jet aircraft, locomotives: 5 to 10 years.[2]

Trade finance can be provided by the supplier or by the buyer directly involved in a transaction, or these parties can bring in a bank to play an intermediary role.

Suppliers' and buyer credits are the most straightforward examples of trade credits. For a supplier's credit, an exporter provides the finance—shipping the product and collecting payment with interest from the buyer at a later date. This time lag allows for transport halfway across the globe in the case of South Africa and gives the buyer an opportunity to assemble the payment money. Sales on open account are a commonly used form of supplier's credit. Here a firm, typically a large corporation, ships goods to a subsidiary or a regular customer and receives payment at a later date. In the case of a buyer's credit, the purchaser obtains the credit and pays the shipper directly.

Banks may participate in supplier's or buyer's credits by lending a firm the funds which allow it to provide suppliers or buyers credits through a credit facility. Banks can also purchase at a discount the paper held by firms which have provided suppliers credits. This practice is known as *forfaiting*.

Banks play a direct role in other types of trade lending through letters of credit, revolving credit facilities and other mechanisms. Under such arrangements, a bank pays the exporter at the time the goods are shipped and later collects payment from the purchaser, in addition to a fee for its services. Banks in the importing and/or exporting country can take a role in such a transaction.

The Role of Government Trade Promotion Agencies

Most industrialized countries have government agencies that promote foreign trade by facilitating trade finance. The structure of these programs varies from country to country. Some agencies primarily insure privately arranged trade credits against losses arising from political turbulence and commercial risks. Most countries offer both insurance and actual trade finance. Table 1 provides a lists of these agencies for South Africa's major trade partners.

Table 1
Government agencies providing guarantees and/or credits for trade of the major trade partners of South Africa

Agency	*Service*
United Kingdom	
Export Credit Guarantee Department (ECGD)	Guarantees only
Federal Republic of Germany	
Hermes Kreditversicherunge	Guarantees
Treuarbeit	Guarantees
Kreditanstalt für Wiederaufbau	Credit
AKA-Ausfuhrkredit (Private)	Credit
Japan	
Export-Import Bank	Credit (Guarantees)
Ministry of International Trade and Industry (MITI)	Guarantees
United States	
Export-Import Bank	Permitted to grant credit or guarantees for South Africa only under very special circumstances

Since capital goods exports require risky financing arrangements with years-long terms, the trade promotion agencies in most countries concentrate on insuring these kinds of sales. Agencies do assist in the export of consumer goods as well as imports that are crucial industrial inputs.

The most important role trade promotion agencies play in regard to South Africa is promoting exports by domestic producers of capital goods. Except for the mining industry, state owned authorities and corporations in South Africa dominate the basic industrial sectors which account for much of the bulk of the country's imports of capital goods. Thus trade promotion agencies in the industrialized countries which facilitate trade finance with South Africa are almost always dealing directly with an agency of the South African government.

The Volume of Outstanding Trade Credits for South Africa

Estimated from Trade Data This calculation is of the basic finance needed to maintain trade at the 1985 level, assuming that trade credits were used for this finance rather than the general purpose borrowing which was common up through much of that year. Thus the estimate is made for the type of credits which are now in use since the time when the debt moratorium was called in September 1985. The general level will be similar to that required for 1986 and subsequent years. A breakdown of South Africa's overall trade by country and major commodity is given in Tables 2 and 3.

Table 2
South African exports by country of destination for 1985

South African Exports to	*Gold (US$ million)*	*Total (US$ million)*
Germany	76	1,006
United Kingdom	2,122	3,420
Switzerland	3,194	3,264
United States	1	2,239
Japan	221	1,852
Italy	1,235	1,842
France	16	644
Other OECD		1,441
Other		671
Total	6,864	16,573

Table 3
South African imports by source for 1985.
Machinery represents SITC 7.[3]

South African Imports from	*Machinery (US$ million)*	*Total (US$ million)*
Germany	1,133	1,690
United Kingdom	622	1,279
United States	573	1,232
Japan	695	1,020
Italy	196	330
France	212	389
Other OECD	661	1,260
Other	296	3,155
Total	4,190	10,356

For most countries the volume of new trade finance will roughly equal the total of imports plus exports. However, gold sales make up roughly 45% of annual South African exports, and we assume that sales of gold do not require normal trade finance.

South African mining companies sell their gold to the South African Reserve Bank (SARB). The SARB probably pays the companies in rand at the time of delivery or very soon thereafter. The SARB sells about 80% of the metal to dealers on the London and Zurich gold markets and most of the remainder to wholesalers in Italy, who resell it to jewelry manufacturers.

Sales by the SARB to the huge financial institutions that control the London and Zurich markets probably take place as follows: gold is flown to the European centers and immediately credited to the SARB's gold bullion account. At the time of sale, the metal is debited from the gold account and the amount of the sale minus a commission is credited to the SARB's currency account. Since payment is immediate, no trade credits are needed. Since the Reserve Bank chooses to sell about 20% of its gold to Italy when it could easily sell all the metal in London and

Zurich, it seems likely that the Bank had similar arrangements for immediate payment with Italian institutions as well.

With no foreign currency credit needed for gold sales, the total amount of trade finance used by South Africa in a year is assumed to be roughly equal to the sum of imports and non-gold exports. In 1985, South African imports totalled $10.5 billion and non-gold exports were equal to $9.3 billion.[4] Thus trade credits for 1985 should equal about $19.8 billion.

The length of these trade credits determines the total credits outstanding at a given moment. Total outstandings, rather than total trade credits allocated in the course of a year, are the crucial figures. The outstanding amount of credit, which is constantly coming due and being reissued, represents the amount of finance needed to keep the foreign trade sector of the South African economy running.

To estimate outstandings, South Africa's foreign trade in 1985 was broken down by major commodity groups and assigned trade credits varying in length according to the guidelines in the *International Finance Handbook*, noted above, and after conferring with a banker involved with trade finance.

Food products and most raw materials were given credit terms of 30 to 60 days. Light consumer goods such as clothing and stereos and intermediate goods such as steel and auto components were assigned terms of 90 to 180 days. Agricultural and industrial machinery were assigned terms of 180 to 360 days. And installations of heavy industrial plants were given terms of five years.

The sum of these categories of trade credits (30 to 60 days, 90 to 180 days, 180 to 360 days, and five years) are added together. This total is then divided by the number of times a credit of this length would roll over in a year. Thus a credit of 30 days would expire and be granted for another transaction 12 times in the course of a year, and a credit of 60 days six times. Hence, the $7.78 billion of South African exports assigned 30 to 60 day credits is divided by 6 to 12 to give a range of $648 million to $1.30 billion for the amount of these credits outstanding.

In the case of credits greater than a year in length, the $558 million in trade that falls under this category is multiplied by the factor needed to keep the amount of outstandings constant. That is a steady state condition with new loans replacing previous ones as they are paid up. For five-year credits the factor is 3 and for seven-year credits 4. This gives total long-term outstandings of $1.67 to $2.23 billion.[5]

This estimation method gives a range of outstanding credits needed to finance all of South Africa's trade of $4.99 billion to $8.31 billion for 1985. South Africa primarily exports raw materials and basic industrial inputs which were assigned 30- to 60-day terms in the above scheme. Its imports, by contrast, include a variety of industrial goods which have trade credits with longer terms. As a result, the outstanding trade credits of $3.41 billion to $5.65 billion needed to finance imports is about three times greater than the $1.02 to $2.05 billion in outstandings needed to finance exports. All these results are scaled to trade figures for 1985 and 1986 and they are summarized in Table 4.

The exporting country provides trade finance in most cases of international sales. Where credit is provided as part of a sales transaction, the exporter or the exporter's bank usually receive delayed payment for goods after they have been shipped.

Since South African imports require about three times the outstanding trade finance as the country's exports, and since the exporting countries generally provide trade finance, it is logical to expect that foreign countries provide about three quarters of the credit needed to finance South Africa's foreign trade while South Africa only provides about one quarter.

Medium- and Long-Term Credits Estimated from Capital Investment Data

The total annual imports of capital goods, requiring medium and long term financing, will now be estimated from entirely different source data in order to provide a better evaluation of the possible error in the figure of $558 million for 1985 estimated above from trade data. Here the starting point will be figures of total investment in machinery and equipment by the South African economy as a whole.

Table 4
Estimates of the trade credits necessary to finance South Africa's credits outstanding in billions of U.S. dollars

	1985		*1986*	
	Trade	*Estimated Financing*	*Trade*	*Estimated Financing*
South Africa Exports (excluding gold)	9.3	ST 1.3-2.1	11.0	ST 1.5-2.5
Imports	10.5	ST 2.0-4.0	10.5	ST 2.1-4.2
		LT 1.7-2.2		LT 1.8-2.4
Total (excluding gold)	19.9	ST 3.3-6.1	22.3	ST 3.6-6.7
		LT 1.7-2.2		LT 1.8-2.4
TOTAL		5.0-8.3		5.5-9.1

Legend
ST: Short-term credits of less than one year.

LT: Medium- and long-term credits of one year or greater. Outstandings of credits with a term of five years represent about three times the annual new lending if in each year the new lending equals the amount of credits paid off.

As can be seen from Table 5, these investment figures lie between $5.1 billion and $5.5 billion for 1985 and 1986, of which between 25% and 30% is investment by public corporations. What fraction of this investment is in foreign purchased machinery and equipment? An estimate of this fraction is only available to us for the Electricity Supply Commission (ESKOM), but it is fortunately the largest public corporation. First ESKOM's investment in machinery and equipment is estimated from that of all public corporations as proportional to their gross investment and is found to be $1.21 billion for 1986. Eskom's foreign borrowing in 1986 was $164 million or 14% of this total investment in machinery and equipment. This borrowing was presumably all through trade credits, since the moratorium had already been called, and thus it represents the type of financing that concerns us now. A figure for the total purchases of foreign machinery and equipment of $693 million is obtained by assuming that this 14% applies to the economy as a whole.

Table 5
South African capital investment in billions of U.S. dollars

Investment in Machines and Equipment	*1985*	*1986*
All sectors[1]	5.45	5.11
Public corporations[1]	2.02	1.73
ESKOM—estimate[2]	1.59	1.21

Sources:

1. South African Reserve Bank, *Quarterly Bulletin.*
2. Calculated by scaling from the Public Corporations on the basis of Gross Investment in billions of dollars:

	1985	1986
Public Corporations[1]	2.72	2.32
ESKOM[3]	2.15	1.62

3. ESKOM Prospekt, *Boersen Zeitung,* 23 December 1987

This figure of $693 million is 25% higher than the figure of $558 million calculated from the trade data. The $693 million could be high because of ESKOM's relatively high capital intensity compared to other sectors of the economy. On the other hand, the ESKOM borrowing of $164 million in 1986 may be low because of carry over from the large amount of borrowing in 1985. Nonetheless, the agreement is quite good considering the different bases of two estimates.

Consistency of the Estimate of Short-Term Credits

The suggestion given above that the South African exports may be primarily financed by South Africa and that imports requiring short-term financing are financed through foreign trade credits can be checked for consistency against the known assets and liabilities of South Africa.

In order to cover their exports, the South African private and banking sector would need short-term assets abroad greater than the required export trade finance of $1 billion to $2 billion. Short-term claims of the South African bank sector on foreign banks were $1.04 billion at the end of 1985 and rose to $1.76 billion by mid-1987.[6] Short-term claims abroad of the non-bank private sector of South Africa were $1.2 billion at the end of 1985.[7] The sum of the bank and private sectors is $2.2 billion for the end of 1985. This amount would just permit the $1 to 2 billion in export financing since part of the non-bank assets represent deposits of individuals abroad that are not available for trade finance.

Certainly there are not sufficient assets in the private bank and non-bank sectors to permit financing the short term imports without using general purpose medium- and long-term assets and borrowings.

Part II. Foreign Debt and Financing Since the Moratorium

Total Debt

The sectors of the foreign creditors of South Africa's foreign debt are shown in Table VI for the end of 1985 and 1986. The total debt decreased during 1986 for several reasons. During this period $0.5 billion was repaid on the $10 billion of the debt which was under a standstill agreement with the foreign banks. This standstill agreement was precipitated by a moratorium on payments declared by South Africa in September 1985 and it has been extended until mid-1990.

Payments were made on bonds and no new issues were floated because of the credit conditions caused by the moratorium. However, the figures in Table 6 seem to belie this, since the amount of outstanding bonds increased in dollar amounts in 1986 when no new bonds were issued. Indeed, bonds falling due during the year were paid off, so the debt should have decreased. This contradiction is explained by the fact that half of the bonds are denominated in Deutsche Marks and they appreciated by 27% against the US dollar during the year. Thus if no bonds were redeemed during the year, the value of the outstanding bonds as expressed in dollars should have appreciated by 13% just because half of them are in Deutsche Marks. The increase would be even greater because other bonds are in Swiss francs and other currencies which have also appreciated relative to the dollar.

Payments were also made on the portion of the debt guaranteed by foreign governments and on recent trade credits. However, Table 6 shows an increase in non-bank credits. Here again the Table reflects an appreciation of foreign currencies of the major trading partners of South Africa relative to the dollar. In reality there has been a slight decrease of this lending.

The following analysis will take up each of these areas of credit in detail and we will want to know whether funds have flowed into or out of South Africa by sector of the creditors and by sector of the borrowers. The only way these flows can be calculated is if the currency distribution of the debt is known, for otherwise currency appreciations can not be distinguished from money flows. Table 7 shows this currency distribution in the debt as a whole and by borrowing sector of the South African economy. The latter is deduced from South African government guarantees of debt by currency, which cover all debt of public authorities and public corporations, like ESKOM, as well as some general trade credits.

When looking at the bank and private sector, the interbank lending can be immediately separated out because it is almost all in U.S. dollars. This contention is supported by the following facts. First, almost all of the interbank debt is under the standstill agreement, so no new lending is likely to have occurred since September 1985. Then when this debt is expressed in dollars it has decreased roughly at the rate of the specified repayment schedule. If the interbank debt were denominated in other currencies, it would have increased greatly in dollar terms under the standstill because of the appreciation of these currencies relative to the dollar. The latter has not been the case, and thus the interbank debt is in dollars.

Table 6
Foreign debt of South Africa in billions of U.S. dollars by source

	End 1985		*End 1986*	
	Total	*OECD Country Guarantees*[a]	*Total*	*OECD Country Guarantees*[a]
Foreign Banks[b]	17.459	1.996	16.126	1.802
BIS reporting countries[c]	17.003		15.618	
Remaining OECD countries[d]	0.456		0.508	
Non-bank lenders including official credit agencies[e]	2.69	1.076	2.881	1.357
Bonds[f]	2.91		3.118	
IMF	0.851		0.468	
Total	23.473[g]	3.172	22.593[g]	3.159

Notes

a. Amounts guaranteed by instrumentalities of the governments of the OECD member countries including credits given by official financing agencies. See notes d and e.

b. The sums of the BIS and OECD data are essentially identical to the IMF data that are reported by the individual debtor countries in *International Financial Statistics* as the sum of "Cross-Border Interbank Liabilities by Residence of Borrowing Bank" and "Cross-Border Bank Credit to Nonbanks by Residence of Borrowers." The IMF sums are $17.47 billion and $16.12 billion for 1985 and 1986, respectively.

c. *Maturity Distribution of International Bank Lending,* Bank for International Settlements (BIS), consolidated accounts of banks in Austria, Belgium, Canada, Denmark, Federal Republic of Germany, Finland, France, Ireland, Italy, Japan, Luxembourg, Netherlands,

Norway, Spain, Sweden, Switzerland, United Kingdom, United States, and major off-shore centers. Further analysis using central bank data yields the following estimates of bank debt in billions of U.S. dollars for the end of 1986: UK, 3.6; US 3.0; Germany 1.9; Switzerland 1.7; France 2.0; Japan 1.6; others 2.4.

d. *Statistics on External Indebtedness: Bank and Trade-Related Non-Bank External Claims on Individual Borrowing Countries and Territories* BIS/OECD, includes BIS reporting area plus claims guaranteed by the governments of Australia, Greece, New Zealand, and Portugal.

e. The total amount of non-bank claims is obtained by difference from the total debt reported by South Africa and all debt that can be allocated by categories. The total amount of non-bank debt given in this table is thus the upper bound for non-bank debt because it represents the remainder and thus the accumulation of errors. The guaranteed portion, from ref. d, includes insured suppliers' credits and credits extended by official export financing institutions.

f. 1986: South African Reserve Bank quoted by *Financial Mail* (supplement), 9 October 1987. 1985: Scaled from 1986 using the list of bonds in J. E. Lind and D. V. Espaldon, *South Africa's Debt at the Time of Crisis* (Caniccor, 1986), Appendix B. Early DM bond issues were assumed to have been called to reduce the outstanding to the 1986 level. The increase in the dollar amount of the bonds between 1985 and 1986 is purely a reflection of the appreciation of the Deutsche Mark in which half the bonds are denominated.

g. South African Reserve Bank, *Quarterly Bulletin*, March 1988.

At the end of 1986 the interbank debt of South African banks amounted to $7.2 billion according to the Bank for International Settlements (BIS).[8] Thus the remaining $8.0 billion, made up of the remaining $3.0 billion of debt in dollars plus $5.0 billion in various other currencies, is the debt of the South African private non-bank sector. The final principle in the following analysis is the fact that the governments of the various OECD member countries, prefer to provide guarantees and trade loans in their own currencies, and in a few cases only deal in their own currency. This fact will assist in separating guaranteed credits from those without guarantees.

Table 7
South African external debt at the end of 1986 by currency and sector of the debtor economy (in US$ billion)

Currency	*Total*	*Public Sector*		*Bank & Private Sectors*
		Bonds	*Public Authorities & Corporations*	
US$	13.5	0.53	2.73	10.2
DM	3.1	1.6	0.2	1.3
UK L	1.2	0.2	0.0	1.0
Swfr	1.7	0.74	0.1	0.8
Frfr	1.0	0.0	0.7	0.4
Japan Y	0.58	0.0	0.41	0.18
Other	1.5	0.2	0.0	1.3
Total	22.6	3.3	4.1	15.2

Sources: *Total debt by currency*: South African Reserve Bank quoted in ESKOM *Prospekt* in the *Boersen Zeitung* (Frankfurt), 23 December 1987; *Bonds*: Bonds are almost entirely public sector financing, for either public authorities or public corporations (see note d in Table 6); *Public Authorities and Public Corporations*: Total debt guaranteed by the South African government, *Government Gazette,* No. 10930, p. 13, 25 September 1987, for 31 March 1987, less bonds.

Total Debt to Foreign Banks

At the end of 1986, the total debt to foreign banks was $16.1 billion, of which $7.2 billion was the debt of South African banks. It should be remembered that this interbank debt was the principal cause of the debt moratorium of 1985, because South African banks had been borrowing excessively in the short term interbank market to finance long term capital lending in South Africa. When this short term debt began to be withdrawn, the resulting liquidity crisis forced the calling of the moratorium.

The portion of these debts that represents trade credits is impossible to ascertain. This is so because what in times of good credit ratings is a general purpose loan becomes, in times of poor credit ratings, trade finance linked to specific trade transaction. However, some information is available on bank trade credits which are insured by government of the OECD member nations, and that is described below.

Insured Bank Credits

The bank credits for trade that are insured by OECD member countries dropped from $2.0 billion at the end of 1985 to about $1.8 billion by mid-1986 and has remained at that level through mid-1987. Unlike interbank lending, which is primarily in US dollars, trade credits tend to be denominated in the local currencies of the country exporting to South Africa. Only two countries provide public data on these guaranteed bank trade credits.

The US does not now generally provide insurance, and has only $0.358 million of a $5.1 million Export-Import Bank guarantee to run off the books.[9]

The only other country that reports insured bank credits is the UK, and they have remained relatively constant, between $0.87 billion and $0.81 billion in dollar terms, since mid-1985. These UK insured bank trade credits made up about 45% of the total OECD-insured bank credits in mid-1987. If all the pounds sterling exposure of banks in the UK is in trade credits rather than general lending to South Africa, then these guaranteed credits are essentially all in pounds sterling. Thus total UK guarantees since mid-1985, expressed in pounds sterling, would have decreased by 30% rather than remaining roughly constant, as they appear in dollar terms.

Mid-1985 is close to the imposition of the moratorium on the South African external debt in September 1985; thus we see a declining trend in the lending of pounds sterling since the moratorium's imposition. This trend is masked by the conversion to a depreciating dollar. The yen and the Deutsche Mark have appreciated with respect to the dollar even more than the pound. Thus it can be said with reasonable certainty that bank credit guarantees have continued to drop throughout the period between mid-1985 and mid-1987 when expressed in the currencies in which these credits are denominated. The total decrease in these currencies between mid-1985 and mid-1987 is at least as great as the 30% that is given by the pound sterling figures for that period.

In the case of Japan, we can assume that insured banks credits are almost zero. First, most trade credits that are guaranteed by Japan are made in the form of official financing of the Export-Import Bank rather than as insured credits of the Ministry of International Trade and Industry (MITI) and the Export-Import Bank. Thus guaranteed bank trade credits are not common. Secondly, it is the lending in yen that is likely to be under Japanese guarantees and two-thirds of it is to the South African public sector. Since Japan has a policy that banks should not make loans to the South African government, this two-thirds should not be guaranteed bank credits.[10] As a result of the weight of these arguments, we assign a value of zero to the Japanese guaranteed bank credits.

What do these various currency figures mean in terms of the amount of goods delivered on the docks in South Africa? Initially, some of the local currency prices are locked in through contracts. However, some exporters in countries whose currencies have appreciated will cut prices to stay competitive with dollar denominated goods in the hope that exchange rates are experiencing only a short fluctuation. These exporters can not maintain these price cuts over a longer time frame because the price cuts reduce exporters' profit margins significantly. Thus in the medium term the graphs of appreciated currencies will somewhat undervalue the amount of physical exports and the graphs of depreciated currencies will tend to overvalued physical exports, leaving the amounts of physical exports lying somewhere between the two. In the long term, the assumption that prices are fixed in the domestic currency of the exporter is probably more accurate.

Non-Bank Credits

Non-bank credits are the other major source of credits now available to South Africa. These include private suppliers' credits and both supplier and buyer credits from government credit agencies like the Japanese Export-Import Bank and the German trade finance agency, Kreditanstalt für Wiederaufbau. The $2.881

billion in non-bank credits at the end of 1986 in Table 6 is estimated by subtracting from the total debt of $22.593 billion the sum of the debt to the foreign banks, the bond holders and the IMF. Since all errors in the various data accumulate in this difference of $2.881 billion, it is not highly accurate.

This non-bank credit appears to rise in Table 6 from $2.25 billion at the end of 1985 to $2.88 billion at the end of 1986, with the OECD member-country-guaranteed-portion rising from $1.08 billion to $1.36 billion. Thus there appears to be an increase of both the total and the insured portion between the end of 1985 and 1986. However, these increases are attributable to currency exchange rate changes as shown below.

Figure 1 shows the insured portion rising rapidly after the debt standstill in late 1985. By converting this debt into various currencies and setting the vertical currency scales on the right hand side of the figure to coincide at the mid-1985 data point, figure 1 shows that if all the guaranteed debt were in Deutsche Marks, there would have been a general decline in the amount of this guaranteed Deutsche Mark debt. Assuming a fixed price for goods in each currency, this means a decrease in the physical amount of goods exported to South Africa with OECD guaranteed financing. If the exports were in pounds or yen, the amount oscillates and is only very slightly higher in mid-1987 than in mid-1985.

The amount of German exports financed by non-bank institutions is plotted in Deutsche Marks at the bottom of figure 1. They amount to about 20% of the total OECD member country guaranteed non-bank credits, assuming that the German data refer mostly to guaranteed credits. The German credits remain relatively constant throughout the time period when expressed in Deutsche Marks, but they would show a spurious increase since 1985 if they were expressed in dollars.

Estimates of the amount of non-bank credits and guarantees in all the various currencies must be made before we can see if the amount of goods delivered has increased or decreased over time. Table 8 gives our estimates with an explanation in the notes to the table. The UK portion of the non-bank credits is roughly estimated at $250 million at the end of 1986, while the largest contributor is Japan with $580 million or 43% of the total as suppliers' credits.

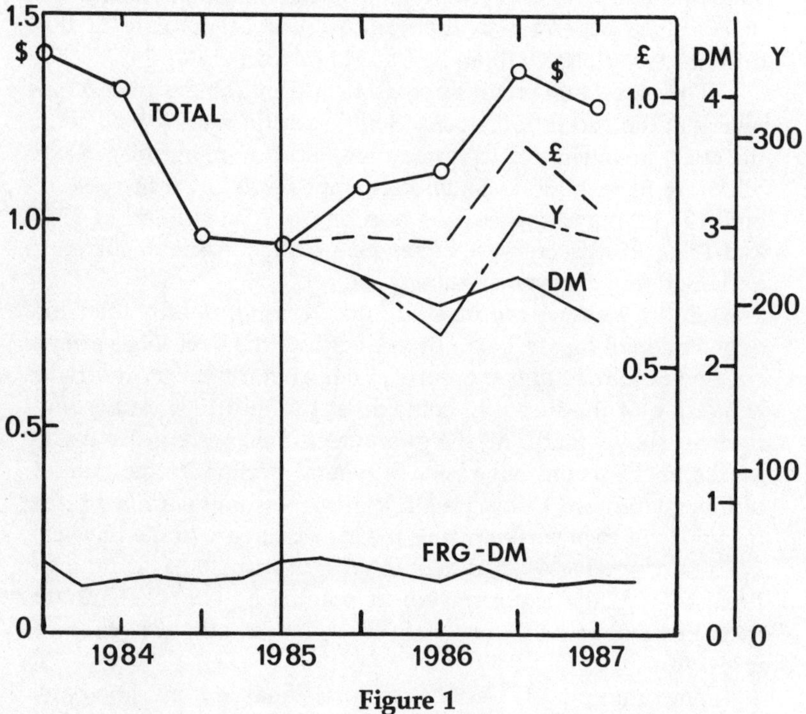

Figure 1

Non-bank credits guaranteed by the member countries of the OECD. Suppliers' credits and credits of official export financing institutions in billions.

Total non-bank insured credits, expressed in US dollars, are taken from reference 2 in Table 6. Scales on the vertical axes for other currencies are set so that they coincide for mid-1985 just before the moratorium. It is thus evident that much of the increase in the insured and guaranteed credits expressed in dollars results from the falling value of the dollar, since these credits remain more or less constant.

Non-bank credits of the Federal Republic of Germany, insurance not specified, are expressed in Deutsche Marks from Table 11c of the *Statistische Beihefte zu den Monatsberichten der Deutschen Bundesbank*, Series 3, *Zahlungsbilanzstatistik*.

Table 8
Insured credits to South Africa by OECD member countries at the end of 1986, by type of creditor and currency exclusive of dollars, expressed in billions of US dollars

Currency	*Total*[a]		*Insured Credits, OECD*[b]	
		Without Bonds	*Bank*	*Non-Bank*
DM	3.1	1.5		0.21
UK L	1.2	1.0	0.75	0.25
Swfr	1.7	0.9		0.0
Frfr	1.0	1.0		0.16
Japan Y	0.58	0.58	0.00	0.58
Other	1.5	1.4		1.36
Total	9.1	6.5	1.80	1.36

Notes

a. See Table 6 for sources.

b. See Table 6, footnote b for source.

DM: Non-bank credits, Table llc, *Statische Beihefte zu den Monatsberichten der Deutschen Bundesbank*, Series 3.

L: See notes to Figure 1 for bank guarantees. Total guarantees are estimated for the end of 1985 from the ECGD-reported amount for all Africa. This amount is scaled by the percent of African trade with South Africa and yields about $1.2 billion for guaranteed suppliers' credits to South Africa. Only $1.0 billion is available in pounds sterling and $0.75 billion is already allocated to bank credits, as explained in the note to Figure 1. This leaves $0.25 billion for non-bank credits. These must be insured suppliers' credits since the UK does not directly provide buyer's credits through a government export bank.

Swfr: Switzerland has little trade with South Africa other than imports of South African gold on account. Therefore non-bank credits are minimal.

Frfr: Non-bank credits in Frfr and "other" currencies are obtained between the total insured amount of $1.36 billion and the estimated credits in DM, L, Swfr, and Y. The remainder is apportioned between francs and "others."

Y: When the outstandings of export credits of The Export-Import Bank of Japan for Africa, given in its annual report for 1985, are scaled by the percentage of African trade with South Africa, the cover for South African suppliers' credits is 30% of the total for Africa, or $0.52 billion. Unfortunately, the 1986 annual report mixes suppliers' and buyers' credits, so that the suppliers' credits cannot be isolated. Within the accuracy of this estimate, the total yen exposure of $0.58 billion is probably insured. Buyers' credits are probably not provided, at least for the $0.40 billion of lending to public corporations shown in Table 7 because of the prohibition by Japan on lending to the South African government. Thus we assume that all the Japanese non-bank credits are suppliers' credits.

Other: Non-bank amount apportioned by difference from the total as in the case of Frfr.

By using the currency distribution at the end of 1986 and assuming that the distribution remains relatively constant over time, the value of the non-bank guarantees and credits at the end of 1986 can be calculated back to mid-1985 through the exchange rates. The result shows that there was no change in the amount of each currency and that the variation in the dollar amounts in Figure 1 is all a result of the exchange rate variation between mid-1985 and the end of 1986. Some decrease then occurs in 1987. If the value of goods is constant in a given currency, this result means that there was no change in the amounts of goods covered from mid-1985 until the end of 1986.

Looking at the total non-bank credits, both insured and uninsured over the year 1986, the total increased in dollar terms from $2.25 billion to $2.88 billion, a 28% increase. However, to determine the real change in the amount of goods delivered, a currency distribution must be obtained for all non-bank credits. Such a distribution is estimated by scaling the machinery exports for OECD member countries from 1985 to 1986 by the ratio of the total exports in those two years and by scaling the $2.88 billion of non-bank credits using these estimates of machinery exports in 1986. The results are listed in Table 9. The distribution of currencies of the exporting countries in the remaining debt is sufficient to cover all these exports in domestic currencies except for the UK where $0.15 billion in US dollars would be required. Using this currency distribution, the $2.88 billion at the end of 1986 would have represented only $2.45 billion worth of currencies a year earlier. Since non-bank trade credit at that time was only $2.25 billion, there was a real increase in non-bank trade credits during 1986 of 8%, assuming that prices remained constant in each currency.

Summary of Foreign Credits

The analysis given above provides a general picture of the South African exposure of foreign banks and non-banks which is outlined in Table 9. If exposure to South African banks is omitted, foreign banks have provided credits of $8.94 billion to the public and private sectors of South Africa at the end of 1986. Non-banks, that is other businesses and official financing agencies, have provided $2.88 billion. Having now analyzed non-bank creditors, further insight can now be gained on the banking sector.

Subtracting all the currencies in the bond and non-bank distribution of the total debt leaves $3.2 billion in various currencies other than dollars (DM 0.6, Swfr 0.6, Frfr 0.8 and other currencies 1.0, all expressed in billions of dollars). These amounts more than adequately cover the unallocated $0.97 billion of guaranteed bank credits not yet accounted for, leaving another $2.2 billion in bank credits which are not guaranteed.

Thus known trade credits amount to $2.88 billion of non-bank credits and $1.80 billion of guaranteed bank credits, totalling $4.68 billion. Of the remaining $7.14 billion of foreign bank credits to the South African non-bank sector, $2.2 billion are not denominated in dollars and are thus more likely to be directly associated with trade. This analysis suggests that outstanding trade credits are about $6.9 billion. This amount is just above the upper bound estimated in Part I for South African import credits in 1986.

Table 9
Total credits (in $US billion) of foreign banks and non-banks in South Africa, 31 December 1986

Country	*Total*	*Banks*		*Non-Banks*		
		Total without Inter-bank	OECD *Govern-ment Guaran-teed*	*Total*[a]	OECD *Govern-ment Guaran-teed*	*Est. Tot. Exp.*
UK	3.62	2.32	0.83	0.4	0.25	4.0
US	2.96	1.06	0.0	0.4[b]	0.0	3.4
Germany	1.87	1.45		0.9	0.21	2.8
Switzerland	1.68			0.1	0.0	1.8
France	2.03			0.2	0.16	2.2
Japan	1.56		0.0	0.6	0.58	2.1
Others	2.41			0.4	0.16	2.8
Total	16.13	8.94	1.80	2.88	1.36	19.1

Notes

Without Interbank: Total bank exposure less interbank lending.

OECD Government Guarantees: Guarantees by governments of OECD member countries given separately for bank and non-bank credits. The latter includes credits by government trade finance agencies.

a. Very rough estimates by scaling the total of $2.8 billion by the machinery exports of each country for 1986. The 1986 values were obtained by scaling the 1985 OECD statistics for machinery to 1986 by total exports for each year.

b. US data for non-bank credits are given as $50 million in Table CM-IV-5 of the *Treasury Bulletin*, Department of the Treasury. However, claims on subsidiaries are not included and thus it is a lower bound.

Known Lending Since the Moratorium

The one sector of the South African economy which is known to have received foreign funds since the moratorium has been the public sector, both public authorities and public corporations.

Hearsay evidence suggests that Swiss and/or German banks lent about $400 million in early 1986 to the public authorities for oil purchases to restock their reserves at a time when the price of oil started dropping rapidly. Since oil is sold in US dollars, these loans were presumably in dollars. When we look at the Bundesbank statistics, an assumption must be made about the currencies in which the South African lending is made in order to permit the calculation of the money flows. Only the figure for banks in the UK is available, and it show that 80% of British bank exposure is in US dollars. Using this same percentage for the German banks, a flow from German banks to South Africa of about $130 million can be seen in the first half of 1986 and this is primarily in the first quarter. This inflow to the South African public sector is against the background of a much larger outflow from South African banks to the German banks. While this calculation is not very accurate, it suggests that the larger portion of these oil loans may be Swiss.

ESKOM, a public corporation, reported $164 million (R371 million) in foreign loans in 1986, and projected a total of $465 million (R929 million) for 1987. The Reserve Bank already reports a net inflow of $340 million to public corporations in the first half of 1987. Where is this money coming from, and can these flows be seen from the side of the supplying banks and other institutions?

First, some of it is generated internally within South Africa. When a South African debtor pays off its foreign currency debt which is under the standstill agreement, the money is deposited with the Public Investment Commission (PIC). If these funds are not needed at that time for payments under the agreement, they will be lent out (reinvested) with South Africa in the public sector. Some of these funds are also being directly acquired by ESKOM. Thus the standstill agreement is providing a pool of foreign funds for the government.

Secondly, export credits are still available from all the major trading partners. Only the US has cut off government guarantees and lending, but private sector trade credits are permitted. As Larry Harper, ESKOM's general manager of finance, stated, "If we place orders overseas using credit lines with overseas institutions we can still fund at least 85% of our import requirements ....

There has been no indication that that sort of finance will be withdrawn."[11]

The exposure of UK banks in the South African public sector has been rising continuously since the end of 1985, especially in the first half of 1987. Using the fact that 80% of UK bank lending to South Africa is in dollars, the flow to the South African public sector in the first half of 1986 would be about $160 million while that in the first half of 1987 would be about $170 million. In the latter case the flow is almost completely compensated by a decrease in unused commitments which suggests that the flow was a result of a draw down on an already committed loan or loans. German bank data suggest a net flow into the South African non-bank sector, including the public sector, of about $40 million in the second quarter of 1987. Remember these flows are net flows or flow into South Africa minus any repayments of existing loans. Thus the actual inflows are larger and have probably risen even more in the second half of 1987.

Three credits for a total of DM 32.8 million are known to have been accorded to the South African Post and Telecommunications Administration in 1987 for financing telephone offices by the German reconstruction bank, the Kreditanstalt fuer Wiederaufbau (KfW).[12] The *Frankfurter Rundschau* in January 1988 had reported that these credits were for ESKOM, but the German Embassy stated that this report was incorrect.[13]

Note that a DM200 million bond issue was floated in December 1987 for ESKOM with a registration date of 1 April 1985. The lead managers were Dresdner and Commerzbank. ESKOM received the funds in 1985 from the underwriters, so the issue does not represent an inflow of funds in 1987.

Part III. The Effect of Cutting off Trade Credits

Dr. Gerhard de Kock, Governor of the South African Reserve Bank, in his "optimistic scenario" for 1988 foresaw the possibility of a 4% growth in the South African economy.[14] This scenario required among other measures "an increased use by South African importers and exporters of foreign trade and suppliers' credits with a consequent improvement in the capital account of balance of payments." The question for this chapter to answer is, Just what effect would the cutting off of trade credits have on the South African economy?

Because many of the present trade credits are in the form of suppliers' credits, such a ban on trade credits would most easily be enforced by each of South Africa's trading partners requiring a proof of payment for each item as it is shipped into or out of their country.

The Economy

The average growth rate of the South African economy during the 1980s has been very low. The best linear fit of the growth of the gross domestic product between 1980 and 1986, inclusive, is 0.88% per year according to Nedbank.[15] In seeking answers as to why the growth rate has been so low, Nedbank enumerates several constraints on the economy. Among these constraints are the "low ebb of entrepreneurial confidence" and "the completion of major infrastructural programmes of the parastatal corporations." The latter point highlights that this small growth has been led by the capital spending of the parastatals like ESKOM. In fact, de Kock in his abovementioned address states that an essential requirement for a take-off of economy in 1988 is a "distinct revival in real fixed and inventory investment" and that a growth rate of 4% can be achieved only if there is a marked increase in the total spending in capital outlays on plant, equipment, and construction.

As was explained in Part I of this chapter, the essential machinery involved in capital outlays must be purchased abroad, and thus financing for these purchases is crucial to the implementation of this plan of economic growth. The lack of sufficient capital outlays is in part the result of the low ebb of entrepreneurial confidence arising from the political problems in South African and from the imposition of sanctions from abroad.

This lack of confidence is exemplified in the IMF figures for errors and omissions in the South African balance of payments figures. The errors and omissions are an indication of unreported capital flight under circumstances like the imposition of US sanctions in the last quarter of 1986. Indeed, in that quarter, the IMF's *International Financial Statistics* reports that errors and omissions were over $1 billion, signifying massive capital flight. Note that the South African Reserve Bank tried to explain this $1 billion outflow as a shift from external to domestic financing of foreign trade by their usual combining of reported short term capital flows with errors and omissions. Thus if sanctions continue to be scaled upward and/or if the political scene continues to worsen, the entrepreneurial confidence will continue to ebb even with funds available from the present positive flow of funds in the balance on current account.

ESKOM's present expansion plans are a transparent use by the government of a parastatal to prime the economic pump through capital investment with hope that the ripple effect will raise the entrepreneurial confidence and create more investment. ESKOM's expansion, with five new power stations under construction, is based upon the premise of a 7% annual increase in the demand for electricity in a country whose central bank governor's most optimistic hope is for a 4% growth rate and whose average real growth has been under 1% for the past seven years.

The financing for capital equipment for these power stations is coming from prior commitments, new suppliers' credits of foreign banks, some suppliers' credits from foreign government export agencies, and foreign funds locked in by the standstill agreement.[16] The prohibition of trade credits by South Africa's major trading partners (US, Germany, UK, and Japan) would exclude most of the sources and force South Africa to depend upon those funds locked in by the standstill agreement. However, these funds all become due in mid-1990, along with $1.1 billion of bonds coming due that year, making the use of these locked in funds very perilous. South Africa is obviously hoping that the economic and political situation will be sufficiently good that these debts can be rolled over at that time. Otherwise, there will be a crisis like the one of September 1985.

Sanctions Against Trade Credits

How much liquidity does South Africa have if trade credits ceased being granted by foreign banks, corporations, and government agencies in the major exporting countries to South Africa? Certainly the overborrowing of the South African banks up until the moratorium in 1985 was prompted by the very high domestic South African interest rates and relatively low international capital market interest rates. This fact suggests that as much trade finance as possible was sought abroad at that time. Foreign dollar and domestic rand interest rates did not begin to converge until late 1986 and early 1987. There have been no large outflows of recorded short term capital since the beginning of 1986 which would suggest, as the Reserve Bank erroneously proposed for the fourth quarter of 1986, that there has been a major shift toward domestic finance of trade since the moratorium.

Thus even if South Africa were providing the $1.8 billion to $2.9 billion of its own export finance in 1987, imports required about $2.7 billion to $5.3 billion of short term outstandings. Annually new medium and long term funding of $0.7 billion to $0.9 billion was required and any cut-off of trade credits would require raising this amount plus an equal amount to pay off long term debt from previous years that is coming due. (Long term outstandings would climb to $2.1 billion to $2.8 billion over five years.) Thus the total bill for imports in the first year after all trade credits were cut off, assuming no other sources of credit, would be $4.1 billion to $7.1 billion. In the succeeding years the amount of new money would be reduced to the amount of medium and long term funds for capital imports and service on the previous debt. However, the economy would be saddled with large amounts of foreign exchange tied up in trade finance and not otherwise available.

The primary effect of the cutting off of trade credits is the sharp impact of raising $4 billion to $7 billion in foreign exchange in the year the sanctions are enforced with most of that capital being necessary in the first three to six months. This assumes that all major trading partners act at the same time and the effect is reduced proportionally if they do not.

As of 30 September 1987, the South African Reserve Bank held foreign assets of $3.70 billion of which $2.61 billion was in gold reserves. For these gold reserves to be utilized, they would need to be swapped for foreign currencies. These reserves are building up partly to keep an oversupply of gold off the market in order to maintain a stable price. The banking system held foreign assets of another $0.96 billion. Finally foreign deposits by non-banks were $1.75 billion. These assets represent the main sources of foreign exchange that can be quickly tapped. The Reserve Bank and banking system assets of $4.66 billion are most accessible while the foreign deposits include individual accounts which have no relation to imports and are thus inaccessible for these purposes. Comparing these numbers with the $4 billion to $7 billion required to finance the trade indicates that South Africa would face a financial crisis if trade credits were cut off by its major trading partners, for South Africa could barely cover the needs at the lower estimate of the trade finance by liquidating almost all of its foreign reserves.

Notes

1. Letter, Embassy of Federal Republic of Germany to authors, 21 March 1988.

2. Abraham M. George and Ian H. Giddy, *International Finance Handbook* (New York, Wiley Interscience, 1983).

3. SITC 7 refers to the Standard International Trade Classification (Revision 2) for machinery and transport equipment.

4. The statistic is drawn from various issues of the *Quarterly Bulletin* of the South African Reserve Bank.

5. Details of these estimates are given in the original monograph of the same title published in March 1988 by CANICCOR Research, P.O. Box 6819, San Francisco, California 94101.

6. *International Financial Statistics* (IMF).

7. *Quarterly Bulletin*, South African Reserve Bank.

8. *Maturity Distribution of International Lending* (Basel, Bank for International Settlement), December 1987.

9. *Contingent Foreign Liabilities of the U.S. Government* (U.S. Department of Treasury), 30 June 1987.

10. *Japan Times*, 19 December 1986.

11. *Financial Mail* (supplement), 24 July 1987.

12. Letter, Embassy of Federal Republic of Germany, 21 March 1988.

13. *Frankfurter Rundschau*, 23 January 1988.

14. Address of 18 September 1987, reprinted in *Quarterly Bulletin* (South African Reserve Bank), September 1987.

15. Nedbank *Guide to the Economy* (November 1987).

16. When a South African debtor pays off any of its debt which is under the standstill agreement, it is normally paid into the Public Investment Commission (PIC). This agency pays any portion of the principal that is due under the agreement. This amount is slightly under 5% per year. The remaining amount is then reinvested with PIC paying an extra 1% interest to the original lender. This reinvestment is a relending of foreign funds, primarily to South African government agencies and parastatal corporations. Technically all remaining principal is due on 30 June 1990.

SANCTIONS AND SOUTH AFRICA: AN ANALYSIS OF SOUTH AFRICA'S STRATEGIC MINERAL EXPORTS

Sanford Wright

Sanctions and South Africa's Strategic Minerals

Several of the minerals that South Africa exports to the Western Countries are considered to be strategic, leading many people to conclude that the West is consequently vulnerable to South Africa. When President Reagan issued his Executive Order on 9 September 1985 to implement sanctions against South Africa, South African President P. W. Botha reacted to these sanctions by threatening to implement his own sanctions—centered around an embargo of strategic mineral exports—against Western countries. He stated, "My message to the United States and the British Commonwealth is that by digging a hole for South Africa they could end up harming themselves. If South Africa were to withhold its chrome exports, one million Americans would lose their jobs, and the motor industry in Europe would be brought to a standstill."[1]

This threat was immediately given credibility by various parties. Rep. Don Fuqua (D-Fla.), chairman of the House Science and Technology Committee, argued that Botha's threat should be taken seriously since a cutoff of chromium could have serious economic consequences for the United States. Sudden and prolonged loss of supplies could hurt the auto industry in particular, he said, and perhaps cost jobs.[2]

This position, which may be termed the "resource denial theory," is also presented from the additional perspective that the Soviet Union, in collusion with socialist governments in southern Africa, would deny these minerals to the West. This argument has been put forth by the South African government in an attempt to discredit its opposition, particularly the liberation forces. This position gained additional support recently when Jonas Savimbi, head of the UNITA guerrilla force that is using South African and United States' support in an attempt to overthrow the Angolan government, visited Washington in February 1986. Reacting to the warm reception by President Reagan and administration officials, Savimbi declared, "If you lose Angola to communism you lose southern Africa. By losing southern Africa, you lose access to strategic minerals that are critical to your economy."[3]

The four minerals considered to be strategic are chromium, vanadium, manganese, and the platinum group metals. The first three are considered to be strategic as a result of their role in the manufacture of steel, and platinum is considered to be strategic because of its use as a catalytic agent.

Recent research has clearly demonstrated that the level of United States' imports from South Africa is more of a convenience than a dependence, since various alternatives to South Africa's exports are available.[4] Western European countries and Japan would be more affected than the United States by a South African cutoff, since their level of South African imports is higher. However, Europe's automobile industry would not be brought to a halt, as the alternatives available to the United States are also available to Europe.[5] The probability of South Africa stopping its exports is very remote, as the various available alternatives, including substitution, alternate supply sources, and recycling industries would permanently diminish the need for South Africa exports.

Congressman Dellums (D-CA) has introduced new legislation that will strengthen sanctions against South Africa. A major section of this bill bans all imports from South Africa

> except for any strategic mineral with respect to which the President certifies to the Congress that the quantities of such mineral which are essential for military uses exceed reasonable secure domestic supplies and that substitutes for such minerals are not available.[6]

The Comprehensive Anti-Apartheid Act of 1986 required a report to Congress on the extent to which the United States is dependent on the importation from South Africa of the four minerals mentioned. This report, which was released in September 1987, highly overstated U.S. dependence on these minerals from South Africa. For example, the report stated that:

> For purposes of this report, dependence is defined as the percentage of U.S. consumption of a given commodity supplied by South Africa. Factors other than production, import levels, and consumption were not considered. Alternative sources of supply from other producers for materials such as chromium and manganese were not taken into account. Possibilities of substitution, inventory changes, variations in trade patterns and effects of price changes were also not considered in preparing this report.[7]

This article's comparative analysis of the major Western countries' reliance on South Africa's strategic mineral exports will utilize 1986 data in order to assess the credibility of South Africa's threats and to assist in the development of current sanctions legislation.

The Research Data

Research on South African exports of strategic minerals is very difficult, since Pretoria refuses to disclose the necessary data and many minerals are retraded among the user countries, making their origins difficult to trace. Several countries that import these minerals refuse to identify their source, which is very likely to be South Africa. In addition, the minerals are divided into various subunits according to such factors as the grade of ore and their processing into ferroalloys. However, data from various reliable sources—the U.S. Bureau of Mines, the Japan Tariff Association, and the European Community—have been utilized to construct tables 1-4.

Analysis and Discussion

The four tables together demonstrate that Japan is more reliant upon South Africa's exports than either the European Community countries or the United States. However, reliance does not mean dependence, as the following analysis will demonstrate.

Table 1 indicates that Western countries have a high reliance upon South Africa's chromium exports. Within the European economic community, Britain is a major importer of South African chromium. However, Britain has a large stockpile of strategic minerals, and it has been reported that the U.K. is disposing of some of these minerals, including chromium.[8]

South Africa accounted for one-third of the world's chromite production in 1986;[9] data for the world's ferrochromium production are unavailable. However, vast chromium reserves exist in other countries, particularly in Zimbabwe, Brazil, India, Turkey, and Albania. In 1986 these four countries produced 3,380,000 short tons of chromite, which would be equivalent to eighty-eight percent of South Africa's productions of 3,840,000 short tons.[10] A cutoff of South African imports would be a stimulus for the development of domestic chromite resources and construction of ferrochromium processing capacity.

A recent U.S. Bureau of Mines study found that the National Defense Stockpile was adequate to meet U.S. demand until new supply sources could be developed, should total disruption of chromium from the Republic of South Africa and Zimbabwe occur.[11] The vast majority of chromium is used for decorative purposes, primarily on automobiles. If this practice were discontinued, then the need for chromium would be substantially diminished.

Table 1
1986 Chromium Imports by Country

Importing Country	*Chromium: Form and Total Imports*	*Imports from South Africa*	
		Amount	*Percent*
United States[a]	Chromite (Short Tons, s.t.) 488,203	340,892	69.8%
	Ferrochromium (s.t.) 348,443	214,084	61.4%
Japan[b]	Chromium (metric tons, m.t.) 670,625	379,867	56.7%
EEC[c]	Chromium Ores (tons) 792,697	312,662	39.4%
(secret countries)		138,572	
TOTALS		451,234	56.9%

Notes

a. Bureau of Mines, *Preprint from the 1986 Bureau of Mines Minerals Yearbook, Chromium,* 1987: Washington, D.C., Superintendent of Documents.
b. Japan Tariff Association, *Japan Exports & Imports, Commodity by Country,* 86.12, 1987: Toyko.
c. European Communities Statistical Office, *Analytical Tables of Foreign Trade: NIMEXE, Imports, Products by Countries, 1986,* 1987.

Table 2
1986 Platinum Imports

Importing	*Platinum*	*Imports from South Africa*	
		Amount	*Percent*
United States[a]	Platinum (Troy Ounces) 2,073,000	1,178,000	57.0%
Japan[b]	Platinum (grams) 31,043,682	17,762,155	57.2%

Notes

a. Bureau of Mines, *Preprint from the 1986 Bureau of Mines Minerals Yearbook, Platinum Group Metals,* 1987: Washington, D.C., Superintendent of Documents.

b. Japan Tariff Association, *Japan Exports & Imports, Commodity by Country,* 86.12, 1987: Toyko.

Under Title III of the Defense Production Act, the US Department of Defense began drafting a request for proposals for the purchase of high-purity chromium metal from superalloy scrap to stimulate domestic recycling of superalloys that contain chromium. Implementation and support of this proposal would greatly assist the development of the domestic recycling industry.

Table 2 presents data on platinum, which is the major metal of the six comprising the platinum-group metals (PGM). The second major metal is palladium. In 1986 the USSR and the Republic of South Africa accounted for ninety-five percent of world mine production of PGM with South Africa accounting for 46 percent of the world's platinum production.[12] Table 2 indicates that the United States and Japan are not highly dependent upon South Africa's platinum exports. Platinum is mined in the United States, but production figures are not known, as the mining companies refuse to disclose this data.

Production from the Stillwater complex in Montana is expected to begin in 1987, which will be a significant addition to current production.

The European Community data on platinum imports is incomplete and consequently it has not been included.

Table 3
1986 Manganese Imports by Country

Importing Country	*Manganese: Form and Total Imports*	*Imports from South Africa*	
		Amount	*Percent*
United States[a]	Manganese Ores (short tons, s.t.) 225,608	13,988	6.2%
	Ferromanganese & Silicomanga-nese (s.t.) 594,295	234,191	39.4%
Japan[b]	Manganese Ores (metric tons, m.t.) 1,287,496	724,406	56.3%
	Ferrouginous Manganese (m.t.) 519,355	293,558	56.5%
EEC[c]	Manganese Ores (tons) 2,690,292	575,484	21.4%
(secret countries)		358,528	
TOTALS		934,012	34.7%

Notes

a. Bureau of Mines, *Preprint from the 1986 Bureau of Mines Minerals Yearbook, Manganese,* 1987: Washington, D.C., Superintendent of Documents.

b. Japan Tariff Association, *Japan Exports & Imports, Commodity by Country, 86.12,* 1987: Toyko.

c. European Communities Statistical Office, *Analytical Tables of Foreign Trade: NIMEXE, Imports, Products by Countries, 1986,* 1987.

Platinum is virtually indestructable, and recycling industries of automobile catalytic converters have begun in the United States.

Industrial use of platinum and palladium is principally for automobile and petrochemical catalytic converters. A majority of platinum is used for non-essential purposes. For example, Japan uses over fifty percent of its platinum for jewelry, a practice that could be easily eliminated.

Platinum is being increasingly viewed as an investor commodity. Johnson Matthey PLC has estimated that investment demand in North America has grown from virtually zero in 1981 to perhaps 220,000 ounces in 1986.[13] The Isle of Man, near the United Kingdom, is marketing a one ounce platinum coin called the Noble, and it has been reported that several countries, including Canada, China, and Mexico were considering issuing platinum coins.[14]

Table 3 indicates that the Western countries have a low to medium level of reliance upon South Africa's manganese exports. South Africa accounted for 15 percent of world manganese ores production in 1986.[15] South Africa produced a large quantity of ferromanganese and silicomanganese; its percentages of world production of these alloys are not available.

Supplies of manganese ores are abundant, which resulted in downward pressure on prices in 1986. The seabed provides an additional source of manganese nodules, and studies are continuing to determine the economic feasibility of mining and processing these metals.

Table 4
1986 Vanadium Imports by Country

Importing Country	*Vanadium: Form and Total Imports*	*Imports from South Africa*	
		Amount	*Percent*
United States[a]	Ferrovanadium & Vanadium Pentoxide (pounds, lbs.) 2,942,570	1,275,226	43.3%
	Vanadium Bearing Materials Vanadium Pent. Content (lbs.) 7,188,764	4,312,056	60.0%
Japan[b]	Vanadium Ore (metric tons, m.t.) 68 670,625	68	100.0%
EEC[c]	n/a	n/a	

Notes

a. Bureau of Mines, *Mineral Industry Surveys, Vanadium In December 1986*, Division of Ferrous Metals, Washington, D.C., March, 1987: pp. 8 & 9.
b. Japan Tariff Association, *Japan Exports & Imports, Commodity by Country, 86.12*, 1987: Toyko.
c. n/a = data not available

The United States imports much of its manganese from Mexico, Brazil, and Gabon.

Table 4 indicates a high level of vanadium imports from South Africa. South Africa provided 46 percent of the world's vandium in 1985.[16] There was a continued downward pressure on vanadium in 1986, which forced major producers in Finland to close their plants because of unprofitability. Finland had supplied 85 percent of US vanadium imports in 1983.[17] The producers in Finland were rendered uncompetitive because of the low price of the rand. Prospective and past producers in North America and Oceania either delayed or shelved plans for new mines and extraction facilities.[18] The US ferrovanadium market was further complicated by the South African producers resuming shipments of the ferroalloy after a hiatus of seven years.

Conclusion

An international boycott of South Africa's strategic minerals would not severely harm the military or industrial capabilities of the Western countries. Short-term disruptions in supplies would expectedly result in higher prices. However, this temporary cost would be offset by the long-range benefits that would occur from the development of recycling industries, the development of substitution industries, and the development of domestic resources. In fact, it is difficult to understand why Western countries, the United States in particular, have allowed South African exports to be promoted at the expense of their own domestic production. Almost all of the uranium-vanadium mines in the Uraven Mineral Belt of western Colorado have been closed permanently or placed on standby as a result of the 1981-84 collapse of the domestic uranium ore market.[20] Domestic producers of these strategic minerals simply could not compete with South Africa's exports.

Western countries could simultaneously confront apartheid and assist Southern African development by replacing their imports of these minerals from South Africa with imports from other Southern African countries. For example, it would appear logical and prudent for Western countries to replace their Chromium imports from South Africa with those from Zimbabwe, which has sufficient chromium deposits to supply one-fourth of the world's requirements.

Failure to include a ban on strategic minerals as an integral part of a sanctions policy will help render the policy ineffective. As divestment policies and trade embargoes decrease the value of the rand, South Africa's mineral exports will become more internationally competitive, which will result in increased sales and increased government revenues; in addition, it will assist South Africa in developing a monopolistic position in international markets. A mandatory comprehensive sanctions policy that includes strategic minerals is the only way to break this cycle and to pressure the Botha regime.

Notes

1. *The Detroit Free Press,* 24 October 1985, p. 15A

2. "South Africa 'Toy' Draws Fire," *Chicago Tribune,* 24 October 1985, Section 1, p. 5.

3. George D. Moffett III, "U.S. Debates Support for Angolan Rebels vs. Broader African Policy," *Christian Science Monitor,* 11 February 1986, p. 6.

4. See Sanford Wright in George Shepherd and Ved Nanda, eds., *Human Rights and Third World Development,* Greenwood Press, 1985.

5. See Sanford Wright, "South Africa's Mineral Embargo Threat: Rhetoric and Reality," *TransAfrica Forum,* Spring 1986, pp. 55-62.

6. See H.R. 1580, 100th Congress, 1st Session, p. 2.

7. See *Report On South African Imports,* The Assistant Secretary of State, Bureau of Economic and Business Affairs, Department of State, Washington, D.C. 1987, p. 1.

8. *The Mineral Industry of the United Kingdom,* Reprint from the 1984 Bureau of Mines *Minerals Yearbook,* 1985: U.S. Government Printing Office, p. 1.

9. Bureau of Mines, *Preprint from the 1986 Bureau of Mines Minerals Yearbook, Chromium,* 1987: Washington, D.C., Superintendent of Documents, Table 16, p. 15.

10. Ibid., Table 15, p. 15.

11. U.S. Bureau of Mines, Division of Minerals Policy Analysis. *South Africa and Critical Materials.* BuMines OFR 76-86, July 1986.

12. Bureau of Mines, *Preprint from the 1986 Bureau of Mines Minerals Yearbook, Platinum-Group Metals,* 1987: Washington, D.C., Superintendent of Documents, Table 11, p. 12.

13. Ibid., p. 4.

14. M. Siconolfi, "With Platinum's Popularity Growing, Several Nations May Soon Issue Coins," *Wall Street Journal,* v. 208, No. 4, July 7, 1986, p. 22.

15. Bureau of Mines, *Preprint from the 1986 Bureau of Mines Minerals Yearbook, Manganese,* 1987: Washington, D.C., Superintendent of Documents, Table 9, p. 13.

16. Bureau of Mines, *Minerals Yearbook, 1985,* Vol. I, Metal and Minerals, "Vanadium," 1986: Washington, D.C., Superintendent of Documents, Table 10, p. 1025.

17. Bureau of Mines, *Preprint from the 1983 Bureau of Mines Yearbook; Vanadium,* 1984: Washington, D.C., Superintendent of Documents.

18. *Minerals Yearbook, 1985,* Vol. 1, op. cit., p. 1014.

19. Ibid., p. 1014.

20. Ibid., p. 1011.

THE FRONTLINE STATES AND SANCTIONS AGAINST SOUTH AFRICA*

Douglas Anglin

The emergence since 1985 of international sanctions against South Africa as a live political option confronted the Frontline States (FLS) with an agonizing dilemma. Politically and ideologically, all the Frontline States are fully committed to complete moral and material support for the liberation struggle inside South Africa. At the same time, they are compelled to weigh in the positive contribution to the common cause that their imposition of punitive sanctions on South Africa would make against the economic, military, and domestic political costs that they would thereby inevitably incur. Yet, the alternative strategy of seeking safety through non-participation in sanctions offered no guarantee of immunity from retribution. Indeed, Pretoria has already demonstrated both its ability and its eagerness to hold its black neighbors hostages as a deterrent against coercive action by

*The support of the Social Sciences and Humanities Research Council of Canada, in enabling me to undertake extensive visits to southern Africa in 1985, 1987, and 1988 is gratefully acknowledged.

the world community. How the Frontline States, individually and collectively, perceive their predicament and have responded to the challenge is the concern of this chapter.[1]

In policy terms, the sanctions debate in southern Africa has revolved around four analytically distinguishable but inextricably interrelated issues. These are the extent to which the Frontline States have been prepared:

1. To commit their diplomatic and other resources to the international campaign for comprehensive, mandatory, and effectively enforced sanctions;
2. To participate actively in meaningful economic measures against South Africa either as part of a coordinated international effort or, if need be, unilaterally;
3. To take pre-emptive action, on the basis of systematic contingency planning, to minimize the adverse consequences of sanctions and reduce FLS vulnerability to South African retaliation; and
4. To act energetically to counter South African stratagems for circumventing sanctions.

The international movement to mobilize world support for coercive measures against South Africa has had a long and checkered history. Sanctions have been central to the endless debates across the full range of South African-related issues. In addition to the challenge apartheid itself posed, Pretoria's earlier open underwriting of rebel Rhodesia during UDI, its continued belligerent occupation of Namibia, and its current purposeful destabilization of its black neighbors have all prompted appeals for punitive action. Since the early 1960s, when independent Africa first made its presence felt on the world stage, peremptory demands for comprehensive mandatory sanctions have been routine features at annual sessions of the UN General Assembly and other international bodies. Yet, despite much eloquent oratory and innumerable ritualistic resolutions, for years there was little progress to record, principally because of the stubborn opposition of South Africa's major trading partners.[2]

The first intimation of Western willingness to appear even slightly more responsive came in the aftermath of the Soweto massacre, with the adoption of a mandatory UN arms embargo in 1977. However, it was not until 1985, following the dramatic escalation in the scope and scale of state repression and popular resistance within South Africa, that the international community came to treat the economic sanctions option seriously. Despite desperate and devious rearguard maneuvering on the part of President Reagan and Prime Minister Thatcher, the Commonwealth, the American Congress, and somewhat timidly the European community[3] were each eventually driven to adopt a series of measures which, while differing in their range and impact, added up to a significant breakthrough. As the domestic crisis in South Africa deepened, sanctions acquired a currency and a credibility that even the most cautious and supine leader could no longer completely ignore.

The more favorable climate of international opinion on sanctions forced Pretoria's neighbors for the first time to face up realistically to the profound implications of even limited economic measures for their fragile political economies. Since the early 1980s, the fate of the Frontline States had been the subject of considerable concern in African and international forums, but little of substance had emerged from the protestations and promises it had generated.[4] Now, with sanctions on the political agenda and South Africa intensifying its cross-border incursions and other destabilization efforts, the prospect could no longer be ignored.

The first serious sounding of government opinion took place at a summit meeting of the Southern African Development Coordination Conference (SADCC) in Arusha in August 1985, when all six Frontline States as well as Lesotho came out firmly in support of full sanctions.[5] Since then, they have continued to add their voices and votes to the chorus of demands for immediate comprehensive mandatory sanctions. Nevertheless, the only politically relevant catalogue of measures has been the Nassau "programme of common action" enshrined in the Commonwealth Accord on Southern Africa of October 1985. This operational agenda provided, first, for an initial installment of nine "measures" intended for immediate adoption and modest enough that even Mrs. Thatcher could safely subscribe to them. The declaration also contained a second contingent list of eight additional and generally more significant items held in reserve for consideration in the likely event that the South African regime failed within six months to record "concrete progress" towards "dismantling apartheid and erecting the structures of democracy."[6] Responsibility for testing Pretoria's intentions in terms of five defined criteria was delegated to a review committee of seven heads of government, including two frontline leaders: President Kaunda of Zambia and Prime Minister Mugabe of Zimbabwe. The committee, in turn, assembled the Eminent Persons Group (EPG), which strove valiantly but unsuccessfully to persuade Pretoria to embark upon a meaningful dialogue with representative South African blacks.

The EPG was finally forced to concede failure when, in May 1986, the South African Defence Force (SADF) demonstrated its utter contempt for the Commonwealth good offices mission by launching simultaneous aerial assaults on three FLS capitals—Gaborone, Harare, and Lusaka—at a time Pretoria was supposedly negotiating in good faith.[7] When, therefore, the mini-summit met in London in August, members were quickly able to agree—with only Mrs. Thatcher dissenting—on full implementation of the Nassau package (augmented by three further measures). They also joined in appealing to the full Commonwealth and the wider international community to follow suit.[8] Accordingly, Robert Mugabe returned to Harare in an exuberant mood, pledging prompt Zimbabwean compliance, and urging other frontline states to join in the great crusade fully and fearlessly. It marked the peak of political commitment by southern African leaders to action on sanctions. Since then, the momentum among southern African states for early implementation of even partial sanctions has slowly slackened. For Zambia and Zimbabwe in particular, this meant an agonizing reappraisal of their obligations and options.

Shortly after the London meeting, the FLS leaders assembled in Luanda to reassess the situation. Kenneth Kaunda as chairman pleaded with his colleagues to endorse the Commonwealth list of sanctions. "Otherwise they are not worth the paper they are written on." The response was disappointing. By now, Botswana and Mozambique had calculated the likely economic and military costs of compliance, and had concluded that their countries simply could not sustain them. Accordingly, the summit had to content itself with a weak and ambiguous communique that merely "expressed satisfaction" with the decisions reached in London.[9] The position was further defined (and clarified) the following day at a meeting of SADCC heads of state. "Although individual SADCC members states may not themselves be in a position to impose sanctions," they declared:

> 1. SADCC member states' vulnerability should not be used as an excuse by others for not imposing sanctions; [and]
> 2. SADCC member states will do nothing to undermine the effectiveness of sanctions imposed on South Africa by the international community.[10]

Since then, modest measures have been taken to loosen ties with South Africa, but inevitably progress has been slow, despite the almost irresistible urge some leaders have felt to tempt fate by striking out boldly with some dramatic gesture of defiance. In appealing to the Commonwealth Conference in Vancouver to institute "*new* and *additional* measures" against South Africa, the Frontline States reported that, for their part, they

> continued to maintain a restrained stance against the apartheid regime. Some of them continue to have no economic relations whatever with the apartheid regime. Others are reducing theirs through the diversion of their exports and imports from the South African ports. More could have been done but for South Africa's policy of destabilization which has disrupted the alternative transport routes.[11]

They might legitimately have added that three of Mozambique's neighbors had already made major military investments in men and money to protect those outlets to the sea. Security of these routes remains an essential precondition for any further FLS action in confronting South Africa.[12]

Assumptions

The optimism that infected the sanctions movement in southern Africa as well as globally during the heady days following the resurgence in 1984 of popular resistance to apartheid within South Africa was grounded in three operational assumptions. These were:

1. That effective international pressure on Pretoria was now politically within the realm of possibility;
2. That as a result, the collapse of the apartheid regime could realistically be envisaged within the forseeable future; and
3. That the costs and consequences of full FLS participation in sanctions would not prove unjustifiably painful or protracted.

However, by late 1986, confidence in each of these pillars of FLS policy had begun to erode, necessitating a radical reassessment of sanctions strategy.

In the first place, international support for sanctions did not prove as solid or as assured as had been expected. Earlier, it had been confidently anticipated that, in the event the initial installment of sanctions turned out to be inadequate, prompt actions would be taken to stiffen them. Instead, the political problem now was not so much how to reinforce them but how to hold the line against the threat of retreat in the face of mounting "sanctions fatigue," especially among South Africa's principal trading partners. Their response to pressures to conform had ranged from halfheartedness to open defiance. Prime Minister Thatcher and President Reagan in particular wasted no opportunity to discredit sanctions in the hope of ultimately dismantling them. In the process, they rendered invaluable service to the Pretoria regime in bolstering its own massive public relations campaign to subvert sanctions—ironically, on the grounds that allegedly they had not worked. Consequently, the climate of support in important sections of Western opinion became steadily less receptive to the logic of sanctions. The use of economic sanctions is now commonly, though wrongly, perceived of as an obstacle to "peaceful negotiations" rather than as the last slim hope of coaxing Pretoria to the conference table and thereby minimizing the danger of an inevitable tragic descent into uncontrolled violence.

A second shift in outlook has been the gradual recognition that the final demise of apartheid is unlikely to be realized as soon as or as certainly as had appeared probable at the height of the turmoil in the townships. The widespread and unrestrained resort to state repression, the partial return of international business confidence (foreshadowed in the shockingly lenient agreement with the banks on foreign debt rescheduling), and the renewed evidence (most obviously in the May 1987 elections) of the blind determination of whites to cling to their undiluted power and privileges have all served to revise forecasts of the probable timescale for achieving fundamental change. Even the resistance movement within South Africa became reconciled to the need to plan for the long haul. The "Prague Spring" was clearly over. Liberation may still be visible on the horizon, but it is no longer wishfully assumed to be around the corner.[13]

Finally, the more the Frontline States analyzed the impact of sanctions on their own political economies, the more perilous their prospects appeared. To drive the lesson home, the South African government pointedly provided them with a sharp reminder of their acute vulnerability to retribution. Simultaneously with the action of the Commonwealth mini-summit in confirming the Nassau sanctions package, Pretoria imposed punitive restrictions on Zambian and Zimbabwean transit trade. The result was chaos at the Beitbridge border until South Africa—its point having been forcefully driven home—rescinded its sanctions three weeks later.[14] Nor was this painful experience the only worry to concern Kaunda and Mugabe. Both faced deteriorating domestic economies. In Zimbabwe, the first signs of the subsequent downturn were emerging, while in Zambia the situation was already truly desperate.[15] Yet, despite these discouraging developments, Harare and Lusaka pressed ahead with their contingency planning. The more formidable the challenge, the more urgent the need for exhaustive study of all the implications.

Contingency Planning

Indications that the world was headed into sanctions precipitated a sharp increase in interest—nationally, regionally, and internationally—in attempts to gauge their probable impact on South Africa's black neighbors. At the *national* level, five of the states most closely concerned took administrative action to assess the magnitude and character of the problems likely to be encountered, and to devise measures to cope with them. Zimbabwe, after some delay, appointed a cabinet committee and created a secretariat within the Ministry of Trade and Commerce to undertake its contingency planning.[16] It also drew upon the expertise and (cautionary) advice of the business community. Zimbabwe alone among SADCC members could boast a private sector sufficiently developed and organized to initiate detailed and carefully documented studies on an industry by industry basis. The Confederation of Zimbabwean Industry (CZI) did, in fact, furnish the government with the earliest and most exhaustive analyses of the likely costs of sanctions to the country.[17] Similarly, Zambia reactivated its long-standing Contingency Planning Organization first established in 1965 in response to UDI,[18] while Botswana designated the Administrative Secretary in the Office of the President to head a Contingency Planning Committee of officials. Similar arrangements were made in Mozambique. Even the recently installed military government in Lesotho—on the front line, but not a Frontline State—appointed a ministerial subcommittee whose activities led to the compilation of two important reports.[19]

At the *regional* level, the looming prospect of sanctions spurred a series of urgent consultations among SADCC members and especially the Frontline States concerning collective contingency planning exercises. For FLS leaders, sanctions strategy and related defensive measures had been recurrent concerns. Nevertheless, the South African assault on three of their capitals in May 1986 added immediacy to their deliberations and decisions making. Matters came to a head on 21 August 1986 at the Luanda summit, at which Kaunda and Mugabe pressed for early concerted action on the Nassau package. With Mozambique and Botswana effectively opting out of active participation and Angola and Tanzania only marginally involved, the detailed planning of contingency measures as well as decisions on the scope and timing of any sanctions contemplated were left to Lusaka and Harare to coordinate between themselves.[20] This they did in the course of frequent close consultations over the subsequent months.

The Frontline States did, however, resolve to seek the cooperation of other key African states, notably Kenya and Cape Verde, in connection with the attempt to ban air flights to and from South Africa.[21] Similarly, they set out to wean Zaire and Malawi away from active collaboration with UNITA dissidents in Angola and MNR bandits in Mozambique respectively. As a result, heads of state missions met with Presidents Mobutu and Banda to warn them, in the event of a final break with Pretoria, not to expect continued access to transit routes through Frontline States, on which they were currently heavily dependent. These not-so-gentle threats appear to have had the desired effect, at least in the case of Malawi. Banda, who is nothing if not a realist, got the message and agreed to cooperate in efforts to reopen his traditional rail outlets through Mozambique.[22] The Zairean response has been more problematical.[23] Despite these demarches, pending the availability of alternative routes bypassing South Africa, the Frontline States were in no position to act on their political instincts. Thus, in their Maputo Declaration of October 1986, they confined themselves to affirming their unwavering "solidarity with the oppressed peoples of Namibia and South Africa." There was no specific reference to joint action on sanctions, though the commitment to comprehensive and mandatory UN sanctions remained.[24]

In a sense, SADCC can rightly claim to have been actively engaged in contingency planning from the outset. Its charter Declaration in 1980 defined its "urgent task" as the necessity to "liberate our economies from their dependence on South Africa," and pinpointed the provision of adequate regional transport and communications links as "the key to the strategy." On the other hand, SADCC's ambitious Programme of Action has not been motivated by the prospect of imminent sanctions. Rather, it envisages a major restructuring of regional infrastructures to be undertaken over the medium term.[25] Nevertheless, faced with the possibility of a sudden closure of the southern routes, SADCC members at their Arusha meeting in August 1985 mandated a ministerial working group to devise a comprehensive contingency plan

> concentrating on upgrading and defending transport routes to the sea, maintaining oil and electricity supplies, securing external sources of finance and supply to replace trade with South Africa and finding alternative employment opportunities for migrant laborers in South Africa.[26]

However, when SADCC leaders came to consider the report in Luanda a year later, they opted instead for accelerating implementation of their existing Programme. Accordingly, the committee was disbanded. As the SADCC Chairman, Botswanan President Quett Masire, explained with a certain impatience,

> Some of our friends in the international community have been asking us whether we have a contingency plan to counteract the effects of sanctions and South Africa's retaliatory measures on our economies and how they can assist us. The SADCC Programme of Action constitutes a contingency plan. This programme comprises high priority projects whose implementation and effective operation and management will free our economies from the current state of dependence on, and vulnerability to South Africa.[27]

Clearly, SADCC members were anxious not to offer donors the opportunity to divert their interest and resources to specifically emergency projects at the expense of the organization's primary thrust. Only in the case of Lesotho was it accepted that special provisions would prove necessary. Here authorization was given to commission detailed studies.[28] Members did, however, pledge to "cooperate closely with each other to lessen the adverse impact of sanctions on their own economies," adding that, in this respect, they expected "the international community to render them maximum assistance."[29]

A third regional organization—the Preferential Trade Area for Eastern and Southern African States (PTA)—also sought to get into the act. In December 1986, its supreme Authority adopted a comprehensive Economic Sanctions Programme which, in substance, committed its Eastern African members to assist its Southern African members (or in PTA jargon, ASNSA—African States Neighboring South Africa) in their sanctions efforts and contingency planning endeavors.[30] Unlike SADCC, the emphasis in the PTA approach is on concrete emergency measures to "lessen the impact of possible South African counter-measures" on frontline states seeking to delink their economies from dependence on the South. The full range of possible policy options was the subject of a comprehensive consultants' report and detailed study by a special meeting of PTA Ministers of Trade, Transport and Finance prior to final approval at an extraordinary summit in Addis Ababa in May 1988.[31] A related proposal to provide military support to the Frontline States in the form of guards for strategic roads, railroads, airports and power plants has proved more contentious. As subsequently reformulated, it refers merely to the "implementation of appropriate measures by non-ASNSA PTA member states to assist the ASNSA in the protection of critical infrastructural facilities and installations within the framework of the decisions of the OAU."[32] Meanwhile, discussions on security support ar continuing (in secret).

The plight of the Frontline States, caught by history and geography between a vengeful Pretoria bent on defending apartheid privileges at all costs and the rising tide of world indignation, also grabbed the attention of international organizations, governments, and peoples far beyond the regional confines of the conflict. Although reactions were typically restricted to rhetoric and resolutions, there was some encouraging evidence of an increased willingness to respond with a greater measure of responsibility and realism. Admittedly, the OAU decision in July 1986 to appoint yet another watchdog committee on southern Africa did not inspire any great confidence.[33] On the other hand, the work of the Commonwealth's energetic Committee on Southern Africa in London did offer hope.[34] Similarly, although the Non-Aligned Movement, at its eighth summit in Harare in September 1986, dispatched a fresh galaxy of foreign ministers on a futile mission to pressure South Africa's major trading partners on sanctions, it also, in an attempt to appear more practical, launched an ambitious AFRICA Fund designed to "assist the Frontline States to enforce sanctions against South Africa and to cope with any retaliatory economic action by the racist regime."[35] In addition, a number of UN bodies embarked on contingency enterprises of varying utility.

Western governments, individually and collectively, were also hard at work on their sums. The consensus, based on these calculations, clearly indicated that any attempt at active FLS participation in sanctions would have calamitous domestic social consequences quite beyond the capacity of any of the states in the region to contain. Nor was an international rescue operation deemed feasible—logistically, financially, or even politically. As Mrs. Thatcher remarked pointedly to Prime Minister Mugabe at Nassau, "If you cut your own throat, don't expect me to provide a bandage." By the following year, London and Washington were even more anxious to deter the threatened disaster. Accordingly, they made it known in no uncertain terms that any frontline state acting precipitously must not look to the international community for salvation. These stern warnings were intended specifically for Kaunda and Mugabe as, by this time, they were the only leaders seriously contemplating taking the plunge.[36]

Zambia and Zimbabwe on the Brink

On their return from the Commonwealth mini-summit in London in August 1986, Kaunda and Mugabe clearly had every intention of grasping the sanctions nettle firmly. Mugabe, in particular, was uncompromising in his public comments. In warning his countrymen of the costs of the coming confrontations with South Africa, he declared defiantly,

> When an economic war has been declared against you, you do not go crawling to those who are waging the war against you. You must fight back, and all thought about luxury and comfort must go. We must just be determined to bear the burden our own way, to

> counteract the measures South Africa will impose against us. It is just like a war. Prepare for it.

He added that, if necessary, Zimbabweans would have to eat "*sadza* without *nyama*," that is maize meal porridge without meat. Kaunda, too, had long talked bravely of Zambians carrying copper wire bars to the coast on their heads.[37]

Although sanctions were accepted in principle, it was still necessary to coordinate actions with FLS colleagues, some of whom needed "a little more time." For this reason, Mugabe reported that "the timing was not yet fixed," though it "could very well be towards the end of the year." In the meantime, as an earnest of his sincerity, he announced his intention of abrogating the preferential trade treaty which had been renewed with Pretoria only a month earlier.[38]

What added to the mounting misgivings in Western capitals as well as among local businessmen was that, while Mugabe acknowledged the inevitability of swift South African reprisals militarily and economically, at the same time he appeared to minimize the gravity of the threat. In any economic encounter, he suggested, South Africa had more to lose than Zimbabwe. "We remit profits and dividends to South Africa annually—huge amounts. We remit pensions to South Africa. Of course, if this is an economic war, all those things will stop." Mugabe's scenario was not entirely fanciful. According to one analyst, Zimbabwe has "the ability to act against South Africa in a number of increasingly influential ways." Nor are other frontline states entirely defenseless. Clearly, Pretoria has "an important long-term economic interest in not retaliating within the region against sanctions imposed internationally." Yet, whether purely financial considerations would constitute adequate deterrents in the event of Zimbabwean sanctions was much more problematical. The harsh reality is that Pretoria is fully capable of crippling Zimbabwe's economy, whereas there is nothing Harare can do that would prove equally damaging.[39]

Despite the awesome risks involved, Kaunda and Mugabe remained deeply committed personally and politically to implementing Nassau. They could conceive of no moral alternative. During the balance of the year, reports of impending decisions percolated to the public almost monthly, precipitating fresh controversies. On at least three occasions, the two presidents marched their countries to the very brink of action but, having peered over the precipice, in the end drew back to await more propitious circumstances. On each occasion, they found themselves sadly isolated, domestically and internationally. At home, each encountered stubborn opposition within his own cabinet and party, and especially within the local business community. Abroad, governments and donor agencies continued to sound the alarm, particularly as Pretoria had already begun to turn the economic screw and was threatening to tighten it even further.

Most of the measures contained in the Nassau package posed no particular problem for either country.[40] A few, like the bans on government procurement in South Africa and contracts with South African companies, promised to be troublesome but not impossible to comply with. The two countries could survive even if the Anglo American Corporation in its many manifestations was denied a share of the government cake. Two of the items, however, presented major difficulties for which there were no easy or early solutions in sight. The first was the projected ban on the import of South African coke, low-sulphur coal, and specialist steels, on which Zimbabwe's strategic ferrochrome and engineering industries critically depended.[41] The second was the ban on air flights and overflights to and from the South.

Although initially the air ban constituted but one item in a catalog of measures, it quickly became the central if not the sole option on the political agenda. The singling out of this one sanction for almost exclusive attention in part reflected its operational complexities, but more importantly its perceived potential in delivering a salutary psychological shock to complacent white opinion. In the ensuing discussions on whether to abrogate the existing air service agreements, three concerns dominated debates in cabinet and caucus, especially in Zimbabwe. The first was the adverse impact the action might have on the morale of white Zimbabweans. For many of them, the existence of close air links with the South was psychologically reassuring; it represented a vital lifeline to safety in uncertain times. While the government was bound to deplore the mentality this revealed, it did accept that it constituted a reality that could not readily be ignored.

Secondly, there were the costs of cancellation to consider. At the time, Air Zimbabwe and South African Airways (SAA) operated a total of 42 direct flights a week between their two countries (compared to the eight weekly Zambia Airways/SAA flights between Lusaka and Johannesburg).[42] Moreover, the South Africa service accounted for fully 80% of Air Zimbabwe's regional passenger traffic, and was the only regional route to register a profit. Nevertheless, the dollar sums involved were not prohibitive. While in revenue terms, the airline stood to lose up to $20 million a year, the net loss would likely amount to less than $4 million.[43] The major problem the airline would face would be the restructuring required consequent upon the loss of such a substantial proportion of its passengers. In addition, the tourist trade would be hard hit.

Finally, there was the factor of effectiveness. If the sealing off of South African air space were to be meaningful three conditions needed to be met. These were:

1. That the air ban should apply to overflights in addition to direct flights, as Mugabe had insisted from the outset;[44]
2. That the closed air belt should stretch the full width of the continent (this implied the participation of Mozambique and Botswana); and
3. That countries to the North—notably Cape Verde, Kenya, Zaire and Cote d'Ivoire—should join in denying transit facilities to aircraft flying to or from South Africa.

Although a ban on air links with South Africa had been official OAU policy since 1963 and repeatedly reaffirmed since,[45] when Kaunda and Mugabe set out to enlist the active cooperation of the key countries concerned, their response was less than enthusiastic.

Cape Verde, which serves as a vital refueling stop for SAA planes skirting the bulge of West Africa, indicated a willingness to sever its South African connection—provided Zambia Airways and Air Zimbabwe made up the loss in landing fees and services by diverting their London flights through Sal airport. "We are for solidarity," President Pereira declared, "but not for suicidal solidarity."[46] Kenya, which provided transit services to many of the international airlines serving South Africa, was equally qualified in its response. It eventually undertook to bear the very considerable costs involved in closing Nairobi airport (and air space) to transit traffic but only if *all other* OAU members did likewise, a condition which the government was well aware was in no danger of being fulfilled.[47] The responses of Kinshasa and Abidjan—the other stopover points—were even less sympathetic.[48]

With respect to the Frontline States, the pleas of Mozambique and Botswana that they were unable to comply with an air ban were more critical, if more understandable, especially in the case of the former. Maputo argued persuasively that an air link with Johannesburg was the price it was compelled to pay to retain the services of South African technical teams at its ports, at the Cabora Bassa dam, and on the railroad. It might also have pointed out that the government was clearly in no position to police its air space which was regularly violated with impunity by South African Air Force aircraft on supply missions to MNR (Mozambique National Resistance) bandits. Botswana was similarly tied in with South Africa so closely that any severance of air services with Johannesburg was considered out of the question, politically and legally. Less reassuring, however, were the intimations that Gaborone anticipated profiting from any air ban instituted by its neighbors (though such a development would have been less subversive of sanctions than appeared at the time). Already, British Caledonian Airways was flying into the new Sir Seretse Khama International Airport (where there were convenient onward connections to Johannesburg), and negotiations were underway to attract Lufthansa and Sabena. Despite its FLS undertaking to "do nothing to undermine the effectiveness of sanctions imposed on South Africa," Botswana was reluctant to give a categorical assurance on this point when pressed by Zambia and Zimbabwe.[49]

Lack of support from other African governments failed to deter Kaunda and Mugabe from continuing to coordinate their plans to cut their air ties with South Africa. On 14 October 1986,

Mugabe persuaded a reluctant cabinet to impose a ban in a month's time, while Zambian spokesmen similarly promised action on sanctions "soon."[50] Although the November target date was missed, the two leaders continued to confer closely, notably in Lusaka on 21 December with their FLS colleagues and separately at Kariba on 30 December.[51] At the first of these meetings, Kaunda and Mugabe indicated their intention of instituting an air ban on New Year's Day, provided Botswana and Mozambique agreed not to take advantage of them by *increasing* the volume of their air traffic with South Africa. When Presidents Masire and Chissano pleaded for more time, Zambia and Zimbabwe felt they had no alternative but to delay their decision. Accordingly, Mugabe revised his New Year's broadcast at the last moment, and announced that the Commonwealth sanctions package

> will be implemented soon, but now obviously no longer at the end of December 1986 as earlier expected, because our [Contingency Planning] Task Force charged with the duty of coordinating various aspects and areas still needs a little more time to complete its task. I shall, as soon as this is done, announce the sanctions commencement date. In the meantime, may I ask you in all seriousness, to gear yourselves for the difficult times ahead of us.

He then added that, "as a member of the Commonwealth, Zimbabwe must be seen to be playing its own part in support of the struggle for liberation in both South Africa and Namibia."[52]

Although assurances continued to be given that sanctions were "coming, and coming soon," the promised announcement failed to materialize. Moreover, the emphasis in public statements shifted to "mobilizing international opinion and pressure."[53] Clearly, Mugabe found himself in an impossible position, caught between his own tough public posture and the harsh economic and political realities confronting the country. While the official explanation for the delay in introducing sanctions was still that they had been postponed "deliberately in order for us to consult with the other Frontline States because some of the sanctions require their cooperation,"[54] obviously other constraints also operated on the government. Particularly humiliating was the need to appeal to Pretoria in early December 1986 for 34,000 tons of petrol, diesel, and aviation fuel to ease the sudden shortage that hit the country as a result of the calculated hostility of the South African government. Not only did its MNR surrogates sabotage the Beira-Feruka oil pipeline and Beira's electricity supply, but it hurriedly recalled its locomotives and rolling stock on loan to the National Railway of Zimbabwe, thus crippling efforts to distribute existing supplies.[55] To compound Mugabe's troubles, Zambia's desperate economic plight, dramatized by the bloody food riots that swept the Copperbelt in December 1986, gravely weakened Kaunda's domestic position.[56]

What finally enabled Mugabe to climb down with some semblance of dignity was, more than anything else, the timely visit of Canadian Prime Minister Brian Mulroney in late January. His message, alluded to in public and expounded at length in private, was that no one in the West expected the Frontline States to commit national suicide. In this, he echoed the arguments of the British and the Americans who had seized every opportunity to hammer the point home. However, unlike them, Mulroney went on to insist that sanctions were first and foremost the responsibility of the wider international community. "The onus is on the industrialized countries who can afford the burden somewhat better," he declared, "to provide a greater degree of leadership than the Frontline States whose economies are relatively fragile and effectively subjugated [to] the economy of South Africa."[57] What made Mulroney's plea for restraint palatable and persuasive was the high personal regard in which he—in marked contrast to Reagan and Thatcher—was held in Harare.

Despite periodic assertions that implementation of the Nassau package had not been shelved but merely delayed pending completion of consultations, consideration of the question had effectively been erased from the active political agenda. It did experience a brief revival in late April 1987 when, following the South African commando raid on Livingstone, economic retaliation was one of the options Zambia entertained but quickly dismissed.[58] Finally, in July, Lusaka and Harare officially conceded that the search for agreement on an air ban had had to be abandoned for the time being. "It is quite clear," Kaunda confessed, "that sanctions on air links will not work."[59]

Although the air links issue had been their principal preoccupation, Kaunda and Mugabe did not overlook other possible actions outside the Nassau Accord. They were particularly impressed with the urgency of lessening their dangerous dependence on South Africa, which Pretoria had striven so hard and with such success to increase.[60] Accordingly, upon returning from London in August 1986, they set about alerting their respective business communities to the prospect of a sudden closure of the southern route as a consequence of sanctions, South African retaliation, or even African National Congress sabotage of the South African Railways. The clear message was that they should act swiftly to search out new routes, sources, and markets. "We have warned you enough," Kaunda told them in November. "There is not much time left before the explosion takes place in South Africa." Nevertheless, in the absence of material inducements to change, the appeals failed to make much of an impact.[61]

To set an example, in November 1986, Lusaka ordered its huge conglomerate, Zambia Consolidated Copper Mines (ZCCM) to cease shipping its copper through South African ports. The results were dramatic. Whereas in 1986 Port Elizabeth had handled up to half of Zambian copper exports, following the ban as much as 80% utilized Dar es Salaam, with the balance—an increasing proportion—being diverted to Beira.[62] It was an impressive achievement, but not one that Lusaka would find easy to repeat. In May 1987, confronted by a further disastrous downward spiralling of the economy and additional impossible demands from the International Monetary Fund (IMF), Kaunda took the drastic step of breaking with "big brother." This has severely circumscribed his capacity to cope with further sanctions. Moreover, when, as is inevitable, negotiations with the IMF resume, Zambia will again be under intense pressure not to disrupt the stability of regional trade relations.[63]

Meanwhile, Mugabe was feeling increasingly frustrated with his inability to implement meaningful sanctions, either unilaterally or in concert with others.[64] Zambia's success in cutting back on its use of South African rail and port facilities only added to his discomfort. Accordingly, on 21 July 1987, immediately upon his return from meeting Kaunda at Victoria Falls on the air ban issue, he secured cabinet agreement for the imposition of limited trade sanctions. Armed with this authority, the Minister of Trade and Commerce promptly added South Africa to the list of countries from which imports would no longer be approved, and so informed officials of the Confederation of Zimbabwe Industries and the Zimbabwe National Chamber of Commerce in an urgent private briefing. Within an hour, Pretoria had learned of the decision, and swiftly responded with a threat to cut off all trade with immediate effect. Confronted with this ominous ultimatum and the anxious representations of an alarmed business community, the cabinet reconvened in emergency session on 28 July. In the ensuing debate, divisions among members proved too great to resolve. This led Mugabe, then in Addis Ababa attending an OAU summit, to cut short his visit and rush home to deal with the crisis. By this time, the contingency planning committee of the cabinet had managed to marshall certain basic data. In particular, it reported that existing stocks of essential commodities were hopelessly inadequate for a siege economy and that the Beira route had only a limited capacity to handle additional traffic beyond the 30% of Zimbabwe trade it was already carrying. In the circumstances, ministers decided simply to scrap the proposed scheme and revert to the *status quo*. At the same time, the government denounced the foreign press for alleging that there had ever been a decision to ban imports. Even if this were technically true, it completely ignored the feverish debate and high drama of the previous ten days.[65] Although there are currently no legal restrictions on trade with or through South Africa, appeals to businessmen to reduce their ties with the South have continued. Moreover, Mugabe has made it clear that he for one has by no means abandoned his commitment to sanctions.[66]

Scope for Sanctions

The dilemma the Frontline States find themselves in has been galling. Much as they would wish to set an example to the world by standing up boldly to South Africa, they have instead been compelled to conduct themselves with the utmost circumspection so as not to invite even more retribution than they already suffer from. In consequence, they are exposed to the taunts of critics who chide them for advocating sanctions for others, while opting out themselves. At the same time, they have equally firmly been admonished—often by the same critics—to resign themselves to the inevitable and accept the reality of South African regional hegemony. What scope then, does this leave for FLS initiatives? Or must they of necessity sit the sanctions game out?

For the Frontline States seriously to contemplate risking sanctions, three conditions would have to be met:

1. The specific measures proposed would have to be capable of inflicting significant damage on the South African economy, or on white morale; otherwise, the exercise would serve no useful purpose.
2. The economic and political costs would have to be within acceptable limits and commensurate with the anticipated benefits.
3. The probability of Pretoria being provoked into crippling reprisals would have to be slight.

In view of these formidable constraints, the task of the Frontline States might appear to be impossible. Only Zimbabwe could conceivably hope to be in a position to participate actively in sanctions. Yet, further reflection indicates that the prospects may not be quite as bleak as initial impressions suggest. Moreover, in any calculation of contributions to the common global effort to end apartheid, it is necessary to acknowledge the high price the Frontline States are already paying for their principles. Estimates of current annual costs of South African destabilization range from $2 billion to $8 billion even without formal action to institute sanctions.[67] The immense burden in financial and human terms of Zimbabwe's military support for Mozambique merits special recognition.

The best hope of the Frontline States sending an unmistakable signal to white South Africans is a modified air ban in which there would be no pretence of imprisoning them in their *laager*. Instead, the intention would simply be to submit air travellers to the maximum personal inconvenience. If the purpose is to register a stinging psychological impact on white opinion, requiring the South African jet set to board their overseas flights in neighboring countries might serve as a potent reminder of the intensity of international disapproval. Moreover, a limited exercise of this kind would appear to be politically feasible. All that would be required would be a FLS ban on overflights to and from third countries. Overseas airlines that now use Johannesburg would be offered a choice of nearby alternatives—Gaborone, Harare, Maputo, and, for some purposes, Maseru, all of which now boast international airports.[66] It might not even be necessary, or desirable, to bar connecting feeder flights, or to ground SAA flights within the region—only beyond it. An incidental benefit of this scheme would be the substantial increase in airport fees that would accrue to the states concerned. More important, there is a reasonable chance that Pretoria would not react too intemperately, for fear the ban would be extended.

In this context, the much-criticized action of Zambia Airways in April 1988 in introducing a weekly New York flight (with convenient Lusaka-Johannesburg connections), following the Congressional ban on US-South Africa flights, is fully consistent with a sound sanctions strategy, though its effectiveness is limited as long as SAA and overseas airlines continue to overfly the Frontline States. A more legitimate criticism of the Zambian initiative is the decision to spurn Sal in favor of Monrovia as the refueling stop. Clearly, Cape Verde is entitled to expect reasonable compensation for the financial losses it incurs as a consequence of sanctions—its own or others.[69]

Another option open to Zimbabwe, and possibly Botswana and Zambia, is to restrict financial transfers destined for residents of South Africa. As one authority has explained, Harare

> could halt the outflow of South African profits, interest and dividends (valued at over $20m a year), freeze the interest and principal repayment of the $120m loan owed to South Africa, interrupt the over $35m worth of annual pension and annuity remittances of former

> residents now living in South Africa [and] confiscate the remaining financial assets of the 60,000 people who have emigrated to South Africa since independence.

He added that "even more dramatically," the Zimbabwe government could (provided it were prepared to accept the risk)

> nationalize the over $850m worth of South African locomotives and rolling stock on Zimbabwe's rail system and take action against the upwards of 4,000 people in Zimbabwe who have South African citizenship or the right to South African passports.[70]

Blocking financial transfers has the advantage that it could readily be excused as a measure to conserve foreign exchange. Already, in May 1987, Harare had reduced remittances of dividends and profits by foreign firms from 50% to 25%.[71]

The case for withholding pension payments to former Rhodesians residing in South Africa has received careful consideration, only to be dismissed. Apart from the complications which the constitutional provisions governing pensions have created, the government has been anxious not to tarnish its reputation for humanitarianism and fair play. It is also reluctant to take any further action that might reflect adversely on the investment climate in the country. The time may come, however, when Harare might have to reconsider its scruples in this respect.[72]

One respect in which the states of southern Africa could play a constructive role without undue risk of arousing Pretoria's active displeasure is by joining more directly in efforts to strengthen the effectiveness of global sanctions. Admittedly, the Frontline States have long been in the forefront of campaigns to widen the sanctions net by seeking to mobilize world opinion and, on occasion, by lobbying South Africa's major trading partners, such as Japan.[73] In 1986, three of the four FLS members of the Commonwealth—Tanzania, Zambia, and Zimbabwe (as well as Lesotho)—boycotted the Commonwealth Games in Edinburgh in protest against Mrs. Thatcher's footdragging on sanctions. However, much more could be done through systematic monitoring to tighten and intensify existing measures, and to expose Pretoria's extensive sanction-busting operations.

Of immediate concern to the Frontline States is the need to ensure that they are not unwitting parties to conspiracies to subvert sanctions. The two most obvious targets of South African attention are Botswana and Mozambique (along with Lesotho and Swaziland). Pretoria has already shown considerable interest and ingenuity in taking advantage of its shared membership with the BLS (Botswana, Lesotho, and Swaziland) countries in the Southern African Customs Union to penetrate SADCC and overseas markets; and the BLS states have been fully receptive to South African capital. As the Botswanan Minister of Commerce and Industry explained with evident approval, in congratulating a South African company on the occasion of the opening of its Gaborone shoe factory: "In this way, Edworks hopes that the products will be exported to EEC and the rest of Africa, thus taking full advantage of Botswana's preference in these markets under the Lome Convention and other special bilateral agreements".[74] Lesotho and Swaziland have been at least as energetic and successful in offering generous financial inducements to enable South African companies to break out of their isolation.

Maputo, too, is reportedly being used once again, as it was by Rhodesia during UDI, as an entrepot for the bogus labelling and false invoicing of South African exports and as a backdoor for embargoed imports. In this connection, suspicions concerning the operations of Renfreight, the South African forwarding and clearing agency that dominates the region, have led SADCC governments to explore ways of loosening the company's grip on their freight handling business.[75] What has so far been overlooked, however, is the extent to which foreign multinationals with interests in the Frontline States also profit from collusion with apartheid. As far as is known, although Lonrho has major investments in every SADCC state except Angola, no FLS leader reacted publicly to its ("dirt cheap") purchase of Western Platinum mine when Falconbridge finally decided to dispose of its South African holdings.[76]

In present circumstances, the scope for FLS action on sanctions is severely circumscribed. Even the few possibilities that do exist carry with them an uncertain risk of triggering swift South African reprisals. Only if the Frontline States succeed in insulating, or at least cushioning, themselves adequately against such an eventuality can they contemplate participating in further measures against South Africa. For this reason, the priority in policy has shifted from sanctions *per se* to disengagement. The greatest challenge the FLS face is how to survive the first months of an emergency, especially if it involves a complete closure of the South African border. To minimize FLS vulnerability in such circumstances, urgent attention is needed in three priority areas.[77]

The first requirement is a stockpile of essential supplies adequate to tide the Frontline States over the first three or four months of a siege. Any such contingency exercise, however, is bound to encounter fierce resistance, as Pretoria has always been careful to keep its neighbors on a short tether, normally rationing them to no more than three week's supply of basics. When Botswana took precautions to increase its oil storage capacity, South Africa ensured that the tanks were never filled. Similarly, Lesotho's attempts to import four months' reserve of refined Algerian oil through Maputo were frustrated by Pretoria's refusal to provide the necessary transit permits.[78] Zambia and Zimbabwe can expect the same systematic obstruction in their current search for alternative sources of supply of mining equipment and spares.[79] Other projects that require acceleration are SADCC's food security program and provisions for assured supplies of fertilizer,[80] medicines, specialty steels, tools, and spare parts generally.

No effort at stockpiling will succeed or suffice, however, unless secure and reliable alternative transport routes and facilities are available. Despite the widespread appreciation of the problems and considerable progress in overcoming them, there are still three aspects occasioning critical concern. These are the current heavy reliance on locomotives and wagons on loan from South Africa, the absence of alternative ports equipped to handle Zimbabwe's and Botswana's chilled beef exports and, more generally, the inability of Mozambican and Tanzanian routes, in their present state of partial rehabilitation, to cope with the full volume and complexity of FLS traffic.

The third area of vulnerability relates to the provision of electricity. The position of Maputo is particularly precarious as the transmission lines from Cabora Bassa pass through South

Africa. Botswana, too, remains dependent on Pretoria's goodwill, although with Morupule power facility now on stream, reliance should end once the interconnector lines tying the country into the Kariba grid become operational.[81]

For the Frontline States, or some of them, to embark on comprehensive sanctions, or to contain a further sharp escalation in South African destabilization, the range of preparatory measures that would first need to be undertaken is formidable. Even in the best of circumstances, the costs in human and monetary terms would be almost intolerable. Clearly, it is beyond the capabilities of any of the countries of the region to gear themselves up adequately for such an ordeal. Nor would it be right to expect them to bear the common burden alone. External support on a scale substantially in excess of that presently available or projected is essential—in three spheres: finance, logistics, and security.

Financial assistance is needed both to enable the Frontline States to achieve major progress in disengaging from economic subservience to South Africa, and to meet the additional costs invariably associated with crises, such as absorbing expelled migrant workers. Logistical support in the form of an emergency airlift would also appear unavoidable, at least during the initial stage.[82]

Finally, the whole exercise would prove futile without adequate provision to deter or restrain Pretoria's predatory instincts. The answer would appear to be an offer to the most threatened Frontline States of military cover in some credible form, or at least a firm commitment to institute comprehensive mandatory sanctions if destabilization persists. Admittedly, Washington, London, and Bonn are far from ready to intervene on this scale or in this way, but the time may come when they will be forced to treat the problem seriously.[83] When it does, the question of full FLS sanctions can be reconsidered. In the meantime, this potentially important instrument of pressure on apartheid can be of only limited benefit to the common cause.

Notes

1. Contingency planning for sanctions is understandably a sensitive subject. Consequently, any study, especially by an outside researcher, must of necessity be confined to publicly available sources. Whether Pretoria is similarly restricted in its access to information is problematical. Not all SADCC governments (or companies) appear equally conscientious where security considerations are concerned.

2. On 9 April 1987, when Britain and the United States (with West German support) vetoed a draft UN Security Council resolution (S/18785) submitted by Zambia, among others, calling for comprehensive mandatory sanctions against South Africa for its illegal occupation of Namibia, France, Italy, and Japan abstained. Earlier, on 20 February, a more modest call for selective mandatory sanctions (S/18705) suffered a similar fate.

3. In May 1987, Britain and Portugal blocked adoption by the European Community of a "charter of principles" for post-apartheid South Africa (*Financial Times* [London], 26 May 1987, 1).

4. *Africa Contemporary Record, 1980-81,* A28-29, 71; *1981-82,* A104; henceforth cited as *ACR.*

5. *ACR, 1985-86,* A115; Phyllis Johnson and David Martin, eds. *Destructive Engagement: Southern Africa at War* (Harare: Zimbabwe Publishing House, 1986), 275. The summit communique made no reference to sanctions (*Africa Research Bulletin: Economic, 1985,* 7832; henceforth cited as *ARB:E*). Malawi and Swaziland maintained a discreet diplomatic silence, while Lesotho reversed its policy following the military coup on 20 January 1986. The commitment of the seven was confirmed by OAU Chairman Abdou Diouf on 9 October 1985 following a tour of SADCC capitals (*Africa Research Bulletin: Political, 1985,* 7813; henceforth cited as *ARB:P*).

6. "The Commonwealth Accord on Southern Africa," Lyford Cay, Nassau, 20 October 1985. The final communique of the conference explained that the Accord was "directed equally towards ensuring South Africa's compliance with the wishes of the international

community on the question of Namibia." (Commonwealth Secretariat, *Commonwealth Heads of Government: The Nassau Communique, October 1985*, 6-8, 13). This was reiterated by the 1987 Commonwealth Conference.

7. *Mission to South Africa: The Commonwealth Report* (Harmondsworth: Penguin Books, 1986), 117-18, 120, 126, 130. According to *Africa Confidential* (London), "the real turning point in the sanctions 'phoney war' was 19 May 1986," with the SADF attack (27(25)), 10 December 1986, 6).

8. *Commonwealth Secretariat, Commonwealth Heads of Government Review Meeting: Communique*, London, [5] August 1986, 5-6.

9. *Courier* (Brussels), no. 99, September-October 1986, IV; *ARB:P, 1986*, 8207-8; *Sunday Times* (London), 24 August 1986, 11; *Observer* (London), 7 September 1986, 13.

10. SADCC *Communique*, Luanda, 22 August 1986, 4, SADCC/S/1/86/4.

11. "The Commonwealth, Apartheid and Sanctions: The View of the Frontline States," Lusaka, 4 October 1987, 7, 10. There was no mention of comprehensive and mandatory UN sanctions, though FLS leaders had reiterated this demand at their meeting in Dar es Salaam on 17 September 1987 (*AIM Bulletin* [Maputo], 135, October 1987, 10). The 1987 Commonwealth Conference did call for a "wider, tighter, and more intensified application" of selective sanctions "pending acceptance of [comprehensive and mandatory sanctions] by the international community as a whole" ("The Okanagan Statement on Southern Africa and Programme of Action," Vancouver, 16 October 1987).

12. Unofficial mid-1988 estimates of troop deployment in Mozambique are: Zimbabwe 6,000-11,000, Tanzania 1,500, and Malawi 300.

13. *Times* (London), 4 May 1986, 7 and 11 June 1987, 12.

14. Zambian imports in transit through South Africa were subject to a cash deposit payable in advance (beginning 4 August), while for South African imports from Zimbabwe a new licensing scheme was instituted (as from 8 August) (*Africa Confidential* 23(17), 20 August 1986, 1; *ARB:E, 1986*, 8306-7; *Times*, 7 August 1986, 1).

15. *Financial Times,* 19 March 1987, 4 and 16 September 1987, 4; "Zimbabwe's Economy," *Times,* 23 and 24 February 1987 and "Economic Crisis in Zambia," ibid., 17, 19, 20, 23, 24 and 25 March 1987. Some Zimbabwean businessmen were quick to attribute the downturn in the country's economy to Mugabe's sanctions rhetoric.

16. The cabinet-level Contingency Planning Task Force was led by the Minister of Trade and Commerce until August 1987, when the Deputy Prime Minister took over. It first met on 6 August 1986, the day after Pretoria instituted its own trade sanctions (*Africa Confidential* 27 (25), 10 December 1986, 7). Much of the ground work was undertaken by an inter-ministry Sanctions Readiness Committee of officials chaired by the Secretary for Trade and Commerce.

17. *Financial Times,* 11 August 1986, 2. Although the consensus within the Zimbabwean business community was that sanctions would prove an unmitigated disaster, the CZI at its annual congress in July 1986 accorded "unequivocal support" to mandatory sanctions. At the same time, it urged that the government first study their implications thoroughly and then plan their implementation carefully so as to minimize the inevitable disruption to the economy that would result (*Guardian* [London], 4 July 1986; *Africa Confidential* 27 (25), 10 December 1986, 6, 7.). In addition to the CZI, a number of individual companies have established in-house sanctions committees of their own.

18. The Director of Contingency Planning operates within the Office of the Prime Minister.

19. Ministry of Planning and Economic Affairs, *Economic Sanctions on South Africa and Their Implications on Lesotho* (July 1986) and *Economic Sanctions on South Africa: Measures and Projects to Cushion Their Effects on Lesotho* (August 1986). Project 16 provided for a Sanctions Emergency Planning Unit within the Ministry.

20. *Southern Africa Report* (Johannesburg), 4 (47), 28 November 1987, 14.

21. President arap Moi of Kenya was invited to Luanda but was unable to attend, as was a Nigerian representative (*Financial Times,* 22 August 1986, 2). President Sassou-Nguesso of the Congo, the current OAU chairman, did attend.

22. Colin Legum, "Africa Frontline States get tough with Malawi and Zaire over links with South Africa," *Third World Reports* (London), 17 September 1986; *Observer*, 24 August 1986, 11 and 30 November 1986, 17; *Financial Times*, 9 October 1986, 4. The Frontline States charged that the "Malawian government . . . organized, facilitated and set up conditions for bandit gangs to occupy frontier zones in the provinces of Tete, Sofala and Zambezia" ("The Maputo Declaration of October 12, 1986" [Harare: Government Printer, 1987], 4). Kaunda, Machel, and Mugabe confronted Banda in Blantyre on 11 September 1986.

23. Kaunda, Machel, Mugabe, and dos Santos met Mobutu at Kasaba Bay, Zambia on 19 October 1986—the fateful day of the Machel air crash. Subsequently, Kaunda, dos Santos, Chissano (or his representative), and Mobutu met in Luanda on 16 April and in Lusaka on 30 April 1987 to discuss the possibilities of reopening the Benguela Railway to the West Coast.

24. "The Maputo Declaration of October 12, 1986"; AIM Bulletin, 135, October 1987, 10.

25. SADCC *Southern Africa: Towards Economic Liberation*, 1 April 1980. The Programme of Action was outlined in skeleton form at the inaugural conference in 1980, and subsequently amplified upon annually.

26. Christopher W. Davids, "Contingency Planning Study for Southern Africa" (Ottawa: CIDA, 12 November 1986) 1, 8. The subcommittee comprised Bernard Chidzero, Zimbabwe's Minister of Finance, Economic Planning and Development as chairman, Peter Mmusi, Botswana's Vice-President and Chairman of SADCC's Council of Ministers, and Abdul Magid Osman, Mozambique's Minister of Finance. Members held several meetings.

27. Sixth SADCC summit, Luanda, 22 August 1986 (*Courier*, no. 99, September-October 1986, III). SADCC's Southern African Transport and Communications Commission (SATCC) in Maputo had less hesitation in drawing up lists of emergency projects.

28. At the request of SADCC (November 1986), the Commonwealth Secretariat prepared a memorandum on Lesotho's precarious situation. Its conclusions inevitably were exceedingly pessimistic. The risk of South African retaliation may now be somewhat reduced as

a result of the more accommodationist stance of the military government that seized power in January 1986. The Luanda summit had received consultant's reports on a number of other issues (*ACR, 1986-87*, A32, 116-17; Johnson and Martin, *Destructive Engagement*, 275-79, for example, B. Setai, "Implications of Sanctions against South Africa on SADCC Member Countries: Focus on Migrant Labour," 30 April 1986.

29. SADCC *Communique*, 22 August 1986, 4. SATCC's revised Programme of Action included seven additional projects "mainly for the purpose of contingency preparation" (*SATCC Amendments January 1987*, 3). A careful reading of other SADCC documents reveals, in more circumspect language, the extent to which sanctions concerns affected project priorities. Thus, we are told that "in the present circumstances, special emphasis has been put on projects which will give the capacity to handle all of the international trade of the member states thorugh the SADCC ports" (SADCC *Transport and Communications*, Gaborone, 5th-6th February 1987, 5).

30. PTA, *Report of the Fifth Meeting of the Authority, Addis Ababa, 3rd to 4th December, 1986*, PTA/AUTH/V/3, 18-20. A list of goods that FLS members were currently importing from South Africa was supplied to PTA states. Three FLS/SADCC members—Angola, Mozambique, and Botswana—have not yet joined PTA.

31. *Measures to be Taken by PTA Member States in Support of Economic Sanctions against South Africa and Assistance to be Provided to African States Neighbouring South Africa ASNSA in order to Lessen the Impact of Possible South African Counter-Measures* PTA/AUTH/VI/7, June 1987 (financed by the Commonwealth Secretariat); *Report of the Meeting of Ministers of Trade, Transport and Finance on Measures to be Taken by PTA Member States in Support of Economic Sanctions against South Africa and Assistance to be Provided to African States Neighbouring South Africa (ASNSA in order to Lessen the Impact of Possible South African Counter-Measures* PTA/ASNSA/M/1/2, April 1988; *ARB:E*, 1988, 9129.

32. The report, prepared by Ben Bardan and financed by the Commonwealth Secretariat, was submitted to PTA in June 1987.

33. AHG/Res. (XXII), 30 July 1986. The Committee on Southern Africa comprised the six FLS leaders plus the presidents of Algeria, Cape Verde, the Congo, Ethiopia, and Senegal. A Committee on

Assistance to Frontline States had been appointed in 1977 and enlarged in 1979 (AHG/Dec.112 [XVI]).

34. Commonwealth Secretariat, *Report of the Commonwealth Committee on Southern Africa, September 1985—September 1987*, September 1987. The Commonwealth Secretariat was prepared to provide much more assistance, but was constrained by SADCC's obvious reluctance to accord priority to specifically emergency projects.

35. *AFRICA: Action for Resisting Invasion, Colonialism and Apartheid* (New Delhi: Ministry of External Affairs, 1987). The Plan of Action outlines 57 emergency and longer term projects in nine priority spheres. Note that AFRICA is an acronym.

36. *Sunday Telegraph* (London), 15 February 1987, 1; *ARB:E, 1986*, 8349. As early as 1985, a mysterious memorandum, detailing the dire consequences of sanctions, circulated in SADCC capitals. Allegedly written by a senior Western diplomat, it was probably the product of South African disinformation (*Southern Africa Report* 3 (35), 13 September 1985, 10.

37. *ARB:E, 1986*, 8307; *Times*, 9 August 1986, 1; *Times of Zambia*, 8 August 1986, 1. Suggestions that Mugabe was merely talking tough to impress the Non-Aligned Movement which was meeting in Harare in a month's time underestimate the strength of his feelings on the matter.

38. *Times*, 9 August 1986, 1 and 30 August 1986, 5. The agreement dated from 1965 but had been amended and reaffirmed on 31 July. When questioned on this, Mugabe claimed that his officials had acted without his knowledge (*Sunday Times*, 31 August, 1). The required six months notice of termination has yet to be given.

39. *ARB:E, 1986*, 8307; *Times*, 4 October 1986, 5; *Africa Analysis* (London) no. 9, 31 October 1986, 6; Overseas Development Institute, "Sanctions and South Africa's Neighbours," *Briefing Paper*, May, 1987, 6.

40. The extended Nassau list consisted of: "(a) a ban on air links with South Africa, (b) a ban on new investment or reinvestment of profits earned in South Africa, (c) a ban on the import of agricultural products from South Africa, (e) the termination of all government assistance to investment in, and trade with, South

Africa, (f) a ban on all government procurements in South Africa, (g) a ban on government contracts with majority-owned South African companies, (h) a ban on the promotion of tourism to South Africa, (i) a ban on all new bank loans to South Africa, whether to the public or private sectors, (j) a ban on the import of uranium, coal, iron and steel from South Africa, and (k) the withdrawal of all consular facilities in South Africa except for our own nationals and nationals of third countries to whom we render consular services" (*Commonwealth Heads of Government Review Meeting: Communique*, 5-6).

41. *Africa Analysis*, no. 17, 6 March 1987, 7. *Africa Economic Digest* (London) estimates AirZim's loss at $10.7 million (8 (2), 10 January 1987, 16).

42. Air Zimbabwe *Timetable*, 1 July 1986. The frequency of direct weekly flights each way was: Harare-Johannesburg 13, Bulawayo-Johannesburg 6, Harare-Durban 1, and Victoria Falls-Johannesburg 1.

43. *ARB:P, 1987*, 8323.

44. *Times*, 9 August 1986, 1. Five airlines use Nairobi on their Johannesburg runs: British Airways (with four flights a week each way), Swissair (with three), and El Al, KLM, and Olympic (each with one flight). Three airlines now fly nonstop to South Africa: Lufthansa (four flights), British Airways (three), and Alitalia (two).

45. OAU resolutions CIAS/Plen.2/Res.2, May 1963; CM/Res. 13 (II), June 1964; ECM/Res. 13 (IV), December 1965; CM/Res. 473 (XXVII), July 1976; CM/Res. 734 (XXXIII), Res. 2, July 1979; CM/Res. 816 (XXXV), June 1980; CM/Res. 1056 (XLIV), July 1986; and AHG/Dec. 2 (XXIII), July 1987.

46. *Economics* (London), 21 February 1987, 42. The US ban on SAA flights reduced Cape Verde's annual airport income by $3.5 million to some $2 million. Cape Verde introduced its own flight (to Boston), but barred passengers whose journeys originated in South Africa (AIM *Bulletin*, 129, April 1987, 14). SAA continued to use Sal for three flights a week to and from Europe. Pereira was a member of the OAU Committee on Southern Africa.

47. *Times*, 28 July 1987, 7. Following the failure of Moi to attend the Luanda FLS meeting (21 August 1986), Kaunda contacted him concerning the air ban (*Financial Times*, 22 August 1986, 2). At the OAU Council of Ministers in February 1987, Ghana berated Kenya for its failure to close Nairobi airport to flights to and from South Africa. To do so would have cost an estimated $30 million in landing fees (or $50 million according to the *Financial Times*, 18 December 1986, 4). Fewer flights to Nairobi would also adversely affect the tourist trade and industries dependent on daily air freight services to Europe.

48. TAP with three flights a week each way, Sabena with two and UTA with one use Kinshasa. UTA and SAA each have one flight a week each way through Abidjan. Brazzaville is no longer used as a transit stop.

49. *Times*, 5 August 1986, 5; *Sunday Mail* (Harare), 1 March 1987, 3; SADCC *Communique*, Luanda, 22 August 1986, 4; *Southern Africa Report* 5 (29), 24 July 1987, 15. Kenya Airways, Air Tanzania, Zambia Airways, and Air Zimbabwe also had flights to Gaborone.

50. *Africa Confidential* 27 (25), 10 December 1986, 7; *Financial Times*, 22 October 1986, 6 and 25 November 1986, 2; *Southern Africa Report* 4 (47), 28 November 1986, 14. Kaunda stated that a joint committee was discussing a coordinated package of sanctions and that it was only "a question of time" before air links would be cut (*Times of Zambia*, 28 November 1986, 1).

51. *Financial Times*, 31 December 1986, 2; *Times*, 31 December 1986, 6. The FLS meeting ended prematurely following news of the death of one of Kaunda's sons.

52. Department of Information, Harare, *Press Statement* 2/87, 7 January 1987, 11.

53. *Southern Africa Report*, 5 (3), 23 January 1987, 11; President Canaan Banana, 13 February 1987 (*Press Statement* 75/87, 2). Banana added that "Zimbabwe will continue to coordinate and plan with other nations" at the same time as it "prepares to implement the Commonwealth package of sanctions." A Zambian-sponsored resolution calling for selective mandatory sanctions was debated (and vetoed) in the UN Security Council, 20 February 1987.

54. *Times*, 20 January 1987, 6. Two months later, Mugabe repeated that, "We are still working at these arrangements and as soon as we are ready, we will make the people know. So the sanctions are coming." "We are going to implement our own package of sanctions jointly with Zambia" (*House of Assembly Debates*, 1 April 1987, col. 1854). Kaunda made similar comments (*Times of Zambia*, 2 March 1987, 1; *Citizen* [Johannesburg], 2 March 1987.

55. *Southern Africa Report* 5 (3), 23 January 1987, 11. On earlier African transport and fuel squeezes, see Joseph Hanlon, *Beggar Your Neighbours: Apartheid Power in Southern Africa* (London: James Currey, 1986), 187-93.

56. *Financial Times*, 15 December 1986, 3, 16 and 24 February 1987, 4; *Africa Confidential* 28 (2), 21 January 1987, 6-7.

57. Press Conference, Harare, 30 January 1987. See also, his address at the official dinner in Harare on 27 January. The two prime ministers conferred for a total of 18 hours, including 6 hours alone without advisors, 27-30 January.

58. *Sunday Times*, 26 April 1987, 13; *Times*, 27 April 1987, 8. The raid, which killed five Zambians, including two nephews of the Prime Minister and a niece of the Defence Minister, appeared to be an election gimmick on the eve of a South African white poll on 6 May. There were unconfirmed reports that the ZAF was eager to bomb Johannesburg following criticism of its failure to challenge the SAAF attack on Lusaka in May 1986 (*Africa Confidential* 27 (17), 20 August 1986, 1).

59. *Times*, 21 July 1987, 1 and 27 July 1987, 7.

60. Between 1981 and 1985, the proportion of extra-regional trade funneled through South Africa increased dramatically as a result of South African destabilization and financial incentives. Since then, determined efforts at diversification have led to a significant reduction but not the virtual end to Zimbabwe transit traffic through South African ports that Mugabe forecast for the end of 1988 (*Globe and Mail* [Toronto] 19 September 1987, A8).

Table 1

	Zimbabwe	*Zambia*	*Six Landlocked States*
1981	67%	36%	50%
1985	92%	60%	85%
1987	70%	n/a	58%

Source: "Sanctions and South Africa's Neighbours," 4; *Financial Times*, 17 September 1987, v..

61. *Times of Zambia*, 27 November 1986, 1 and 2 March 1987, 1. In August 1986, Zambia introduced foreign exchange curbs on imports from South Africa (*ARB:E, 1986*, 8307). It also allowed (until June 1987) exporters to retain 50% of the foreign exchange "earned" when exporting to PTA countries through the Clearing House.

62. *ARB:E, 1987* Annual Report, 5. The loss of Zambian traffic was a serious blow to Port Elizabeth's economy.

63. K. D. Kaunda, "New Economic Recovery Programme," 1 May 1987; *Africa Analysis* no. 22, 15 May 1987, 6-7; *Africa Confidential* 28 (19), 23 September 1987, 6-7.

64.*House of Assembly Debates*, 8 July 1987, col. 201.

65. *Times*, 28 July 1987, 1, 18; *Southern Africa Report* 5 (30, 31 July 1987, 3 and 5 (31), 7 August 1987, 5; *Star* (Johannesburg), weekly, 1 August 1987, 1 and 15 August 1987, 3; *Financial Times*, 1 August 1987, 3; *Africa Confidential* 28 (17), 19 August 1987, 3. Import Licenses were rubber stamped "Not for use in South Africa, Taiwan, South Korea and Israel." Since 1984, Zimbabwe has made provision for a special foreign exchange allocation to finance imports from PTA countries (*EASA* [London], 1 (4), 23 February, 5).

66. *Financial Times*, 6 August 1987, 4; *Globe and Mail*, 19 September 1987, A8. Zimbabwean imports from South Africa declined from 28% of the total in 1981 to 19% in 1985, while exports to South Africa fell from 22% to 11% over the same period. Since then, the trends appear to have been reversed.

67. *Children on the Front Line* (New York: UNICEF, 1987), 32-34.

68. The distance in air miles from Johannesburg to Gaborone is 182, to Maseru 224, to Maputo 270, and to Harare 596. The new airport at Gaborone was built partly with contingency considerations in mind (*Times*, 27 May 1987, 20). Moshoeshoe I International Airport was built for Boeing 727 type aircraft, and would require an extension to its runway to handle larger aircraft (Economic Sanctions against *South Africa: Measures and Projects to Cushion their Effects on Lesotho*, Project Proposal 4).

69. *Sunday Times*, 1 May 1988, A1, 18; *Washington Post*, 30 July 1988, A17-18. The shift of Qantas Airways' terminus from Johannesburg to Harare is similarly to be welcomed.

70. "Sanctions and South Africa's Neighbours," 3, 6.

71. *Financial Times*, 5 June 1987, 4.

72. *The Constitution of Zimbabwe*, sections 16 and 112, and schedule 6, *House of Assembly Debates*, 1 April 1987, col. 1863; *Sunday Times*, 17 August 1986, 11; *Times*, 11 September 1986, 7.

73. In February 1986, Kaunda hosted a meeting of EEC-FLS foreign ministers in Lusaka (*Times*, 6 February 1986, 5).

74. Ministry of Commerce and Industry, *Botswana Business News* 7 (2 & 3), 1986, 6; *African Business* (London) no. 101, January 1987, 49; *Citizen*, 3 February 1987.

75. AIM *Bulletin* 131, June 1987, 11; Hanlon, *Beggar Your Neighbours*, 138-39, 195-96. Swaziland is already a major conduit for sanctions busting (ibid., 73, 100; *Observer*, 6 July 1986, 5; *Star* (weekly) 16 September 1987, 9). Whether or not Renfreight's offices (or their employees) in Maputo or Beira have been engaged in subversive activities, the company has certainly sought to divert traffic to South African ports and away from Mozambican ports.

76. *Financial Times*, 12 February 1987, 1.

77. "Sanctions and South Africa's Neighbours"; Hanlon, *Beggar Your Neighbours*, 271-76; Johnson and Martin, *Destructive Engagement*, 273-

80; J. P. Hayes, *Economic Effects of Sanctions on Southern Africa* (London: Gower, 1987), 43-66.

78. Hanlon, *Beggar Your Neighbours*, 75, 220; *Africa Confidential* 24 (7), 30 March 1983, 2. The oil was purchased at concessionary rates and after 18 months of futile negotiations, sold. South Africa insisted that all oil imports be pooled.

79. On 12 August 1986, Kaunda discussed the threat of South African curbs on the supply of mining equipment with Gavin Relly, chairman of the Anglo American Corporation (*Times*, 13 August 1986, 5; *Times of Zambia*, 3 November 1987, 1).

80. Zimbabwe established a strategic stockpile of chemical raw material essential for its (and Zambian) industry (*Financial Gazette* [Harare], 5 August 1988, 5).

81. In July 1987, Beitbridge (in Zimbabwe ended its dependence on the supply of South African electricity (*Herald*, 1 August 1988, 5).

82. Nyerere suggested this for Lesotho in August 1986 (Hanlon, *Beggar Your Neighbours*, 275; Johnson and Martin, *Destructive Engagement*, 279), but it may be required elsewhere, for example, to deliver aviation fuels or mining spares, or to market frozen beef.

83. Roger Martin, *Southern Africa: The Price of Apartheid* (London: Economist Intelligence Unit, 1988).

THE POTENTIAL FOR SOUTH AFRICAN SANCTIONS BUSTING IN SOUTHERN AFRICA: THE CASE OF BOTSWANA[*]

Jack Parson

Introduction

The important question about sanctions against South Africa is not whether one or even a combination of sanctions can in a singular way destroy apartheid. Rather, the question is the extent to which sanctions play a role in that process. The imposition of sanctions is a crucial but only a first step. The monitoring and management of sanctions over time will determine their effectiveness.

---

[*]Some of the research for this chapter was conducted in Botswana under a grant from the College of Charleston Faculty Research and Development Committee during May and early June 1987. The support of the College for this research is gratefully acknowledged. An earlier version of this chapter was presented at the annual meeting of the African Studies Association, Denver, 1987.

Given that fact, a primary concern is whether limited sanctions will increase the cost of apartheid sufficiently to play a role in forcing change in a progressive direction. A large part of the answer turns on whether or not South Africa, through various means, will be able to avoid or subvert the sanctions effort. Will its explicit policy of sanctions "busting" be successful? The answer will depend upon the extent to which it is able to directly engage in "illegal" trade as against its success in finding legal means to trade banned commodities.

Because of this, sanctions against South Africa have a direct impact on the southern African regional system. Sanctions make South African direct importing and exporting more difficult and expensive. The cost of maintaining apartheid is therefore increased. The extent to which this increased cost results in changes toward an equal society depends on whether or not the South African government is able to reduce the cost to acceptable levels. The management of the sanctions environment has much to do with South Africa's ability to manipulate its southern African regional political and economic relationships.

The regional factor in a South African sanctions busting program has to do with whether or not South Africa will be able to engage in those activities through neighboring territories, particularly those which are historically economically tied to the South African economy—Botswana, Lesotho, and Swaziland—but also more generally through existing economic relations with many of the other nations in the Southern African Development Coordination Conference (SADCC).

This chapter explores the extent to which South Africa may be able to engage in sanctions busting through its relations with the Republic of Botswana. It argues that the internal class structure and class state relations in Botswana create contradictions which open opportunities for sanction-busting activity while at the same time supporting the government of Botswana's policy advocating the imposition of sanctions by the international community. This analysis also argues that the economic relations between the government of Botswana and South African capital and the South African state have the partial effect of insulating the South African economy from the effects of sanctions.

Botswana and South Africa in Recent History

This is not the place to rehearse the details of the history of relations between Botswana and South Africa. However it is important to summarize that history if contemporary relations are to be understood. Most especially it is important to understand the contours of the historical relation in understanding the conditions which create both the opportunities for and limits to South Africa's use of Botswana for sanctions busting.

Botswana occupies a territory the size of Kenya, France or Texas with a population of about one million people and triple that number of cattle and small stock. The country's geography has long had a determinant effect on its political history, economic fortunes, and international relations. Semiarid conditions prevail over most of the land, much of it in the Kalahari Desert, where limited and unpredictable rainfall and deep sand limit both human and animal habitation. As a result, agricultural production is very risky and there are periodic multiyear droughts such as that which occurred in the 1980s. Most of the population lives in a narrow corridor running north and south where permanent water supplies and most of the arable land are to be found. The only other part of the country with regular water supplies is in the north, in particular in the relatively remote northwest area, the Okavango Delta.

The peopling and political and economic history of this rather inhospitable physical environment owes much to the history of southern Africa, most especially the history of what is now South Africa. The difaqane and subsequent expansion of the Afrikaner Republics pushed a Batswana population into the territory. The attempt to retain independence, at least autonomy, in 1885 led certain of the Dikgosi (Kings) to ask for British "protection." The British Empire's southern African interests desired to protect the "road to the north" from South Africa into the interior (what became northern and southern Rhodesia) from incursions by the Boer Republics from the east. Thus the territory became the colonial Bechuanaland Protectorate.

British interest in Bechuanaland derived primarily from its strategic geographical location. The main British interests were in the developing mining industry in South Africa and the development of Southern Rhodesia. A north-south railway was built on a strip of land ceded to Rhodesia Railways thus providing an essential transport link in the development of Bechuanaland's northeastern neighbor. At the same time, the future of the Protectorate was tied to the fortunes of the South African economy and polity in a variety of ways. In 1910 the Protectorate was brought into the Southern African Customs Union, creating a single southern African economy with South Africa at its core. The currency of the Protectorate was South African currency, a situation which only changed in the 1970s, well after independence, when Botswana withdrew from the Rand Monetary Area and created a central Bank of Botswana and national currency, the Pula. Most importantly, restrictions on Batswana economic activity, including the marketing of cattle, combined with the imposition of taxation and the development of other cash requirements, accelerated what had been a trickle of labor migration from Bechuanaland to South Africa. The Bechuanaland Protectorate became a "labor reserve" for South Africa—so much so that by 1947 Isaac Schapera estimated that about forty-five percent of the adult males of Bechuanaland were working in South Africa.[1] As a result, almost nothing was done by the British to develop the territory. It was viewed as an appendage to the South African economy and in fact the Act of Union creating modern South Africa provided for the likelihood of Bechuanaland's eventual incorporation into the Union of South Africa. Bechuanaland's international relations were handled through the Dominions—not the Colonial—Office for most of its existence and Britain's chief representative to the Union was, for much of the time, also the High Commissioner responsible for Bechuanaland. Even the capital of the colonial territory was located in South Africa, at the "Imperial Reserve" in Mafeking.

Botswana's contemporary situation owes much to this history. Its economic dependence on South Africa is longstanding and runs both wide and deep. Its politics also reflect its proximity to its neighbor. Late colonial nationalist politics reflected the coming to power of the National Party in the 1948 Apartheid election. As a result, Seretse Khama, Kgosi of the Bangwato, was banned from the territory until 1956 for marrying an Englishwoman. Certain leaders of the nationalist parties had themselves been involved in South African politics. Part of the urgency in bringing Botswana to independence in 1966 resulted from the need to create a measure of political sovereignty to protect the nation from South African machinations. In that same period began the political process of defining Botswana's relationship to the liberation struggle in South Africa itself, a theme that has persisted and increased in importance particularly in the 1980s.

It is in this context of Botswana's long-term integration into a southern African regional political economy dominated by South Africa that the country's contemporary situation must be evaluated. As will become evident below, the widening of economic relationships with South Africa after independence occurred not so much from a desire to embrace that system but from economic necessity. The persistence of migratory labor to South Africa from Botswana in 1988 reflects the fact that overcoming the years of colonial underdevelopment is not something that happens overnight or even in two decades. At the same time, as will also become evident below, contemporary Botswana reflects this history in a more positive way. Much of the government's development planning and intentions are designed to reduce and eventually eliminate its dependence and to play a positive role in the liberation of South Africa. The country's active membership in the SADCC reflects these desires, as does its policy of accepting political refugees from South Africa and for this and other reasons subjecting itself to military attacks from South Africa. The contradictions of living with the victimization of the colonial legacy and of struggling against it create the environment in which sanctions against South Africa and sanctions-busting activity have to be evaluated.

Conceptualizing Sanctions Busting in Botswana: Who Will Do It and Why?

The question of the extent to which Botswana may become involved in sanctions busting is not simply a question of principle. Indeed, if it were a matter of principle then the answer would be that the likelihood that Botswana would become involved in sanctions busting is very low, virtually zero. The Botswana government has maintained and continues to maintain the principle that international sanctions are a legitimate and useful weapon to bring about change in South Africa. Botswana has consistently supported the international movement to impose economic sanctions on South Africa. It has resisted the argument that there should not be sanctions because southern African countries outside of South Africa would be hurt. Recently Botswana's Minister of External Affairs, Dr. Gaositwe Chiepe, while in the United States, said that the US Anti-Apartheid Act of 1986 was a "most encouraging and welcome" move by the United States and that these sanctions had not hurt Botswana.[2] The government under the presidencies of both Seretse Khama and Quett Masire have maintained the principle that while Botswana cannot itself impose mandatory economic sanctions without committing economic suicide, Botswana does in principle support the use of sanctions to bring about a change in South Africa. The principle involved in Botswana policy regarding sanctions is one precluding an official policy of sanctions busting. Botswana insists that it will do and is doing everything it realistically can to support the political, military, and economic pressure on South Africa in the direction of bringing about a dismantling of the policy and practice of apartheid.

The possibility that Botswana might become a venue for sanctions-busting activities arises not from principle but from the fact that activities which amount to sanctions busting derive from a material set of interests in the relationship between external and internal class economic and political relations which can take place and thrive alongside an official and principled governmental commitment to sanctions themselves. While this is contradictory (not merely in appearance but also in actual fact), it is so because of the history of the state structure in Botswana and its international relations. This chapter takes this as a beginning point in an investigation of the internal and external interests and pressures the result of which may be what is in effect sanctions busting.

The Sanctions-Busting Environment: South Africa's Perspective

There are a broad range of existing commercial entities and arrangements linking South African business to business in Botswana. These include a spectrum of arrangements from direct government to government agreements (such as the Southern African Customs Union Agreement) through purely commercial operations such as the large number of "joint" ventures between South African and Batswana capital to direct and singular South African-owned business ventures. The extent to which these could be turned to effective sanctions busting is related to the economic imperatives for the businesses themselves as well as to the types of inducements the South African government can make available to engage in sanctions busting whether directly or indirectly.

The South African interest would be related as well to the extent to which its economic relationship with Botswana supports the overall economy of South Africa (for example, in terms of foreign exchange earnings) and the extent to which it supports specific sectors of or firms in that economy.

The sorts of enterprises which might have an interest in using a Botswana base in order to export goods "made in Botswana" in defiance of sanctions would be quite diverse and would include the following: commodities for which final stage assembly is labor intensive and where the components do not entail burdensome transport charges; commodities for which there is pre-existing manufacturing capacity in Botswana requiring only expansion or use at full capacity; commodities where the raw materials are imported from abroad and which might suffer if those raw materials were restricted; commodities where the raw materials are available in South Africa for manufacture in the export market and where the cost of transporting raw materials is not excessive.

At the macro-economic level the South African economy would derive a benefit from economic relationships which substituted local (southern African) production of raw materials and finished goods for goods imported from abroad. In addition, South Africa would be interested in production which contributed to the integrity of the South African Rand and southern Africa's foreign exchange situation.

From a South African perspective the means to induce cooperation fall into categories of both carrots and sticks—of reward and of punishment. On the one hand, carrot-like inducements would be the promise of additional foreign investment, generating both employment and new tax revenue as well as opportunities for Batswana entrepreneurs. There might be secondary linkages created and the opportunity to utilize previously untapped raw materials in the Botswana economy. The goal of developing a more diversified and integrated economic system with the direct involvement of Batswana capital would provide a broad economic inducement.

At the same time, but on the other hand, South Africa has consistently shown itself capable of wielding a heavy "stick." What has become a persistent policy of destabilization in the region has sought to punish neighbors for their misdeeds. An increase in the threat or use of military action could easily become a part of government-to-government relations in a sanctions environment of increasing intensity. There is every reason to believe that the South African government is prepared to use its military apparatus to achieve its goals and the goals of specific economic entities in the South African economy. Botswana has been a regular target for such actions since June 1985, although so far apparently for political rather than economic reasons. An intensifying sanctions environment in fact increases the likelihood that this pattern will persist and perhaps become more frequent. The instruments of coercion available to South Africa are not solely military. There are economic "levers" which South Africa can manipulate. Lewis, for examples, sees the primary point of leverage in the South African control of the main railway transportation system in southern Africa.[3]

The Internal Calculus: Botswana in a Sanctions-Busting Environment

Botswana experienced tremendous growth in the post-colonial period (i.e., since 1966 and particularly since 1969). A number of factors caused and conditioned this growth. One was the development of a political relationship with South Africa conducive (although not in all respects) to Botswana's economic growth. Most importantly here was the renegotiation of the customs union agreement in 1969, the creation of a congenial "climate" for South African investment, and a relationship conducive to the development of a close partnership between certain sections of South African mining capital and the Botswana government. A second factor was the Botswana government's ability to conclude several major deals with South African capital around the exploitation of mineral deposits in Botswana, most notably diamonds but also copper/nickel. A third factor was the Botswana government's ability to generate foreign aid from the West, from both bilateral and multilateral aid agencies.

While the rate of economic growth has been nothing short of spectacular, the distribution of resulting incomes and opportunities was highly unequal. A high rate of unemployment persisted. The most recent estimate of the unemployment situation, that for 1984/85, concluded that the unemployment rate in Botswana was 25.3%, including an unemployment rate of 19.3% for males and 30.6% for females. The rate was significantly higher in urban as compared to rural areas and for the labor force under 25 years of age, whether male or female: 46.1% of the labor force under 25 years of age in urban areas and 32% of the same force in rural areas were unemployed.[4] Wage employment creation for unskilled and semiskilled workers continued to be an issue for both supporters and opponents of the government. The result has been continual pressure to generate the macroeconomic resources to alleviate the problem in the shortest possible time. This has in practice directed attention to the search for additional mineral resources that can be exploited to sustain existing levels of employment and increase the ranks of the employed, directly in mining employment and indirectly through creating jobs with the revenue accruing to the state.

A consequence of the development of this network of relations is a pattern of economic growth that depends heavily upon maintaining these relationships. It also creates a "natural" tendency to view such relationships as on balance worthy of development and expansion. Finally, and most importantly, it creates a material position and ideology that regards these relationships as matters of national economic interest unrelated to the whole question of the apartheid economy. After all, there is little or no direct engagement with the apartheid state and the economic interests are those of "enlightened" South African capital. In such circumstances it is easy to persuade oneself that a direct government of Botswana-South African capital partnership is one which is excluded from consideration in the debate about sanctions. If the benefits are big enough and if the government is a partner, then it is a matter of national security and not of apartheid, thus excluding the issue from debate.

These factors and resulting patterns create an environment congenial to the further development of economic activities which might have the effect, in certain respects, of supporting the South African economy in the face of economic sanctions.

Botswana's growth was also rooted in the assumption that a national capitalist transformation was both possible and desirable and that what was politically required was to create a "climate" for both private investment and the emergence of those investors. Batswana entrepreneurs were encouraged and private initiatives welcomed. Decisions about what to produce, how to produce it, to whom to sell it, and the distribution and use of resulting resources were to be in private hands. Thus the control and use of private productive property was a primary basis for much economic activity, particularly in the commercial and manufacturing sectors. Batswana businessmen therefore were encouraged and strongly motivated to make a profit.

The reliance on capitalism was associated with the ideology of the separation of politics and economics. The economic motivation of entrepreneurs was primary in their and the government's eyes. Business is business and they could not be expected to judge the value of an investment through the prism of political change in South Africa. The outcome was the existence of a class in Botswana in whose interest it might be to engage in economic activities the effect of which was sanctions busting as long as that was not clearly the only thing those activities constituted. This class engaged in joint ventures with South African capital and could be easily persuaded to improve its own ability to develop by developing new productive capacity for the purpose of developing export markets. That such activities increased the parameters of the macro-Botswana economy, including jobs, provided the final evidence that such activities were necessary and legitimate.

The ideological and public policy parameters for economic activity in Botswana were congruent with the capitalist parameters of the South African economy. The structure of production, patterns of labor relations, low wages, and even migratory patterns were not so different. The Botswana economy was not an apartheid economy nor was the government an apartheid one. But the class outlook and interest of South African and Batswana entrepreneurs were not so different. The language of business created a shared perception of at least the broad means to engage in economic growth and development.

Patterns of Economic Growth and Change in the Sanctions-Busting Environment

The evidence, direct and indirect, bearing on the issues raised above is both sparse and inconclusive but does suggest an overall pattern. The South African government does not publish data on such matters. The South African press would be shut down if it did so in any form. Public data on imports and exports in Botswana is more readily and probably reliably available, but time lags mean that it is available in any detail only for about 1984. In addition, the public data is not detailed enough to definitively show exactly what is going on. Press reports in Botswana are more candid than in South Africa, but cannot be regarded as comprehensive and definitive. There is, therefore, overall, a significant problem of data collection. However, the topic and issues are sufficiently important to use data which is available to discuss the issues, bearing in mind the extremely tentative nature of the interpretation of that data.

If significant direct sanctions busting were going on, one would expect to see it reflected in significant shifts in the value and direction of trade in Botswana's export figures, particularly since the export figures also include re-exports. Botswana's exports rose sharply in recent years from a total of UA347,837,000 in 1981[5] to UA969,127,000 in 1984 and P1,383,134,000 approximately UA1,257,394,000) in 1985.[6] However, the bulk of this substantial increase was due to dramatic increases in the export of diamonds. Just over 90% of the increase in exports between 1981 and 1984 was due to increased diamond sales. There were significant increases in sales of wood, wood articles, and basketry, but much of that increase (UA1.7 million) would be in the form of sales of baskets. Of somewhat more interest were increases in the exportation of textiles and textile articles (up by a factor of 2.75 from UA16.9 million to UA46.6 million), machinery and appliances (up by a factor of 3.34 from UA2.6 million to UA8.9 million), vehicles (up by a factor of 2.15 from UA6 million to UA12.96 million), and photographic, musical, and surgical equipment (up by a factor of 13.6 from UA98,231 in 1981 to UA1.34 million in 1984).

The direction of export trade offers some additional data[7] which may help explain the gross figures on exports. The value of exports to the common customs area (mainly South Africa) increased from P55 million in 1981 to P77.5 million in 1985. The increase in the value of this trade was probably explained by the increase in the number of joint Botswana-South Africa ventures in light manufacturing, with the bulk of the raw materials coming from South Africa for final stage processing or packaging, the commodity then in turn being sold in the South African market. Exports to "other Africa"[8] increased from a value P35 million in 1981 to about P54 million in 1984, most of which I think would have been re-exports of South African goods to Zimbabwe (as Gaborone became the shopping district for many Zimbabweans) and also the export of textile products to Zimbabwe with the relocation of several textile manufacturers from Zimbabwe to northeastern Botswana. These features had as much to do with the economic situation in Zimbabwe as with sanctions busting but did result in an indirect trade between South Africa and Zimbabwe via Botswana. Zimbabwe itself became concerned about this and challenged the "local content" of textiles being exported from Botswana. After a series of acrimonious exchanges on the subject, the countries reached a modus vivendi which slowed down the growth of exports of textiles from Botswana to Zimbabwe based on South African and/or Zimbabwean raw materials.[9] The remainder of the increase in terms of the direction of trade was an increase in exports to "other Europe" (i.e., not the UK) from P138 million in 1981 to P1,118 million in 1985, which was almost certainly the result of the drastic increase in the export of diamonds.

The manufacturing sector could be the origin of export commodities which have the effect of avoiding sanctions. There was ample scope for that for a variety of reasons. The manufacturing sector in Botswana continued to be small and "light," comprising in 1984 a total of 209 companies with an average investment per company of P551,000. It included textiles, chemical and rubber products, wood and wood products, paper and paper products, electrical products, plastic products, and metal products, all activities that could become important in a strict sanctions environment. If one assumes that foreign (for the most part South African) owned firms or joint ventures would be most directly interested in and amenable to sanctions busting, then the manufacturing sector in Botswana offered significant opportunities. In 1984 the proportion of the 209 firms which were foreign owned was 58% with an additional 26% of joint foreign/Batswana ownership. Only 15% of firms were wholly owned by Batswana. In addition, 40% of the wholesale establishments (which were not within the data on manufacturing), including the largest firms, were foreign owned.[10]

The pattern of manufacturing capacity based on foreign investment or joint Batswana/foreign ventures was an increasing one, at least up to 1984. The number of foreign firms increased from 47 in 1979 to 122 in 1984 as the proportion of firms which were wholly Batswana-owned declined from 17% to 15%.[11] More recent data, particularly since the intensification of the international sanctions movement in 1985 and 1986, might yield a clue as to whether or not speculation on the likely sanctions-busting behavior of foreign investment is accurate; however, that data is not presently available.

There can be little doubt that certain foreign capital has moved into Botswana as a result of the sanctions environment. The extension of British Caledonian's (now British Airways') DC-10 flight from London to Lusaka to Gaborone in 1987 seemed to be premised on picking up traffic from South Africa without flying to Johannesburg. The British Airways manager in mid-1988 declined to comment on the present profitability of the flight but was quoted as saying that "I think the best way to put it is to say it is successful. We anticipate that it will be very busy very soon. It is a very important development."[12] A rumor in May of 1987 that a five star hotel would be built near the airport lends credence to this view, as does the announcement more recently that the Botswana Development Corporation in partnership with the Sheraton Corporation and Bouygyes France would build a P30 million hotel of 200 rooms incorporating a gymnasium and conference facilities as well as shops, a golf course, and swimming pool.[13]

Another example of what might be effectively sanctions busting through disinvestment in South Africa and/or reinvestment in Botswana is a new subsidiary (one of six in Africa) of the American multinational Colgate Palmolive built in Gaborone. The factory was reported to represent an investment of P1 million and would employ about 100 citizens.[14] It seems doubtful that Colgate Palmolive would locate one of only six African subsidiaries in Botswana unless it saw a market developing beyond the boundaries of Botswana itself. From Botswana it could perhaps develop markets in the SADCC countries and in the common customs area, i.e., in South Africa. Its South African business then would be shielded from criticism on the grounds that its production is located there. This might be indicative of a move by international capital to disinvest in the South African economy coupled with a re-investment in its immediate periphery.

It would therefore appear that the productive infrastructure to engage in sanctions busting, if on a modest scale, exists in the Botswana economy. More importantly, the ownership and possession of that infrastructure indicates that there is a real potential for its use in that way. This applies not only to direct South African interests in the Botswana economy but also to international capital as well, which has taken a recent and serious interest in "development opportunities" in Botswana.

Against the existence of the opportunities available and costs of breaking sanctions through Botswana must be set a comparison of similar opportunities and costs elsewhere. Swaziland, for example, appears to be a more congenial environment for South African manufacturing investment. The Swaziland government has been more open to turning a blind eye to sanctions busting efforts. The "country of origin" rules appear to be more lenient there than in Botswana. In addition, the public pronouncements of the government in Swaziland appear to be more welcoming of investments where the sanctions-busting implications are clear.[15] Furthermore, both Swaziland and Lesotho remained in the Rand Monetary Area, easing the flow of money to and from South Africa in comparison with the situation in Botswana.

Botswana's most important macroeconomic relationship with South Africa was that between the government of Botswana and South African mining capital, on the one hand, and the government of Botswana and the South African government on the other hand. Botswana's diamond-led economic growth is a direct outcome of the partnership of the government in Botswana and the DeBeers Diamond Mining Company. They jointly own Debswana, which operates the diamond mines in Botswana, the produce of which is marketed through the DeBeers-controlled Central Selling Organisation (CSO). DeBeers is part of the Anglo American Corporation economic empire in South Africa, whose fortunes are critical to the South African economy. The government of Botswana, in its own national economic interest, associated itself closely with the policies of DeBeers and the activities of the CSO through Debswana. This continued to be a most profitable relationship.

The relationship between the Botswana government and DeBeers became closer in July of 1987 with the announcement that Debswana had disposed of its diamond stocks for an undisclosed amount of cash and 20 million shares (5% of the stock) in the DeBeers Diamond Mining Company together with the right to appoint two directors to the DeBeers board of directors. Whatever additional economic benefits will accrue to Botswana from this deal, including access to information in DeBeers which was hitherto unavailable, it also ties Botswana's economic fortunes even more closely to the economic fortunes of the South African economy and inevitably draws Botswana closer to political interests comparable to certain important economic and political interests in South Africa itself. As an editorial in

Mmegi wa Dikgang/The Reporter put it, such a deal could be seen as undermining disinvestment strategies at a time when many Western multinationals were pulling out of South Africa; some observers have asked how Debswana's Batswana representatives would have dealt with questions about the attitude of Anglo American, 30% owned by DeBeers, during the recent (South African National Union of Mineworkers) miners' strike.[16]

As Morton pointed out,[17] the strictly economic advantage to Botswana of this deepening relationship with DeBeers is undoubted; but the advantage to South Africa is similarly undeniable. The debate in the United States in 1988 about intensifying sanctions against South Africa partially involved a proposal to impose sanctions on South African diamonds. That proposal was defeated partially on the argument that it would be difficult if not impossible to distinguish between South African and Botswana diamonds, particularly industrial diamonds, marketed through the CSO. Therefore blanket sanctions would be likely to harm Botswana more than South Africa, as Botswana industrial diamonds were the ones most likely to be directly imported into the United States.[18] This seemed to confirm, as *Mmegi wa Dikgang/The Reporter* pointed out, that the close relationship between the government of Botswana and DeBeers contained a "hidden spin-off advantage for South Africa in protecting Pretoria from what would, potentially, be an extremely damaging form of sanctions."[19]

Even more recently it appeared that a new and very large deal involving the governments of Botswana and South Africa as well as South African capital was nearing completion. For several years the government of Botswana has been attempting to put together a deal to exploit the very substantial soda ash deposits at Sua Pan. The planned capacity of the plant would yield 300,000 tons of soda ash per year. This is sufficient to supply the entire regional market although the main market is South Africa. Soda ash is a raw material used in the manufacture of, for example, glass, paper, and certain steel products.[20]

A stumbling block to developing the mining project has been that although production would be sufficient to supply the South African market, South Africa was importing its soda ash from the United States at a price below the price which would be charged for Botswana supplies. The South African government had been reportedly asking for a year or more that its agreement to stop waiving the normal tariff on soda ash in the common customs area should be linked to agreements on other issues of bilateral interest, most importantly security issues including at one point reports that South Africa was insisting that Botswana sign a Nkomati-type agreement. Botswana refused to do so and the deal was stalled. Those conditions appeared to be lifted and South Africa apparently agreed to a protective tariff.

The deal would result in a Debswana-like arrangement, with the Botswana government holding substantial shares in partnership with the South African African Explosives and Chemical Industries, which is jointly owned by the Anglo American Corporation and the British Imperial Chemical Industries. With a protective tariff, which means the active involvement of the South African government, the project would be economically viable and would secure southern African sources of soda ash for the South African economy. It could then be argued that this is a case of directly investing in apartheid although that is not part of the intention, ideology, or policy of the Botswana government.

Taken together with the diamond deal, the Sua Pan project does seem to deepen the cooperative relationship which has developed over the years between the government of Botswana and South African capital, specifically with the Anglo American Corporation as well as the relationship with the government of South Africa. As one Botswana newspaper put it, "Observers . . . note that the soda ash project, coming soon after the diamond deal, announced in July, in terms of which Botswana acquired cash, shares and Board seats in DeBeers, ties this country even more closely to the South African economy."[21]

At the same time it must be more than coincidental that the South African government should drop its insistence on signing security agreements with Botswana and agree to protective tariffs at a time when it is coming under increasing pressure in the world at large. The threat of sanctions could at some early date result in US supplies of soda ash being cut off. In order to forestall the possibility of that affecting domestic policies, it would appear that the South African government now actively sought supplies of soda ash which would be more or less secure, at least in relative (if somewhat more expensive) terms. If so, then the new cooperative attitude of the South African government was directly related to the imposition and threat of imposition of sanctions. The additional cost to the South African economy through the protective tariff was deemed to be less than the benefit of finding that the economy could be held for ransom over soda ash. This, in combination with other economic pressures, will increase the cost of apartheid; sanctions, or their threat, can work.

More generally, the Sua Pan Project seems to be a good example of the ambiguities of the whole sanctions-busting debate. While the advantage to South Africa is clear and the economic reasons for Botswana's interest are obvious, the deal stands to create in addition new and long-term production opportunities for the entire SADCC region. Soda ash from Sua Pan will meet the requirements for that raw material for the whole of SADCC as well as South Africa. Zimbabwe, the most industrially developed of the SADCC countries, was reportedly offered a ten-percent stake in the Project,[22] thus recognizing the importance of Sua Pan for the development of the liberated states in the region. Arguing against Sua Pan because it will allow South Africa to avoid sanctions means at the same time arguing against the development of industrial productive capacity of SADCC as well as the benefits to Botswana in jobs, development revenue, and the opportunity to develop backward and forward linkages. Support for Sua Pan to benefit Botswana and the SADCC's development—which it will do—means at the same time furthering the insulation of the apartheid economy from the effects of sanctions. In the long run, Sua Pan is a small step in the development of a southern African productive capacity more autonomously than can be expected given the present domination of the world economic structure by the advanced capitalist countries (here specifically the US). If, however, grasping this opportunity merely makes more permanent the apartheid regime and South Africa's sub-imperialist role in the region, then its value has to be questioned. It is probably the case that Sua Pan may become part of a more progressive pattern of development and therefore worthy of support, its effect in insulating the South African economy from at least one sanction notwithstanding.

Perspectives on Botswana and Sanctions Against South Africa in Southern Africa

The evidence suggests five broad conclusions. One is that the internal, indigenous political economy of Botswana may be amenable to economic activities the effect of which is sanctions busting. An economically and politically important fraction of the petty-bourgeoisie already has an economic partnership with South African capital and this range of joint ventures can relatively easily be turned to activities which would amount to sanctions busting. This fraction is politically well located to reinforce policies which can accommodate those activities.[23] Resting on the benefits to Botswana in terms of macroeconomic growth and the alleviation of the persistent unemployment problem, this fraction of the petty-bourgeoisie may expand its economic interests through intrusive joint partnerships with South African capital. The recent debate over the razing of the Gaborone Hotel to make way for a mall the centerpiece of which will be a (South African) OK Bazaar is a case in point. Criticism was heaped upon this South African investment from all points of view (imperialism, competition with budding Batswana entrepreneurs, etc.). In the end these arguments lost their appeal as OK negotiated with the parastatal Botswana Development Corporation and what has been described as a "group of citizens." The result was reported to be an agreement wherein this "group of citizens" will hold 40% of OK's shares. In addition, DBN Developments, "wholly owned by [in June 1988 unnamed] citizens," will apparently own the P9 million complex and OK will pay rent to DBN Developments as the anchor tenant. Furthermore, 30% of the shop space will be preferentially leased to "citizen shop owners." Finally, Tswana Construction, two-thirds of whose shareholders are citizens, will be the main contractor. OK's concessions create security for the investment in the long run. In the meantime, a fraction of the Botswana national bourgeoisie participates in the profits and the joint agreement forges another material and deep tie between Botswana and South Africa, but one which becomes immune to criticism within the Batswana elite as their own economic interests are equated with the national economic interest.[24]

A second conclusion is that the direct presence of South African capital in the manufacturing sector opens up the opportunity to collude in sanctions busting in South Africa using Botswana as the venue without any direct collusion of the Botswana government or governing class. I have presented no evidence that indicates that firms have been or are being established in Botswana for this purpose. But the openness of the Botswana economy and policies of more or less unrestricted foreign investment in manufacturing create the opportunity to do just that.

What is not clear is the extent to which this can be done without its becoming clear that the intent of such increased business is indeed sanctions busting. The small Botswana market and its openness will make dramatic expansion for export or import stand out. It will not be easy to hide sanctions-busting operations within the economy. Given that fact it will be difficult to politically insulate such ventures from public criticism. The openness of the political environment is likely to make such ventures a target for opposition parties and the press. These difficulties must also be seen in relation to the possibility of their relative absence elsewhere, in Swaziland or Lesotho for instance. Thus, while the opportunity for sanctions-busting operations are present because of the position of an important fraction of the governing class and the presence of South African capital, their ability to capitalize on the opportunity is problematic.

At the same time the Botswana government sees no apparent problem with non-South African foreign investment in a sanctions environment. According to the *Botswana Daily News*, for example, the Minister of Commerce and Industry "appealed to American companies withdrawing from South Africa to reinvest their capital in Botswana."[25] It is likely that the sanction-busting implications of such investment would be denied. As *Mmegi wa Dikgang/The Reporter* editorialized recently:

> The Government could argue—and quite truthfully—that it had tried very hard in the past to secure investments from outside southern Africa, in our

> copper-nickel mines (American Metal Climax), our vast coal deposits (Shell Coal), in Sua Pan, and even in the Breweries, but had failed. Is Botswana supposed to forgo such development until South Africa is liberated, it could ask?
>
> The country is historically a part of the Southern Africa Customs Union and the point has been made on many occasions by both President Masire and the late President Khama, that Batswana did not choose their neighbours. This is a situation that most of our allies and friends have accepted and understood in the past.[26]

Third, the continuing importance of growing joint government of Botswana/South African capital ventures to the overall macroeconomic development of Botswana will be of importance in a growing international sanctions environment. The effect of such ventures in a sanctions environment is not so much that of sanctions busting as it is an effect of insulating the South African economy from the effects of sanctions. The Sua Pan soda ash project, for example, will substitute Botswana for American supplies of an important raw material. Secure supplies of soda ash in Botswana will prevent sanctions on imports from affecting the South African economy in that respect.

The effect of the Sua Pan soda ash project is to make the South African economy more self-sufficient in the southern African region. This marks it off as different in degree if not kind from the diamond deal and the partnership with DeBeers in Debswana. The diamond deal was struck before the sanctions issue was squarely on the international agenda, and in the first instance the Botswana government was rather desperate to conclude a deal. The first mine was opened under an agreement which gave the government only 15% of the mine and DeBeers had absolute control including agreement to have a closed mining compound. As the mine was very successful, and additional ores were found, Botswana became increasingly important to DeBeers itself, and it was at that point in the mid-1970s that DeBeers agreed to a fifty-fifty partnership through Debswana. DeBeers was interested in profits but also its position in the world of diamond marketing. The partnership turned out to be very good for both sides. The deal lent general support to the South African economy indirectly through the contribution of DeBeers to that economy. But the production of diamonds in Botswana was not important for the linkages in production within South Africa. Diamonds were not an important raw material for the manufacturing sector. An international boycott of diamonds would not automatically affect the productive capacity of South African industry.

The same cannot be said for the soda ash deal. Soda ash is an important raw material and if there were a boycott of US supplies it would affect—if not fatally then at least in some way—production in South Africa. The effect of supplying South Africa with that raw material is to make a direct contribution to the maintenance of the present South African economy in the event of international sanctions. Further, this deal is taking place in the full glare of a world where the question of sanctions against South Africa is very much on the agenda. The overall implication of the Sua Pan project is somewhat different from that represented by the diamond deals.

The distinction is important. It is analogous to that raised by Judy Seidman with regard to the display of Botswana tapestries in a South African state-owned museum. It is one thing to feel compelled to sell your goods in South Africa for sound historic and economic reasons. The long history of the "web of dependency" is not to be denied. It is quite another thing to give the appearance of colluding with the South African government and South African capital, legitimating it and at the same time being victimized by it, by collaborating in cultural (or economic) relations.[27] Such a consideration raises important questions about what *Mmegi wa Dikgang/The Reporter* calls the "dangers" arising from closer ties (for whatever reasons) with South Africa:

> There are general dangers that arise out of our closer ties to South Africa. It does make it increasingly difficult to take independent stands because in increasing our dependency, we increase our vulnerability.
>
> There is also the danger that many ordinary people might be beguiled into forgetting how odious apartheid is, and into muting their criticisms of it as

> they slip into more and more dealings with South Africa at many levels and in many ways.[28]

The additional implication of the insulation of the South African economy from outside pressure in this way is to force the further regional integration of economic development based on the South African economy. In a post-apartheid South (Southern) Africa this could turn out to be a positive development, not unlike the effect of sanctions on Southern Rhodesia, although now on a regional scale. The question, however, is whether this might delay the emergence of that post-apartheid society through the support it gives to the continuation of the apartheid economy in the present era.

Fourth, it is important to consider the subtlety of the Botswana government position. Its forging of partnerships with South African capital, which directly involves agreements with the South African state, is deemed to be a matter of national interest and economic security. From the point of view of the government, this places the issue in a category different from that of normal sanctions policy. Such agreements are viewed as necessary to strengthen the Botswana economy as a mechanism to resist pressure from South Africa. From two points of view this may be correct. For one thing it does generate resources in Botswana lessening the need to export labor and making it easier to maintain an independent economic and monetary policy. After all, the Pula is stronger than the Rand and is the strongest currency in the common customs area. Increased economic strength also makes it easier to resist overtures for direct sanctions busting.

Secondly, the macro-collaboration in the diamond and soda ash deals is not as one-sided as may appear at first blush. It is clear that Botswana diamond production has become crucial to the economic health of DeBeers itself and DeBeers efforts to retain control of the market in diamonds. As a result the Botswana government has achieved a partnership which yields economic benefits that are substantial. DeBeers does not have it all their own way. Likewise the soda ash deal which seems set to operate much like that in diamonds (i.e., the Debswana model) is not one which has it all South Africa's way. Had that been so and had Botswana needed the soda ash deal badly, then there would probably have been a Nkomati-type agreement long ago between South Africa and Botswana. South Africa needs the productive base in soda ash in Botswana. That it deepens Botswana's dependence in general (which it does) and that it helps South Africa withstand the pressure of sanctions (which it does) are therefore not the only issues to be considered. It also strengthens Botswana in certain ways in its relations with South Africa. That this is contradictory should not be surprising, given the contradictory nature of relations in this regional capitalist periphery.

Finally, and most speculatively, some of the evidence would suggest that South Africa's regional policy may be changing somewhat. Some years ago South Africa proposed a political and economic "constellation" of states in southern Africa, to be formed through diplomacy and with the carrot of South African aid. When that initiative failed, South Africa turned to the policy of destabilization and set about systematically attacking its neighbors for the real and supposed excuse that they were providing aid and comfort to South Africa's enemies, the African National Congress in particular. Punitive raids, the funding and training of so-called "freedom fighters" like UNITA in Angola and RENAMO in Mozambique, and other forms of subversion were repayment for the southern African nations' refusal to go along with apartheid.

Now, however, the arena of the struggle against apartheid has widened (very marginally in most respects) to include what has become world opinion on the side of imposing some kind of sanctions on South Africa. The cost of maintaining apartheid has gone up, if marginally. The South African economy has to respond to the sanctions environment and one means of doing so is to return to its regional base. It needs to protect and expand its market in southern Africa as a cushion against the loss of overseas markets. It needs to secure as wide a net of raw materials in southern Africa as possible in order to cushion the effects of overseas supplies drying up with sanctions. It needs to create positive economic inducements to gain the cooperation, if indirect, of its neighbors. Perhaps we are in for another shift in South African policy because of the sanctions environment. It might be appropriate to finish with an extract of an opinion piece from *The Gazette* subsequent to the visit to Botswana in October, 1987 by South African foreign minister Pik Botha, purportedly to finalize details of the Sua Pan project:

> Thus Mr. Botha's visit on October 13 marks a significant change and a possible shift in policy on the part of Pretoria, according to regional analysis.
>
> Critics of the Government expressed strong verbal protests over a visit three months earlier by Mr. Botha to Botswana.
>
> External Affairs Minister Dr. Gaositwe Chiepe told angry Opposition Members of Parliament that Mr. Botha had flown into the diamond mining town of Jwaneng, on a private visit to see Mr. Basimanyana Peter Masire, a brother of President Masire.
>
> Dr. Chiepe vigorously denied that the Government had prior knowledge of the visit. Government spokesmen in Gaborone attempted to play down the importance of Mr. Botha's latest visit, saying he had come to finalise details of the Sua Pan soda ash project in which South Africa is expected to have a major financial and technical stake.
>
> The South African minister's visit, however, has taken on extra significance with earlier announcements of a major acquisition of shares by the Botswana Government in Anglo American the South African diamond conglomerate and new commercial investments in Gaborone by Johannesburg-based companies.
>
> Other observers said the combination of these factors and Mr. Botha's forays into Botswana were clear indicators that South Africa was laying the foundation for a modus vivendi with Botswana.[29]

Is he perhaps laying also the foundation for a modus vivendi for other states in the region as well? Perhaps. But the fact also is that South African military action against Botswana has also continued.

The effect of such events is also not solely to secure economic ends in South Africa. There is, in addition, from South Africa's point of view an effect in confusing the issue with regard to the anti-apartheid movement worldwide. The trip to Gaborone by the South African Foreign Minister, Pik Botha, in October, is a case in point, as *Mmegi wa Dikgang/The Reporter* points out:

> For one thing he [Pik Botha] was here during the very week that all the Commonwealth Heads of State and Government, apart from Britain's Mrs. Thatcher, were calling for increased sanctions, to discuss action by the Customs Union which would result in tying Botswana economically, ever more closely to South Africa. He chose to claim on his return to Pretoria that South Africa was doing more to help Front Line States than the Commonwealth and other donors are doing, quoting Sua Pan and railways cooperation as two such measures, and this claim was supported by the more sycophantic of the South African newspapers. He was also able to accuse the American Soda Ash Consortium of hypocrisy in trying to label Botswana's proposed project an "investment in apartheid", calling it an alibi for continuing their own exports to the land of apartheid.[30]

The ambiguity which results is in the end a recognition that relations between Botswana and South Africa—economic and political—are part of a continuing struggle rooted in the contradictions of the national, regional, and international systems. The resulting analytical minefield can only be effectively mapped by keeping one's eyes on the prize of a liberated South Africa and a peaceful and progressive pattern of development in the future for the region as a whole.

Notes

1. *Migrant Labour and Tribal Life: A Study of Conditions in the Bechuanaland Protectorate* (London: Oxford University Press, 1947). I have developed certain of these themes at more length in my *Botswana:*

Liberal Democracy and the Labor Reserve in Southern Africa (Boulder: Westview Press, 1984). The most useful collection of essays on the colonial period is Fred Morton and Jeff Ramsey (Editors), *The Birth of Botswana: A History of the Bechuanaland Protectorate from 1910 to 1966* (Gaborone: Longman Botswana, 1987).

2. Reported in *Mmegi wa Dikgang/The Reporter* (Gaborone), Volume 4, No. 36, 19-25 September 1987, 1 and 4. See also the report of the speech in the *Daily News*, 16 September 1987, 1.

3. Stephen R. Lewis, Jr., "Some Economic Realities in Southern Africa: One Hundred Million Futures," in *Poverty, Policy and Food Security in Southern Africa*, ed. Coralie Bryant (Boulder, Co.: Lynne Rienner Publishers, 1988), 39-92.

4. "Unemployment" was defined as "those aged 12 years or more who were not employed during the reference week but who wanted to work and were available to work." See Central Statistics Office, *Labour Force Survey 1984-85* (Gaborone: The Government Printer, n.d.), 9. The statistics on unemployment are found on p. 17.

5. Values are reported in units of account (UA) which are defined as "equal to a unit of the currency in circulation in the remainder of the common customs area." The Pula value of 1 UA in 1981 was 1.04, 1.05 in 1982, 1.01 in 1983, and 1.13 in 1984. The definition and data reported unless otherwise noted are published by the Central Statistics Office, Ministry of Finance and Development Planning for the Department of Customs and Excise, *External Trade Statistics 1983/84* (Gaborone: The Government Printer, n.d.).

6. 1985 figures from *Statistical Bulletin*, Vol. 12, No. 1, March, 1987 (Gaborone: The Government Printer for the Central Statistics Office, 1987), 10.

7. Unless otherwise noted the figures referred to are from Ibid.

8. It is worth noting that this category appears to be almost exclusively Zimbabwe for in the 1983/84 trade statistics, op. cit., in 1984 the proportion of imports accounted for by Zimbabwe in the "other Africa" category was 97.8% and for exports 95.1%. Thus "other Africa" is Zimbabwe.

9. See the discussion of this issue in Fred Morton, "South African Capital in Southern Africa: Botswana's Sua Pan Project", paper presented at the Third Symposium on Post-Apartheid South Africa, University of Pittsburgh, 17-19 March 1988.

10. Data on manufacturing and the wholesale trade is from *National Development Plan*, 1985-1991 (Gaborone: The Government Printer, December 1985), 236-237. In October 1987, it was reported that there were a total of 5,000 businesses registered in the previous ten months. According to the Senior Commercial Officer in the Ministry of Commerce and Industry, the new businesses included ventures in meat and meat products, dairy and agricultural implements, beverages, Bakery products, textiles, and chemical and rubber products. See *Botswana Daily News*, 20 October 1987, 1.

11. Ibid.

12. *Mmegi wa Dikgang/The Reporter*, Vol. 5, No. 20, 28 May—3 June 1988, 4.

13. *Botswana Daily News*, 31 August 1987, 2.

14. *The Gazette*, "Business Gazette", 9 September 1987, 11-12.

15. See Alan Booth's chapter in this volume.

16. Editorial in *Mmegi wa Dikgang/The Reporter* ,Vol. 4, no. 37, 26 September—3 October, 1987, 2.

17. Fred Morton, "South African Capital in Southern Africa . . .", op. cit.

18. It was also pointed out that under existing rules the cutting and polishing of gems, done largely outside of South Africa in countries like Israel, Belgium, and India, conferred country of origin status on the diamonds in the country where the cutting and polishing took place. Therefore it would not be possible to identify South African stones under the present General Agreement on Tariffs and Trade (GATT). It was reported that 85% of U.S. imports of polished stones came from the three countries mentioned. See *Mmegi wa Dikgang/The Reporter*, Vol. 5, No. 20, 28 May—3 June, 1988, 4.

19. Ibid.

20. See *Botswana Daily News,* 19 October 1987, 1.

21. "Soda Ash: A Debswana-style Deal?", *Mmegi wa Dikgang/The Reporter,* Vol. 4, No. 39, 17-23 October 1987, 2. That article is the general source for the description of the deal presented above.

22. See Morton, op. cit., 3.

23. I make this case elsewhere in some detail. See for example *Botswana: Liberal Democracy and the Labor Reserve in Southern Africa* (Boulder: Westview Press, 1984), and, "The Trajectory of Class and State in Dependent Development: The Consequences of New Wealth for Botswana", in *The Journal of Commonwealth & Comparative Politics,* Vol. XXI, Number 3, November, 1983, 39-60.

24. Details of the agreement contained in a Botswana Development Corporation news release reported in *Mmegi wa Dikgang/The Reporter,* Vol. 5, No. 20, 28 May—3 June, 1988, 4.

25. *Botswana Daily News,* 16 October 1987, 3.

26. *Mmegi wa Dikgang/The Reporter,* Vol. 4, No. 40, 24-30 October 1987, 2.

27. See Judy Seidman, "Biting the Hand that bleeds you; or when do we talk about Cultural Boycott in Botswana?" *Mmegi wa Dikgang/The Reporter,* Vol. 4, No. 41, 30 October—7 November, 1987, 10.

28. *Mmegi wa Dikgang/The Reporter,* Vol. 4, no. 40, 24-30 October, 1987, 2.

29. See "A Modus vivendi after the bombs?" *The Gazette,* Wednesday, 28 October 1987, 6.

30. *Mmegi wa Dikgang/The Reporter,* Vol. 4, No. 40, 24-30 October 1987, 2.

SOUTH AFRICAN SANCTIONS BREAKING IN SOUTHERN AFRICA: THE CASE OF SWAZILAND

Alan R. Booth

Introduction

Of all the uncertainties and ambiguities surrounding the Western world's slapping of economic sanctions on South Africa during 1986, one thing is definite. South African attempts to obscure their effects on its economy, and to cover its tracks in evading them, have been quite effective.

Government censorship of the South African press has made it quite useless as a source for "sanctions-breaking" research. Government figures on foreign trade, which were always obscured, became increasingly secret—the first casualty, really, of sanctions. Customs and excise figures have continued to be published, but information on harbor traffic and shipping schedules, for instance, have been curbed; while South Africa and its trade partners' figures have begun to include Namibia and other neighboring states.[1]

So statisticians have had to make do with summary figures. Export statistics indicate that when gold is factored out, some of South Africa's commodity exports are feeling the pinch of sanctions. Coal (South Africa's second largest export earner) has been hardest hit—by sanctions on top of a general slump in the world market for fuels—leading to the cutback of production in one large mine. Other exports have been "sharply" hit, with a total drop in exports reckoned at from 3% to over 10%, depending on one's source.[2]

How worried the South African government is about all this is hard to say. A drop in exports of less than 10%, limited to a few commodities, would appear manageable. Certainly, to hear top government officials talk—which is not a lot—one could conclude that sanctions have been a mere pinprick. Indeed, sanctions have made some South African whites quite rich—those managers of foreign-owned corporations who have picked them up at fire sale prices, complete with ongoing franchise agreements, from foreign "divestors." "Beware Sanctions Euphoria," cautioned *The Star* (Johannesburg), hardly a supporter of government apartheid policies, to its white readers.[3]

South African Sanctions Breaking

Yet underneath this veneer of official calm and optimism lies a South African state which is feverishly engaged in evading world sanctions. In the absence of statistics and press accounts of "sanctions busting" (since revealing those secrets is a crime in South Africa, the few that appear are denatured and unhelpful), other signs are meaningful. One was the appointment of prominent figures as czars of two vital areas of government sanctions-breaking efforts. One, Fred Bell, former chief of Armscor (the renowned breaker of sanctions in the 1970s and 1980s), was given the task of freeing South African industrialists from their dependence on foreign technology. The other, Desmond Krogh (once governor of the Rhodesia Reserve Bank) was made coordinator of the Department of Finance's anti-sanctions effort.[4]

In the short run, Krogh is surely the more important of the two. For if the South African government could attempt to pass off as little more than a nuisance, it cannot hide the fact that the capital boycotts of 1985-87 have constituted an extremely serious obstacle to growth. In 1985, when the townships exploded into violence, 9 billion Rand (R) flowed out of the country. Another R6 billion fled in 1986.

Capital flight has been so serious that the ban on new investment by the Americans and the European Community (except for Britain) has yet to be tested, foreign and South African companies preferring to invest elsewhere. "Without foreign capital," *The Economist* warned recently, "South Africa's economy cannot manage the 5% growth a year it needs to create jobs for its burgeoning population; most economists agree that the 5% target can be met only if 10% of total investment—R3 billion a year—comes from abroad.[5]

Clearly Mr. Krogh has his work cut out for him. Just as clearly he and his murky colleagues are hard at work drumming up export business—sanctions or no—wherever they can get it, to amass the required investment income. They are, by all accounts, being aided by a "steady stream of sanctions busters," filing into this country, "offering their services in thinly disguised advertisements in the financial papers."[6]

It would appear that the greater number of these opportunities come from the second and third worlds, especially nations in the Far East. There, fierce price cutting by the South Africans is displacing Australian coal exporters. In southeast Asia, Thailand, not previously a pipemaker, appears to be using South African steel to manufacture pipe.[7]

Nearer home, South Africa is actively seeking friends on small islands off Africa's coasts which possess both airfields and harbors. By 1987 the republic had already moved into Equatorial Guinea, the Comoros, and Mauritius, with generous aid projects involving roadworking, medical assistance, and cattle breeding projects. In return the South Africans sought air landing rights which, combined with port access, would give them insurance of sorts against tougher sanctions, the ability to transship imports and exports through the islands.[8]

In particular, South Africa's fellow nations on the outs with the United Nations establishment,namely, Israel and Taiwan, seem to be responding with a ready hand to the Republic's need. At least they are the most heavily invested in the new factories springing up in the homelands, fostered and heavily subsidized by the South African Decentralization Board, where they are reputedly "worse than the Boers" when it comes to wages and working conditions.[9] And Israel is claimed to have been "systematically hoodwinking the Israeli public" by disguising its multimillion-dollar steel deals with South Africa through an intricate network of Swiss-based straw companies, and to be using its free trade agreement with the United States to funnel South African goods there—accounting for a 70 percent increase in South African exports to Israel.[10]

The Swaziland Connection

South Africa's alleged ties with Israel in any event fit into the pattern of what is now seen to be its sanctions-breaking strategy. That strategy has been summarized as follows:

> A new approach to [South Africa's] foreign trade policy in the face of sanctions includes the promotion of exports in non-traditional markets and in markets where trade is limited by the shortage of foreign currency by using 'non-conventional methods' .... The government ... has ... made it clear that it intends to try to maintain and strengthen its world trade links rather than retreating into attempted self-sufficiency .... Attention is also being given to strengthening existing trade links, *particularly with neighboring African states.*[11]

Swaziland has come to play a key role—perhaps the strongest role—in this "neighboring state" strategy.

The imminence of sanctions in 1986 made Swazi officialdom apprehensive that they would hurt Swaziland as much as they would South Africa. Attached to South Africa by a network of dependencies (migrant labor; the Customs Union; monetary [lilangeni-rand] linkage; energy; 90% reliance on South African imports), Swaziland felt sure to feel far more than the ripples of any sanctions waves striking South Africa.[12]

The fact of Swaziland's dilemma was repeated by its senior ministers at every opportunity. "Swaziland understands," the

Labour and Public Service Minister told an International Labour Organization [ILO] Conference in Geneva in mid-1986, "that [the] object of economic sanctions against South Africa is to dismantle apartheid." But, he added, they would "hit hard" on the victims they aimed at saving; and "in the final analysis, it "destroys [sic] the economies of neighboring states."[13]

South African threats to extend the effects of sanctions to its hinterland were taken seriously by the Swaziland business community, which was well aware that increased unemployment carried with it the threat of social and political unrest, and where fearful speculation touched on Berlin-type airlifts to combat a rumored South African grain embargo.[14] When British foreign secretary Sir Geoffrey Howe visited southern Africa in July 1986, the Swazi foreign minister, Prince Bhekimpi, told him flatly that Swaziland would not support any action that would ultimately harm its own people—thus placing his country out of step with most of the frontline (and other Southern African Development Coordination Conference [SADCC]) states.[15]

By October, as both Europe and the United States applied sanctions, Swaziland's worst fears seemed about to be realized. Finland's trade unions refused to handle goods destined for Swaziland, and other Scandinavian countries threatened slowdowns on Swazi products shipped through Durban. In March 1987, Japan embargoed Swaziland citrus, ostensibly because of the kingdom's economic ties with South Africa.[16]

"Sanctions Have Been Good to Swaziland"

Those incidents turned out to be the exceptions to, rather than the pattern of, the effects of anti-South African sanctions on Swaziland. Overall, the events of 1987 have proved that Swaziland had decidedly more to gain from sanctions than to fear. In fact, it would not be out of line to conclude that—to strain a sports metaphor—sanctions have been good to Swaziland. There are several reasons for this. First and foremost, sanctions have brought a wave of increased South African investment into the kingdom, which has in turn helped to stimulate a return to growth in its stagnating economy, a decline in inflation, and creation of a significant number of new jobs.

The employment estimates are particularly dramatic. Paid employment in Swaziland, averaging 89,500 during 1981-1983, fell to 87,399 in 1984-1985. Government estimates are that as many as 3,000 new jobs have been created by the current investment boom. Several of the kingdom's prime industrial estates (Matsapha, Mbabane, and Sidwashini) are running out of serviced building sites, and there is speculation that a new site will have to be developed along the rail line, perhaps in the lowveld near Phuzumaya.[17]

Actually, the beginning of this new industrial growth predated the actual imposition of sanctions (which is not to say that prudent South African businessmen had not seen them coming and acted). In early 1985, acknowledging its inability to match South African investment incentives for its "homelands," and after a series of industrial reverses, including the cutback or collapse of fertilizer, furniture, and TV production, the Swaziland government implemented a new incentive package to attract investment. Its new features included a tax holiday for manufactures, and an extension of residence permits for foreign investors from two to five years.[18]

The timing of the new Swazi incentives could not have been more fortuitous, coming as they did on top of the eruption of the South African townships (September 1984) and their ominous effects on the business climate. In 1985 Kirsh Industries reversed an earlier decision to set up its projected new cotton textile mill in the Transkei, and established it instead in Swaziland ("Swatex," at the Matsapha industrial estate). Its product, premium quality cloth, was to be marketed in South Africa, Europe, and the United States.[19] In 1986 Taiwanese investors (following a 1985 promotion trip by the Swazi prime minister) opened four new textile-related manufacturing plants in Swaziland. Its products aimed primarily at the European and North American markets, creating 850 new jobs. Other firms locating in Swaziland manufactured shoes, locks, cooking utensils, nuts and bolts, school desks, and appliances.[20]

If it was the anticipation of sanctions which fueled the flurry of investments in Swaziland during 1985-86, the realization of sanctions in late 1986, as if confirming the wisdom of the investors, touched off a new wave. As the details of sanctions against South Africa became understood, the soundness of Swaziland as a locus for investment became more widely recognized.

Most important was the quick assurance by the Reagan administration that the United States would regard goods produced in Swaziland and exported through South Africa as exempt from the United States sanctions against Pretoria. The exemption encompassed such products of Swaziland as were "transported, graded, packaged, repackaged, marked, containerized, or otherwise serviced" in South Africa; and it included goods produced in Swaziland by private South African capital.

Those guarantees simply added to the allure which Swaziland had traditionally offered during the 1970s and 1980s to the South African investor. Those included free exchange of goods and movement of funds between the two countries. Moreover, independent of South Africa (to which it was linked by a monetary and Customs Union), Swaziland, as a signatory to the Lome Conventions, had tariff and quota preferences for agricultural produce and manufactured goods to the 12-member European Community (EC). It was also a member of the 15-nation Preferential Trade Area for eastern and southern Africa, which allowed for a graded reduction of between 10% and 70% on a common list of trade items. Finally, under the General System of Preferences of the UN Conference on Trade and Development, Swaziland was a beneficiary of the non-reciprocal tariff preferences offered by the US, EC, Austria, Sweden, Switzerland, and Australia.

Moreover, Swaziland offered a liberal interpretation of what qualified goods to be regarded as the "product" or "manufacture of Swaziland." "Rules of Origin" of preferential trade areas or countries required that about 35% of the direct production costs of such goods as represented by "materials purchased or labour performed" be attributable to Swaziland.[22] Other countries required even less: a "certificate of origin," which stipulated only that the product be "finished in Swaziland and contain at least 25% local value added."

Finally, goods could legally be exported from Swaziland and marked "made in Swaziland" even if they did not qualify for a certificate of origin. And, a local economic newsletter observed, "Swaziland does not know and cannot enforce the rules for each country. It must trust that if the destination country has any questions it will contact the government of Swaziland to ascertain whether the goods are legitimate."[23]

Under those regulations, it was possible for South African firms with warehouses in Swaziland to use the kingdom as a conduit to and from the republic: consigning goods bound to and from South Africa to Swaziland instead, for transshipment. Industries in Swaziland even found it possible to import items from their South African branches and export via Swaziland without those items having the proper 25% local content.[24]

South African industries have consequently turned to Swaziland in large numbers during the past year. By October 1987, the government-owned Swaziland Industrial Development Company (SIDCO) was processing 15 new foreign investment projects, most of them South African, amounting to 150 million emalangeni (E) ($75 million). Several more were at the discussion stage. One of the new South African-capitalized projects, Interboard Swaziland (Pty.) Ltd., opened its E47 million ($23.5 million) Nhlangano plant for the manufacture and export of chip board, 50% to Europe, 50% to South Africa.[25]

A large paper mill (presumably South African as well) was to be set up on the former Matsapha premises of the liquidated Swaziland Chemical Industries—whose assets, it was reported, the US chemical multinational Dupont was interested in acquiring. British capital, Lonrho and the Commonwealth Development Corporation, announced the establishment of two ethanol fuel distilleries in the sugar-producing lowveld, the market for which was surely South Africa.[25]

The potential for Swazi ethanol in future efforts by South Africa to breach tougher sanctions (not to mention Lonrho's and the Thatcher government's roles in its development) raise a number of interesting questions, which are outside the scope of this paper. But ethanol is not the only new strategic commodity to be produced in Swaziland with the potential for shock value.

It was announced in July 1987 that the newly-formed Swazi Chrome Company would establish a E14 million ($7 million) charge chrome plant in the lowveld near the north-south rail link to Richard's Bay, South Africa, and the rich coal field at Mpaka. Designed to produce up to 60,000 tons of charge chrome per year, it was headed by John Vorster, a former director of South Africa's Samancor ferrochrome plant, and was to use feed from South Africa (which produced 50% of ores and concentrates outside the Eastern bloc).[26] It was the clearest example to date of the ways in which South African industry was using Swaziland to position itself in anticipation of more damaging sanctions in the future.

"Going Half-Way"

But in 1986 and 1987 it was also for the Americans that "sanctions, at long last, had put Swaziland on the map."[27] United States-owned multinationals, which pulled out of South Africa with such an initial flurry of favorable publicity during 1986, were also quietly looking at what Swaziland had to offer. One was Coca-Cola, which announced with great fanfare in September 1986, that its pullout would involve selling R10 million ($5 million) worth of shares to black South Africans. In November 1986, the corporation announced its intention to build a E15 million ($7.5 million) concentrates plant at Matsapha, which would supply all of southern and central Africa, as well as the Indian Ocean islands. Swaziland's free access to South Africa would, of course, allow Coke to ship its product to the republic, where the corporation had retained its franchising rights.[28]

Other U.S. multinationals have observed these goings-on with more than a modicum of interest. General Electric, which announced its departure from South Africa in late 1986, is cited by Swazi officials as planning to base itself in Swaziland. Most interesting is the case of Kodak, which in November 1986, announced its exit. In doing so it went a step further than other US divestors—at least in the area of public relations. While they had carefully preserved upon leaving their licensing, component supply, franchising, and trademark agreements with their South African purchasers, Kodak announced that, in addition to selling its assets, it would halt and prevent further shipments of its products to South Africa as well. "We decided we would not go half-way," a company spokesman announced to a press conference.[29]

But "going half-way" was just what Kodak subsequently appeared to be doing, when in late 1987 it was reported to be contacting Swazi officials about re-establishing itself in Swaziland.[30]

The future marketing strategies of Coca-Cola (and Kodak, if it invests) in Swaziland over the next few years will reveal a great deal about the actual strategies of U.S. multinational "divestors" from South Africa, and the role those plans provide for Swaziland. Perhaps the two American corporations have at last found the optimum way to, in the words of South African economist Duncan Innes, "retain access to our markets without any longer having to deal with anti-apartheid harrassment at home."[31]

Conclusion

The stealth with which South Africa is going about evading sanctions makes any analysis of its strategy a difficult undertaking. So, too, have the "magic lantern show" departures of US multinationals from South Africa obscured their true intentions. It will take a while for the smoke to clear, but certain outlines are already discernible. One is that Swaziland's role in Pretoria's sanctions-breaking efforts, and in international capital's relocation and repositioning in the South African market (for that is for the most part what "disinvestment" has turned out to be), is a significant one. The chances are that the kingdom's role will increase over the next several years, and that its economy will be the richer for it.

The reasons are fairly obvious. Swaziland's open border with Pretoria, its preferential access to U.S., European, and Third World markets, and its keenness to attract African and other foreign capital, make it an ideal instrument.

There is nothing in its recent relations with Pretoria to preclude Swaziland's playing this role of collaborator. Since 1980, during the declining years of King Sobhuza II (d. 1982) and the early reign of his successor, Mswati III, Swaziland's relations with Pretoria have increasingly been seen as those of the client. The policy of the dying King Sobhuza of accepting the incorporation of the KaNgwane homeland from Pretoria in return for Swaziland's suppression of the African National Congress (ANC) continues under Mswati, who has publicly re-endorsed the land deal. The 1982 secret accord with South Africa remains in force. The bodycount from Pretoria's kidnap and death squads roaming the kingdoms, seemingly at will and with no more than perfunctory Swazi protest, continues by the month. Swaziland's new rail links connecting it with the South African transport system carry more and more tonnage.[32]

It is as if Swaziland's rulers, while decrying apartheid and maintaining their ties with SADCC, have managed to balance off those positions with the more pressing needs for peace with their powerful and edgy neighbor, and for as much of a share of Pretoria's investment as it can get. So the kingdom's increasingly open role in South Africa's sanctions-breaking efforts and in the repositioning of international capital is not all that inconsistent with its recent diplomatic maneuverings.

By all accounts it is becoming a profitable position to take. Swazi headlines ("Economic Boom in '87") and those from South Africa ("Sanctions Boost Swazi Economy") tell of a far rosier outcome for the kingdom in the face of sanctions breaking than was once feared. In fact the government, in its current economic forecast, expects production from "recently established new businesses" to offset the predicted 20% drop in sugar production, reduce the inflation rate, and maintain a real annual growth rate of 3.2% through 1990.[34]

What this prospect of new prosperity omits is the factor of dependency on a country which has become ever increasingly the pariah of the civilized world, which will force Swaziland to make some hard choices as Pretoria becomes increasingly isolated in the future.

Notes

1. Economist Intelligence Unit, Country Report: *South Africa* [hereafter EIUCR-RSA] 4-1986, 16; EIUCR-RSA 2-1987, 19.

2. EIUCR-RSA 2-1987, 21; EIUCR-RSA 3-1987, 7, 28-29; "Whatever Happened to Sanctions?" *Economist*, 22 August 1987, 39-40. South African exports, January-May 1987, were R5.65 billion, compared to R4.92 billion for the same period in 1986. But the average gold price jumped from $343 per oz. in 1986 (January-May) to $443 per oz. in 1987 [each $50 increase bringing $2 billion into South Africa]. That price rise, coupled with an altered rand/dollar exchange rate, was good for an extra $1.3 billion to South Africa, meaning that non-gold exports were off for the period by R570 million. Total losses in coal export earnings in 1987 may run to R900 million. The coalmine cut back was the Welgedacht, at Utrecht, causing a retrenchment of 530 workers.

3. "Why South Africa Shrugs at Sanctions," *Forbes Magazine*, 9 March 1987, 101.

4. *Star Weekly* (Johannesburg), 3 January 1987; "South Africa Shrugs at Sanctions," 103.

5. EIUCR-RSA 4-1986, 17; "Whatever Happened to Sanctions?", 40.

6. EIUCR-RSA 1-1987, 17.

7. "South Africa Shrugs at Sanctions," 103.

8. "South African Seeks Friends With Airstrip," *New York Times*, 21 October 1987. The reported activities by South Africa give further credence to reports that it had entered negotiations with the Manx (Isle of Man) government with the intention of taking over its free port and importing South African goods to the island, processing food, changing labels, and then reporting to EEC countries. ("Manx Denies Sanctions-Busting Plan," *Star Weekly*, 24 January 1987.) Similarly, a West German firm, LIAT Finance Trade and Construction Ltd., with strong ties to Israel and South Africa (through Bophuthatswana) is suspected of being the vehicle by which South

Africa is allegedly seeking transshipping and re-exporting arrangements in Sierra Leone ("Sierre Leone/South Africa: The Strange Story of LIAT," *Africa Confidential*, XVIII, 13 [24 June 1987]; "Sierre Leone: Wide Open to South Africa?", *Review of African Political Economy*, XXXVIII [April 1987], 86-89). For similar South African intrigues in the Seychelles, see "Spy Hired to Bust Sanctions," *Observer* (London), 26 April 1987; "South Africa: The Network of a Master Spy," *Africa Confidential*, XVIII, 8 (15 April 1987).

9. "Taiwanese, Israelis Exploit Cheap Black Labor in South Africa," *Manchester Guardian Weekly*, 26 April 1987.

10. "Israel Loophole in Sanctions Net Denied," *Star Weekly*, 20 December 1986: "SA Straw Company Steel Deals Hoodwink Israeli Public—MP," *Star* (Johannesburg), 4 August 1987.

11. EIUCR-RSA 4-1986, 16-17; EIUCR-RSA 1-1987, 18 [italics mine]. It apparently is also South African strategy to maintain a foothold in sanctioning countries by resorting to false invoicing. It is alleged, for instance, that South Africa is breaking France's 1985 embargo by shipping 600,000 tons of coal (1986) and 800,000 tons (first half of 1987) invoiced as originating in Australia ("Aussie Coal in France Allegedly from SA," *Star*, 14 August 1987).

12. Swaziland delinked from the South African rand on 1 July 1986.

13. The minister was Mhlangano Matsebula ("Sanctions Can Be a Big Blow To Us—Matsebula," *Swazi Observer*, 27 June 1986).

14. "Why Swazis Are Jittery Over the Prospect of Anti-SA Sanctions," *Star Weekly*, 30 June 1986; "Could Our Wheat Be Blockaded?" *Times of Swaziland*, 3 October 1986.

15. Economist Intelligence Unit, *Country Report: Namibia, Botswana, Lesotho, Swaziland* [hereafter, EIUCR-SWD] 3-1986, 51. Swaziland's regional neighbors (with the exception of post-coup Lesotho) were at the same time reaffirming their commitment to sanctions, despite the threat of serious economic repercussions. See, for instance, "SA Ban Could Hit Over 1-M Mozambicans," *Star Weekly*, 11 October 1986.

16. *Econews* (Swaziland), IV, 1 (October 1986), 3-4, 6, 10; "Citrus Board Loses Japan Market," *Swazi Observer*, 18 March 1987. The

Swaziland Citrus Board markets mainly through South Africa's Cooperative Exchange ("Outspan"), some of its product sold with a "Produce of Swaziland" label, the rest marketed under the "Outspan" label.

17. *Econews*, 9. Economist Intelligence Unit, *Country Profile: Botswana, Lesotho, Swaziland* [hereafter EIUCP-SWD] 1987-88, 67; "Matsapha Is Centre-Stage," *Times of Swaziland*, 25 February 1987; "Economic Boom in '87," *Swazi Observer*, 6 August 1987.

18. EIUCP-SWD 1987-88, 75.

19. Interviews, Nathan Kirsh, Johannesburg, 2 March 1983 and 24 February 1986. "Swatex" was a new company formed by Kirsh Industries Swaziland ("Swaki"). For Nathan Kirsh in Swaziland, see Alan R. Booth, "Capitalism and the Competition for Swazi Labour, 1945-1960," *Journal of Southern African Studies*, XIII, 1 (October 1986), 148.

20. *Econews*, 9; EIUCR-SWD 4-1986, 48. The four Taiwanese enterprises were: More Industries Ltd. (Mbabane; gloves [USA]; 100 workers); Garment Industries Swaziland Ltd. (Matsapha; shirts [USA]; 500 workers); Oriental Swaziland Ltd. (light clothes; 200 workers); and Francois Fashions Ltd. (Matsapha; knit sweaters [USA/Europe/South Africa]; 50 workers). "450 Jobs Soon to Be Available," *Swazi Observer*, 17 June 1986.

21. EIUCR-SWD 1-1987, 49.

22. EIUCP-SWD 1987-88, 84-86; "Swazis Wary of Letting in SA Sanctions-Busters," *Business Day* (Johannesburg), 21 April 1987.

23. *Econews*, 10.

24. Ibid.

25. "What is Swaziland? Well, For One Thing, It Isn't Switzerland," *Wall Street Journal*, 1 October 1987; "Development for the South," *Swazi Observer*, 24 September 1987; EIUCR-SWD 3-1987, 52; "Big Bend Gets New Fuel Plant," *Times of Swaziland*, 2 September 1987.

26. *African Economic Digest*, 10 July 1987; EIUCR-SWD 3-1987, 52. A substantial portion of the new venture's financing was reported to

be West German. The undertaking would eventually use up to 36,000 tons of Swazi coal annually, giving local production a substantial boost.

27. "What is Swaziland?", *Wall Street Journal,* 1 October 1987.

28. "Giant Coke is Here," *Times of Swaziland,* 6 November 1986; "E15 M Gets Coca-Cola Going," ibid., 21 January 1987; "Coke's Conco Settles In," ibid., 16 March 1987. Coca-Cola has had a substantial stake in sugar production in Swaziland since 1980, when the giant sugar mill at Simunye, in which it was part owner, commenced production.

29. "Kodak Sets Pretoria Pullout," *New York Times,* 20 November 1986. Kodak's sales in South Africa were in the neighborhood of $10 million annually, in addition to which it had marketing and photofinishing facilities in Johannesburg, Durban, Port Elizabeth, Cape Town, and Bloemfontein. In 1985 Kodak had agreed to stop marketing film and cameras on South African military bases in order to win an $8 million contract to supply photocopiers to New York City.

30. "What Is Swaziland?", *Wall Street Journal,* 1 October 1987; interview with Dr. Timothy J. Diamini, Swaziland Permanent Representative to the United Nations, Athens, Ohio, 24 October 1987.

31. Quoted in "The Ambiguity of South African Divestment," in *New York Times,* 31 December 1986. Innes was referring to IBM, which had "left" South Africa while retaining an array of licensing and components supply arrangements with the purchasers ("the barons of corporate power in South Africa"). The Coca-Cola arrangements for "divestment" allowed it to withdraw and still sell its products. Its bottling operations in South Africa were bought by franchised bottlers, while its syrup plant was relocated in Swaziland, so that Coke had no visible corporate presence in South Africa. But a new company, National Beverages Services Ltd., was created to buy Coca-Cola's assets, take over its trademark, and monitor product quality. ("U.S. Goods in South Africa: Little Impact of Divestiture," *New York Times,* 27 July 1987.)

32. "Railway Traffic Coup," *Times of Swaziland,* 23 April 1987.

33. Indeed, if one accepts the proposition that apartheid is at base a system of labor exploitation, Swazi industry might be said (albeit tongue-in-cheek) to be, on occasion, outdoing the South Africans. At least that was the perception of the Federation of Swaziland Employers, which accused local South African-owned companies of paying wages "a lot better" than their non-South African counterparts, and allowed that Swazis so fortunately employed "jealously guard their jobs." In his annual report, Federation president Neville Crowther complained that such differential wage scales "undermine[d] the economy of the kingdom" and posed "substantial hazards" to the system. "Why Pay is Better on the SA Scale," *Times of Swaziland*, 17 September 1987.

34. "Economic Boom in '87," *Swazi Observer*, 6 August 1987; "Sanctions Boost Swazi Economy," *Star* (Johannesburg), 16 September 1987; Swaziland Government (Prime Minister's Office; Department of Economic Planning and Statistics), *Economic Review and Outlook* (January 1987), 50.

SANCTIONS AGAINST SOUTH AFRICA: LESOTHO'S ROLE

James Cobbe

Introduction

Lesotho is widely regarded as the SADCC state most dependent on South Africa, for obvious reasons of geography and history.[1] It is not necessary to recount in detail the well-documented story of its history, economy, and politics that produced this result. It will suffice to note that Lesotho is physically an enclave wholly surrounded by South African territory, that over half of Lesotho's national income is earned by migrant workers in South Africa, and that Lesotho imports all its electricity and petroleum products, around half of its food, and over half of its total consumption goods from South Africa. Lesotho is a member of the Southern African Customs Union (SACU) (with South Africa, Botswana, and Swaziland) and the Common Monetary Area (with South Africa and Swaziland; informally known as the Rand Area).

However, "dependence" is a very slippery concept, and the bald statement that in a gross sense Lesotho is extraordinarily dependent on South Africa does not tell us anything about the actual behavior of the Lesotho government, or the actual nature of the constraints on that behavior caused by dependence on South Africa. Superficial analyses notwithstanding, any careful study of the history of Lesotho's behavior since independence will show that Lesotho is far from being a client state of Pretoria in any meaningful sense. This basic conclusion remains as true after the 1986 coup in Lesotho as it did before.[2] General Lekhanya's regime may be more accommodating of Pretoria's wishes on some dimensions (notably behavior toward the ANC) than Leabua Jonathan's was, but it still retains considerable freedom of action in both domestic policy and international relations, and it has exercised that freedom.

Thus, the actual and prospective application of economic sanctions against South Africa by the international community and specific countries raises some interesting questions about Lesotho that do not all have easily determined or clear-cut answers. The objective of this chapter is to raise some of these questions, and explore some tentative attempts at answers to a few of them.

The kinds of questions that will be addressed can be grouped into three sets:

1. What will be the probable effects of sanctions against South Africa on Lesotho, both direct and indirect, and both in narrow economic terms and in terms of political conditions and international relations between Lesotho and both South Africa and the other countries of SADCC in particular?
2. To what extent will the South African government, and private South African firms and individuals, seek to use Lesotho and its residents to evade the effects of sanctions?
3. What attitude in practice will the government of Lesotho adopt toward the enforcement of sanctions imposed by others, and toward evasion activities engaged in on its territory by its own nationals, South African nationals, and third country nationals?

It may seem surprising that I have omitted any question concerning whether Lesotho itself will introduce economic sanctions against South Africa. This should not be surprising, because it is the one question to which the answer does appear completely clear-cut. Lesotho will not. It cannot afford to, it would be economic and political suicide for the government to attempt to do so, and the new government stated very clearly in 1986 that it would not. The international community has always accepted that Lesotho is a special case in so far as its relations with South Africa are concerned. It is universally agreed that economic and geographic realities leave Lesotho no choice but to have, as far as possible, "normal" commercial and economic relations with the Republic of South Africa, and it was widely accepted during the latter part of Jonathan's rule that the existence of such relations in no sense reduced the legitimacy of his government's anti-apartheid credentials. The present government does not, as yet, have as clearly established anti-apartheid credentials as Jonathan was eventually able to acquire, and indeed is regarded by some observers as "in bed with" the South Africans. Certainly, it is true that the current Lesotho Government has far better relations with Pretoria than Jonathan did in the latter part of his rule. However, to a large extent this may be a question of pragmatism and military insensitivity to political concerns of those who do not have direct responsibility for the governance of a country in a very difficult situation. Refugees seeking to join the ANC still cross the Lesotho border, at a rate of around 15 to 20 a month, and are shipped out by air to destinations further north after fairly loose detention in Maseru until a flight is available. On the other hand, some of the pragmatism is a little extreme in public relations terms. The South African Trade Mission in Maseru quite openly performs full consular functions, and the South African Defense Force is openly present in the country (in uniform) for certain purposes [helicopter flights to villages in the mountains cut off by snow and flooded rivers, construction of a military hospital for the Royal Lesotho Defense Force (RLDF) in Maseru] for the first time in many years. Further, some incidents involving ANC members within the country raise serious questions about Lesotho's current stance.

The assassination of ANC member Mazizi Maqekeza in his hospital bed in Maseru, where he was being treated for wounds sustained in a clash with RLDF members, and the angry response in the government paper *Lesotho Today* (7 April 1988) to the allegations about his death in the Johannesburg *Weekly Mail* (25 March 1988), is perhaps the most disturbing incident. The *Lesotho Today* editorial makes clear that although the government of Lesotho's policy is "to give refuge to genuine political refugees as a signatory of the UN convention on refugees," in its view all "refugees" must report themselves to the "relevant authorities" on arrival, and may not carry firearms without an official government license (which clearly will not be issued to South African refugees). To quote the editorial, "Lesotho has neither the wish nor the power to keep refugees whose intention is to use Lesotho as a launching pad for attacks on other countries." The inclusion of "nor the power" in this sentence is of some interest, suggesting that armed ANC members in Lesotho are vulnerable to South African actions.

Although the Lesotho government is very far from a homogeneous entity, with the Council of Ministers encompassing both relatively politically neutral technocrats and persons of clear political identification ranging all the way across the Lesotho political spectrum from highly "right wing" former ministers of Jonathan (e.g., E. R. Sekhonyana, Minister of Finance) to "left wing" graduates of Moscow State University (e.g., Michael Sefali, ironically Minister of Planning and Economic Affairs), it is clear that on important matters of policy it is the Military Council, consisting of five career military officers, that has the final say on policy. However, it is also widely believed in Lesotho that the members of the Military Council are themselves not wholly in agreement on the appropriate political strategies to adopt toward South Africa and domestic constitutional arrangements. Some sources allege that the King, in alliance with his cousins, the Lieutenant-Colonels Letsie, wishes to retain the current system that gives him substantial power, whereas Lekhanya and others would like a return to some form of democracy, and that South Africa sides with Lekhanya because of a desire for democratic legitimacy to its agreements concerning the Highlands Water Scheme.[3] However, when it comes to economic relations with the Republic, and the desirability of Highlands Water, there does not appear to be much disagreement, and this suggestion has a distinct aroma of South African disinformation. Pretoria in practice as opposed to rhetoric has displayed little interest in encouraging democracy in its neighbors, and is much more likely to be opposed to King Moshoeshoe II for the simple reason that he, sometimes dubbed the "mildly marxist monarch" by irreverent expatriates in Lesotho, is well known to espouse views very inimical to Pretoria.

Effects of Sanctions

The starting point for any discussion of the effects of sanctions has to be the disclaimer that it is very difficult to discuss the effects of sanctions in the best of circumstances, because of the substantial uncertainties involved, but it is almost impossible to be at all precise if the exact specification of the sanctions under discussion is unknown. One is forced, therefore, to make some assumptions about the nature of the sanctions to be considered.

The types of sanctions we will consider are two, namely those that close markets to South African exports, and those that deny South Africa legal access to imports from certain sources, typically of high technology products. In addition, we will make some comments on effects of campaigns against investment in South Africa.

The first of these kinds of sanction is by far the more important for Lesotho, and, to be blunt, their imposition is easily the most positive development for the Lesotho economy for several years. It is crucial to carefully explain why this is so, and how it can be without Lesotho doing anything that, in its view at least, could reasonably be regarded as attempting to defeat the purposes of sanctions against South Africa—although opinions might differ about that, even if one had complete sympathy with Lesotho's decision about policy.

To understand why this should be so, we will need to review briefly the economic situation of Lesotho and the economic development strategy it has pursued since independence. Lesotho now has a population of approximately 1.6 million people, about 84% of whom live in rural areas. However, even in rural areas, agriculture is the main source of income for only about 42% of households; remittances from absent migrants or support from relatives is the main source of income for about 43.6% of rural households, and even 29.5% of urban households. 25.4% of rural households have no access to land, which is very limited because of the small size and mountainous topography of the country; two-thirds of these unfortunates do not have livestock either. Over a third of those who do have land do not have livestock.[4]

In these circumstances, Lesotho is highly dependent on the earnings of temporary migrants in the mining industry in South Africa, as it has been since before independence. However, the access of Lesotho to this market for her labor is, and has been since at least the early 1970s, somewhat uncertain. This is highly problematic for Lesotho because of the magnitudes involved. As already noted, migrant earnings are roughly equal to domestic output within Lesotho, and even now close to half of all households in Lesotho are dependent to some extent on remittances from migrants in South Africa.

South Africa in the long run has no need for migrant workers from Lesotho. It has considerable black unemployment (variously estimated from 8.1% to 22% of the black labor force) within its borders, and since the increases in real mine earnings of the mid to late 70s, TEBA (The Employment Bureau of Africa, the recruitment agency for the Chamber of Mines) has no difficulty in supplying adequate numbers of novice recruits from within the borders of the Republic of South Africa. In the short run, other things equal, the mines would like to retain the services of their miners from Lesotho, because they are experienced, have a reputation as good workers, live within a relatively short distance from the mines, and represent a useful diversification of sources of labor, which is a worthwhile insurance policy for the mines given the unsettled political climate in southern Africa. Replacing them with novices would be expensive and undesirable for the mines in the short to medium term.

However, the mines are not given a completely free hand in their choice of labor by the government of the Republic of South Africa. Pretoria can dictate what the mines will do with respect to foreign labor, subject to negotiation to some extent. Thus the number of miners from Mozambique has been reduced at Pretoria's dictate, and it has been alleged by some observers that some of the fluctuation in numbers of Basotho miners in recent years (e.g., the decline in numbers after Lesotho failed to sign an agreement similar to the Nkomati Accords) has been attributable to political decisions by Pretoria.[5] Thus there is a risk that Pretoria will carry through with the threats it has made at times to repatriate miners to Lesotho, either to induce Lesotho to behave in ways more acceptable to Pretoria or as "retaliation" for actions taken against Pretoria by others. Overall, it is projected by de Vletter that foreign workers on the mines could easily drop to only around 20 per cent of the total by the early 1990s, even without action by the South African government.[6]

Furthermore, things are not always equal. Basotho have been prominent in the rise and leadership of the National Union of Mineworkers of South Africa (NUM), and took a conspicuous part in the 1987 strike by NUM against the gold mines. As it happens, the mining house most severely hit by the strike was the Anglo American Corporation, which before the strike employed about 29% of all Basotho miners. Anglo American, which had given some support to the NUM earlier, was apparently very unhappy with the behavior of the Union, and appears to have reacted to the strike and Basotho involvement in it by reducing its employment of Basotho. The extent of the change in total numbers of Basotho migrants following the strike is not yet clear, but in the view of TEBA management in Maseru the former slow upward trend (numbers of Basotho miners peaked in the second quarter of 1987 at 131,134, the highest figure of the decade) was likely to be reversed. This may, however, be alarmist, because in the latter half of 1987 migrants numbered 122,640, with no strong downward trend between the third and fourth quarters; and Anglo American does seem to have reached an accommodation of sorts with the NUM, rehiring 30,000 miners fired during the strike.[7] By the third quarter of 1988, the number of Basotho miners was in fact some 3,000 higher than a year earlier.

These incidents illustrate Lesotho's vulnerability arising from its dependence on migrant labor, and explain to some extent why, at least in its official statements, the government of Lesotho has, ever since independence, put great emphasis on promoting alternative, domestic sources of wage employment. One can argue that this emphasis has been mistaken, that in fact the majority of nonmigrant Basotho are self-employed or unpaid family workers, and that the best emphasis would have been on horticulture, intensive non-traditional non-fieldcrop agriculture, rural nonfarm activities, and the informal sector in towns; but nevertheless it has been wage employment that in practice the government has emphasized.

Within the wage employment sector, manufacturing has always been the great hope of the government, and South African fear of "a little Hong Kong" within its borders has at times encouraged it. Unfortunately, the record of manufacturing growth since independence in Lesotho has been extremely disappointing, reflecting Lesotho's relatively disadvantageous position as a location for manufacturing industry in Southern Africa as a whole. In the twenty years after independence, manufacturing averaged a job-creation rate of only about 300 a year, barely 2% of the annual net additions to the labor force.

Lesotho's disadvantages as a location arise from its geographical position and consequent high transport costs for inputs and outputs, its relative lack of suitable infrastructure, shortages of skilled and supervisory labor, and less attractive incentive packages than the decentralization areas and bantustans in the Republic of South Africa. However, the beginnings of the imposition of sanctions against South Africa's exports radically changed this situation, which was quickly recognized in Lesotho. Goods of Lesotho origin are not only given free access to the southern African market under SACU, but also have preferential access to the European Community Market under the Lome Convention, and to other African markets under the Preferential Trade Agreement for Eastern and Southern Africa (PTA), and are fully acceptable in all other markets worldwide, even though they are transported through South Africa and exported through South African ports. In fact, a statement issued by the US Embassy in Maseru, and publicized by the Lesotho government's parastatal Lesotho National Development Corporation (LNDC) in South Africa, made clear that the official interpretation of the 1986 US Anti-Apartheid Act not only meant that goods of

Lesotho origin were exempted from the restrictions of the Act even though they had transited South Africa, but that they could even be packaged, repackaged, or graded in South Africa and still be acceptable to the US authorities, regardless of whether the manufacturer in Lesotho was South African-owned. US Department of Treasury regulations provided that "as a general rule, imports of products of third countries which were transshipped through South Africa will not be prohibited when such products were merely transported, graded, packaged, repackaged, containerized, marked, or otherwise serviced in transit in South Africa," even if the goods were produced in third countries with private South African capital.[8]

Overall economic conditions from 1986 created a favorable climate for attracting so-called flight capital to Lesotho (and also Swaziland, which, in the view of most observers in Lesotho, has done much better at this, reflecting better location for transport purposes to export markets, better infrastructure, and—in South African eyes—a more disciplined labor force). Macroeconomic conditions in southern Africa were very depressed, and simultaneously the exchange rate of the Rand, at around 50 US cents, made export markets very attractive to South African manufacturers. The issue, of course, from a South African point of view, is access to the export markets, because of sanctions and consumer boycotts (far more important in the UK and Europe than in the US).

Location of final assembly in Lesotho (or Swaziland) is an ideal, and relatively low-cost, solution to the problem from the point of view of the South African manufacturer. They both are within the customs union and the Rand area, so there are no complications with customs, trade restrictions, or foreign exchange, and yet their goods have access to markets worldwide. This process of transfer of capacity, or attraction of flight capital (or whatever label one wants to use for it) is what both Lesotho and Swaziland are trying to encourage, and the major way in which they stand to gain from the imposition of sanctions against their neighbor. In the case of Lesotho, at least, the process is quite open, and civil servants and high government officials bring it up spontaneously, being not in the least apologetic about it, even when their own opposition to the apartheid system in South Africa is beyond question.

The issue then becomes how this process should be viewed. The Lesotho interpretation is very straightforward. South African manufacturers who establish operations in Lesotho are employing Basotho, and bringing Lesotho needed value added, exports, and (through the operations of the SACU) revenue as a result of their intermediate imports. At the same time, South African firms and their employees are having to deal with a truly independent African government, operate under color-blind law, and cope with labor legislation quite unlike that of South Africa. That the South African manufacturer is also to some extent defeating the purpose of sanctions, by continuing to make exports from the SACU and thereby help the foreign exchange position of the Rand area and the South African government in particular, is unfortunate but a consequence of geography and institutional arrangements that are quite beyond the control of the government of Lesotho.

What one has, in effect, is a situation somewhat akin to the distinction often made with respect to income tax between tax evasion, which is illegal, and tax avoidance, which defeats the actual objective of the tax legislation but is—in terms of the letter of the law—legal. Lesotho (and Swaziland), in seeking to attract South African manufacturers to set up shop in order to have access to export markets, are acting in a fashion similar to the tax lawyers and accountants who facilitate tax avoidance. Tax lawyers and accountants, although they may not be popular people, are generally regarded as respectable. In fact, the government of Lesotho can legitimately claim that its behavior is far less disreputable than that of the tax avoidance advisor because it is not acting in its individual venal interest, but in the interest of promoting the general development objectives of the country as a whole and of the unemployed in particular.

How then should outsiders view this behavior? Does it constitute "being in bed with the South Africans," or is it rather perfectly reasonable given the situation Lesotho finds itself in? Different observers will obviously react differently, but I find it very hard to criticize the government of Lesotho for managing to find something positive for its own economic development out of South Africa's difficulties. More to the point, so far at least Lesotho does not seem to be having much success in this strategy, at least in relation to Swaziland or what might be possible. As of late 1987, the only well documented cases involved textiles and apparel, at least six export-oriented South African companies being reported as having moved to Lesotho since the 1986 coup.[9] Nevertheless, LNDC is upbeat about the prospects, which include not only South African firms, but new investments by firms from third countries choosing a Lesotho location over a South African one for partly political reasons. The largest known case is a Chinese-Hong Kong joint venture to produce cotton cloth and denim for US and European markets, employing 300 Basotho with an investment of $11 million.[10] Apart from its infrastructural problems, Lesotho is not too bad a location for serving the major South African markets, and the possibility that Japan may restrict investment in South Africa by its firms more strictly than in the past may present some opportunities for Lesotho to acquire overseas manufacturing investments aimed at the South African market.

Apart from these possible positive consequences of restrictions on South Africa's exports, what other effects will sanctions have on Lesotho? It depends, of course, on what the sanctions are, and how the government of South Africa reacts to their imposition. A true oil embargo, for example, would be potentially devastating because Lesotho receives all its petroleum products through normal commercial channels from the big five foreign oil companies in South Africa. It is unlikely that it would be easy to get oil through to Lesotho if it were not available in South Africa.

Restrictions on imports into South Africa of high-tech products will tend to raise costs for such goods to Lesotho. In theory, Lesotho could be used as a route to break sanctions on imports into South Africa, and at least for small quantities this would be hard to detect. In practice, indications are that the reverse is more likely; the embargoed goods will remain on sale in South Africa (namely, Apple computers or Kodak film) brought in by South African entrepreneurs by simpler routes than airfreight or sealed container to Lesotho, and Lesotho will continue to buy these goods from South African sources at slightly higher than normal prices because that will still be cheaper than arranging direct imports for small quantities.

In as much as the bulk of migrants from Lesotho who make remittances to Lesotho are working in gold mines, and it is unlikely that sales of gold by South Africa will in fact be affected by sanctions, any depressive effect on the southern African economy of sanctions will probably have little effect on Lesotho. Some impact might be felt through effects on customs revenue and the exchange rate, but this will be minor.

Political Implications

As yet, there is little evidence as to how Lesotho's relations with South Africa, SADCC, and other countries will be affected by its behavior in reaction to sanctions. One is thus forced to make some inferences based on past events and reasoning about the interests of the parties concerned.

With respect to South Africa, one would expect that there would be a positive response from the authorities to Lesotho accepting South African investments aimed at overseas markets, because the effect is to improve the South African foreign exchange position. On the other hand, if Lesotho succeeds in attracting substantial amounts of such investment, this may damage Lesotho's standing with black South Africans who may lose their jobs, and both black and white South Africans who see Lesotho's actions as defeating the objectives of sanctions. With respect to overseas investments aimed at serving the entire southern African market, past experience is an ambivalent guide. As long ago as the early 1970s, South African opposition prevented some proposed Japanese investments in Lesotho of this type. However, in the current situation, much will depend on the specifics of particular investments, and the degree of political difficulty the investor would be likely to encounter in the relevant home country if the investment were to occur in South Africa. Pretoria does not seem to have objected very strongly to Swaziland's successful wooing of some prominent American corporations seeking to "divest" from South Africa while retaining their South African markets from their new Swazi bases. At issue may be whether the investment in question will continue to make available to the South African market things which, for either economic or political-morale reasons of the white electorate, Pretoria wishes to continue to have on sale in South Africa.

With respect to the SADCC countries, there is probably no reason for the Lesotho government to be too concerned, unless they get involved in some activity clearly seen as directly assisting the current regime in South Africa to stay in power. Export-oriented investments that merely help South Africa's foreign exchange position a little will not particularly alienate other SADCC members, because they all engage in commercial transactions with South Africa when it is in their economic interest to a sufficient extent. If Lesotho were to succeed in a very large way, or be seen to be too accommodating to South African interests, this might change, but it is unlikely. Other aspects of Lesotho's behavior with respect to South Africa, particularly the degree of freedom it gives South Africa's security services to operate within Lesotho and how Lesotho deals with, and protects, refugees and ANC members, is much more likely to offend other SADCC members (with the probably exception of Swaziland, which is probably at least as bad as Lesotho in these terms).

With respect to the rest of Africa, the reactions will probably depend on how well informed about the general southern Africa situation the commentator is, how well Lesotho succeeds in continuing to make a case for the uniqueness of its situation, and how blatant Lesotho's behavior appears to be. Lesotho will probably get some ill-informed criticism, but again issues of other kinds of South African influence and actions in Lesotho are much more likely to cause the Lesotho government problems.

With respect to the rest of the world, there will probably be at least three different kinds of reaction. The US and the UK will almost certainly encourage Lesotho to seek out South African investment to produce for overseas markets, as the US statement above suggests. West Germany, France, and Italy will probably take similar attitudes. To the extent that Lesotho succeeds, its economy improves, and the potential calls on Western aid to prevent economic disaster are reduced. On the other hand, those Western governments that have stronger commitments to the overthrow of apartheid will find themselves in a more awkward position. Sweden, Denmark, Canada, and Holland are possible examples: how will they react if they find that their aid to Lesotho is in fact being used to facilitate investment by South African companies in order for those companies to continue to be able to export to their markets? This might be very hard for them to explain to their domestic electorates and therefore they are hardly likely to encourage this kind of behavior by Lesotho, even if in pragmatic terms they accept the logic of Lesotho's reasoning. It would probably be wise for Lesotho to ensure that there can be no direct link between aid received from such countries and new investments by South African companies.

The third type of reaction is the wholly pragmatic one, which essentially ignores the issues of effects on South Africa's position and asks only whether this situation represents any potential advantages. Perhaps the majority of countries, to the extent that they have any reason to interact with Lesotho, will take this approach. Interestingly, that appears to be the position of both Taiwan and the People's Republic of China, the former already having investments in Lesotho and the latter, as noted above, currently proposing them.

Evasion

There is very little more than can be said about evasion. The very nature of evasion means that if it is successful, it will not be detected. Further, it is unlikely that anyone in Lesotho is really looking hard to find out whether Lesotho is being used for evasion purposes; there are more important things for government to do and there are very few other people who might be interested and would have the resources to find out. There are some rumors about evasion circulating in Maseru. A wholly unconfirmed example, so absurd that I originally regarded it as apocryphal, was that oranges had been seen on sale in Denmark labeled "product of Lesotho"; this is roughly equivalent to claiming that oranges are grown in West Virginia. However, a confirmed report of grapes labelled "produce of Botswana" (in English and Afrikaans!) from the United Kingdom, which is equally unlikely, gives some credence to the Lesotho story.[11] It is entirely possible that Lesotho's name—or simple repackaging represented as manufacturing, maybe not even in Lesotho—will be used for evasion purposes, but at this stage it is not possible to say anything firm.

One particular problem that will make detection harder, and needs to be addressed, is the trade data recording system in southern Africa. South Africa reports the external trade of the entire SACU region, and this is accepted by most gatherers of international economic data (e.g., the IMF, the World Bank). The other countries in SACU do collect and publish their own trade data, including direction of trade data, but this data is not generally available outside the region. Further, in the particular case of Lesotho, the trade data collection process leaves a great deal to be desired and the external trade statistics are several years behind in publication (in early 1988, 1983 was the last year for which final data had been published). Lesotho's trade statistics are therefore not going to be much help for detection of evasion, and the lack of any data for Lesotho in both IMF and OECD direction-of-trade statistical publications will make one standard technique—comparisons of X's reports of imports from Y to Y's reports of exports to X—impossible in the Lesotho case.

Attitude of Lesotho Government

As noted above, the Lesotho government cannot be said to be a homogeneous body with a single clear policy and ideology. The best that can be said of it is probably that it is extremely pragmatic and, faced with enormous actual and potential economic problems, concentrates on attempting to improve its economic position and reduce the danger of economic catastrophe. Its dependence on South Africa for economic wellbeing is enormous; not only now the employment of the migrant mineworkers, but also the Highlands Water Scheme, a huge project to reroute the headwaters of the Orange (in Lesotho, Senqu) River system into the Vaal to sell water to South Africa and generate electricity for Lesotho. This project is by far the largest capital project ever to be undertaken in Lesotho, the South

African government has made clear that its approval of it was in some sense a reward for Jonathan's overthrow and the more accommodating stance of Lekhanya's government, and it is wholly dependent on the cooperation of the South African government. Of course, the project is of vital significance to continued industrial development in the core PWV (Rand) region of South Africa, but South Africa could withstand a short delay, whereas a Lesotho government cannot necessarily withstand even temporary disruptions to normal commercial relations with South Africa.

It would seem, therefore, that in the absence of evidence to the contrary, the best assumption to make is that the government of Lesotho will defend sanctions avoidance via capital flight to the hilt and will condemn any instances of sanctions evasion that come to light, but will make no great efforts to detect the latter. Time will show if this is correct.

Notes

1. John E. Bardill and James H. Cobbe, *Lesotho: Dilemmas of Dependence in Southern Africa* (Boulder, Co.; Westview Publishing Co., 1985); James Cobbe, "Economic Aspects of Lesotho's Relations with South Africa," *Journal of Modern African Studies*, XXVI, 1 (1988), 71-90.

2. Cobbe, "Economic Aspects of Lesotho's Relations." For a slightly different view, see Robert Edgar, "The Lesotho Coup of 1986," *South African Review IV* (Johannesburg: Ravan Press, 1987), 373-382.

3. *Africa Confidential*, 4 March 1988.

4. 1986 Population Census Preliminary Results, Bureau of Statistics (Maseru, Lesotho Government Printer, 1987); Unpublished working tables, 1985/86 Labour Force Survey, Bureau of Statistics.

5. See Fion de Vletter's chapter in Carl Keyter, ed., *The Report on the Proceedings of the Second Consultation on Migration and Development,*

Roma, Lesotho, June 1986 (Maseru: AIM and Transformation Resource Centre, 1986), 85-87.

6. Fion de Vletter, "Foreign Labour on the South African Gold Mines: New Insights on an Old Problem," *International Labour Review,* 126, 2 (1987).

7. These numbers come from the Central Bank of Lesotho's *Quarterly Review,* VI, 4 (December 1987), 61; *International Herald Tribune,* 14 March 1988.

8. "Lesotho industrialists protected against sanctions hardships," *Lesotho National Development Corporation Newsletter,* First Quarter, 1987.

9. *Weekly Mail,* 12 November 1987.

10. *Lesotho Today,* 7 April 1988.

11. *Anti-Apartheid News* (London), March 1988.

ZIMBABWE IN THE FRONTLINE

Roger C. Riddell

Introduction

Zimbabwe has no diplomatic relations with South Africa, yet the South African flag flutters in the breeze on one of the main streets of the city center of Harare. Zimbabwe has an excellent university well able to train its doctors, accountants, and engineers to world-recognized standards, yet scores of its young students attend universities in South Africa using the country's scarce foreign exchange. To the outside world there appears to be little love lost between Zimbabwe and South Africa, yet more visitors come to Zimbabwe from South Africa than from any other country, accounting for one third of all foreign visitors and one third of all spending by foreign individuals, while nearly half of all Zimbabweans venturing abroad go to South Africa—a destination twice as popular as any other country. For every Zimbabwean visiting Britain, ten go to South Africa, and for every Zimbabwean visiting neighboring Southern African Development Coordination Conference (SADCC) countries, two visit South Africa.[1]

If these elements of contemporary relations between Zimbabwe and South Africa seem ironical, of greater significance appears to be the contrast over time between major political and policy objectives enunciated by Zimbabwe and evolving economic reality. Since Independence in April 1980, Zimbabwe has articulated as one of its major economic and foreign policy objectives the loosening of bonds with its southern neighbor and the reduction of economic dependence. Since then, however, many of the links between the two countries, already widespread and strong, have become even stronger, while South African aggression is highlighted by writers sympathetic to SADCC's aims and objectives as the major obstacle frustrating attempts to reduce dependence upon their powerful neighbor.[2] In the case of Zimbabwe, trade agreements with South Africa have been renewed, adapted, and signed by senior officials of both countries, total trade between the two has doubled in value and a substantially greater proportion of transit traffic flows through South Africa today than it did at Independence.

It is in the context of these ideas and perceptions that I thought it would be interesting to develop three interlinked theses raised by the evolving relationship between Zimbabwe and South Africa. First, what appears to be the growing dichotomy in a number of key areas between what is happening on the ground and Zimbabwe's objective of disengagement arises more because of the relative strength of South Africa and its interest in frustrating the process of disengagement than to failure by Zimbabwe to attempt to de-link from South Africa. Indeed what has been most remarkable is that in spite of South African attempts to frustrate disengagement, substantial delinking has occurred.

Second, there are sound economic reasons for Zimbabwe to wish to reduce its economic dependence upon South Africa besides the well-known repugnance its President, Robert Mugabe, and its people have for the apartheid policies of the South African government. Indeed, although conventional wisdom would tend to hold the view that (especially since the start of the UDI period in 1965) Zimbabwe and South Africa have become more closely bound together, the contemporary Zimbabwean policy of economic disengagement bears a striking resemblance to policies of previous governments stretching back for many decades.

Third, even though successes in disengaging have been achieved, under present and expected future circumstances Zimbabwe's ability substantially to reduce further its dependence on South Africa is going to continue to be difficult not only because of South African action to prevent or slow down the process but also because contradictions between this and other different policy objectives will continue to manifest themselves.

Perhaps I can preface my discussion of these different ideas with a few remarks on the critical role of Zimbabwe in understanding South Africa's overall links with its neighbors. Although Zimbabwe contains only 12% of the total SADCC population and covers only 8% of the total surface area of the SADCC countries, its economic significance is far greater. It is responsible for 21% of the gross domestic product (GDP) of the nine SADCC-member countries, 20% of all the exports of the SADCC countries, and 17% of the total imports of the SADCC countries. And of total trade between the different SADCC countries, over half of all exports originate in Zimbabwe while Zimbabwe purchases over a quarter of intra-SADCC imports. As for the direct trade links with South Africa, Zimbabwe provides South Africa with over half of all products SADCC countries export to South Africa while it absorbs 10% of all the exports of South African goods to SADCC countries.[3] The various figures from which these percentage contributions are derived are shown in Table 1.

South African Policy and Practice and Its Effects on Zimbabwe

There would appear to be an array of political, military and economic reasons why South Africa would wish to increase its control over Zimbabwe and, more particularly, to maintain and even increase the dependent relationship. At the political level, South Africa is challenged in the ideological debate among South Africa's white electorate to the extent that Zimbabwe succeeds in its stated objective of establishing a flourishing multiracial and multiethnic society and prosperous economy so close to home.

Such success gives the lie to South Africa's claims of white superiority and black incompetence.

Table 1
Basic economic data: Zimbabwe, SADCC and South Africa (US $ million)

	South Africa	*SADCC*	*Zimbabwe*	*Zimbabwe as %*
Gross Domestic Product (1985, $ billion)	54.4	19.3	4.1	21.2
Intra-SADCC exports $million		245	131	53.4
Intra-SADCC imports $million		245	67	27.3
Total SADCC exports $million		5,734	1,156	20.2
Total SADCC imports $million		5,801	955	16.5
South African exports to		1,723	184	10.7
South African imports from		415	212	51.1

Source: Lewis (1987, Tables 1 to 4) and ODI (1987, Box 1).

A peaceful, stable, united, and prosperous Zimbabwe also poses a greater military threat to South Africa for at least three reasons: because Zimbabwe will be in a better position to receive and welcome political refugees from South Africa; because of the greater likelihood of it following through on its well-known political support for political groupings banned in South Africa with the provision of military assistance; and, perhaps of greatest importance, because Zimbabwe will be better able to both strengthen its armed and air forces and to focus that strength in a concerted manner to the defence of its borders against South African attack.

Substantive political and military gains to South Africa can be greatly assisted by action on the economic front: to the extent that Zimbabwe's economic progress can be held in check, halted, or reversed, and to the extent that this can be achieved without leading to retaliatory action by either Zimbabwe (or its more powerful allies), then South Africa's political and military objectives would be the better achieved. Two general and interconnected ways of achieving these economic objectives would be to raise the costs of economic development and to bring the Zimbabwean economy more into the direct control of South Africa. The first would help to ferment any social disharmony existing in the country and reduce Zimbabwe's ability to defend itself against South African attacks, the second would provide South Africa with greater power to inflict economic damage to Zimbabwe should the need arise. This latter objective also has a broader goal: to the extent that Zimbabwe in particular and the SADCC states more generally are bound and beholden to South Africa, the less able are they either to impose economic sanctions themselves upon South Africa or to influence those western nations unwilling to impose their own sanctions upon South Africa.[4]

Over the nine years since Zimbabwe achieved Independence, there has accumulated a wealth of evidence suggesting that South Africa has acted on all three fronts against Zimbabwe. Without going into a litany of facts and figures, reference can be made to a few of the more significant events. Even before Independence, South Africa in 1977/78 loaned the then Rhodesian government 200 million Zimbabwe dollars to help support the anti-ZANU/ZAPU war effort and, in the runup to the Independence election, provided over three million Rand and scores of vehicles to try to ensure an election victory by Bishop Muzorewa's United African National Council (UANC).[5]

To attempt to disrupt the Zimbabwe government's attempts to create a unified nation, the South Africans have funded, trained, and armed Zimbabwean insurgents who have re-entered the country to operate mainly in the south-west of the country. They were implicated in the attempt to assassinate the then

Prime Minister and senior party officials at the ZANU(PF) party headquarters in 1982 and they have established and funded a radio station beamed to Zimbabwe to broadcast anti-Zimbabwean material in both English and Shona/Ndebele.

While the training and funding of insurgents has led to Zimbabwe having to divert defense resources to keeping the domestic peace in the south-west of the country, South African support for the Mozambique National Resistance (MNR) movement, over 700 miles to the east in Mozambique—leading to the disruption of land-locked Zimbabwe's closest and cheapest road, rail, and oil pipeline links to the coast—forced the Zimbabwean government to commit some one quarter of its army to semipermanent occupation of northern Mozambique. Not only has this action raised the costs of defence expenditure substantially (increasing the defence vote 2 1/2 times from Z$291 million in 1982/83 to Z$720 million in the financial year 1987/88, raising it from 10% of total government expenditure to 14% this year) but it has led to the Zimbabwean army having to spread itself over an even wider geographical area. More recently, attacks by the MNR in both the north and eastern border areas of the country have further stretched the resources of the National Army of Zimbabwe. As for Zimbabwe's air strength, much of this was destroyed in 1982 in an attack by the South African airforce on fighter aircraft only recently acquired. The result of all these different types of action is that South Africa has been better able to deploy both its own troops and those of its surrogates within the borders of Zimbabwe and that its airforce has been able to strike at targets even within the main cities of the country, as it did in 1986, with minimal fear of Zimbabwean retaliation.

The increase in the defense vote gives some idea of one aspect of the costs to Zimbabwe of South African action. Another identifiable and critical cost is that caused by the disruption of transport routes. Whereas in 1981, 67% of Zimbabwe's extraregional trade had to use South African transport routes, by 1985 92% was forced to use these longer and more expensive routes, adding some Z$100 million to freight and insurance costs. The war in Mozambique has also led to an influx of upwards of 80,000 refugees entering Zimbabwe and requiring food, medicine, and shelter.

Less tangible but still substantial economic costs to Zimbabwe have also resulted from this and other types of South African action. For instance the loss to Mozambique of transit traffic from neighboring SADCC countries has reduced its own rail and port revenues (by over $80 million), reducing its ability to purchase Zimbabwe exports. Similarly the perhaps 5% increase in the overseas price of Zimbabwean exports caused by the forced rerouting of freight through South Africa has adversely affected Zimbabwe's export competitiveness while higher priced imports have reduced further the quantity of foreign exchange available to buy already scarce foreign goods. Other types of action would include the following: the withdrawal of locomotives on "semi-permanent loan" to the National Railways of Zimbabwe in 1981; the engineering of a substantial slowdown in goods traffic at the busiest Beit Bridge border in August 1986, when South Africa imposed (without warning) a cash in advance levy on extraterritorial goods passing through South Africa and demanded that all Zimbabwean-destined goods be subject to a detailed and unprecedented search; and, in April 1987, the announcement at the start of tobacco auctions that Zimbabwean tobacco exports would be subject to a Zimbabwe-specific R2 per kilogram levy.[6]

To these increased economic costs of South African action need to be added the absolute rise in trade flows between the two countries. Between 1978 (the last complete year for which figures are available in the pre-Independence period) and 1987, total external trade between Zimbabwe and South Africa rose from Z$240 million to Z$562 million, more than a doubling of total trade, with imports from South Africa trebling in value. Additionally, as the data in Figure 1 clearly show, a small pre-Independence surplus has been changed into a substantial (over Z$100 million) deficit.

Zimbabwe's Achievements in De-Linking

Although both South Africa's acts of aggression and its grip on the Zimbabwean economy remain significant, it would be mistaken to suppose that Zimbabwe's policy of disengagement

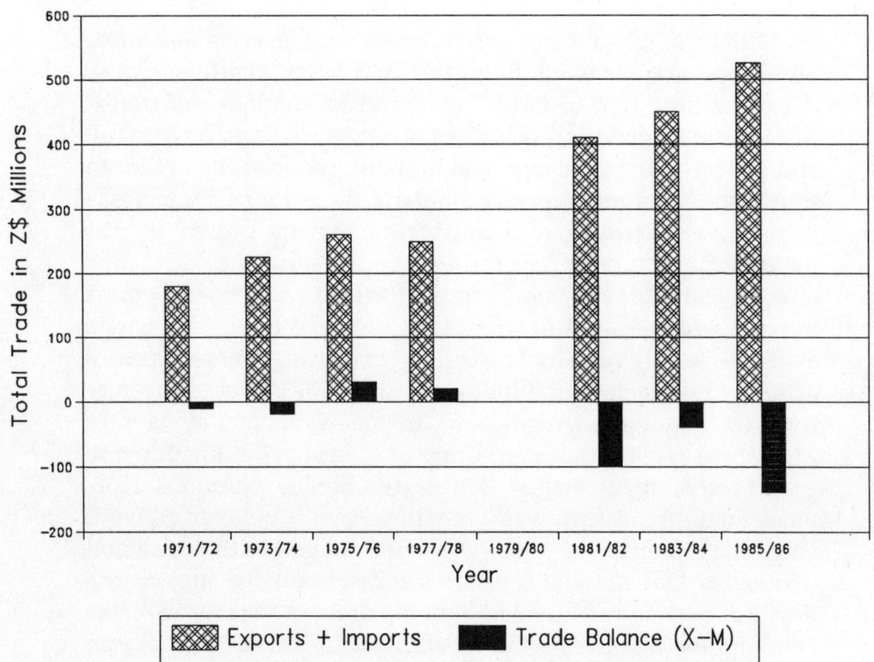

Figure 1 Zimbabwe trade with South Africa (two year averages, 1971 to 1986, in (Z$ millions).

Source: *Quarterly Digest of Statistics, March 1987, Monthly Digest of Statistics* and *Statement of External Trade* (various issues).

has been without impact. I shall consider in turn four elements of importance: tourism, investment, transport routes and trade.

Tourism

While it remains true that South Africa is the major destination of Zimbabwean tourists, the single most important source of supply of foreign tourists and the major earner of tourist dollars, there has been considerable de-linking in recent years. For instance, whereas in 1980, 70% of all Zimbabweans going abroad went to South Africa, the proportion had dropped to 58% by 1987, with absolute numbers halved from over 200,000 to around 100,000. And of those Zimbabweans visiting African countries, the proportion going to South Africa had fallen from 80% to 65% over the same period. Similarly, whereas 45% of all visitors to Zimbabwe in 1980 were South African residents, the proportion had dropped to 33% by 1987, the absolute numbers dropping by perhaps a few thousand.[7]

Investment

At Independence, South African private capital interests in Zimbabwe were valued at some US$590 million, about one quarter of total private capital in Zimbabwe and well over 15% of total national assets.[8] These interests ranged right across the economy from banking, insurance, mining, agricultural, manufacturing, and freight and transport interests, as well as in publishing.

Progressively since 1980, substantial South African assets have been acquired by Zimbabweans, a high proportion by central government, and through purchase agreements with the South African owners of the assets. For instance, in 1981 the government purchased 61% share in Zimbank[9] (with assets valued at the end of 1980 at Z$209 million and responsible for 20% of commercial banking business in the country) from the Netherlands Bank of South Africa. The government also established in that year the Mass Media Trust, which purchased both Zimbabwe Newspapers and Kingstons, the booksellers, from South Africa's Argus Printing and Publishing. In the mining sector, the government acquired one of the major South African companies, MTD Mangula, while it also purchased a share in the ownership of the Hwange Colliery.

It is, however, in the manufacturing sector, where the largest quantities of South African assets were located, that disengagement has been of most significance. Besides acquiring interests in a host of smaller holdings (often through the parastatal Industrial Development Corporation), such as Central Film Laboratories and the largest pharmaceutical company, CAPS Holdings, recent acquisitions include an 80% holding in the large Astra Corporation for Z$26 million from the Barlow Rand group and the initial purchase of a 31% stake in the Delta Corporation, Zimbabwe's biggest conglomerate (with the aim of building up its share to up to 60%) for US$14 million from South African Breweries.

Together, Zimbabwe's purchases of quoted South African owned or controlled companies since Independence has led to a shift in ownership to Zimbabwe of at least 25% of the total asset value of Zimbabwe's top companies.[10] Additionally, a not inconsiderable number of large companies either owned or part-owned by South African companies or subsidiaries have reduced or are currently in the process of reducing or eliminating their South African holdings. More recently these have included Hunyani, owned by Barlow Rand, with assets of over Z$30 million, and Woolworths. Overall, few, if any, would dispute the view that at least 30% of South African assets held in Zimbabwe at the time of Independence have now been acquired by Zimbabwe, thus decreasing substantially not only South Africa's investments in the country but reducing, too, the outflow of profit and dividends.

Direct Trade

How about the direct Zimbabwe-South African trade links? As the data in Figure 1 reveal a steady expansion in trade, it would appear that in this major area Zimbabwe's efforts at de-linking have not been successful. These figures, however, tell only part of the story. While in absolute terms, direct trading links have certainly increased, as a proportion of total trade, South Africa has been responsible for a falling share of both exports and imports. Whereas at Independence, 19% of Zimbabwe's exports went to South Africa, the share had fallen to 9% by last year, and whereas imports from South Africa at Independence amounted to 28% of the total, they had fallen to 21% by 1986.[11]

For some sub-sectors of the economy the switch away from South Africa has been even more dramatic than these aggregate figures indicate. For instance, whereas in the two year period 1964 and 1965, 92% of all Zimbabwe's manufactured exports went to either South Africa or SADCC countries, in the period 1981 to 1983, only 43% of all manufactured exports went to Zimbabwe's southern African neighbors.

In late 1987, comprehensive trade data by seven digit classification for each country destination were made available for the years 1984, 1985, and 1986, enabling a far greater depth of analysis of manufacturing exports than has been possible for any year since 1964. In aggregate these data confirm the UDI trends just mentioned. In 1984, only 41% of all manufactured exports went to countries in southern Africa, falling to 34% by 1986. If all exports of cotton lint, ferrochrome and steel products are excluded, dependence on southern African markets increases significantly although the reduction in dependence is clearly observable over recent years. Whereas in 1984, 69% of all such exports went to southern African countries, this ratio had dropped to 61% by 1986. As the data in Tables 2 and 3 indicate, the most important changes observable in recent years have been the decrease in dependence upon South Africa as a destination for manufactured exports (estimated to be taking about 32% of total manufactured exports in 1980, with the exclusion of cotton lint) and the significant rise in the share of nontraditional manufactured exports being sold to destinations outside Africa. In 1986, 34% of nontraditional manufactured exports went to non-African countries compared with 23% in 1984 and for five manufacturing sub-sectors over 40% of all manufactured exports were sold outside Africa.

Transport Routes

The fourth element of de-linking concerns transport routes. As we have seen, one of the most effective measures of South African-induced action against Zimbabwe has been to succeed in diverting most of Zimbabwe's extraterritorial trade through South Africa. To counter this trade diversion, a number of approaches have been tried. Within the context of the SADCC, the development of transport links has received the highest priority with Zimbabwe's potential gain being maximized because of the highest priority being accorded to the repair, rehabilitation, and development of Mozambique's ports, railways, and associated facilities (such as telecommunications and electricity). Increasingly over the past few years, aid donors have given priority to the funding of these transport links, particularly concentrating on the port of Beira facilities and the transport links between Zimbabwe and Beira. Linked to this SADCC/donor initiative have been two more Zimbabwe-specific initiatives. The first has been the deployment of the Zimbabwe National Army across the border into Mozambique to defend the road, rail, and pipeline links to Beira. The second has been the establishment of the Beira Corridor Group, funded in part by Zimbabwean businessmen, one of whose main objectives is to accelerate the use of the Beira outlet for the sea for exports and imports of the major land-locked SADCC states.

Table 2
Manufactured Exports by area of destination, 1980, 1984 and 1986 (U.S.$ million)

Market	*Total Manufactured Exports*				*Total Manufactured Exports Less Cotton, Lint, Ferrochrome & Steel*			
	1984	*%*	*1986*	*%*	*1984*	*%*	*1986*	*%*
South Africa	137.4	23	101.7	14	82.3	30	65.1	20
SADCC	114.5	19	144.6	20	106.9	39	134.9	41
Other Africa	23.6	4	32.7	4	22.3	8	19.3	6
Non-African	318.6	54	462.0	62	63.3	23	112.9	34
Total	594.1	100	741.0	100	274.8	100	332.2	100

Total Manufactured Exports:

	Less Cotton Lint						*Less Cotton Lint and ferrochrome*					
	1980	*%*	*1984*	*%*	*1986*	*%*	*1980*	*%*	*1984*	*%*	*1986*	*%*
South Africa	93.7	32	100.7	21	69.4	11	89.2	41	97.5	30	65.6	16
SADCC			114.5	24	144.6	24			114.5	35	144.4	36
Other Africa			23.6	5	32.7	5			23.3	7	32.4	8
Non-Africa			240.0	50	363.8	60			88.8	27	158.1	40
Total	288.9	100	478.8	100	610.5	100	218.7	100	324.1	100	400.5	100

Source: "Domestic Exports Valued FOR by Item/Country," CSO, Harare, 1988 (mimeo) and R. Riddell "Zimbabwe's Manufactured Exports and The Ending of The Trade Agreement With South Africa," Confederation of Zimbabwe Industries, December 1981, (mimeo).

Table 3
Manufactured exports by industrial sub-sector and destination 1980, 1984 and 1986 ($ million)

	Percentage Export by Respective Destination											
	South Africa			*SADCC*		*Other African*		*Non-African*		*Total Exports $ million*		
Sub-sector	1980	1984	1986	1984	1986	1984	1986	1984	1986	1980	1984	1986
1	37	16	12	33	34	22	9	29	45	6.8	70.4	98.5
2	73	83	69	6	6	3	10	8	15	5.6	3.5	2.8
3	—	33	22	9	8	—	—	58	70	—	154.5	179.7
3[a]	58	36	14	37	38	—	1	27	46	10.7	39.2	49.2
4	93	55	36	12	15	1	1	32	48	15.4	20.5	28.9
5	86	60	43	30	41	5	4	5	12	8.8	11.8	9.1
6	56	7	14	80	76	1	3	12	7	1.2	8.6	6.7
7	26	8	9	78	77	2	4	12	10	1.8	31.2	30.6
8	15	54	4	40	75	5	3	1	18	0.6	10.0	11.5
9	—	14	6	11	11	2	5	73	78	—	248.3	324.3
9[b]	27	34	12	16	30	4	14	46	44	23.8	93.6	114.3
10	61	14	5	66	67	20	27	0	1	9.4	10.4	16.2
11	90	31	32	6	4	1	1	62	63	5.1	25.0	32.2

Notes

a. Sub-sector 3 with cotton lint export data omitted.
b. Sub-sector 9 with ferrochrome exports omitted.

Legend

Sub-sectors: 1 foodstuffs; 2 drink and tobacco; 3 textiles; 4 clothing and footwear; 5 wood and furniture; 6 paper, printing, publishing; 7 chemicals and pharmaceuticals; 8 non-metallic minerals; 9 metals and metal products; 10 transport equipment; 11 other.

Source: As for Table 2.

While action by both South African and MNR personnel directed at Mozambique's transport system still continues and while the southern Chicualacuala-Maputo rail link between Mozambique and Zimbabwe remains effectively closed (as it has since mid-1983), some substantial progress can be recorded. Although both the pipeline and the railway line are subject to attack, the presence of Zimbabwean troops has meant that these tend to be relatively small-scale and repairs are effectively concluded within 24 hours.[12] On the port end, major land engineering and dredging works have been taking place and by early October 1987 the first phase of the rehabilitation of the port of Beira had been completed, raising its capacity by 30% to 3.2 million tons of cargo a year.

But perhaps the most significant indication of success in the transport field is the fact that whereas in 1985 over 90% of Zimbabwe's overseas trade had to use South African routes, the Beira Corridor was carrying 30% of Zimbabwe's overseas trade by September 1987, according to the BCG and 20% of total regional traffic,[13] both reducing the foreign exchange costs of freight to Zimbabwe and, at the same time, providing Mozambique with much-needed foreign exchange.

De-linking From South Africa: The Longer Term Perspective

Figures 2 and 3 show the manner in which in relative terms Zimbabwe has been successful in reducing its external trade links with South Africa since Independence. The trends recorded there reveal not only that this reduction was taking place during the UDI period—a time of economic sanctions and when one might have thought trade relations would have been strengthened—but that it has been a pattern observable at a number of different time periods over the past 70-odd years. Furthermore, as recently documented historical evidence shows, a major objective of successive governments from the 1920s onwards has been to attempt to reduce South African trade dependence, a desire that led to a differing record of success at different time periods. For instance, Ian Phimister points out that as the pre-independent Zimbabwean economy developed and diversified throughout this century, South Africa viewed its growth and diversity as a threat to itself and sought repeatedly to reduce both competition and the threat of competition from its northern neighbor.[14] As long ago as 1929, Southern Rhodesia's Legislative Assembly was told that South African policy "is inimical to the interests of the people of this Colony, whether they were producers, traders, consumers, or the Treasury itself."

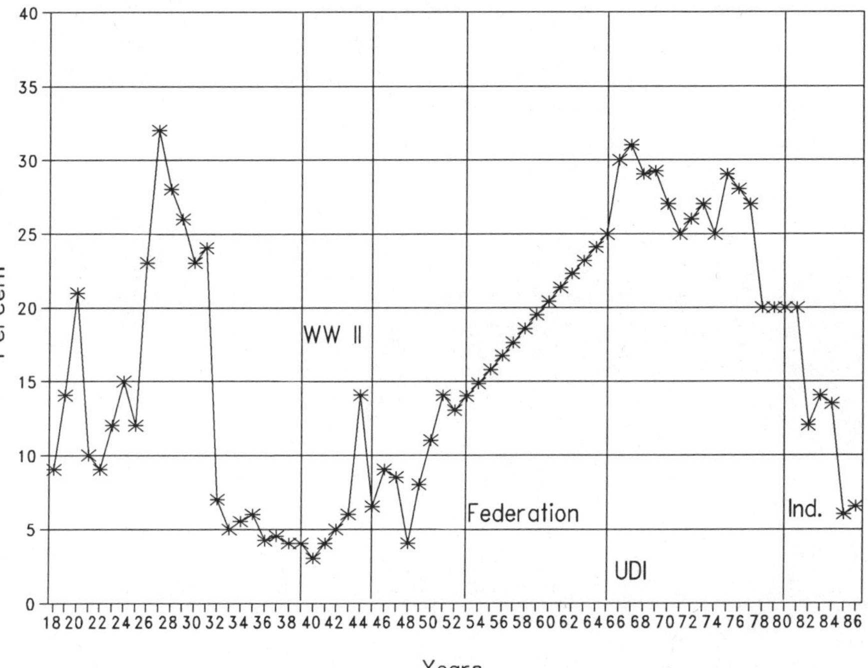

Figure 2 Ratio of exports to South Africa over total percentage, 1918 to 1986.

Why should successive governments have been so keen to attempt to reduce dependence upon South Africa and, relatedly, why should it be in the economic interests of the Mugabe government to follow the same policy of de-linking? Development theory suggests that to be overly dependent upon one market for either or both imports or exports is a high risk strategy because one becomes extremely vulnerable to changes in that economy's fortunes as well as one's own and, relatedly, to policies introduced to reduce external exposure. Also, when the two countries are at different stages of development, manipulation of trade arrangements by the stronger will tend to frustrate the process of industrialisation in the weaker, thereby exacerbating the dependent relationship. Furthermore when the countries are adjacent to each other, as in the case of Zimbabwe and South Africa, and when the differential transport, freight, and insurance costs from importing goods from South Africa and from overseas are substantial, the opportunity arises for South Africa to use its monopoly position to extract higher than normal profits.[15]

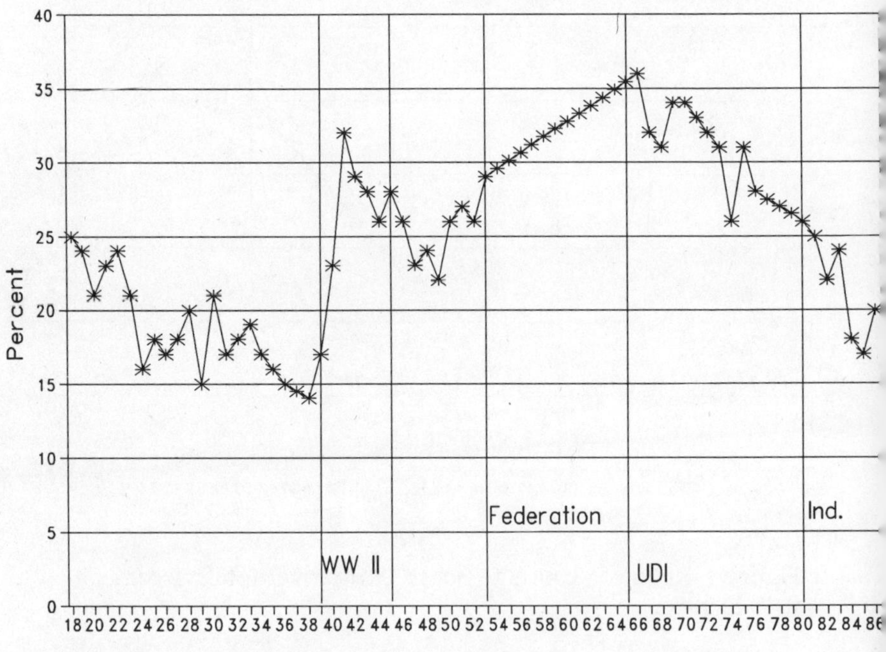

Figure 3 Ratio of imports to South Africa over total percentage, 1918 to 1986.

All these factors have been present in the Zimbabwe/South African case for many decades. Trade agreements have been a source of almost continual friction and South Africa has persistently put up trade barriers to prevent access of more competitive products from Zimbabwe into its markets. Other adverse factors have also arisen. Close trading links existing to exchange goods produced in the respective countries have led to Zimbabwe using South African agents to purchase goods from third countries rather than purchasing them directly, thereby raising their cost—a practice which became more widespread during the UDI period. Similarly, to purchase a high proportion of capital equipment (for instance mining equipment in the case of Zimbabwe) from South Africa means that Zimbabwe has tied itself into South African sources of supply for the provision of spares and replacement parts. Yet another adverse effect has arisen from the extensive presence of South African company subsidiaries in Zimbabwe. Since Independence, there have been cases where the South African parent company has prevented their Zimbabwean subsidiary company from expanding into export markets within the southern African region because market allocation decisions made by the South African head office had previously determined that those markets would be supplied from South Africa. Reports suggest, for instance, that this occurred with the pharmaceutical company, Datlabs.

The Future

There would appear to be little doubt both that South Africa would wish to maintain and even increase Zimbabwe's dependence upon it and also that Mr. Mugabe would like to see the process of de-linking accelerated. But for both sides dramatic moves to shift reality nearer to their respective objectives has its costs.

This can be seen clearly in relation to some recent developments. For his part, President Mugabe's attempt in August 1987 to all but halt imports from South Africa (by ceasing to issue import licenses for goods coming from South Africa) was turned down by his Cabinet colleagues, after a barrage of pressure from the Zimbabwean business community. The government's eventual decision to maintain the status quo arose not because of any widespread opposition to the principle of further disengagement but rather because the economic effects—in terms of increased foreign exchange costs of obtaining goods from alternative sources, immediate shortages of basic and intermediate inputs and spare parts, and possible retaliation from South Africa—were thought to be far too severe for the country, already suffering from drought, economic contraction, severe foreign exchange shortages, and rapidly rising levels of unemployment.

Similarly, with the far higher international profile currently being given to the economic problems of Mozambique, the rehabilitation of its transport system and the manner in which the donor community has publicly committed itself to supporting these projects makes it more difficult for the South Africans dramatically to disrupt especially the Beira Corridor and reverse SADCC successes in rechannelling overseas trade away from South Africa. To do so would be likely to increase pressure for Western action to be taken against South Africa, for instance by tightening the US sanctions legislation and by Congress pressing harder for the President to encourage other OECD nations to impose similar sanctions.[16] It would also help to place the sanctions debate high on the international agenda once more.

The likely course of events over the short term, therefore, would appear to be for Zimbabwe's process of *economic* disengagement and de-linking from South Africa to continue and thus for major aspects of its dependence on its southern neighbor to continue to be reduced. However on the *political* and *military* fronts, there are few if any grounds for believing that South Africa's mostly covert actions against Zimbabwe will either halt or be scaled down. Indeed, to the extent that Zimbabwe continues to make gains on the trade, transport, and investment fronts—and in the process strengthens its economic independence from South Africa—its threat to South Africa is likely to intensify. This in turn will increase the likelihood of action by South Africa on the military/political front.

Contradictions

Perhaps a final word should be added about contradictions. In practice, because events in southern Africa have evolved in a far less clear-cut manner than the analysis presented here would suggest, contradictions are just as likely to continue to arise in the future. These can arise because some policies *are* illogical and inconsistent—perhaps because communication between different government departments is not as efficient and open as it would be in an ideal world and perhaps, too, because differing policies reflect contradictions between different elements of government, each with some power and each with different ideas about how to combine the carrying out of objectives with policy execution. However, other contradictions can and do arise because of tension or conflict between particular policy goals for southern Africa and other policy goals.

For instance, from Zimbabwe's perspective, it would appear that the decision taken in early October 1987 to hire 10 diesel locomotives from South Africa was directly at variance with Zimbabwe's interests and policies, because it substantially increases Zimbabwe's dependence upon South Africa and, as occurred in 1981, provides South Africa with the opportunity to inflict widespread trade disruption if it chooses suddenly to withdraw them from Zimbabwe. However, from the Zimbabwean perspective, with some one half of its 200 locomotives off the tracks because of age, more locomotives required for the Beira line,[17] and a lack of spares, and an ever growing need to maximize foreign exchange earnings from higher exports, these other considerations overrode the objective of de-linking from South Africa.

A potential contradiction is also developing for Zimbabwe as a direct result of the *success* of part of its policy of de-linking from South Africa. As already noted, Zimbabwe is accelerating the domestic acquisition of private (foreign) South African capital in the country. While this leads both to greater domestic control of capital and to a decrease in remittance outflows to South Africa, the reduction in South African interests has the adverse effect for Zimbabwe of also reducing the lobby of South African business interests pressing the South African government to desist from harming Zimbabwe and its economy because of the financial repercussions for South African stakeholders. In short, the success of this aspect of de-linking makes Zimbabwe more vulnerable to South African attacks of economic sabotage.

Another contradiction has recently manifested itself with the announcement by Zimbabwe's Minister of Finance in his July 1987 budget speech that, as of January 1988, import licenses would be issued for the CIF value of imports rather than, for the FOB value of imported goods. The objective behind this move is to attempt to reduce the escalating costs (especially the foreign exchange costs) of freight and insurance charges by requiring the user of the imports to pay for these charges out of the total value of the license.[18] While this new initiative should go some way to reduce freight and insurance costs and thus make it relatively more attractive for importers to purchase goods from a closer source, the indirect effect of such a move will be to make South African goods relatively more attractive than similar goods available overseas.

Contradictions to perceived national interests, however, are not all one-sided. For instance, just as the throughput of traffic along the Beira Corridor was beginning to expand in April 1987, the South African Transport Services raised their special low contract freight rates by 15% and by 20% for tobacco containers.[19] While this was needed because of increasing costs (SATS ran a deficit of R367 million in the 1985 financial year), it was clearly a move in contradiction to the frequently successful attempts by South Africa to increase transport dependence by cutting the SADCC road and rail links.[20] Similarly in September 1987, MNR guerrillas destroyed a rail bridge on the main South African rail line from Komatipoort to Maputo. While this action seriously affected Zimbabwe's trade, it also affected South African trade, especially from the Rand and the north-east Transvaal for whom that route to the sea is the most cost effective. It also came after South African trade sources stated that they wished to encourage an increase of exports through Maputo.[21]

Important though these various incidents are, the argument of this chapter is that they can be better understood within a broader context, on the one hand, of Zimbabwe's attempting to de-link from South Africa and, on the other, of South Africa trying to weaken and maintain or increase its power over Zimbabwe. They do not reflect any substantial change of attitude or broad policy on the part of either country or its government.

Notes

1. The SADCC countries are: Angola, Botswana, Lesotho, Malawi, Mozambique, Swaziland, Tanzania, Zambia, and Zimbabwe.

2. See, for instance, J. Hanlon, *Beggar Your Neighbours* (London, CIIR and James Currey, 1985) and J. Hanlon and R. Omond, *The Sanctions Handbook* (London, Penguin, 1987).

3. Figures from *Sanctions and South Africa's Neighbours*, ODI Briefing Paper, May 1987 and S.R. Lewis, *Economic Realities in Southern Africa (or One Hundred Million Futures)*, IDS Discussion Paper, DP 232, IDS, Sussex, June 1987.

4. An argument frequently used by the British Prime Minister, Mrs. Thatcher to resist either extending British sanctions to South Africa or using its influence to encourage her EEC partners to do so is that Zimbabwe and Zambia have failed to impose their own sanctions against South Africa. The argument was heard, for instance, at the Commonwealth Heads of State meeting in Vancouver in October 1987.

5. This was revealed in a book by Professor Deon Geldenhuys, *The Diplomacy of Isolation: South African Foreign Policy-Making*, reviewed by Major Michael Evans of the University of Zimbabwe in *The Financial Gazette*, 14 November 1986.

6. South Africa was, until that time, the fourth largest importer of Zimbabwean tobacco. No similar tax was levied on tobacco imported to South Africa from Malawi.

7. These latter figures include travellers arriving from Botswana and Swaziland. For all the figures in this paragraph, see *Zimbabwe: Monthly Migration and Tourist Statistics* (Harare, Central Statistical Office [various years]).

8. Figures from D. G. Clarke, *Foreign Companies and International Investment in Zimbabwe* (London, CIIR, 1980).

9. Previously called Rhobank.

10. The market capitalization value of the Zimbabwe stock exchange in July 1987 was Z$ 629 mn. Of this, over Z$150 mn was made up of the contributions from the *Delta Corporation*, *CAPS Holdings*, *Zimbabwe Newspapers*, *Zimbank* and *Apex*.

11. Of course one needs to be careful about drawing specific conclusions from aggregate trends; in a number of fields Zimbabwe remains as dependent upon South Africa for imported inputs now as it was at Independence.

12. For instance, the rail bridge 45 miles from Maputo on the route to Zimbabwe via Ressano Garcia was sabotaged on 19 September 1987 and repair work was completed by 3 October while a minor derailment on the Beira line in late September only halted traffic for a few days (see *The Financial Gazette*, 16 October 1987).

13. Report to the first annual meeting of the BCG, reported in *The Financial Gazette*, 18 September 1987.

14. See, for example, I Phimister, "Industrialisation and Sub-Imperialism: Southern Rhodesia and South African Trade Relations Between The Wars," paper presented to the workshop on Alternative Development Strategies in Africa, Queen Elizabeth House, Oxford, September 1987 (mimeo).

15. For instance, if South Africa is able to manufacture goods required by Zimbabwe at internationally competitive prices but, as was the case in 1986, transport, freight and insurance costs of bringing South African goods to the Zimbabwe border are 10% of the ex-factory cost but for European goods are 30% of the ex-factory cost, then South African companies are able to increase the price they charge to just below the landed cost of European goods and still be cheaper for Zimbabwean purchasers.

16. The *Comprehensive Anti-Apartheid Act of 1986* required the President to impose tighter sanctions against South Africa in the event of no progress being made to eliminate apartheid and for him to work with U.S. allies to implement wider sanctions against South Africa.

17. The increased use of locomotives on the Beira line is only partly related to the increased use of the line. For security reasons, the

line is only used for eight hours of daylight each day, necessitating the use of three times more locomotives than if the line could be used for 24 hours a day.

18. As under the old system the foreign exchange cost of getting the goods to the factory gate or the shop are incurred by freight and forwarding agents, and foreign exchange is in far shorter supply than domestic currency, the objective of importers has been to maximize their foreign exchange allocation. Thus, it has been relatively immaterial where the goods are purchased from—South Africa, Zambia, Sweden or Alaska—provided the fob prices are lower. While this helps to provide the maximum quantity of goods to be brought into the country, it does not provide for the most efficient use of foreign exchange. Hence the proposed changes.

19. New rates quoted in *The Financial Gazette*, 10 April 1987.

20. It should be noted that Mozambique has not gained overall from the increased flow of traffic through the Beira Corridor. A September 1987 report by Mozambique's Prime Minister to the Peoples Assembly observed that while in the year to September, traffic using the Beira Corridor had increased by 50%, compared with 1986, there had been on overall traffic decline of 35% because of the re-routing of South African trade away from Mozambique's ports. *The Financial Gazette*, 23 October 1987.

21. See *The Financial Gazette*, 2 October 1987 and *SOUTHSCAN*, Vol. 2, No. 6, 21 October 1987.

THE CULTURAL BOYCOTT OF SOUTH AFRICA (I)

Mbulelo Vizikhungo Mzamane

Culture may be seen as

> the ensemble of meaningful practices and 'uniformities of behaviour' through which self-defined groups within or across social classes express themselves within an identifiable 'field of significations.' It is the process which informs the way meanings and definitions are socially constructed and historically transformed by social actors themselves. Cultures are distinguished in terms of differing responses to the same social, material and environmental conditions. Culture is not a static or even a necessarily coherent phenomenon: it is subject to change, fragmentation, reformulation. It is both adaptive, offering ways of coping and making sense, and strategic, capable of being mobilized for political, economic and social ends.[1]

Neither in traditional nor in modern or contemporary society has culture, in the comprehensive sense just defined, ever existed as an entity separate from other social structures. It has always been in the interest of the ruling classes, however, to keep art and culture, like religion, as apolitical as possible; for then such a dichotomy, which in reality does not exist, confirms them in their unchallenged position of dominance. Culture is not a neutral commodity, although this may be seen to be the case in societies where a social truce appears to exist between various classes in the society. Culture can be a repressive or a liberating force; it can either retard or facilitate social transformation. The artist or cultural worker, consciously or unwittingly, is the vehicle for the expression and propagation of certain values. Every artist is committed to such values long before sitting in front of a typewriter, stepping on a stage, or pulling out a canvas and paints; what the artist produces affirms or opposes dominant social relations.[2] In societies that are in the grip of social and political upheaval, the fallacy of cultural neutrality, of culture free of ideological leanings, becomes clear for all to see. Such an understanding of how culture and society interact is necessary to our appreciation of the political importance of the cultural boycott against South Africa.

South Africa has a long and venerable history of resistance to imperial domination, a tradition that has given rise to an alternative culture of liberation—alternative only in the sense of being opposed to the establishment culture of repression. The alternative culture in South Africa has always enjoyed primacy and dominance, by virtue of the fact that it is the majority culture, but has not always been accorded the recognition to which it is entitled among all sectors of the community. The establishment culture of repression, on the other hand, has always relied upon propaganda and state coercion because it is a minority, unpopular culture. The alternative culture derives from a democratic tradition that is as ancient as the institution of the traditional *mbizo, kgotla,* or *pitso,* the village square where matters of social significance were always thrashed out in any community. The alternative culture is as old as the theatrical tradition of *izibongo* or *lithothokiso* (heroic Poetry) and the story-telling performing art of the *intsomi, tsomo* or *inganekwane* (traditional tales), *imilando* (oral history), and *amabali* (legends). This alternative culture has survived more than three centuries of settler-colonial repression by building a new base in each new era, by digging in its transplanted but firm roots on new soil made fertile by the blood of a people schooled in sacrifice. It is dynamic, and not as stagnant as the settler colonial culture, and promises far-reaching social changes; it is already providing "the infrastructure for the new order." This alternative, majority culture is accommodating and life-giving; it is not exclusive and life-denying, like the culture of repression. The majority culture will triumph in the end. Because the battle lines are drawn out so starkly, a clear choice faces everyone concerned with South Africa.

What, then, is an appropriate approach to relationships with South Africa in terms of the music, literature, theatre, academic, and sports boycott? It is much simpler to deal with absolutes, that is, the status quo or blanket boycotts, than to construct a strategy that achieves maximum economic, political, and social pressure without doing terrible harm to the youth, the workers, the unions, and the alternative structures who must ultimately provide the leadership for the country. Barbara Masekela, ANC Cultural Secretary, sets out the principles underlying the cultural boycott against South Africa in the following terms:

> The cultural boycott of South Africa cannot be viewed outside the demands of our developing and intensifying struggle for national liberation and the establishment of a united, democratic and non-racial South African state. The boycott issue must be understood in the context of that aspect of the African National Congress's strategies and tactics that have promoted united action at home and mobilization of the international community for the isolation of the racist regime. It is a supplement to the struggle waged by workers, youth, students, professionals, churches, community and civic groups.[3]

This seems a reasonable principle to accept, whatever one's party political affiliation happens to be. It is a principle that should inform all opposition to apartheid.

The cultural boycott of South Africa is designed to counteract apartheid culture by passing the initiative to—and weighing the scales in favor of—the forces ranged against the vicious white minority racist regime. Apartheid culture, Barbara Masekela continues, sanctions "the instruments of torture: breathing tear gas, suffering the pangs of hunger in the land of plenty, the torment of homelessness in the face of empty 'white' housing, lack of classrooms and overcrowding of schools in spite of the fact that white schools are underpopulated, and worse, political repression including the imprisonment of children. That is apartheid culture."[4]

Apartheid culture sustains white political dominance; it is also designed to keep blacks economically weak and confined to low-paid jobs. It severely restricts their educational, business, and professional opportunities, and ensures cheap labor for white-owned industry, farming, and commerce.

Apartheid culture gives some 86.3% of the land to whites and a meagre 13.7% to about six times as many Africans. The 86.3% becomes a "white" country, a white South Africa; the 13.7% fragmented into ten "self-governing homelands" for Africans, each destined to achieve "independence." Thus a predominantly black country becomes white, and the African becomes an alien in his native land.

Apartheid culture is the Internal Security Act of 1982, which, among other formidable powers, allows for indefinite detention "for interrogation," a power much abused by the security forces. The same Act empowers the Minister of Law and Order to "ban" organizations and individuals. A banned individual can be required to stay in a certain place, prohibited from attending gatherings, and prevented from being quoted. Such an array of state powers, many of which are expressly not subject to review by the courts, coupled with extraordinarily wide definitions of "communism," "terrorism," "treason," and "sedition," render the country a police state with a permanent state of emergency in terms of the ordinary laws of the land. That is apartheid culture.

Clearly, no group, let alone a majority of the population, could be expected to acquiesce to such treatment. Certainly, blacks are no longer prepared to tolerate either exploitation or gross disparity. There have been waves of protests in the past, invariably put down by the security forces. The current wave of protests are without precedence in scale and intensity, even after government decided on February 24, 1988 to curtail the activities of eighteen black opposition groups. That is the alternative culture of liberation.

In protest at housing conditions, rent offices have been ransacked and stand, roofless and windowless, in townships where arrears of "rent" run into millions of rand, rent on houses paid for many times over by their black occupants with no prospects that they can ever own these houses.

In frustration at those who have aided the system by joining government-backed "town councils," collaborators have been hounded out of office—frequently out of house and home and often, tragically, "necklaced."

Students have often been on strike over educational issues; schools have been burnt down and destroyed and teachers paid to do nothing. Calls for work stay-aways, consumer boycotts and general strikes achieve increasingly unprecedented levels of response and solidarity. The dependence of white-owned shops on black purchasing power has been brought home to the white community as never before.

The government has been driven to a point where it is unable to police its own laws in some black townships, where its policies inevitably lead to systematic repression by the security forces. A *de facto coup d'etat* has occurred in South Africa and repression by the regime has reached its peak. This repression is paralleled by violent vigilante action by favored blacks, with active support from the government, against people rebelling against apartheid and forcing the pace for a democratic, non-racial South Africa.

Yet after constant and recurring cycles of repression, states of emergencies, bannings, and arrests, black resistance has not only been maintained, it has been strengthened and made more resolute. It has resolved into a new and telling strategy for change: to make apartheid unworkable.

The beast called apartheid has been hurt, and hurt badly, by the blows of a mobilized and militant people, schooled in the arena of sacrifice and struggle. But the beast has not yet died and, in its thrashing death throes, spreads terror and destruction over an oppressed and mutilated people. Things have fallen apart and the center is not holding. Much worse than anarchy has been let loose upon the earth, air, and waterways of South Africa.

Apartheid culture continues to derive sustenance, nonetheless, from the support it has enjoyed from Western governments and their allies: "This support in all its aspects, particularly the economic and military sector, has prolonged the tenure of the minority regime and emboldened it to carry out even more aggressive and repressive acts not only against its opponents, and in particular the majority population, but also against the frontline states with impunity."[5]

The South African government says it demands of its opponents a renunciation of violence—or a "commitment to non-violence"—as a precondition to negotiation; its opponents point out that their violence has been reactive, and call upon the government to abandon its violence first. The grand design of apartheid has always been to make South Africa a "white" country. The implementation of this design over the years, with the government riding roughshod over the wishes and traditions of the people affected, necessitated coercion by the state in a manner and on a scale which reveal the inherent violence of the system. The call for a cultural boycott of South Africa is a response to apartheid atrocities; it is a measure, very mild by comparison, adopted against a people who continue to flout civilized standards of government by the consent of the governed and to spread terrorism throughout the subcontinent.

The findings of the Commonwealth Eminent Persons Group (EPG) on Southern Africa further point to the fact that "the Government of South Africa has itself used economic (and other boycott) measures and that such measures are patently instruments of its own national policy."[6] The same observation holds true for other Western governments who have declared their opposition to sanctions and the cultural boycott against South Africa. Against Poland, Nicaragua, Libya, and more recently, Panama, President Ronald Reagan's administration considered every form of boycott action as an important weapon in its arsenal; similarly, Prime Minister Margaret Thatcher's government retaliated against Argentina by imposing comprehensive mandatory sanctions to supplement their war effort during the "Falklands Crisis."

"We are convinced that the South African Government is concerned about the adoption of effective economic measures against it," the Commonwealth Report concludes. "If it comes to the conclusion that it would always remain protected from such measures, the process of change in South Africa is unlikely to increase in momentum and the descent into violence would be accelerated. In these circumstances, the cost in lives may have to be counted in millions."[7] The resolution of the conflict by peaceful means must lie, to some extent, with the imposition of cultural boycott, along with other boycott measures, by the international community.

The liberation movement has, indeed, "already come to the view that diplomatic persuasion has not and will not move the South African Government sufficiently. If it also comes to believe that the world community will never exercise sufficient effective pressure through other measures in support of their cause, they will have only one option remaining: that of ever increasing violence. Once decisions involving greater violence are made on both sides, they carry an inevitability of their own and are difficult, if not impossible, to reverse, except as a result of exhaustion through prolonged conflict."[8] The argument is frightfully compelling and must be viewed seriously by people committed to peaceful change in South Africa.

"The question . . . is not whether such measures will compel change; it is already the case that their absence and Pretoria's belief that they need not be feared, defers change." We may well ask, along with the Commonwealth Eminent Persons Group, whether the international community will "stand by and allow the cycle of violence to spiral? Or will it take concerted action of an effective kind? Such action may offer the last opportunity to avert what could be the worst bloodbath since the Second World War."[9]

The cultural boycott undermines the unqualified support right wing Western regimes accord South Africa, by pointing to the abnormality of the situation and the brutality of the apartheid regime.

"Reforms" envisaged by South Africa fall far short of reasonable black expectations and are a ploy to buy time in a bid to update apartheid by co-opting "moderates"—in reality collaborators—from the ranks of the oppressed. The government has sought consistently to dictate both the content and pace of change. Its approach seeks not to unify the country but to divide. It is an approach which seeks to preserve the whites in their position of political and economic privilege and domination.

The Mixed Marriages Act has ostensibly been repealed, but the Group Areas Act remains, so that a white who marries a "coloured" must move to a "coloured" township with Ministerial permission. All this makes no difference to the impact of apartheid on the lives of the black majority. In a country where white income per capita is ten times that of a black person, what proportion of blacks can afford to dine at Johannesburg's Carlton Hotel or Durban's Maharani; what proportion can send their children to multiracial private schools, or attend a mixed concert by some overseas group at some inflated price?

The much heralded reforms are designed to buy time for the regime that has rejected a non-racial, democratic dispensation based on the principle of "one man one vote in a unitary state." They manifest a determination not to give up white control. In many of its manifestations, the harshness of apartheid may have softened for a select few. But the essential pillars remain: the "homelands" policy, the Population Registration Act or race classification, the Group Areas Act. "In the Government's thinking," the Commonwealth Report confirms, "there were a number of non-negotiables; for example, the concept of group rights—the very basis of the apartheid system—was sacrosanct; the 'homelands' created in furtherance of that concept would not disappear, but be reinforced with the emergence of an 'independent' KwaNdebele; the principle of one man one vote in a unitary state was beyond the realm of possibility; the Population Registration Act would continue; and the present Tricameral Constitution which institutionalized racism must be the vehicle for future constitutional reform."[10]

Apartheid cannot be reformed any more than Nazism could. The South African government has established no basis for negotiation and must be coerced to do so: "From these and other recent developments, we draw the conclusion that while the Government claims to be ready to negotiate, it is in truth not yet prepared to negotiate fundamental change, nor to countenance the creation of genuine democratic structures, nor to face the prospect of the end of white domination and white power in the foreseeable future. Its programme of reform does not end apartheid, but seeks to give it a less inhuman face. Its quest is power-sharing, but without surrendering overall white control."[11]

The cultural boycott, like the call for mandatory and comprehensive sanctions against the apartheid regime, is an appeal, as Barbara Masekela points out, "to the international community to take actions that go beyond condemnatory press statements and speeches at international fora, to hasten the demise of apartheid and stop the conflict which the minority regime is actively promoting."[12]

The cultural boycott is also a statement to affluent whites in South Africa who, for the most part, are able to go about their daily lives without any direct exposure to the deplorable conditions in the black townships where, as in Soweto, two million people are compressed into housing designed for 800,000; and where, as in Crossroads, thousands of destitute families, in defiance of the "homelands" policy and the Group Areas Act, have chosen to squat crowded into crude shanties put together from discarded sheets of corrugated iron, and lined with cardboard and polythene in a futile effort to keep out the cold.

Within the white community there is a desperate need for international recognition. The South African passion for "contact" sports, especially rugby, nurtures such craving for acceptance by the international community. The EPG filed the following report after their 1986 visit to South Africa:

> On the arrival of a "rebel" New Zealand rugby team, a Rugby Board official was reported as exulting that rugby had "changed the face of South Africa" by driving Nelson Mandela from the front page on to page six. As "white" South Africa basked in the illusion of an imagined international respectability, the death toll continued to mount unabated in the townships and in the "homelands." The response of whites to the presence of overseas sportsmen—whether representative or not—brought home to us the impact and importance of the international sports boycott of which the Gleneagles Agreement is a vital part. The lengths to which the

> South African authorities are prepared to go in elevating the importance of visiting teams, and the huge financial inducements they offer, reveal their craving for supposed international recognition. That alone demonstrates the continuing need for this form of pressure, including the strict observance of the Gleneagles Agreement.[13]

The argument holds true for music, literature, theatre, and the academic field.

The double standards in dealing with South Africa displayed by certain Western governments are a betrayal of the democratic ideals to which such societies profess to adhere. To protest Soviet occupation of Afghanistan, for instance, the US stayed away from the Moscow Olympics in 1980. Not to have done so would have been tantamount to condoning Soviet actions which the US claimed to deplore. Few Americans dared, then, to exercise their constitutional prerogatives to run, freely and democratically, in the Soviet Union. The liberation movement asks the US and its Western allies to act consistently, in accordance with their oft proclaimed ideals. To protest apartheid repression, Western governments must support the cultural boycott of South Africa. Not to do so is to condone apartheid, which such governments profess to deplore. And that is objectionable and unprincipled.

"The sports boycott is a direct result of the intransigence of the apartheid establishment," as Reggie Feldman, President of the Transvaal Council on Sport, points out. "The boycott was designed to put the state and the citizen-voter and white sportsperson under pressure with the aim of bringing an end to apartheid and apartheid sport."[14]

The slogan "no normal sports in an abnormal society" adopted by the South African Council of Sports and other progressive organizations remains valid as long as Race classification, the Group Areas Act, the Separate Amenities Act, and the Tricameral parliamentary system remain on the statute books.

Every black person in South Africa knows that whites have the best schools with the best sports facilities, that white parents have the best jobs because they have also had the best education, but sometimes have the best jobs even without the benefit of a sound education, and can therefore afford the best coaching and equipment for their children. They can also build and maintain the best sports facilities. And all this because they wield political power and can vote themselves the good things in life. Blacks, too, want that power.

The sports boycott is not purely vindictive and punitive, designed to avenge past and present wrongs or to reduce white sportspeople to nervous wrecks. Reggie Feldman is correct to point out that Zola Budd is not a victim of the evil machinations of the Anti-Apartheid Movement; she is a victim of apartheid.

Sports isolation was meant to punish those people who wish to maintain white privilege. It is also unfortunately true that it deprives black sports people of the opportunity to display their wares to the outside world, as the case of Jomo Sono barred from playing soccer in Zimbabwe indicates. Such acrimonious incidents, though, can be averted by prior consultation between South African non-racial sports organizers, progressive community organizations within the country, the external wing of the liberation movement, and the international Anti-Apartheid Movement. In addressing tactical issues in the implementation of the cultural boycott in general, Barbara Masekela mentions "the need 'to act together' between the ANC, the broad democratic movement in its various formations within South Africa, and the international solidarity movement."[15]

A creative response to the cultural boycott needs to be devised. As a matter or urgency and strategy, a structure for such consultation across the board needs to be set up by the Cultural Secretariat of the liberation movement. Unless the movement against apartheid in its various formations, internally and externally, can act in concert, the implementation of the cultural boycott can be embarrassing and divisive.

The sports boycott, like the cultural boycott in general, must also be prosecuted in such a way that it can be educative, as much to the international community as to local sportspeople, all of whom must be made to realize why it is vital to sacrifice international sports in pursuit of a non-racial South Africa, and why sports and politics continue to mix in South Africa.

All sportspeople, especially prominent ones, have an opportunity to make a contribution to the struggle, and the boycott carried out, as far as possible, after due consultation can be an effective weapon in the struggle; but the struggle for equal rights requires willing, dedicated people and not unwilling, frustrated "partners" in struggle. Prominent sportspeople, like Zola Budd and Jomo Sono, must be persuaded to appreciate the necessity, where it is unavoidable, to make this sacrifice in the interests of the black community and a better South Africa. We are not on "an easy road to freedom."

Sports people by themselves, like other cultural activists working in isolation, cannot bring about the radical changes needed to make South Africa truly non-racial and democratic: "We are not naive. We do not think that the cultural boycott will bring about instant liberation to South Africa (anymore than mandatory comprehensive sanctions will). We know that ultimately we must and will liberate ourselves from racial and economic oppression. In view of the prolonged suffering of our people, we believe the cultural boycott—in conjunction with other mandatory and comprehensive sanctions—will have a cumulative effect that will force a speedy resolution of the South African crisis. Unarguably, this would mean less bloodshed. For those then who profess support of the South African people in struggle, it is incumbent to show their solidarity in practical terms."[16]

In accordance with the principle of consultation already outlined, sports administrators within South Africa need to cultivate close relations with progressive community organizations, consulting them and commemorating all the national days of solidarity with the oppressed that mean so much to the communities. We are in a period when eighteen organizations and the trade union movement have been severely restricted. Sports and other cultural organizations cannot stand aloof from the country's political crisis. The solution is for representatives of voteless sportsmen and women to sit around a table where non-racial sports organizations can draw up a sports "charter."[17]

In South Africa the academic field becomes another arena of struggle. In general, academic exchanges must be subject to the same principles as cultural exchanges. We cannot stop the regime from inviting right wing academics. But we can expose their evil machinations and discredit the "academics" concerned.

In addition, we can establish academic programs more responsive to the needs of the downtrodden and oppressed. The operation of such programs, however, requires consultation between the responsible institutions, on the one hand, and representatives of the internal and external wings of the liberation movement, on the other hand.

In the final analysis, the cultural boycott must be so prosecuted that it accelerates the "changing balance of strength in our country and the shift of strategic initiatives into our hands."[18]

As the fortunes of the regime decline, it undertakes desperate experiments with new propaganda ploys aimed at destroying the growing liberation movement inside and outside South Africa. For one thing, whites would like to enjoy the best that Western culture can provide in music, literature, sports, and theatre. Barbara Masekela's call for international solidarity against apartheid in this regard is quite pertinent: "We say: Support our cause—deprive them of these amenities which at best have negligible exposure in the majority of the population."[19]

Various success stories in prosecuting the cultural boycott deserve mention and are worthy of emulation: "In 1985, 54 artists in the US made their viewpoint very clear. As Artists United Against Apartheid through the 'Sun City' project, they said loudly and clearly, 'I ain't gonna play Sun City.' We applaud the actions of Artists United Against Apartheid because they are exposing the obscenity of Sun City built in the midst of apartheid-made hunger, suffering, repression, torture and death."[20]

We must also applaud efforts by the international solidarity movement which have led to maximum exposure given overseas to South African resistance culture: nominations for five 1988 Tony Awards given to such a production as *Sarafina* that highlights the liberation struggle; the 1988 Cannes Film Festival success of *A World Apart*, that is centered on the struggle against apartheid; solidarity concerts such as "FreedomFest" to commemorate Mandela's seventieth birthday; and many other similar successes abroad.

Along the same lines, anti-apartheid workers and artists in Sweden, Holland, Denmark, England, France, Nigeria, Senegal, and many other countries have organized projects to make their voices heard against apartheid.

Inside South Africa, cultural workers continue to set the pace. The years since the emergence of Black Consciousness have seen "the founding of a number of cultural groups aimed at tackling the apartheid monster. It is the South African people who signalled the time for this activity when they boycotted foreign cultural mercenaries who performed in South Africa at the invitation of the regime."[21]

We must take into account these changes that have taken place over time:

> There has emerged a definable alternative democratic culture—the people's culture—permeated with and giving expression to the deepest aspirations of our people in struggle, immersed in democratic and enduring human values . . . the alternative structures that our people have created and are creating through struggle and sacrifice as the genuine representatives of these masses in all field of human activity. Not only should these not be boycotted, but more they should be supported, encouraged, and treated as the democratic counterparts within South Africa of similar institutions and organizations internationally.[22]

We must also educate ourselves to recognize anti-apartheid culture in all its subtle nuances:

> In other words, we would like to stress that we are not dour-faced dogmatists calling for a rigorous code that every song and poem should reverberate with heavy revolutionary fervor. Neither do we have a secret formula which advocates percentages or quotas for humor, slogans, names of leaders, history, and so forth. After all, where would we be without the optimism which carries us from one struggle to the next? Our South African languages are replete with humor, satire, and sheer poetry.[23]
>
> In general we must remain firmly opposed to visits by artists, academics, and sportspersons to South

> Africa. Such visits only serve to legitimize the regime and make nonsense of the objective to isolate Pretoria. Any visits to South Africa should be discussed beforehand with the liberation movement and the appropriate international solidarity organization.[24]

But we must open the doors of culture and learning everywhere to the downtrodden and oppressed people of South Africa.

Notes

1. *Contemporary Cultural Studies* (Birmingham, U.K.), No. 5 (1985), n.p.

2. Alex La Guma, "Culture and Liberation in South Africa," *Sechaba*, X (1976), 50-59.

3. Barbara Masekela, "The Cultural Boycott of South Africa," *Africa Report*, XXXII, 4 (July—August 1987), 19; See also Barbara Masekela, "Isolate Apartheid Culture," *Rixaka* (Cultural Journal of the African National Congress), 3/1986.

4. Masekela, "The Cultural Boycott," 20.

5. Ibid.

6. *Mission to South Africa: The Commonwealth Report* (Harmondsworth, Penguin, 1986).

7. Ibid., 140.

8. Ibid.

9. Ibid., 140-41.

10. Ibid., 132.

11. Ibid., 132-33.

12. Masekela, "The Cultural Boycott," 19.

13. *Mission to South Africa*, 44.

14. Reggie Feldman, "SACOS Never Said Sport Alone Can Change Society," *Weekly Mail*, 27 May—June 2 1988, 31.

15. Masekela, "The Cultural Boycott," 21.

16. Ibid., 19.

17. Dennis Cruywagen, "SACOS Needs Marketing: the NSL Needs a Heart," *Weekly Mail*, 10 June-16 June 1988, 35.

18. Masekela, "The Cultural Boycott," 20.

19. Ibid.

20. Ibid.

21. Ibid.

22. Ibid., 21.

23. Ibid.

24. Ibid.

THE CULTURAL BOYCOTT OF SOUTH AFRICA (II)

Larry Shore

The struggle against the apartheid system in South Africa has necessitated actions on a broad front. One of these has been the call for a cultural boycott of South Africa. This article will attempt to briefly lay out some of the issues and debates involved in the cultural boycott of South Africa, with the hope that further discussion can take place on this important question.

There have been various activities in the decades since the Second World War to punish South Africa for its inhuman policies towards its majority black population. South African sports teams have been denied international competition through banning South African participation in international events, and international sports teams have been prevented or discouraged from visiting South Africa.[1] Many musicians have refused to perform in South Africa, and many playwrights have not allowed their works to be performed in South Africa.

In 1968, the United Nations General Assembly formally adopted a resolution requesting all states and organizations to "suspend cultural, educational, sporting and other exchanges with the racist regime . . . ."[2] A 1980 resolution called for "writers, artists, musicians, and others to boycott South Africa."

In recent years, this cultural boycott has been more vigorously monitored by the UN Anti-Apartheid Committee, which keeps a list of international artists and sportspeople who violated the call for a boycott and performed in South Africa. Those on the list are likely to be the object of pickets and boycotts of their performances, or at least of negative publicity.

The cultural boycott has two essential components which are often not separated out. The first is a boycott of all culture going to South Africa, and the second is a boycott of all culture coming out of South Africa. Although they both have the objective of weakening and contributing to the overthrow of the apartheid system, it is necessary to consider these two issues separately.

The Boycott of Culture Going to South Africa

The argument in favor of boycotting all forms of culture going to South Africa is seen as part of the larger objective of totally isolating South Africa economically, politically, and culturally as a form of pressure on the South African government to dismantle the apartheid system. This position is based on the historic intransigence of the South African government in bringing about anything more than superficial reforms of apartheid, and their lack of serious response to quieter forms of persuasion. In response to this intransigence, it seems apparent to many in the West seeking the end of apartheid, that the South African government and the white population that supports it (or the even more extreme forms of white supremacy)[3] will only make significant changes if there are significant costs involved in the continuation of apartheid.

The cultural boycott seeks to "destabilize South Africa's access to cultural enrichment"[4] as a form of punishment for the continuation of apartheid, even in its newly "dressed-up" versions. Undoubtedly, part of the intent of the cultural boycott is to act as a form of psychological pressure on white South Africans by means of denying them the comfort of feeling that they are accepted members of Western cultural and moral traditions. White South Africans, despite the condemnation they have received, like to see themselves as part of the West politically and culturally. White South Africans are also very assimilated into Western popular culture, in particular American culture. Most white South Africans have grown up watching American films and listening to Anglo-American popular music. More recently, many have become avid fans of American TV programs.[5] The boycott thus seeks to deny apartheid South Africa any legitimacy and normal relations with the West.

In particular, the boycott has sought to deny any legitimacy to the South African government's aggressive propaganda campaign to promote its "reforms." In recent years, the government has undertaken certain reforms, in an attempt to portray to South Africans and the outside world that it is moving away from apartheid. In the cultural arena, this has resulted in allowing, in certain locations, multiracial performers, audiences, and spectators for theatres, movie houses, musical performances, and sports events. The most publicized of these venues is Sun City, the entertainment complex located in Bophuthatswana, one of the supposed "independent homelands" set up by the South African government as part of its apartheid/Bantustan masterplan. The South African government has tried to promote these and other reforms as proof of their desire to move away from apartheid.[6] The hope of this campaign was that it would placate South Africa's internal and external critics and ease the pressure on South Africa, or at least prevent a further increase in pressure. Presumably the government believed that it could offer these types of reforms without dealing with the fundamental issue of political and economic power.

When unravelled, the argument for the boycott of culture going to South Africa calls for essentially three things: for artists, musicians, and sportspeople not to perform in South Africa; for artists such as playwrights and filmmakers not to allow their work to be performed or screened in South Africa; and that musicians and writers not allow their recordings and books to be sold in South Africa. Most of the debate and publicity has been about not performing in South Africa and not allowing films and plays to be screened or performed. Much less attention has been focused on the question of selling popular music and books in South Africa, although these issues have come up in debates within the music and publishing industries.

Supporters of the boycott believe that any performance by someone from outside South Africa at any venues in South Africa, even if multiracial, grants a degree of legitimacy to the government strategy of reforms without fundamental changes. Any performance at one of these sites provides the South African government with the ideological victory it seeks, and suggests to white South Africans that these types of changes are sufficient. The cultural boycott has sought to let South Africans know that although there are now multiracial sports teams and cultural venues, "there can be no normal cultural interaction in an abnormal society."[7] Participation, however well intentioned, will ultimately serve as a form of collaboration with the current version of "Reformed Apartheid."

In the United States, most of the negative publicity on those who have defied the boycott has been focused on musicians. One reason for this might be the publicity surrounding the "Sun City" record album and videotape which made an anti-apartheid musical statement and appealed to musicians not to play Sun City. There has been some pressure on black American boxers not to perform in South Africa, but relatively little publicity has focused on tennis players and golfers who play in South Africa.[8] In the West Indies, Britain, and Australia, much attention has been focused on the "rebel" cricket tours which have gone to South Africa, and in New Zealand controversy has been created by the "rebel" rugby tour to South Africa.[9]

The debate over Paul Simon's visit to South Africa, and the subsequent enormously successful "Graceland" album and tour, for which Simon collaborated with a number of black South African musicians, is an illustration of the complexity of the issue of what performing in South Africa means. Simon was initially put on the U.N. list for having broken the boycott by going to South Africa. Those who opposed this action (including, of course, Paul Simon himself) argued for the important distinction between performing at a live concert in Sun City or in Johannesburg as opposed to privately playing and recording with black musicians in South Africa. Simon also argued that he turned down offers to play Sun City, and that he was invited to go to South Africa by black South African musicians. Simon was taken off the list, although there were calls for boycotting the concert in London during the Graceland Tour.

Some supporters of the cultural boycott have pushed for pressuring American and European record companies to divest their interests in South Africa, and for record companies and film and TV distributors not to allow their products to be sold in the South African market. This is seen as giving comfort to white South Africans, contributing to the apartheid economy, and giving support and profits to a culture industry dominated by white South African interests. This aspect of the cultural boycott has been more difficult to enforce than putting pressure on individual artists not to perform in South Africa, although some American media companies have sold their subsidiaries in South Africa as part of the more general foreign divestment from the South African economy. This, of course, has not prevented South African companies and authorities from obtaining these products through licensing arrangements if foreign companies and distributors are willing to sell to them.[10]

Some people in the music industry in South Africa believe that the absence of foreign repertoire in the South African record market would lead to an increase in local recordings, except for the fact that foreign recordings would within a short period of time be widely available through pirated recordings or expensive imports. The availability of pirated recordings would undermine any real benefits to the local recording industry.[11]

In the publishing industry, a number of book publishers have not allowed their books to be sold in South Africa, but generally speaking there has not been much focus on this question. Some publishers and writers have not prevented their books being sold in South Africa, including many who are staunchly opposed to the system in South Africa.

Another site of debate on the cultural boycott, particularly within the South African and international film community, has been participation in events like the Durban Film Festival. This annual festival organized by progressive white South Africans "sells some 40,000 tickets and shows about 50 films from all over the world."[12] The organizers attempt to show films which challenge the ideology of apartheid and contribute to a change in the consciousness of white South Africans "or at least that they can be persuaded of their vested interest in the possibility of peaceful revolution."[13] The organizers of the conference also make considerable attempts to screen the films in the black townships of Durban due to the cost and difficulty for blacks to travel to the screenings and discussions in Durban. The festival apparently receives some funding from the South African government and special dispensation from the film censors board.[14] Film people who oppose participation in this festival argue that it gives legitimacy to the government's reformist image. As one critic suggests, "There is no dividing line between this festival of Apartheid and the Apartheid system itself."[15] (Arguments in support of the Durban Film Festival will be discussed further in the next section.)

Opposition to a Total Cultural Boycott

The cultural boycott has been criticized from various perspectives. It is important to distinguish between those who oppose the cultural boycott altogether, and those who call for a selective boycott. There are certainly those who oppose the cultural boycott of South Africa because they are ultimately friends of the South African government and oppose all pressure on South Africa, either political, economic, or cultural. There are others, however, equally opponents of apartheid, who believe that keeping the cultural gates open to South Africa does more good than harm in contributing to a new society in South Africa. This argument is based on the belief that cutting white South Africans off from the outside world forces them into a "laager"[16] where they become more intransigent and defiant and thus less likely to take the steps necessary to move towards a post-apartheid South Africa. In contrast, it is argued, by exposing South Africans to cultural experiences, ideas, and images which overtly or subtly propose an alternative to the dominant ideology of racial superiority, white South Africans will become more receptive to these possibilities.

This view suggests the educational value of exposure to culture from outside South Africa that promotes a positive image of blacks. Exposure to such media will teach whites to accept the legitimacy of black demands for an equal status in society. This line of thinking has been evident in discussions about the impact of American movies and TV shows like "The Cosby Show" in South Africa. The Cosby Show is one of the most popular TV shows in South Africa. Representatives of the show have suggested that the show has a positive effect on race relations in South Africa in that within the context of South Africa it promotes a positive image of blacks in a multiracial society, so absent from South African media. Supporters of the show believe that it empowers blacks and forces white South Africans to confront their negative stereotypes of blacks. Critics argue against this interpretation of the impact of the show. They suggest that it gives credibility to the South African government's claims of reform and openness, while a large number of white South African viewers continue to make a distinction between black Americans and black South Africans. Most opponents of the cultural boycott would also argue that performances and screenings before multiracial audiences encourages this practice and contributes to a breakdown of the racial barriers particularly in the minds of white South Africans.

Others take a different approach to the cultural boycott, suggesting that there should be a boycott, but a selective boycott which analyzes each situation separately. This position emerges out of a concern that a boycott which aims to weaken the state should not also weaken the progressive cultural forces within South Africa that are on the frontline in the cultural war against the system. This position argues that whereas it is important where possible to isolate and weaken the South African state apparatus, it is important at the same time not to cut off ties to the many groups in South Africa, which are contributing to a progressive post-apartheid cultural vision. Sometimes observers in the West, in their haste to make South Africa a pariah nation, ignore or underestimate the many people, black and white, working for serious change in South Africa against difficult circumstances in all kinds of cultural settings—in literature and the theatre, in alternate film productions, and in the vibrant music scene. In many ways cultural politics is at the cutting edge of the new society waiting to be born in South Africa. Through these cultural expressions, it is argued, those South

Africans committed to a new society are helping people to resist, survive, and, ultimately, contemplate alternatives.

This view argues that it is important that the cultural boycott not just be determined externally, but be developed in consultation with the needs of progressives within South Africa whose work is in support of the broader movement for the liberation of South Africa.

One example cited in which a boycott might be counterproductive is the availability of books and journals in bookstores and in the liberal universities in South Africa. Such materials are helpful to the forces working for change in South Africa. If such externally printed materials are beneficial for progressive forces in South Africa, then it is arguable that a similar effect might result from the presence of other cultural items such as films and records. The problem is how to get these materials to the progressive forces without also making them available to repressive forces.

The argument in favor of the value to progressive forces in South Africa having access to foreign media has been made in defense of the value of the Durban Film Festival discussed previously. In a letter to *The Independent* and signed by a number of filmmakers and videomakers, actors, directors, media workers, and cultural activists in South Africa, the authors suggest that "the sentiments behind the boycott reflect, more often than not, romantic gestures by groups and individuals whose links to the structural complexities are remote."[17,18]

They argue that despite the special dispensation of the state censors for the festival, and even possible state financial assistance, events like the Durban Film Festival offer "a site for the propagation of progressive ideas," where activists can "exploit the contradictions and turn them to democratic advantage."[19] The authors of this letter argue that not all cultural events are co-optable by the state, and, because cultural struggle takes place at different levels, in these instances, progressive filmmakers and videomakers should not boycott the festival. Allowing their films to be screened contributes to the democratic forces within South Africa. This view suggests that events like the Durban Film Festival should not be boycotted, but that commercial forms of media should be boycotted because they act as a source of comfort and escape for those who support the status quo in South Africa.[20,21]

Some people in the music industry who are concerned about the situation in South Africa have proposed that, instead of not selling foreign popular music in South Africa, an arrangement should be made with record companies and recording artists whereby revenues from the sale of these records in South Africa be given to a credible anti-apartheid group for dispersement to worthy organizations involved in the struggle for a democratic South Africa.

Some suggest that there is an inconsistent standard applied as to who should visit South Africa. Few in the anti-apartheid movement (except perhaps AZAPO[22]) seem to question that, under appropriate circumstances and invitations, it is helpful to the democratic forces in South Africa for prominent black leaders like Jesse Jackson to visit South Africa. If it sometimes empowers anti-apartheid forces in South Africa for people like Jackson to visit South Africa, could this not also be extended to include people in the cultural sphere (provided, of course, that they were allowed in by the South African government)? For example, if a prominent black American writer, playwright, filmmaker, or musician were invited by a credible organization to teach a workshop or even perform in black areas, it could be argued that such a visit could be helpful for black South Africans in much the same way as a visit by Jesse Jackson, on the invitation of prominent people like Archbishop Desmond Tutu or Alan Boesak, might be.[23]

The possibility of an effective selective boycott seems to be contingent on the existence of credible organizations in South Africa which, working with external forces, could invite specific people to South Africa, if in their judgement it would be helpful to them and not be co-opted by the state, or take the pressure off those South Africans who continue to support the system of white supremacy. In such a situation a careful case-by-case analysis could be made in place of an all-encompassing total boycott.

The Boycott of Culture Coming Out of South Africa

The other side of the cultural boycott debate has been the question of whether to boycott artists and productions coming out of South Africa. At the extreme, the argument has been advanced that all culture from South Africa, whether performers or films and recordings, should be boycotted in the same way as other South African products should be boycotted. This position seeks to exclude all performances by South African musicians and actors, and opportunities for South African filmmakers to screen their films outside South Africa. This position has called for boycotting performances by both black and white South Africans and multiracial groups. This type of boycott has been more visible in Britain than in the United States. South African bands, including multiracial bands like Juluka, sometimes had difficulties performing in Britain, very often opposed by local musicians and political organizations.

In the United States there seems to have been less support for an indiscriminate boycott of all South African performers. There was a boycott of the South African musical "Ipi Tombi" in the United States in 1977[24] and, more recently, there was a call for the boycott of the very successful film "The Gods Must be Crazy," made by the South African filmmaker, Jamie Uys.[25]

Other recent performances of South African theatre by resident South Africans have not faced this type of opposition. These include Athol Fugard's plays[26] and the performances of "Woza Albert," "Asinamali," and the festival of South African theatre, "Woza Africa," which took place in New York in 1986. On the musical level, South African bands seem to have had less "political" difficulty touring the United States than Britain.

In literary circles, to this author's knowledge, no one has ever publicly called for banning the works or personal appearances of well known white South African writers like Nadine Gordimer and J. M. Coetzee. Nor has their been a boycott of the photographs of well known photojournalists like Peter Magubane. Clearly, in certain fields, people are able to distinguish between spokespeople or apologists for the South African government and those who, through their work, oppose the system and are contributing to another vision of South Africa's future. Most people would agree that knowledge of their work outside South Africa contributes in some way to their potential influence in South Africa. This flexibility, or selectivity, might be expanded to include other cultural forms.

The issue of South African performers performing outside South Africa came up again with the "Graceland" Tour that Paul Simon did with exiled South Africans Miriam Makeba and Hugh Masekela and resident popular South African musicians, such as Ray Phiri and Ladysmith Black Mambazo, who were major contributors to the "Graceland" album. The tour specifically did not attempt to perform in South Africa, but played a well publicized concert in neighboring Zimbabwe. The issue of whether Paul Simon "broke" the cultural boycott by recording in South Africa was discussed previously. There seems to have been more opposition to the tour in Britain than in the United States. Most observers in the United States seemed to feel, perhaps because of the credibility of the South African musicians involved both inside and outside South Africa, that it would be foolish to deny the opportunity for South African black musicians, who are popular in South Africa and have no links to the apartheid regime, not to be able to receive acclaim outside South Africa. This publicity and focus on South Africa's vibrant black music has the potential to open up the doors for other South African musicians to become known outside South Africa and to show another part of South Africa to outside audiences. It is difficult to see how this is detrimental to the anti-apartheid movement.

There is a danger, of course, in the success of the "Graceland" album—that Americans will only pay attention to South African music if it is brought to them by people like Paul Simon,[27] while the original musicians playing this music remain unknown. However well meaning and artistically successful musicians like Simon might be, this would be reminiscent of the 1950s in America where white performers found success with watered-down cover records of black rhythm and blues artists, while the original artists remained unknown and penniless. It is important to see to it that a phenomenon like the "Graceland" album open up doors for the originators of the music and not just those talented foreigners who appreciate the music and are able to incorporate the sounds of black South Africa into their own music.

The argument for a total boycott of all South African culture argues that artists should be boycotted irrespective of who they are, the subject matter of their music, and their relationship to the struggle inside South Africa. It seems ironic to punish musicians and artists who have never supported apartheid and who in their work constitute an important part of the struggle for a new South Africa. It is doubly ironic if black South African musicians[28] are boycotted merely because they are from South Africa. This is a case of being twice victimized. Black South African musicians struggle against all kinds of odds in a society that denies them full citizenship in the land of their birth, only to be told that they shouldn't perform overseas because of their country of origin. Critics of this type of boycott argue that it is a mistake to label indiscriminantly all South African artists as tainted by apartheid. This denies people outside South Africa the opportunity to experience the range of activities going on in South Africa. A total boycott of all South African culture denies the opportunity for progressives in South Africa to make contacts and get support for the work they are doing in South Africa. Giving them credibility and support outside South Africa empowers them in relation to the powers back home. This is not that different from the type of credibility and "power" that people like Archbishop Tutu and Alan Boesak receive by their connections and support outside South Africa. Although the extent of the state's repressive capacities cannot be underestimated, it is that much more difficult for the South African Government to silence or imprison them, due to their renown in the outside world. The same might be said for writers like Nadine Gordimer and Athol Fugard. If people in the anti-apartheid movement are not calling for excluding these people from access to the outside world, this might be extended to include other, lesser known South African musicians, writers, and filmmakers, in particular black South African artists, who face the most difficult circumstances.

Some voices calling for a total boycott have argued that only South Africans in exile should be allowed to perform or screen their work. Others argue that this position ignores or undervalues the work being done inside South Africa. The vast majority of South African artists want to remain in South Africa, but this position forces them either to leave permanently and take them away from the very place where their work is most effective, or else deny them support and connections with external forces and influences that can assist them in doing cultural battle in South Africa.

To cut off the South African artistic and cultural community seems in fact to be cutting off one of the most progressive sectors in the South African situation. The vitality of current South African literature, theatre, alternative filmmaking, and popular music, in the face of difficult circumstances, is testament to the fact that in South Africa, as in any repressive society, cultural expressions provide not only a way to resist and survive the ravages of apartheid, but a way of articulating an alternative social reality.

If a new South African culture is stirring, do those outside South Africa try to support it, or cut it off as a part of the cost of pressuring the regime to end its inhuman system?

Notes

1. South Africa was thrown out of the Olympic Movement in 1960.

2. Resolution 2396.

3. There are three white parties in South Africa to the right of the ruling Nationalist Party: the Herstigte Nasionale Party, the Conservative Party (which both compete in all white elections), and the Afrikaner Weerstandsbeweging (The Afrikaner Resistance Movement).

4. Charlayne Haynes, "The Culture Boycott of South Africa," *The Independent*, Jan./Feb. 1986.

5. Television first arrived in South Africa in 1976.

6. The government has dropped the Immorality Act, which made sex across racial lines a criminal offense. They have also eased the pass laws and allowed for legal unions, although these unions face ongoing harrassment. Other aspects of "Petty Apartheid" have been removed. One of the government's most touted "reforms" was the creation of separate "parliaments" for so-called coloreds and Indians, which are subservient to the white government.

7. Ashwin Desai, "The Cultural Boycott," *The SAFTA Journal* (The South African Film and Television Technicians Association), Vol. 4, Nos. 1 & 2 (Dec. 1984), 14.

8. It is interesting to note that the "bad boy" of the tennis world, John McEnroe, is one of the few top tennis players to refuse to play in South Africa.

9. These rebel tours have been enormously well financed by large South African corporations. Players have earned sums well beyond what they could earn as professionals in their home countries, at the cost of a few years suspension and bad publicity.

10. Some artists have written into their contracts specific clauses preventing release of their work in South Africa. For example, Woody Allen, the American filmmaker, had a clause entered in his most recent three-film contract with Orion Pictures prohibiting distribution of his films in South Africa.

11. Conversation with Hilton Rosenthal, South African record producer, October 1985.

12. Haynes, op. cit., 19.

13. *SAFTA Journal*, Vol. 4, op. cit., 23.

14. Haynes, op. cit., 20.

15. Ibid., 20.

16. Reminiscent of the circle of wagons that the Voortrekkers (the "heroic" ancestors of the Afrikaners who left the Cape for the interior in the 1830s) drew around themselves in times of danger.

17. *The Independent*, December, 1986, 21.

18. The majority of people who signed this letter seemed to be progressive white South Africans, so it is difficult to assess how widely held this position is amongst black artists and cultural workers.

19. *The Independent*, December 1986, 21.

20. This argument ends up trying to draw a sharp distinction between the political values of so-called popular culture as opposed to mass culture—seen as commercially produced culture. This question is debated in various academic fora. Space does not allow for a discussion of this issue, but suffice it to say that a strong argument can be made that certain forms of commercially produced culture (such as popular music) can have progressive effects in South Africa.

21. *The Independent*, op. cit., 22.

22. Azanian People's Organization.

23. This is not to suggest that progressive white Americans might not also be invited to visit particular groups or organizations in South Africa, if such a system were in place.

24. Most of the objections to the show seem to have been not just that it came from South Africa, but that the theme of the musical was the "happy homeland black," which played into the South African government's propaganda about how contented blacks are in South Africa, or else that they are not ready to be equals or to run the country.

25. "The Gods Must Be Crazy" has been by far the most successful South African film in the international film market. Critics of the film argued that despite the fact that very little of the film actually takes place in South Africa, the very act of making an apolitical comedy promotes an "equal opportunity South African workplace," is patronizing towards the "bushmen" in the film, and makes the black government and guerillas portrayed in the film look like incompetent buffoons.

26. Most recently, "Sizwe Banzi is Dead," "Harold and the Boys," and "The Bloodknot."

27. This is not meant to suggest, counter to what this author believes, that "Graceland" is not musically a remarkable success. The album is too original and collaborative to be called a very good cover record. Some of the criticisms of the album have been aimed at the essentially apolitical nature of the lyrics and the virtual lack of reference to the society from which the music emerges. Others have criticized the participation of Linda Ronstadt on the album; she played Sun City and, unlike some others who have defied the boycott, has refused to "apologize." The "Graceland" album has been the subject of much debate in the popular music press. It won the 1986 Grammy Award for Album of the Year.

28. This is not to suggest that all white musicians are well off. Some pioneering white musicians such as Johnny Clegg of Juluka (and now Savuka), like their black counterparts, have faced substantial difficulties: having their songs censored, not being heard on the radio, or not being able to perform wherever and with whomever they choose.

EDITOR

Robert Edgar is Associate Professor of African Studies at Howard University, Washington, D.C. He was Fulbright Professor of History at the National University of Lesotho, 1984-1986. He has written on twentieth century Southern African history. His recent publications include *Prophets With Honour A Documentary History of Lekhotla la Bafo* (1987) and *Because They Chose the Plan of God* (1988).

CONTRIBUTORS

Douglas Anglin is Professor of Political Science at Carleton University. He was Vice-Chancellor of the University of Zambia, 1965-1969. He has co-authored *Zambia's Foreign Policy* (1979) and co-edited *Conflict and Change in Southern Africa* (1978) and *Canada, Scandinavia, and Southern Africa* (1979).

Benjamin Beit-Hallahmi received his PhD in Clinical Pschology from Michigan State University in 1970. Since then, he has been affiliated with the University of Michigan, the University of Pennsylvania, and Columbia University, and he has taught at several Israeli universities. He writes on Israeli politics and

Middle East affairs. His latest book is *The Israeli Connection* (1987).

Alan Booth is Professor of History at Ohio University. He was Fulbright Professor at the University of Swaziland, 1980-1981. He has written extensively on Swaziland, including *Swaziland: Tradition and Change in a Southern African Kingdom* (1983).

Thomas Conrad is a researcher with the American Friends Service Committee in Philadelphia, Pennsylvania. He has researched on military and high-tech sales to South Africa and contributed to *Automating Apartheid: U.S. Computer Sales to South Africa and the Arms Embargo* (1982).

David Hirschmann is Associate Professor in the School of International Service at American University, Washington, D.C. He has taught at the University of Malawi and the National University of Lesotho. He has written on development and planning issues and women and development and, in 1986-1987, he carried out a study on black South African attitudes.

Richard Knight is a research associate with the Africa Fund in New York City, where he has worked since 1979. He is co-author of the *Unified List of United States Corporations Doing Business in South Africa and Namibia* (1988).

David Koistinen is a research associate with CANICCOR. He received his B.A. in Economics and History at the University of California, Berkeley. He has co-authored several reports on South Africa, including *South Africa's Gold and Diamond Trade* (1988) and *Financing South Africa's Foreign Trade* (1988).

Ian Lepper has written widely on corporations and southern African issues for Counter Information Services. He is the author of *Black South Africa Explodes* and *Partner in Apartheid* and co-author of *South Africa Inc.* (1988), a study of the Anglo American empire.

John Lind is the executive director of CANICCOR, an inter-church agency which specializes in banking issues. He was trained as a chemical engineer and a physical chemist and taught at Cornell University and Stanford University. In the 1970s, he joined what is now CANICCOR and focused his research on corporate responsibility in international banking. His writings include *The Debt Crisis and Credit Risk in Countries with Human Rights Abuses* (1983), *Phillipine Debt to Foreign Banks* (1984), and *Financing South Africa's Foreign Trade* (1988).

Gay McDougall is Director of the Southern Africa Project of the Lawyers Committee for Civil Rights Under Law. She has a J.D. from Yale University and a L.L.M. from the London School of Economics. Her project provides financial resources for defense attorneys and political detainees in South Africa and Namibia, initiates legal proceedings in actions opposing South Africa, and educates people who are concerned with the erosion of the rule of law in South Africa.

Mbulelo Mzamane is Professor of Comparative Literature at the University of Georgia. He is the author of *Children of Soweto* (1982) and *My Cousin Comes to Johannesburg* (1981). He is the editor of *Selected Poems of Mongane Serote, Selected Poems of Sipho Sepamla* (1984), and *Hungry Flames and Other South African Stories.*

Jack Parson is Associate Professor of Political Science and Director of the Institute for Public Affairs at the College of Charleston, Charleston, South Carolina. He taught at the University of Botwana from 1973 to 1978 and returned there again in 1984-1985 as a Fulbright researcher. He has published numerous articles on Botswana and *Botswana: Liberal Democarcy and the Labor Reserve in Southern Africa* (1984).

Roger Riddell is a Research Fellow at the Overseas Development Institute, London, England. He has long professional associations with southern Africa going back several decades, most especially in Zimbabwe, where he has worked for the Zimbabwe government, the private sector, and the university. He is currently completing a book on industry in Africa entitled *Manufacturing Africa.* He recently published *Foreign Aid Reconsidered* (1987).

Peter Robbins has been a dealer in rare and precious metals for over twenty years. He has acted as a consultant for the United Nations and Commonwealth on various aspects of the metals markets. He is the author of *The Guide to Non-Ferrous Metals and Their Markets* and *The Guide to Precious Metals and their Markets,* and is the co-author of *Trading in Metals.* He is now chairman of the World Gold Commission.

Ann Seidman is Professor in the Department of International Development and Social Change at Clark University. She has also taught at universities in Ghana, Zambia, China, Tanzania, and Zimbabwe. She has authored numerous articles and books on African economics, including *South Africa and U.S. Multinational Corporations* (1978), *Outposts of Monopoly Capitalism: Southern Africa in the Changing Global Economy* (1980), *Money, Banking and Public Finance in Africa* (1986), and *The Roots of Crisis in Southern Africa* (1985). She will begin a term as president of the African Studies Association in 1989.

Larry Shore is a graduate of Witwatersrand University. He left South Africa in 1975. He teaches Media Studies at Hunter College in New York City.

Jaap Woldendorp is Director of the Shipping Research Bureau, Amsterdam, Holland. He was trained as a sociologist and political scientist at Amsterdam University, where he comeleted B.A. and M.A. degrees. After working at Amsterdam University for four years, he joined the Shipping Research Bureau in March 1985.

Sanford Wright has been Associate Professor in the Center for Afro-American Studies, Indiana State University, Terre Haute, Indiana and currently teaches at Chico St. University in California. His articles on South Africa have appeared in numerous journals. "The Case for International Comprehensive Sanctions Against South Africa" will appear in George Shepherd, ed.,

People's Rights in an Unjust World: the African Experience (forthcoming).

INDEX